Praise for *A World Elsewhere*

"Using her parents' letters written during ~~~~~~~~~~~~~~~~, Mac-
Rae does a fine job of portraying the fear and uncertainty felt by her
mother, living in a strange land and torn by loyalties."

—*Kirkus Reviews*

"How [her parents] fell in love and lived, until separated by war and
death, is the story told in *A World Elsewhere*, by Sigrid MacRae, their
sixth child, and it is a remarkable and touching book."

—*The New York Times*

"Fascinating . . . Drawing from a collection of letters and diary entries
given to [MacRae] by her mother, [a] thought-provoking chronicle."

—*Publishers Weekly*

"MacRae is an elegant writer with a sharp eye for revealing details. . . .
A World Elsewhere [is] a vivid tale of voyages through war-torn
Europe." —*The Christian Science Monitor*

"*A World Elsewhere* is a literary masterpiece, fully realized, and a
perfect work of art, a daughter's eloquent monument to her coura-
geous mother. It is also a reminder that war spares no one but wounds
everyone it touches." —Edmund White, author of *Inside a Pearl*

"Only a person of superb literary gifts and exquisite sensibility could
have done justice to this great story. The excitements and horrors of
wartime are brought vividly to life, and the reader remains spellbound
with each turn of the von Hoyningen-Huene family saga. The heroic
mother, the romantic, idealistic father, the band of beautiful spunky
children—I will never forget any of them."

—Sigrid Nunez, author of *Sempre Susan:
A Memoir of Susan Sontag*

"This subtle, beautifully crafted book tells a moving story of love, exile, and survival from the frozen Neva river to the Loire valley, from Hitler's Berlin to the shores of Maine. A vivid family memoir and an unforgettable portrait of a woman who braved all to bring her family to safety."   —Caroline de Margerie, author of *American Lady*

"Sigrid MacRae manages to find a window into Germany during World War II we've never looked through before, an unputdownable true story of courage and love, beautifully realized on the page, and a reading experience that will break your heart in a good way."

—Mary-Rose MacColl, author of *In Falling Snow*

"In this compulsively readable telling of an American mother's escape with six children from wartime Germany, Sigrid MacRae brings to life the struggle faced by refugees everywhere, as well as acts of kindness that redeem the atrocities of war. I rooted for Aimée's ingenuity and courage all the way home!"

—April Smith, author of *A Star for Mrs. Blake*

"[*A World Elsewhere*] leaves one with a profound sense of the importance of home—of the danger of being too nostalgic about home, of the horror of having your home taken away, and of the battle to belong and start afresh, creating a home out of the most unlikely circumstances."

—*The History Vault*

PENGUIN BOOKS

A WORLD ELSEWHERE

Sigrid MacRae is the coauthor of *Alliance of Enemies,* about the undercover collaboration between the American OSS and the German Resistance to end World War II. She holds a graduate degree in art history from Columbia. She lives in New York City.

Sigrid MacRae

A WORLD ELSEWHERE

An American Woman
in
Wartime Germany

PENGUIN BOOKS

PENGUIN BOOKS
An imprint of Penguin Random House LLC
375 Hudson Street
New York, New York 10014
penguin.com

First published in the United States of America by Viking Penguin,
an imprint of Penguin Random House LLC, 2014
Published in Penguin Books 2015

THE LIBRARY OF CONGRESS HAS CATALOGED THE HARDCOVER EDITION AS FOLLOWS:
MacRae, Sigrid von Hoyningen-Huene.
A world elsewhere : an American woman in wartime Germany / Sigrid MacRae.
pages cm
Includes bibliographical references and index.
ISBN 978-0-670-01583-2 (hc.)
ISBN 978-0-14-312748-2 (pbk.)
1. Hoyningen-Huene, Aimée von, 1903– 2. Hoyningen-Huene, Heinrich Alexis
Nikolai von, 1904–1941. 3. MacRae, Sigrid von Hoyningen-Huene—Family. 4. Married
people—Germany—Biography. 5. Americans—Germany—Biography. 6. Aristocracy
(Social class)—Baltic Provinces (Russia)—Biography. 7. Intercountry marriage—
History—20th century. 8. Love-letters. 9. World War, 1939–1945—Germany—
Biography. 10. World War, 1939–1945—Refugees—Biography. I. Title.
CT1097.H69M33 2014
943.086'4—dc23   2014004501

Printed in the United States of America
3 5 7 9 10 8 6 4 2

Set in Aldus LT Std   Designed by Francesca Belanger
Map by Jeffrey L. Ward

*To those who went before,
especially my mother, and to
those who will come after.*

Contents

Prologue   1

1: Mademoiselle Sophie's Hat   7

2: I Want My Mother! Give Me Back My Mother!   16

3: Widening Circles   20

4: Forfeits   37

5: The Bread of Exile   43

6: I Never Knew—Ooh, Ooh—
What Love Could Do—Ooh, Ooh . . .   47

7: Life Is a Beautiful Dream   61

8: Abie's Irish Rose   69

9: In a Thousand Ways an Exile   73

10: No Ground Under Anyone's Feet   82

11: Such Fearful Need   87

12: Conditions Are Terrifying   94

13: War Anxiety   111

14: More's the Pity   119

15: Intermezzo   134

16: Barbarossa   141

17: The Home Front   156

18: Keep Your Mouth Shut   174

19: Give Me Ten Years   180

20: Flight   194

21: Everything Passes   204

22: She and Her Kind   217

23: A Labyrinth Without an Exit   232

24: America   249

25: The Mail Must Go Through   268

     Epilogue   277

     Acknowledgments   285

     Glossary   287

     Notes   289

     Bibliography   299

     Index   305

A WORLD ELSEWHERE

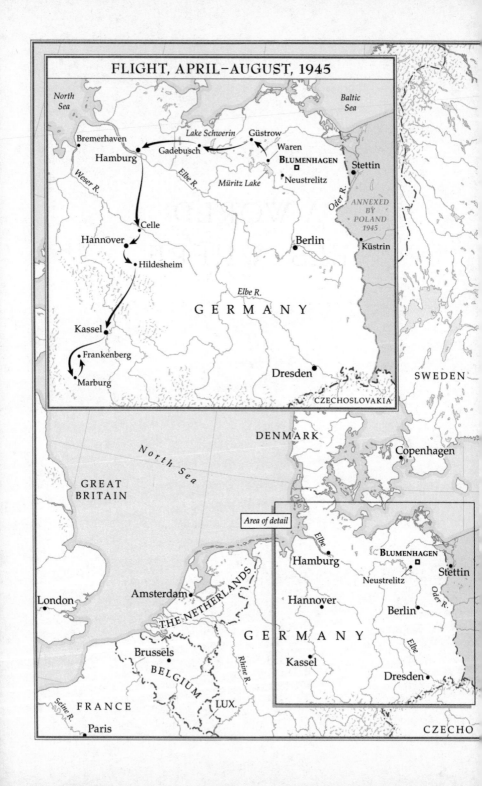

LANDS OF HOME, LANDS OF EXILE

FINLAND

FINLAND UNTIL 1940

RÄISÄLÄ

Lake Ladoga

Vuoksi R.

St. Petersburg

Helsinki

Tallinn

Stockholm

ESTONIA

OTTENHOF   Rujen

Walk

Salis R.   Lake Burtneck

Pskov

Riga

LATVIA

Baltic Sea

LITHUANIA

Vilnius

ANNEXED BY
SOVIET UNION
1945

ANNEXED BY
POLAND
1945

ANNEXED
BY
POLAND
1945

ANNEXED BY
SOVIET UNION
1945

RUSSIA

Vistula R.

Warsaw

POLAND

Oder R.

Breslau

0 Miles   100   200

0 Kilometers   200

SLOVAKIA

© 2014 Jeffrey L. Ward

Prologue

The box was beautiful. My mother had bought it in Morocco many years ago, and as a child, I admired it in secret, stroking the tiny pieces of mother-of-pearl inlay on the surface, its patterns conjuring far-away places. Its ivory keyhole held a key with a striped ribbon attached. Turning the key always produced a soft *pling-plong*, but never opened the box. After many decades, my eighty-five-year-old mother was tired of Maine winters and was moving to Arizona. Parceling out her possessions and the memories they held to her five surviving children, she now held the box out to me, saying simply, "Your father's letters."

I had always suspected that the box held them. Exotic and mysterious, it was the perfect receptacle for the treasured relics of a husband long dead and a father I had never known. It contained a chapter of my mother's life that she had closed long since, one I was reluctant to re-open. The moment was freighted with feeling; her expression suggested things that I was afraid I could respond to only with tears. Neither of us felt comfortable in such emotional territory, and we cut it short. I stowed the box tenderly in the car along with the other pieces of her life she had designated for me: a miscellany of books, pictures, rugs, silver. As the car pulled away, she stood, small and contained, the enormous firs by the garage dwarfing her as she waved good-bye. Behind her, morning sunlight skittered across the bay.

At home the box sat—still beautiful, but still steadfastly, stubbornly locked—keeping its secrets. Though my mother had given it to me, I felt that breaking this family reliquary open by force was wrong. Besides, I was reluctant to discover what the box held. Inside was the person who had changed the shape of my mother's life, whom my older brothers and sisters loved and remembered, a real person to everyone in the family except me, the youngest. For years his mythical presence had loomed large, but as an absence—an immense absence. Time had gradually healed my mother's wounds, but I was wary of causing pain by asking about him. In fact, I realized that I bore some resentment toward the man I had held responsible for many miseries.

My mother had moved on, but for me he remained unfinished business. Opening the box—resurrecting him—would mean finding not only the man who became my father, but also the man responsible for the "Nazi!" a first-grade classmate had yelled at me as a six-year-old, newly arrived in the States from Germany. I didn't know then what that was, but whatever it was, I knew it wasn't good. The taunt stayed with me. It was thrown at me in many other guises, and eventually I blamed my father.

I always felt different growing up. My family was an anomaly in rural Maine—a clan of outsiders. There was my unfamiliar, unpronounceable last name: von Hoyningen-Huene. Even just von Huene was bad enough; I longed to be Linda or Susan, Smith, Jones, or Brown. There was the language, and there was the taint of being German. And in spite of my mother's tireless efforts to always provide a beautiful place to come home to, my sense of dislocation never budged. There was nowhere that felt unmistakably like "home."

My father's parents, Baltic Germans exiled from Saint Petersburg to Germany after the Bolshevik Revolution, had suffered exile bitterly, feeling displaced, lost, and alien—an awareness that also left an indelible mark on my father's life. His younger sister once told me that the only place she ever felt homesick for was Saint Petersburg, a city she had last seen as a twelve-year-old, more than seventy-five years before. Such feelings and memories were endemic; they came with the territory, demanding the lion's share of space in the exile's little bundle of belongings. Maybe for us, as for so many, they ran in the family.

My persistent hunt for home began long before my mother gave me the Moroccan box, and much of it circled around my father. He had always been a presence, if iconic, and I was hardly ignorant about him. His portrait hung in our living room along with one of my parents as a young couple in Paris in 1929, by a celebrated photographer cousin, George Hoyningen-Huene. Assorted forebears kept them company on the walls. I knew about his past; stories about him were family lore. There were letters, diaries, and poems from his turbulent early years. I had read his letters from France as an officer in Hitler's army, where an occasional passage sounding alarmingly like Nazi propaganda had made me squirm, yet his awareness of history, his wide learning, his sympathy for people, and his enviable optimism shone from every page. His brief diary from the Russian front had also made me question what his being in Hitler's army really meant. Still, for me, he remained buried in the uneasy murk of history.

I had read about the backdrop to his life in his father's elegiac memoir. Spinning a magical lost world, it detailed life in tsarist Russia—a civilization that disappeared like Brigadoon beneath the Bolshevik mists. Typed by my father's younger sister, with annotations and a genealogy, it had been privately printed and distributed to all far-flung family households. Along with memoirs by other ancestors, aunts and uncles, and many letters, it was part of a jumble of suggestive ephemera: portraits; poems; a small double-headed imperial Russian eagle in diamonds, once part of a tsarist medal presented to some forebear. Individually, these items all spoke, offering pieces of a puzzle, spurring my imagination, but providing little narrative. Together, they acted as a mute chorus, nudging me to become their amanuensis. It occurred to me that putting the pieces together might help me find where home lay.

My mother died about ten years after she gave me the box of letters, and not long after, turning the key opened it. Inexplicable, I thought, magical, until my husband confessed that he had tinkered with the lock.

After all these years, my father revealed himself quickly. Always dating his letters, numbering pages, he sometimes noted the day of the week, even the time of day. He had been a trained historian after all, yet this was not mere record-keeping; he was also truly sharing his days. His was an ordered mind and a giving nature. The voice of my mother's young lover, so long silent, emerged from his letters like a genie out of a bottle. From the pages of one letter slipped silken, nearly transparent poppy petals of the palest salmon pink—the tender gesture of a long-ago love.

So this was the person who had lurked inside the box all those years:

no bland Hartford, Connecticut, swain, no dull future captain of an insurance empire. Small wonder my mother was *bouleversée* when they met in France; more than seven decades later, he was charming me. His habit of enclosing flowers in letters was one she later adopted, but here, though she would have foreseen my eventual intrusion, I still felt I was prying. A flurry of envelopes, addressed to Hartford in June, July, and August of 1928, was meticulously dated in my mother's hand; this batch was clearly important. My mother was ushering me into their young love.

I began to read. As I came to grips with his loose, generous hand, the father I had never known came spectacularly, breathtakingly alive. Finding sleep after such an introduction was nearly impossible. In the dark, I grappled with this vivid interloper I had known only as a kind of household god. His letters destroyed that status completely, shifting the emotional landscape I had established over a lifetime as the child of a single parent. This was the other side of the parental equation. It changed everything, demanding a revision of my views of my mother and a rearrangement of the family constellation.

One letter stood out. Postmarked London, February 11, 1928, it was addressed to my mother in Paris. Their young romance is blossoming quickly. If she will meet him,

> . . . your great wish will be fulfilled: You shall put on your best clothes . . . and we shall go and do something grand and brilliant. Do you insist on my wearing full dress? Won't this be an historic night: Miss Mayflower flirting with the "Hun."

Apart from shattering his remoteness completely, the letter put its finger squarely on my own puzzling provenance. Clearly the man who had left me his name and his profile was no cliché Hun at all, no bellicose militarist with monocle and bristling moustache, not even absolutely German—as his Russian diary attested. Young, lively, fully aware of the label history had affixed to him, and with an acute sense of humor, he was demolishing all my preconceived notions. The Miss Mayflower he was referring to in impeccable English, though of Mayflower stock, was obviously not my worn, hard-pressed, ever-practical mother, but a carefree spirit, wanting, as she had written him, "to put on my best clothes and go on a bat with you," adding, "It must be most romantic to have a young and ravishing female creature, head-over-heels in love and following you all over Europe."

The pieces on my mother's side of the puzzle were varied too, if less exotic. An American cousin spent many hours interviewing my mother, meticulously transcribing the result; another put together a comprehensive genealogy. Late in her long life when she woke early, my mother often spent those mornings writing recollections on a pad propped against her knees in bed. After she left Maine for Arizona, I tried to make sense of her scrappy, loose-leaf pages, but with a continent between us, distance, my own reticence, and life intervened, leaving me with regrets that I know many share. I asked questions—never enough questions, and never the right ones. The confessional mode was terra incognita in our family, and my mother had a talent for closing doors on what was over. I was reluctant to pry those doors open, no matter the cost.

Apart from those to an American friend, Mary, few of my mother's letters survived. But these—written between 1928 and 1947—are a record of extraordinary times. Had I not found them cached in a rusty file cabinet as I helped clean out Mary's apartment after her death, this window onto my mother's evolution from breathless fiancée to expatriate wife and mother, observing Germany's 1930s and '40s, would never have opened for me. The carefree, playful young thing I encountered in the early missives was unrecognizable as the mother I knew. Her letters added to the clamor of voices driving this book forward, pushing the story further, if not anywhere near its end. Without them, there might never have been a book, just fragments without a narrative, no story at all.

Who were these people? What had brought such an unlikely pair together? And where did their eventual alliance leave me? Accidents of history had joined them, and the entangled mysteries of love, sex, and money. How they had shaped me was yet to be determined, but where should the story of two lives whose strands ran separately far longer than they had been knitted together begin? And how should other lives—those of the parents, aunts and uncles, brothers and sisters, and grandparents—be woven into the fabric? Tangents, vagaries, shifts, and turns are uncomfortable in the tyranny of chronology, yet history is tyranny too, and the convulsive history of the century that shaped my parents' lives refused to obey any other imperative.

"One lives so many different lives," my mother used to say. "Life is a verb. Everyone has a story."

This book is theirs.

1

Mademoiselle Sophie's Hat

The world was more or less whole in 1927, still healing from World War I, but on the mend. Aimée Ellis and an old school friend, an actress named Hope Cary, began their trip in Sicily, and then planned to follow spring up the Italian boot. Easter week found them among Palermo's dim churches and golden mosaics. All Sicily was in bloom. At Agrigento they traipsed through flowering meadows to picnic in the great temple's shadow. They lolled on deserted beaches looking out toward Africa. On Aimée's nickel they spent a few days at a splendid old grande dame of a hotel bellied up against the amphitheater in Taormina, the windows of their baroque room looking out on Mount Etna, smoldering in the distance. They sashayed around Capri, sauntered through Rome, then on to Florence and the hill towns of Assisi and Orvieto. The world seemed miraculously beautiful.

All along the way, Hope kept saying that she'd met a Russian in Providence, Rhode Island, who was studying at the Sorbonne now. Aimée must meet him when they got to Paris. She imagined Hope's Russian in his late thirties, compact, dark, and intense. Instead he was twenty-three, tall, and handsome as a young god.

Baron Heinrich Alexis Nikolai von Hoyningen-Huene was in fact only somewhat Russian. His family was Baltic German aristocracy, a particular caste whose lives had always gravitated toward the tsarist court, and who divided their time between Saint Petersburg and their estates in the Baltic countries. In flawless English, he explained that Germans, many of them like his family, descendants of the crusading Teutonic knights, had been settled in the Baltics since the thirteenth century. After Peter the Great crushed Swedish supremacy in the region, he encouraged more Germans to immigrate, promising them an independent administration with German language and laws. The Baltic nobility profited enormously and played a significant part in the imperial Russian civil and military services ever after. At one point, Heinrich's family was one of the largest landowners in the Baltics.

In the Russian capital, Saint Petersburg, Baltic Germans established German churches, schools, and cultural institutions. The fight against Napoleon—many of Heinrich's ancestors had fought for Russia—only reinforced their influence. But when Tsar Alexander III ascended the throne in 1881, his fervent Russian patriotism and anti-German stance rattled their privilege and independence. Despite reforms, the revolutionary unrest of 1905 only foreshadowed 1917, when the Bolsheviks seized power and many Baltic Germans went into exile.

The riddle of how Heinrich came to meet Hope in Providence, Rhode Island, was explained by an entertaining story about Mlle. Sophie, a longtime governess in Heinrich's father's family. In the semidarkness of a train compartment en route to Vienna, a young American gentleman accidentally sat on Mlle. Sophie's hat. Her lighthearted reaction to his gaffe charmed the embarrassed Mr. Alfred Lorand-Lustig, and for the rest of their journey the two young people talked animatedly. In Vienna, Alfred introduced Sophie to his mother and sister; several weeks later, she and Alfred were engaged. Having stayed in touch with the Hoyningen-Huenes, she was aware that revolution had left the family refugees, without home, lands, or money. In 1924, as Mrs. Lorand-Lustig, she wrote to suggest that Heinrich's extraordinary language abilities could earn him American dollars as representative to the new foreign operations of the Nicholson File Company in Providence, where her well-to-do husband held an important position.

In Providence, Heinrich became "Henry" and lived on charm. Scrimping to save money, he shared a room at the YMCA with a large box of Quaker Oats. Mixed with hot water in his toothbrush glass, it kept his stomach from complaining too much if he had no dinner invitation. But he was lucky. Providence was more than happy to have a charming, handsome baron at its dinner parties, and invited him often. At one such party he met Hope Cary—"Beautiful Hope" everyone called her—in town with Walter Hampden's New York theater company. By the time Henry's stint in Providence came to an end, he had sent money home to the family and saved enough to pursue studies in history, international law, and economics. So here he was, studying in Paris.

Aimée was intrigued. He was utterly impoverished, but that was never an issue. His attitude—"We have no money, but it's a beautiful day, and we won't let that stand in our way"—was like nothing she had ever encountered. She was taken with the buoyant charm that endeared him to everyone he met. His title may have played a part in her interest too, but she knew that there was no shortage of aristocratic dullards, and he was not one of them. Irrepressible, with a storehouse of knowledge, and always up for adventure, he was fascinated by others, and by her. And to think that she had met this extraordinary man only because of a string of coincidences cascading from Mlle. Sophie's squashed hat—amazing.

When he asked her about herself and her family, she felt she had nothing to say. No exotic background, no family to speak of, really. Heinrich said that if she was going to be so reluctant to tell him about herself, they would have to establish a rule: Revelations about self and family from one of them deserved the same from the other. It was only fair. But in her memory, her childhood stretched as a lonely monochromatic landscape. She said nothing.

Hope had exhausted her resources and was due in New York for rehearsals. When Aimée decided to stay on alone in France, Heinrich suggested she join the group enrolled in a summer program for serious students wanting to polish their French at the château at Lestion, a village near Beaugency. Though all the rooms at the little château were taken, he found her a room with an old couple in the village.

Père and Mère Fenique's house was at the end of the village's single street. According to legend, Heinrich said, Joan of Arc had spent the night before the battle of Beaugency, in 1429, in this house. To Aimée, it looked as if it had not changed much since. Joan may not have slept in the same bed, but she must have slept in the same room, for there were only two. The house was built on a south-facing slope, with an entrance to the upper floor on the street side, for the donkey and his fodder, but no windows. Windows on the street were taxed. To the south, the living quarters' windows and doors looked out across meadows sloping down to the Loire River. As he helped get her settled, Heinrich told her that almost a thousand years before Joan, local tribes under the Romans had repulsed the Hun on these very meadows.

A little brook spilling to the river served for bathing. In the mornings, Mère Fenique brought breakfast to a bench outside in the sun— milk still warm from the cow, and fresh, slightly ashy bread, baked in the shallow, open fireplace in the Feniques' room, which mirrored hers. On Wednesdays, stripped down above the waist to marvelously intricate stays, Mère Fenique boiled her washing in an enormous cauldron over an open fire. She had not been to the next village—about two miles away—in years. In lieu of newspapers, a small uniformed man came down the village's one street, his drum roll calling the villagers from their fields or out their doors to hear his reports.

Père Fenique, a veteran of the Franco-Prussian War, was ailing. Only rarely did Aimée hear his sabots clumping in the other room. He was too old to take part in the *vendange*—the grape harvest—already in full swing. (His image survives in a tiny photograph found in the Moroccan box. He sits near voluminous bed curtains, knees apart, cane firmly in hand, under an impressive thatch of white hair.)

Did they have a doctor for Père? Aimée asked Mère.

"Oh no," Mère replied. If the donkey got sick, of course they would get a doctor. The old man wasn't going to last anyway, but the donkey— that was different, she said simply, enunciating a pragmatic, peasant philosophy.

After French classes, Heinrich and Aimée explored Lestion's little church and bicycled along roads barely traveled except for farm wagons bringing in the harvest. Following one wagon laden with sacks of grain, Heinrich told her it was built on a Roman model. When it stopped at a windmill, they left their bicycles and went inside. Wind roared in the sails; the entire structure creaked and groaned. It was like stepping aboard a sixteenth-century galleon in a storm. The grinding stones, the massive beams and joists—every single surface—was white with the dust of powdered grain. Heinrich shared his knowledge enthusiastically, opening dimensions in history, in architecture, in almost everything they saw, ushering Aimée into a rich, new world. She was suddenly, overwhelmingly in love.

The idyllic countryside around Lestion offered endless opportunities for sketching: a young girl knitting as she tended sheep, a dolmen looming behind her; a late summer sun casting a glow over the *pigeonnier* of a big farm. Leaning over to admire her sketch, Heinrich asked, "Where did you learn to draw so beautifully?"

She blushed. He had touched on what she thought of as her one accomplishment. A treasured gift of colored pencils from her uncle Bill had encouraged her as a child, and she had studied and taken George Bridgman's life classes at the Art Students League in New York. He had never had such formal training, he said, only lessons from his adored grandmama Marie, always sympathetic to the frustrations of bringing three dimensions into two.

Those few words about himself opened a floodgate. Heinrich began to talk about his family, painting lively word-portraits of his parents and four siblings, of Saint Petersburg's long dark winters, where night came early and dawn dragged its feet. Even in the bitterest cold, the governess took the children out to make the circuit of *le carrée*, one of Saint Petersburg's vast squares. At the Tavrichesky Gardens, rink attendants in thick padded coats helped get skates on and off, while the Chevalier Guards played waltzes, mazurkas, and marches that accompanied skaters across the ice and drifted through the trees at the lake's edge. Heinrich and his siblings knew that their parents had courted there. On the small nearby stream called the "Tour du Monde," which branched off to afford young Ernst and Mima a few moments of unchaperoned privacy, their mother had delighted Papa with her "yes" to his burning question.

Before the First World War, much of Saint Petersburg gave the impression of a wealthy city. Pink and cream and pistachio-green palaces perched along the canals like oversize petits fours, their pale, delicious colors reflected in the Neva River's green water. The Nevsky Prospekt's shops offered English soaps, fine leathers, Italian ices, champagnes. At Yeliseev, a temple of gastronomy, *style moderne* lamps of glass flowers drooped over an epicurean array. Though the contrast between rich and poor was huge, some prosperity trickled even to the city's beggars; the Orthodox belief that beggars, habitually congregated on church steps, were messengers from God reinforced traditional Russian generosity.

At the core of Heinrich's young life lay an enormous extended family, a multitude of cousins—close and distant—aunts, uncles, grandmothers. Long winter nights meant quiet evenings in cheerful intimacy at home, Papa reading aloud from his favorite Russian writers. Soft lamplight spilled over them like a blanket, reflecting in a mirror or on polished wood, but leaving most of the room wonderfully, mysteriously dark. If aunts and uncles joined the gatherings, a musical soirée might be quite ambitious, with Uncle Emil playing flute, Uncle Rudolph cello, and Tante Marie at the grand piano. The little ones lay on the bearskin rug beneath, letting the resonances roll over their heads. Snow tumbling out of the blackness outside swirled in the light of the streetlamp like a personal snow globe, the stuff of private reveries.

The weeks of Advent before Christmas were filled with preparation, festivities, and great excitement. At the entrance to Gostiny Dvor, the city's biggest department store, stood a stuffed bear, immense and upright, and inside were enough treasures to delight the most jaded child. Even the youngest children accompanied their father to the Christmas market to choose the big Christmas tree, and for several days, ornaments and nuts were gilded for hanging on Christmas Eve. There were visits to his mother's father, Grandpapa Nikolai Sievers, in the house a great-grandfather had bought around 1800, said to have been the house of Peter the Great's doctor. Heinrich's mother, Marie—"Mima"—had been born there, and they visited often.

Grandpapa Nikolai was an enthusiastic naturalist and huntsman who still enjoyed multigenerational mushrooming expeditions with his children, grandchildren, and ever-present manservant, Dimenty Zacharievitch. Deep in the woods, the cool air redolent of moss, soft earth, and resin, with baskets filled with mushrooms, they would find a spot among towering firs for a picnic. Everyone except Grandpapa sat on the spongy forest floor; for him, Dimenty Zacharievitch brought a folding stool to keep his aged joints off the damp ground. A cloth was spread, and bottles, pâtés, and chickens were brought out of hampers while Grand-papa recalled mushroom hunts of long ago.

In 1913, the Romanov dynasty celebrated its three-hundred-year jubilee with a parade even more fabulous than usual. Shining carriages, coachmen in grand liveries, and troops in brilliant dress uniform passed in front of the Winter Palace; sun glinted on thousands of gold buttons; horse flanks gleamed. The glorious show went on for hours. Grandpapa Emil (Papa's father) was dressed for a ball. The children went to the floor below in the apartment building to see him, resplendent in his uniform, a scarlet coat with gold embroidery, white pants with a scarlet stripe. Clustered around his magnificence, the children reached to touch this or that medal pinned to the broad blue ribbon draped across his chest. It was thrilling—all of it.

Carriages and sleighs crowded the streets alongside streetcars, some still horse-drawn. If the Neva River was frozen, much of the traffic, in-cluding the horse-drawn streetcar, the *konka*, could cross the meter-thick ice. When the ice began to break, the cannons of the Peter and Paul Fortress boomed to announce the event; floes from Lake Ladoga sent mountainous chunks of ice crashing against bridge pilings. The nearby Liteiny Bridge might hold them for a time, but the children and their father loved to watch the swollen Neva's current rip the thudding, crunching ice away. The excitement was tremendous: Winter was losing its grip.

Maslenitsa—butter week—or Carnival, was another sign that win-ter was giving way, promising spring and Easter, the highest feast day of the Russian calendar. In this madcap week of entertainments and balls, itinerant entertainers and masked and costumed people crowded streets that were often still under deep snow. At the colorful *Verba*, the Easter market, the children weighed how best to spend their extra bit of pocket money. After the Lenten fast, the city's church bells rang almost inces-santly. It was time for feasting again on the painted eggs, on *pashka*—the traditional Russian Easter dessert—with its paper flowers, and *kulich*—the accompanying yeast cake—laid out on white cloths to be sprinkled with holy water.

Spring made the children restless. The apartment was large and pleasant, there were many fine things to do in the city, but they were always shepherded by a nurse or governess. They yearned for the long days of summer at Ottenhof, the family estate in Latvia, without city constraints, where time was all theirs, where they were free. Then came the great day of the pilgrimage. First the *droschke* to the Baltika Station, then wheels clacking across the miles, through the night. With a railroad car to themselves, the children tried to sleep in the wide reclining seats, but the excitement was great, and lights flickering in glass lanterns cast moving shadows and inspired restless dreams.

Morning sun gleamed on the samovar at the station at Walk, the *zakuska* table laid out with delicious tidbits as they waited for the little train to Rujen, where the coachman would be waiting in the calèche. A second carriage would bring the luggage. The last twenty kilometers were achingly familiar: Emerging from the forest on the height, the children were nearly drunk at the first glimpse of the lake shining below. On either side of the river, meadows swept away to a distant church. Already they could see the allée of larches, then the turn at the so-called heathen oak—so huge it surely predated Christianity.

At the wide bridge over the Salis, the horses slowed. Their solemn tread prolonged the excitement as the river moved in swift counterpoint below, glittering in the sunlight. The ride along the park fence and through the park's great trees to reach the vine-covered house would be exactly as always: the scent of white lilacs, roses, and mock orange; a hundred different birdsongs; the silver willow by the pond; the chuckling millstream. Then lunch on the big veranda with a view across the rose beds, past Grandpapa Nikolai's oak, to the rich meadows along the river and the lake's satin sheen.

Long hours of daylight meant almost limitless pleasures. The roomy "picnic" carriage took them to Salisburg, clattering across the cobbles to buy the baker's special *Kringel*. Then along sandy paths to the Sievers burial ground, where Heinrich's mother, Mima—the children called her Mimama—put roses from Ottenhof on the family graves. Past the Vietinghoffs', rolling into the vast park, with picnic baskets unloaded at the little round temple, coachman and horses resting in shade, the horses' tails switching at flies. Sailing expeditions to the mouth of the Ruje River, where still, salmon-rich waters mirrored red sandstone cliffs and white water lilies nodded on stems reaching into the deep. Elk roamed the forests where gentians bloomed.

The days were nearly endless; the white nights meant little darkness, but the evening still had its special sounds. The call "*Maya, Maya*" brought the russet cattle to their stalls, bellowing. Crickets enlivened the dusk with their immense chorus, and along the so-called Philosopher's Walk the nightingale sang his own melancholy song. It had all seemed immutable. Then it was gone.

2

I Want My Mother!
Give Me Back My Mother!

As Heinrich talked, images and sounds flooded Aimée's consciousness. Light or dark, cozy or exotic, for her they all had a magical quality. His stories told of people moving through their lives together. His Christmases were a family undertaking, lasting for weeks. This was a family, not isolated souls colliding occasionally in the same house.

The house at 820 Prospect Avenue in Hartford was never festive or jolly. What she remembered about Christmas was wondering what distant, happy family would receive the packages piled in the snow by the overstuffed postbox on Prospect Avenue. Apart from the postman, no one would have dreamt of taking them. After church on Christmas Day, they had dinner with her mother's older brother, Uncle Bill, and Aunt Marion on Beacon Street, where things were much livelier, with family, friends, and guests coming and going. After a predinner sherry, Uncle Bill would rise and hold out his arm to Aunt Marion, saying, "Sweetie, it's time to *eat!*" and they would two-step off to the dining room.

On Sundays, Aimée and her brother, Corson, four years older, were dragged over to a large high-ceilinged brownstone adjoining 820 to see Great-Uncle James Brewster Cone and Aunt Lizzie. Saracen coats of mail, helmets, and weapons hung on the walls of the gloomy "den," and to her undying fascination, a life-size sculpture of Isaac awaiting sacrifice before a pile of very white marble logs stood in the large, dim drawing room. Uncle Jim had a Napoleon III moustache, a goatee, chilling, protuberant, pale blue eyes, and an erect bearing. The hope behind the visits was that Uncle Jim would leave them some of the very large portion of the Cone money he had inherited.

When Aimée met Heinrich, her parents were dead; her mother had died at the age of thirty-five, when Aimée was not yet three, and her father when she was twenty-three. As she talked about her family, it was in pain at her mother's death, disappointment with her distant father, or anger at her brother, Corson, her childhood tormentor. She was so small when her mother died that each memory of her tenderness was immortalized: a laughing kiss planted under her chin; her mother's arms lifting her up into a brilliant sky, gulls wheeling; a slight body on a white bed in a white room, a blue ribbon in her hair, asking her to take good care of her brother. All were cherished in the emotional void that followed. Sometimes she spoke with residual sadness for her desolate younger self, bereft and inconsolable, running through the big, dark house, wailing, "I want my mother! Give me back my mother!"

There was no comfort. A string of changing governesses failed to bring calm, order, or emotional support. One young Swiss woman who taught her to knit and filled her head with the Latin names of flowers was remembered fondly, but was sent packing, like those before and after her. Peace returned only when "Mis' Walker" at last came to 820 Prospect Avenue and stayed for seven years.

Mis' Walker taught her to read, and books became both blissful refuge and inspiration. With few little girls along Prospect Avenue's shady length, books were her companions, her comfort, her escape. At six, she was enrolled at the local public school, but a diagnosis of scoliosis, accurate or not, removed her from school and condemned her to a series of body casts until she was twelve. Out of school for years, she was then sent to a newfangled open-air school on the Prospect Avenue trolley line. The wintry outdoor lessons intended to create vigorous, healthy pupils kept them bundled up as for an Arctic expedition, and hard put to hold pencils. The only thing she remembered from this regimen was the Twenty-third Psalm in Latin, "Frère Jacques," and writing according to Palmer Method rules with stiff, chilled fingers. Without much of an education, or even a start on an education, she was left with the sense of being abysmally uneducated years after anyone could have thought that of her. Her father considered neither the regimen nor the schooling successful, but she had discovered that she liked to draw. Her facility was noticed, and drawing became a pleasure and a lasting pursuit.

No one came to the house; there was little talk at home. The only

dinner conversation she remembered was between Corson and her father about the last notes from Captain Scott's failed Antarctic expedition, very masculine, very remote. Otherwise her father's conversation
had mostly to do with annoyances: at breakfast and dinner, annoyances
about food or money. After dinner he communed with his newspaper in
silence. Widowed young, not gregarious, he buried himself in money-
making, lamenting constantly, in spite of her mother's significant legacy, that they were on their way to the poorhouse. Any expenditure
beyond household bills was a reminder of that fact. It was hard for her to
make much sense of this at the time. They lived in a large and comfortable house with a number of servants; there was no obvious explanation
for his worry, but it was a constant refrain.

Her real source of love and support was Uncle Bill, a magical presence
in her life, the cleverest, most cheerful person she knew, and he made a
special project of his younger sister's child. Almost always wreathed in
smoke from his little pipe, he was warm, generous, and upright. The enthusiasm and bonhomie that had made him president of the Yale Banjo
Club as a young man brought him friends and admiration in the Hartford community all his life.

Aunt Marion was Aimée's godmother, and their eldest daughter, Dorothy, radiated physical capability. Lithe and strong and an excellent tennis
player, she seemed to Aimée to be everything that she herself wasn't. The
shy, constricted child, captive to disabilities, was astounded by Dorothy's
dash and sporty demeanor. Her panache in dealing with the crank of her
Model T—giving it a smart turn to kick the engine into activity to take
Aimée out for a drive—was positively awe-inspiring. Those drives built a
bridge for the younger girl; partaking in the glow of her amazing older
cousin, she crept cautiously across it, and expanded a little in her company.

Still imprisoned in plaster, different from everyone, she felt an
outsider—always an outsider. When the final body cast came off, she
underwent a program of wholesale rehabilitation: riding lessons, ballet
lessons, all designed to reengineer her and erase all residue of awkwardness after years of physical constraints. Her teeth were straightened, her
arches supported. She was irredeemably imperfect; her name might be
Aimée, but she knew she was utterly unlovable.

She should have been born into his family, Heinrich interrupted passionately. There were his older sisters, Mira and Ebba, his younger sister, Margarethe, and, of course, Heinrich and his little brother, Georg. They were watched over by governesses too, but also by a mother who was an angel and by a gentle, loving father. With grandparents, uncles, aunts, and so many cousins, she could never have felt lonely or sad or unlovable.

3

Widening Circles

The summer of 1914 was hot at Ottenhof. One particularly sultry July afternoon, Papa and Heinrich were returning from a distant field with Jaeger, the overseer, when they saw Mimama hurrying toward them along the edge of the Kille Wood, an enormous tract of dark forest. Her summer dress flickered white when a shaft of sunlight pierced the black-green firs, then dimmed again in their deep shadows. Watching her approach was like watching a butterfly dart and float.

From her quick step, they sensed that she was bringing happy news. Her face was flushed from her long walk, and soft strands of fair hair escaped from her chignon, wreathing her face. She was waving a letter from Papa's brother, Rudolph. Having asked for the hand of a girl he had come to love on an earlier visit to Germany, he was triumphant; he was engaged! He was coming in ten days, bringing his fiancée and her mother to meet his family. Papa's parents and sister would be at Ottenhof then too. It would be a real family occasion.

The children were gathering flowers to fill the house when word came that Germany had announced a state of war readiness. Borders were sealed; Rudolph, his Ruth, and her mother had to cancel their travel plans. Everyone had been so certain that war would be avoided. Even when war was actually declared, they hoped everything could be resolved quickly, but the conflagration spread in widening circles. Then Rudolph was arrested in Germany on suspicion of being a Russian spy. Anxious weeks passed before the extraordinary efforts of a friend in a Dresden ministry pried Rudolph out of prison. But Ruth's family refused to give their daughter in marriage to a possible Russian spy; the engagement was broken off.

With the outbreak of war, Saint Petersburg's Exercise Square was filled with recruits running at straw figures with bayonets. The German-sounding name of Saint Petersburg was changed to Petrograd, and as the war and the hardships intensified, so did anti-German sentiment. Soon it was forbidden to speak German in the streets. They all spoke Russian, of course, but as *nemetskoye zasilye*—the German plague— now replaced anti-Semitism as the national bugaboo, it was intimidating. At least as a government employee, Papa was not drafted for military service, and for that they were deeply grateful.

Early on, the war was universally expected to be short, yet it went on, and it was going badly. By 1916, troops were strung out along a front that stretched from Riga in the Baltic to the Black Sea and beyond. Every day brought trainloads of casualties, overwhelming a city already teeming with refugees. Prices had quadrupled; the economy was tottering. The winter was bitter and there was no wood. People were hungry and there was no bread.

February 1917 was bleak and frigid. Wrapped in fog, snow, and melancholy, Petrograd was in ferment. Heavy snows kept freight trains from Russia's breadbasket from reaching the city, and the inflated price of potatoes and wood put these essentials completely out of reach for many. Hungry people, strikers, and Cossacks roamed the icy streets, yet soldiers often refused to act against the disorder. Unrest and disturbances were not new, but now the stage seemed to be set for something bigger. The magical, picture-book Saint Petersburg, already scarred by the revolution of 1905, seemed a phantasm.

On February 27, 1917 (Old Style)—according to Russia's prerevolutionary Julian calendar—Papa was due at the Duma, resuming that day, when the children called excitedly to their parents. Below their windows, the Volynsky Guards were getting into formation. A band struck up "La Marseillaise" and they marched off to the stirring, revolutionary tune to quash a revolutionary mob. Just after noon, the maid Irina found their neighbor, Baroness Nina Engelhard-Toróschino, trembling on their doorstep. Ushering her into the salon, Irina alerted Mimama, and went off to fetch tea. The shaken woman sat silent for a few minutes, then, haltingly, began to talk.

Hurrying home from an errand, she had seen a crowd of revolutionaries fighting heavily outnumbered tsarist troops at the barricades surrounding the officers' casino on their corner of the Liteiny Prospekt. A young officer flew up into the air, his elite Preobrazhensky Guards uniform bright against a dim sky, his body controlled, arms tucked in, as if expecting to land comfortably in the arms of his comrades below. She assumed, in spite of the times, that it was youthful celebratory high jinks, tossing a companion skyward to honor an important occasion—a promotion or an engagement. He flew heavenward again, limbs looser this time. Then again—legs and arms now flapping, inert—like a dummy. Leaning back into the sofa cushions, Nina closed her eyes and brought both hands to her temples, struggling for control. The young officer was being tossed on bayonets, she said at last. He was dead.

Terrible times followed that first wild day. Revolutionaries opened prison gates, set fire to police and law buildings, pillaged and plundered. Outside their windows, shaggy little Siberian ponies stamped in the courtyard of Saint Anne's next door, and a horde of soldiers and workers, with bits of red cloth tied at the ends of bayonets or around necks or sleeves, marched past toward the Duma, demanding the tsar's abdication.

One morning the house was suddenly sprayed with machine gun fire. The children pressed against the windows of their parents' corner bedroom, then bullets shattered the panes. A burst of gunfire sent a chandelier crashing to the floor; bullets thudded into the large mahogany armoire against the back wall. Revolutionaries were shooting at the house. At Papa's order, the family dropped to the floor, motionless but for their eyes, moving from one to another of their parents and siblings, looking for answers and reassurance.

A sharp crack from a rifle butt, and the door opened. A band of about twenty ruffians burst in, crowding around them, loud and unruly. Jostling, cursing, and making rough threats, they spread through the rooms, their movements punctuated by the sound of breaking glass and china. Papa's desk was rifled, Mama's writing table was overturned, scattering invitations, letters. Then they found shell casings Uncle Emil had brought the boys from his regiment at Tsarskoye Selo.

The apparent leader of the crew was a burly tough, incongruously dressed in the long gray overcoat of a police officer, immaculate but for a huge bloodstain on the shoulder. The shell casings glinting in his rough palm, he began to rage: They had been shot at from the roof of the house; this was proof. They had been forced to defend themselves. Papa must take them to the attic. They would see for themselves where the shooting had come from and who had done it. Two thugs held Papa's arms and shoved him forward. One of the gang yanked his gold watch and chain from him. When Papa insisted that no one in the house had shot at them, one struck him hard with a rifle butt. The children watched in horror as their slender father collapsed into an unconscious heap.

After hefty kicks restored him to consciousness, he was muscled down the stairs to the floor below, where they seized seventy-six-year-old Grandpapa Emil and shoved both men into the street. The women and children followed hesitantly, both terrified and fascinated. As the family huddled, speechless, on the pavement glittering with broken glass, the Red leader commandeered a passing car, roughly pushed Papa and Grandpapa in, and lurched off down the street.

They were brought to Tavrichesky Palace, recently serving as the lower house of the Duma, now the highest revolutionary tribunal and wildly overcrowded, then on to the nearby offices of the ultraconservative newspaper *Semstchina*, already overflowing with seized police officials. Outside, an enormous revolutionary rabble threatened to shoot them all. Knowing that they could expect only gruesome, lynch-mob justice from such a crowd, many prisoners were afraid. But Papa realized that while the Reds directed a stream of venom at them, promising to shoot them all next day on the Neva ice, they actually served as some protection against the mob.

The day's terrors had exhausted Grandpapa. Not long after they arrived, he wrapped himself in his heavy winter coat, lay down on the stone floor, and fell asleep immediately. Papa lay down beside him, resolved to see about getting his father released in the morning. It was long past midnight before the prison quieted. Waking a few hours later, he saw a pale, solemn Jewish student moving quietly among the revolutionaries, remarkably calm and sensible in the midst of the mayhem. This might be the right person to address about releasing his father, but he wanted to be sure. He circled and watched, and finally approached.

Slowly but determinedly, he made his plea. His father was an old man. Papa could prove that his father had never belonged to any radical nationalistic party. Could something be done to have him released? The student looked down at his own feet and said nothing. He was not arguing for himself, Papa explained, but he would be grateful for any consideration that could be shown his aged father. The student said nothing, but caught Papa's eye for a moment before he turned away.

In wintry early morning darkness, father and son were brought separately before a tribunal consisting of excitable students, reserve officers, and a hodgepodge of young people who had been interrogating prisoners all night. Grandpapa later explained that in a brief second round of questioning, a very quiet student had simply asked a few questions about his political affiliations and activities. Revolution was still young; the Bolshevik terror had not yet reached its full fury, and there were still remnants of sanity and reason to hope. After a hushed consultation, the committee decided to let him go home.

Eventually Papa was brought to the tribunal for further interrogation. Technically, he said, it was true that he and his family seemed to be on the wrong side of the revolution, connected to the *pridvorny*—the court folk. His father-in-law was a steward of the Imperial House, and his wife had been a lady-in-waiting to the tsaritsa, but that was not the whole story.

He was an Octobrist, committed since 1905 to Russia's peaceful, steady regeneration along constitutional lines, and drafting legislation to that end. More questions, then hurried conferences punctuated by occasional brief outbursts. Finally, the committee dismissed him. Hours later, he was told he would be released. Hunched over a small, scarred table, the cluster of scruffy young revolutionaries had already set up a makeshift little bureaucracy. He was handed a certificate saying he was permitted to live and move about in Petrograd. Red stamps were affixed, a signature scrawled. He was free to go.

Reliving the experience for the family at home, Papa told them that the rifle butt against his skull had brought him a wonderful sense of release; the ring of thuggish faces had simply disappeared and he had sunk into a soothing, limitless space filled with blue circles.

The weeks following those nightmarish days had their own air of unreality. The first bitter hours of fighting had left many casualties. Rumor claimed that all the policemen and officers of the gendarmerie with whom Papa had been imprisoned had been led through jeering crowds and shot. But there was no reliable news, no newspapers.

Drunken soldiers reeled everywhere, shooting wildly, randomly. Smoke from the burning law courts and prisons drifted across the city, darkening a sky heavy with incipient snow. Occasionally a commandeered car careered through the streets, honking loudly, soldiers flung across the front fenders, guns at the ready, red flags at the ends of bayonets. Boys with pistols looted from the arsenal took potshots at the pigeons lined up, as always, on the tramlines. The pigeons fluttered up nervously, circling, waiting, circling again, uncertain whether to resume their perches. Open red coffins bore bodies of dead revolutionaries to Exercise Square, often with a small ragtag crew alongside, some of them "mourners," promised bread or a little money for their services.

At the military headquarters at Mogilev, the tsar told his advisers that if it was what the people wanted, he would abdicate and withdraw to Livadia, and dedicate himself to his beloved flowers. When the army marching toward Petrograd to quell the rioting went over to the revolutionaries without firing a shot, he delivered his declaration of abdication. Then the *tsar batiushka*—the tsar, the Little Father—and his family withdrew to Tsarskoye Selo as prisoners.

Petrograd's blue, white, and red tsarist banners disappeared. "La Marseillaise" replaced the august cadences of the tsarist anthem. The Volynsky Guards they had seen marching off to its stirring strains to quell what they thought was a revolutionary skirmish had, in fact, already joined "the people." Whistled everywhere, its familiar bars welcomed Lenin back from exile at the Finland Station that April to find that the tsar's abdication had done nothing to slow revolutionary fervor. Red flags blanketed the city.

Grandpapa Emil told Papa that the news was so discouraging he did not want to hear it anymore. Then he developed pneumonia. When the provisional government dissolved the Senate, of which Grandpapa had long been a member, Papa did not have the heart to tell him. In May, spared that bitter knowledge, he died quietly in his sleep. All this time, Papa's brother, Uncle Rudolph, had been under strict surveillance in Germany. Alone, far from home, broken and unable to recover equilibrium, he killed himself.

Gradually, mercifully, it became clear that there were limits to the energies of even the most fire-breathing revolutionaries. Wild gunfire gave way to occasional shooting, usually at night. A deceptive air of normalcy returned, and the children even went back to school, with orders to shelter in a courtyard if they heard gunshots.

Heinrich hesitated. He and Aimée were sitting in a French meadow in glorious sunshine. All this had happened ten years ago, and while it was as fresh to him as an open wound, it sounded unbelievable, almost grotesque. In the here and now, it seemed impossible to convey to anyone what it had really been like.

Aimée waited. She had only a vague notion of the Russian Revolution and of Communism as a great evil. To her, war had meant occasionally rolling bandages at the Junior League with other socially acceptable girls. Heinrich not only knew history, he had also lived it. This was infinitely more interesting than anything plain-vanilla Hartford, or even New York, had to offer. She was fascinated, but did not press him. Clearly, he needed to tell it all, and would tell it in good time, when he was ready. She looked down, combing the tangle of grasses between them with her fingertips; there was no hurry.

They were both silent. The softness of the countryside, the occasional bird, the river curling past, tranquil under the late summer sun, slowly consigned the sounds of desperation and gunfire to the past. When he began to talk again, it was of a gentler time, a reprieve from the fright and hardship they had suffered. He told her about the summer of 1917, the last period of peace and refuge before the real conflagration.

That summer, as so often in their history, the Baltics were a war zone. Ottenhof was out of reach, on the other side of the front. But the family had an escape hatch, a familiar haven stemming from Grandpapa Nikolai Sievers's firm religious convictions. Grandpapa's wife, Grandmama Lisa, had a Russified family tree that sprouted Maxims, Feodors, Constantins,

Tatianas, but more important, they were Russian Orthodox. Tsar Alexander III, determined to undo his father's liberalizing reforms and diminish European influences, wanted a return to *narodnost*—an untranslatable concept meaning roughly nationality, or Russianness. There would be one language: Russian; one rule: tsarist autocracy; one religion: Russian Orthodoxy. His decree that children of marriages between partners of the Russian Orthodox and Protestant faiths must be baptized Orthodox was a clear threat to the Protestant Baltic German aristocracy.

The Sievers family's wealth had always allowed them to move comfortably between Saint Petersburg and their various estates: Georgievsk, with its beautiful allée of birches; Feodorovsk, called Belaya Mysa by local peasants for its massive white house; Savolchino; and Ottenhof. All these properties were under Russian rule, but acquiring Räisälä, in Finland, gave Grandpapa Nikolai Finnish citizenship. By this sleight of hand, he could baptize his children legally in his Protestant faith, even as Grandmama Lisa held to her devout Orthodoxy. For the time being, Räisälä let the family hold its own.

Räisälä, on the Vuoksi River, was pristine and beautiful, yet relatively easy to reach from Saint Petersburg, even by train, though traveling by steamer on Lake Ladoga was a delicious adventure. Draining waters from the myriad lakes of southeast Finland, the Vuoksi, interrupted by occasional outcrops of rosy granite or rapids deftly negotiated by Finns in narrow kayaks, ran through the magnificent evergreen and birch forests of the Karelian Isthmus, all the way to Lake Ladoga. Old photographs of well-to-do Russians summering there show children in sailor suits, women in long dresses with high collars and long sleeves. They stand, squinting slightly, on the white gravel in front of the dachas they built there, all with the same fancy woodwork trim and canvas veranda awnings that sheltered their summer days in dachas throughout the empire.

For the children, Räisälä was bliss, with its stands of silver birches, deep, clear water, and a forest floor carpeted with soft, spongy moss that muffled footfalls and voices alike. Dimenty Zacharievitch was usually attached to Grandpapa, but he was always willing to explain some aspect of woods or wildlife. Finland's extraordinarily rich aquatic life kept him talking for hours, with details on all the varieties of fish that lured passionate fishermen from as far away as England. Such talk always ended with a sighed *"Bozhe moy"*—"my God"—the alpha and omega of the wondrous natural world he inhabited.

Dimenty Zacharievitch was more than a manservant, valet, or retainer. One great-uncle called him "our Bismarck" on account of his wisdom, his great bald pate, and his remarkable depth of human understanding. For him and for Grandpapa, their different stations in life were a matter of sheer happenstance and, as so often in such Russian relationships, had no bearing on their bond. Dimenty was always where Grandpapa Nikolai was, whether at Räisälä, Georgievsk, Feodorovsk, or Ottenhof. Man to man, they traveled life's path together as companions and equals.

Papa stayed behind that summer, working for the new government on a commission charged with drafting legislation for the proposed Constituent Assembly. The provisional government had been promising free elections and universal suffrage since February, but people were still hungry, land remained in the hands of big landowners, and the disastrous war went on and on. German troops had reached Reval—now Tallinn—on the Baltic; next to nothing now stood between them and Petrograd. Inflation was close to a thousand percent. Russia was disintegrating.

October was ushered in by cold rain. Then came a second revolution—Red October. An election scheduled for November installed the Constituent Assembly, and it met—once. Bolsheviks in no mood to abide by elections that did not go their way broke up the proceedings, disbanded the assembly, arrested the provisional government, and murdered two of its ministers. Now it was "death to the *burzhui*"—bourgeois. In one stroke, people of property were reduced to poverty.

Papa lost his job and the family's assets were expropriated. Papa's mother and sister lost Grandpapa's pension; all bonds and stocks were voided. With no job, Papa had no salary. As a member of the former upper house of government, detested by the new government, he had not the slightest possibility of finding any government work, no matter how apolitical. In any case, he said, there was no position in the new Bolshevik government that he could accept with a clear conscience.

To earn a bit to support his family—wife, five children, and now his mother and sister too—he finally found work as a day laborer, chipping ice from the sidewalks with a heavy iron bar. He was paid his paltry earnings by their oldest household servant, Grigory Petrovitch, to whom Papa had previously given his usual New Year's gratuity. Papa claimed that, to Grigory's credit, he did so with characteristic Russian delicacy of feeling.

After so many weeks of anxious sleeplessness, Papa insisted that the hard physical labor in the cold allowed him to sleep soundly again, a great blessing, and something to be grateful for. In spite of his brave attitude, the family wondered how long their slight father could hold out. Heinrich dragooned Georg into taking some toys and other things to sell at the market for much-needed money. They were among the younger members of the former "classes" now selling whatever pieces of their former lives remained—a little silver, a medal, some jewelry, vermeil embroidery scissors—to bring in money for food. For the time being, church services were still permitted, and on Sundays, the boys also sold circulars for a few kopeks at the church door.

There were no newspapers, but rumors, often wildly exaggerated, swirled through the city. Food became even scarcer; flour was completely unaffordable. They subsisted mostly on potatoes and dried vegetables. With no hope of financial help or food from Ottenhof, the hunger that had become the family's constant companion took on terrifying proportions. They discovered firsthand that hunger steals courage, makes people irritable, petty, and numb to anything beyond the immediate.

The city was starving. That winter they learned the true meaning of "Give us this day our daily bread." Yet the daily bread ration—fifty grams of rye—left them so weak that sometimes they could muster only enough energy to climb a few stairs at a time. Mimama spent much of the day lying down to save her strength. Still Papa dragged himself out to the icy streets, his hands raw from the brutal work. They could not afford suitable gloves, but Mimama made a lining for his worn woolen ones from an old leather pair of hers that helped a little. Just as it seemed they could not keep body and soul together much longer, help came from a family friend.

Sweden's ambassador to the Russian court, Edvard Brändström, was struggling to organize the Swedish Red Cross to deal with the many German, Austrian, Hungarian, and Turkish prisoners of war in Russia. He was a friend, he needed help, and he offered Papa a job. Not only was the work less exhausting, it also paid enough to feed the family, and sometimes Papa was given food, even a bit of meat. The Red Cross was headquartered in the splendid Yusupov Palace on the Moika embankment, where Rasputin had been murdered the year before. Visiting his father at work one day, ten-year-old Georg marveled at the palace's vast splendor and magnificent white marble staircase, but the grandeur paled in comparison to the small glass of milk he was given there.

The German army had taken Riga in September 1917. In February 1918, the family celebrated Papa's forty-fifth birthday with little cookies made of potato peels instead of the traditional yeasty, golden, pretzel-shaped birthday *Kringel* studded with almonds and raisins. Their Siberian "brick" tea had to be broken up with an axe, but when they learned that German troops had arrived at Ottenhof with horses and sleds exactly on his birthday, they hardly minded. They would live on hope; if they could get to Ottenhof, the nightmare would be over.

They survived the winter, barely, in icy darkness, living on dried vegetables, frozen beets, frozen potatoes, very rarely salt fish brought from Siberia by train, or horse lung. For weeks at a time, even the quarter-kilo ration of coarse bread was not available; bread was reserved for revolutionaries. In early March, with the Treaty of Brest-Litovsk, the Bolsheviks ceded control of the Baltic provinces to Germany. The long-term future of the Baltics was unclear, but the family decided to leave Petrograd for Ottenhof. There, at least for the moment, there was peace and food. One last time, Mimama was allowed to open the bank vault that held her jewels and the diamond brooch of the tsaritsa's *shifr*—imperial cipher—worn on the left shoulder of her lady-in-waiting dress, to turn its contents and key over to the "expropriators." Everything disappeared into the Bolshevik maw.

That terrible winter of 1917–18 was followed by a glorious spring. For the whole family, but especially for the children, the summer exodus was anticipated with even more excitement and impatience than usual. Petrograd was definitely not Saint Petersburg; it felt like a prison and they were desperate to escape. The patterns of preparing for departure were familiar: The maids Olga and Irina rushed back and forth, sorting and packing clothes, linens, and miscellany into trunks and baskets. But this time, vast uncertainty lay behind the eager preparations. The hope—even the assumption—that the Bolsheviks would not last, that at some point the mayhem would be over and the old ways would be restored, helped sustain them. But all certainties had been erased; they had no idea when they might actually return. In preparation for departure, the largest paintings and the Della Robbia Madonna had already been packed and sent to Saint Anne's next door for safekeeping.

Their wait for escape was long. Month after month, the government delayed. Spring turned to summer, and yet their exit visas came only after food shortages had completely overwhelmed the revolutionary authorities and the harvest was still just a promise. Papa decided to stay on at the Red Cross and join them later. On July 9, their train rolled into Toróschino, a border station near where Russia, Latvia, and Estonia met. After pass control and an exhaustive luggage search, they clambered aboard a freight train, and a hard-faced young Bolshevik soldier rammed the heavy door of the boxcar into the lock behind them. It felt as if a critical chapter of their life had ended. Slowly, the train chuffed off toward Pskov.

At the railroad station where the tsar had abdicated, they were met by German troops. Mimama, Tante Marie, the five children, Grandmama, and assorted female relatives were housed in barracks, subjected to registration, vaccination, and an official delousing. At Ottenhof, the sign announcing home was not in the usual Cyrillic but in the Roman alphabet. Arriving in the silence of the meadows beside the languid flow of the Salis, and in the green of the park, was more than a relief. Familiar faces welcomed them; there was food. Life had been restored to them.

Papa came to join them on a Red Cross hospital train in mid-August. Worried that his name would be recognized and cause difficulties, he was traveling under an alias: Anton Werner, actor. Asked to declare all Russian currency at a checkpoint, he knew that his one thousand rubles were well in excess of the amount permitted, but declared it anyway. He simply could not overcome his own honesty. What good was his alias, he wondered, if he was unable to lie about some rubles?

Two Red Guards hurried him off the train to the station house. Behind a desk in a small room stood a big man, his back turned, gazing out across the dingy clutter of the rail yard. Papa felt nearly faint with dread; the Bolsheviks were routinely shooting anyone caught smuggling significant sums across the border. Even if they did not shoot him outright, the train was leaving soon. If he missed it, he might not get another.

One guard announced him as "Werner," and the burly Russian turned. Startled, he came around the desk and rushed toward Papa. "Huene!" he roared, hand outstretched. "Don't you recognize me? We were in school together! I was two years behind you, remember?" They talked, Papa halting, tremulous, his schoolmate animated and garrulous, his face nearly swallowed by an immense grin. Glancing at his watch, he thumped Papa cheerfully on the back. Papa must hurry! The train was leaving, and travel arrangements were so difficult these days.

The guards escorted him back to the train, uninterested in whether he was Werner or Huene. Light-headed, astounded by his good fortune, Papa took his seat, anxious that his luck not turn before the train pulled out. What an extraordinary coincidence—encountering a friendly former schoolmate instead of some wild-eyed Bolshevik in this derelict little station so far from the real Saint Petersburg! Trying to calm down, he breathed deep and thanked God; he could live another day and go home to his family. At a station farther along the line, he saw German military helmets outside the train window. The region was under German control. After the fear and anxiety of the last months, he could barely contain his relief.

At Toróschino, like all travelers, he had to endure a true test of patience: three nights in wretched barracks for medical inspection and delousing. The fields beyond the station had turned into a shantytown, thousands of refugees swarming in a no-man's-land at the westernmost edge of a now defunct empire. Crude huts of scavenged wood and blankets provided ad hoc shelter for families huddled in the dust. Arranging themselves as best they could, they besieged the one remaining vestige of an earlier, civilized era: *kipyatok*—the hot water always available at the station for tea. Campfires lighted the dusk, occasionally a little homemade music lightened the mood, but hope was dwindling. Without exit visas, they were trapped; they could go no farther. The canned meat the Red Cross had given Papa for his journey was stolen on the first night. He was hungry and disheveled, but he felt blessed that his detention was only temporary. At last he was on his way.

At Walk there was no welcoming samovar or *zakuska* table as in the old days, so he bought some bread and an end of sausage. Hungry, exhausted, thankful not to be among Bolsheviks, he sank down on the grass of the familiar little cemetery nearby to wait for the train to Rujen and eat his humble and very satisfying meal. On the fourth day, from the heights at Osthof, the familiar lake shone below him like liquid silver and he could make out the ancient trees of Ottenhof's park. Three more kilometers. The summer air was pungent with the scent of resin, of earth and grass. He rushed across the high wooden bridge over the Salis, along the allée and through the park toward the beloved, vine-covered house. He was home.

Summer turned to fall but they did not return to what they still called Saint Petersburg, making educational arrangements for the children complicated. Mira had finished at the Gymnasium with distinction, and was set to teaching her younger sister, Ebba. Heinrich and a neighbor's son went off to boarding school in Fellin. During the week, Margarethe and Georg stayed at a neighboring estate to join other children for tutoring. Their dream of staying at Ottenhof forever seemed to be coming true. With great excitement and anticipation, Papa even invited the neighbors to a hunt.

October tottered into November. They heard news of a mutiny in the German imperial navy at Kiel that triggered revolution and sparked uprisings in Hamburg and Bremen. New councils of soldiers and workers were established that sounded alarmingly like the "Soviets" they thought they had just escaped. On November 9, Kaiser Wilhelm II abdicated.

Two days later, an armistice was signed; the war was over, but it brought no peace to the Baltics. An Allied Commission urged German troops to stay to keep the Red Army from reoccupying the region. The British even sent a squadron under Admiral Edwyn Alexander-Sinclair to Estonia with a shipment of arms, but German troops began to withdraw, and as they did, the Reds flooded in. Heinrich's boarding school was dissolved and he came home, desperate to volunteer for the Baltic Land Defense, like his cousin George and others. But Papa would not allow it: He was fourteen—much too young. Neighbors brought Margarethe and Georg home on rain-soaked roads. Everyone was happy to be together again, but the days of peace and relative plenty of Ottenhof threatened to be short-lived.

Days were cooler now, the nights cold, and keeping the house warm was impossible. Papa had most of the house's thirty rooms closed off, and set the carpenter to making shutters for the verandas along the entry and facing the river to help keep out the chill. Already limited to a few rooms by the cold, the family experienced an increasing anxiety that conspired to draw them into an ever-smaller circle.

On dark December nights, the skies northeast of Ottenhof glowed with flames of the estates and farms set afire by the Reds. The threat came closer every day. Some neighbors and friends were gone already, others were on the point of fleeing, yet leaving seemed unthinkable. When a nearby landowner asked Papa whether he thought the Bolsheviks were coming to slaughter them next, Papa realized that huddling anxiously around the big tiled stove, hoping at least to spend Christmas at home, was foolishness. They must leave now.

The house was decked with firs and candles for the Advent season, but there was no candlelight, no singing. Only seventy-five-year-old Tante Sophie refused to come with them, determined to live out her days in whatever way God had decided she should conclude her time on earth. She would stay behind with Gania, the Russian girl who had been with the family for years, to look after her. A cold wind rattled the panes as they gathered to pray in the great salon.

Some treasured possessions were bundled into a farm wagon. In wintry darkness, Heinrich rushed back to the great hall to take the portraits of revered ancestors off the walls. Over the centuries, they had brought this magical place into being. Their benign spirits had watched over his early years. If the houses they built were to be laid to waste, their graves desecrated, and the land alone remain as their monument, he would at least take their familiar likenesses into the unknown. His childhood was over.

The Salis flowed past Ottenhof to empty into the Baltic Sea, where the family found lodgings at Riga. At Christmas, a sleigh—a last greeting from home—brought them staples, flour, and some gifts. Their holiday dessert was a "fortifying" flour-based pudding, facetiously named after Hindenburg, whose wartime government had rationed flour and bread since 1915. It did little for their spirits. They were so close and yet so far from home, and Riga was roiling. The British still protected the harbor, but for how long?

On New Year's Day, 1919, they learned that the last German troops were withdrawing, the British squadron leaving the next morning. Flames from the burning Riga Theater were shooting high into the lowering sky that night, as they and nearly two thousand other refugees clambered aboard a clunky freighter, the *Roma*. Under the play of searchlights of British warships, the shoreline glittered with hoarfrost, like a dusting of sugar crystals. Occasionally, there was a great splash in the darkness, when luggage hastily, carelessly loaded toppled into the water. A baby carriage laden with bedding rolled almost soundlessly off the pile of boxes and luggage, splashed down, then bobbed and finally settled on the calming surface like a tiny coracle. Slowly, the water drew a white blanket out of the carriage to perform a ghostly ballet on the surface, until currents folded it in on itself and sucked it into the darkness beneath.

With no room below for the many passengers jostling aboard, they spent the icy night on deck. In the early morning hours, the British ships turned and steamed slowly out of the harbor. Riga was defenseless. As the *Roma* cast off, they heard wild gunfire. Apparently, the Reds were trying to force them to turn back. A machine gun mounted on the *Roma*'s deck returned ineffectual token fire. Gradually, at what felt like an impossibly slow rate, they moved out of range. The shooting became sporadic and finally stopped, leaving the deck in eerie silence.

The enormous tension eased a little, but an immense, almost palpable sadness fell over the assembled passengers. In an attempt to lighten the mood, the ship's band struck up a World War I tune; its familiar lyrics asked, *"Wer weiss ob wir uns wiedersehen"*—"Who knows if we'll see each other again?" It was an unhappy choice. The music, quavering out over the decks and across the icy water into the bitter morning air, gave voice to the desperate questions on everyone's mind.

4

Forfeits

What was Aimée doing while the world was at war and Heinrich's life was turned inside out? Living in oblivion: kissing Sammy Ferguson by the big oak tree in Elizabeth Park as part of some forgotten game of forfeits they were playing with Anita Dewing and Gilbert Gillette; coming home after seeing Nijinksy in *Le Spectre de la Rose* to announce breathlessly to her father that she was going to marry a dancer. With few dreams of personal glory, maybe she could marry a star. Her father was not impressed.

In the spring of 1914, her father remarried. Molly Staples, only eighteen years older than Aimée, brought energy, life, and sunshine into the silent house. The two "girls" developed a comfortable camaraderie, unlike any Aimée had ever experienced. As sticky summer heat descended on Hartford, they would submerge in a tub of cold water in their white batiste nightgowns, to spend an idle day letting the cooling damp evaporate slowly. Like companionable ghosts, they wafted silently through the big dark house, their bare feet leaving fleeting footprints on gleaming floors.

Corson was finally shipped off to Saint Paul's that fall. Though Aimée never understood why, there seemed to be nothing but bad blood between them, and his absence removed a huge source of tension and anxiety for her. But Molly was agreeable, and a placid well-being descended on the household. Aimée spent time with her books and her piano, and all was as well as—actually better than—it had been in recent memory.

For all her father's reserve and shyness, they did share one passion: books. He had written stories in college, dedicating one to her mother, and worked for several months as a journalist. His father's death had overwhelmed him with responsibility, but even after he was trapped at Travelers Insurance Company—a misfit in *the* company in a company town—he published *King Philip's War*, about relations between settlers and Indians in seventeenth-century New England.

He was still a great reader who had amassed a serious library, and he let his daughter loose in it. She could read anything she wanted, and did—continually scrunched into the cushions of the small settee. On the walls above her hung prints her father had collected. A Whistler Venetian scene and a Rembrandt etching of *The Blind Tobit* became familiar companions during the solitary hours she spent there, reading, reading, reading, until she too was shipped off to boarding school.

It was 1917. Fourteen seemed to be the age at which parents wanted you out. She could understand why. Corson's departure had been a relief, and she knew she was no prize. The riding and ballet lessons had done nothing to soften her sense of awkwardness. Braces on her teeth, inserts in her shoes, she was no glamour girl. She was wretched about her long nose and her inability to make even an approximation of small talk. There was no mystery about why they wanted her out of the house, but why, oh why, did they have to send her to the Masters School at Dobbs Ferry?

The mid-Victorian school for girls, Spartan, unbendingly puritanical, was ruled by the two Miss Masters. Miss Lizzie, the older of the two, had piercing black eyes. She was a diminutive creature with an imposing presence who behaved like a grand duchess. The other, Miss Sally, was incapable of keeping her foot out of her mouth. The girls wore long, scratchy woolen underwear down to their ankles and were to keep a diary of their bowel movements—exact times if you please—to be submitted once a week. Just before the appointed hour, the girls scrambled to fill in detailed, purely fictional accounts. They were permitted to leave the campus, a hodgepodge of imitation Elizabethan and Gothic architecture, only on so-called French Walks, a teacher in front, a teacher behind, and speaking only French. Before departure, one of the Miss Masters went down the line lifting the girls' skirts to be sure they all had on their woolies. In winter, with ice in the washbasins, no long woolies or high-button shoes kept an unending series of colds from making the rounds.

Bells regulated the girls' lives. Bells to get up, bells for breakfast, bells for class, bells for lights-out. From the moment a bell rang for class or study hall, communicating by word, look, or deed was forbidden. Any infringement of the countless rules was to be reported. The local hairdresser inspected them for lice after every vacation, and one returnee—horror!—brought some back with her. Sundays meant a parade to church in alphabetical order, then sermons, lectures on morals, Bible classes, visiting missionaries, hymns, Bible verses to be memorized and meditated upon. A Miss Masters dictum: "Never sit on the same sofa with a young man; the devil sits between you."

War was happening elsewhere; revolution had no echo here. The girls were so completely isolated that during the 1918 flu epidemic they had not a single case. The only thing that penetrated that hermetically sealed world occurred on one of the carefully monitored French Walks, when, out of nowhere, a girl—maybe eleven years old—came running toward the line of uniformed girls, dark hair flying, a look of utter terror on her small face. Then she was gone. Aimée had no idea who she was, what had frightened her, or where she was running, but she never forgot this startling, deeply unsettling intrusion into a life walled and buttressed against the real world.

Her irregular schooling meant she did not fit into any regular class, and she struggled to keep up, studying late in the bathroom, the only place where a light burned at night. She still did poorly, and was excluded from the dramatic society she was desperate to join. A longed-for weekend visit with another girl was canceled because she flunked an exam. She spent the weekend in her closet, weeping bitter tears; she would never escape Dobbs.

After two wretched years she pleaded with Molly and her father: "Send me anywhere, just not back to Dobbs!" When they relented, her only regret was leaving Nina Howell, her one good friend. But at Dana Hall, near Boston, her haphazard education meant that she was still considerably behind, and she took five years to graduate. Her graduation present in 1923 was Cook's grand tour of Europe with her great Hartford childhood friend, Anita, and Anita's adored mother, Mrs. Dewing.

Southampton, Chichester, Winchester, and Canterbury, tea in London on the terrace of Parliament, with not one, but two English lords. On to Oxford and Stratford by car, with a lugubrious chauffeur named Tear, then the North Cape cruise.

When they arrived in Hamburg with their many suitcases, their porter had his own suitcase stuffed with his tips: millions of marks, small change in Germany's postwar inflation. For well-heeled American girls, this was eye-opening. The hollow-eyed faces on the streets only underlined the contrast between their own well-fed privilege and the hunger and raging inflation in Germany. It was truly the grand tour: Paris, Montreux, Venice, Florence, Paris again. Long before they reached Cherbourg for the return voyage, Aimée had caught the bug; Europe had entered her bloodstream. The world was huge and intoxicating, and there was a great deal in it that she knew nothing about. She would be back.

Her father wanted her to go to college, but she would have none of it. With too much to catch up on at school, she had never taken the prerequisite Latin. Besides, she did not want to be part of a gaggle of girls anymore. The family surrendered on college, but insisted on a debutante season. You went to finishing school and you came out. They had done so much for her; now she could do something for them. One day, she would thank them for it. It was an essential ingredient of the ideal life.

The ideal life meant marrying one of the boys now finishing Yale or Trinity before they all went into the insurance business. They all had what was called a "good line." After you told them what fabulous creatures they were, you got married in style at Saint John's, with lots of bridesmaids. Then you had two children, two houses, two cars. You played bridge and you played tennis and you talked about them all the time, and you wound up in the family plot in Pearl Street Cemetery.

Had the family known the effect of their graduation present, they might have reconsidered, for it plucked her irretrievably out of the bridge and tennis circuit. The family plot was not for her. Life, she was convinced, was being lived elsewhere.

Under pressure, she caved in to the family imperative to "come out," but on one condition: Afterwards, she would go to New York and do as she pleased. It was a deal. Sensitive about the long nose Corson referred to as her "proboscis," she was also unenthusiastic about the flapper fashion. The

style of string-straight dresses with fringes meant that girls like her had
to bind their breasts to achieve the flat "look." Not only that, but "tango,"
the color du jour, was a nasty shade of orangy-brown that did nothing for
her blond coloring. Still, a deal was a deal.

As soon as the "season" wound down, she began packing for New
York. As she sat among the clothes and shoes strewn helter-skelter in
her room, Molly came in and asked if she knew where babies came from.
Yes, she knew where babies came from, she told her stepmother, and that
was the end of that. She was ready for the big world.

The big world was New York. She felt wildly lucky to find a room at the
Allerton, a hotel for women at the southwest corner of Fifty-Seventh
Street and Lexington Avenue, much sought after for its location and re-
spectability. She was wildly lucky because she was willing to risk the
consequences of taking the thirteenth room on the thirteenth floor when
no one else would chance it. Five days a week, she walked across Fifty-
Seventh Street to the Art Students League. Enrolled in the legendary
George Bridgman's life class and a class in portraiture, she found a new
friend, Mary Russell, from California. Soon enough, the two young ladies alone in the city were sharing an apartment at 121 East Eightieth
Street.

New York was bubbling with cultural crosscurrents and activity. The
twenties roared; she reveled in her escape, her new freedom and discovery of the world. A trust from her mother provided enough income for
her to indulge in theater, music, and whatever captured her interest,
even her weakness for elegant shoes. There were about seventy-five theaters in New York at the time, and she wanted to go to them all—to see
The Great God Brown, Desire Under the Elms, Grand Hotel. And there
were musicals: *The Student Prince, The Vagabond King*. She was out
almost every night, soaking up drama, dance, music, hearing and seeing
the great performers of the moment: Nijinsky, Landowska, Rachmaninoff, Katharine Cornell in *The Green Hat*, Walter Hampden in *Cyrano*,
Sacha Guitry, and Yvonne Printemps.

Nina Howell, her one friend from Dobbs, was at Barnard College in
the city, and on Friday afternoons, sitting high up in Carnegie Hall with

Nina and her mother, Aimée let music roll over her. She met Everest Haight, warm, lively, interested in much that interested her, and a member of the Metropolitan Opera Club. They went to the opera, they went riding, they waltzed, they danced the Charleston and listened to Lee Morse. In Greenwich Village they heard Edna St. Vincent Millay reciting sonorously about burning her candle at both ends. Tossing her red hair, baring her long white throat, Millay was a startling presence in Aimée's new, liberated life, and became a lifetime source of poetic quotations on the stark New England landscape and the vagaries inherent in erotic quest.

She liked Everest enormously. Many dinners, evenings, and weekends later, they were, if not an item, at least good friends, perhaps more. He was a very suitable young man in the family's view: old colonial stock, more than socially acceptable, and very "comfortably fixed" with funds from family mills. Her father was delighted. She liked him enormously, but she was not ready to get married; there was too much world to explore.

It was 1925. For two and a half years, she saw and heard everything New York had to offer. Though the family was not sure it was either safe or proper, she even took a tiny studio on Minetta Lane in Greenwich Village, painting and drawing to her heart's content. It was a dilettante's luxury; she never imagined herself a major artist, but she had escaped Hartford. She felt free; life was intoxicating, she was on top of the world.

5

The Bread of Exile

Heinrich's first footsteps on German soil were accompanied by curiosity and excitement. German was being spoken on Stettin's icy streets, yet everything about his family seemed to be conspicuously alien. Passersby nudged each other and commented. For the first of many times, he was pointed out as a refugee. Marked as a homeless outsider, he felt as if his very self had been erased. That first night, sleeping on one of many iron bedsteads set up in a local school, its thin mattress covered with paper, he tasted the bitter bread of exile.

As he told Aimée about it, she realized that she had always felt the outsider too, for reasons she could never enunciate. Nothing obvious marked her exile, yet whatever gulfs of experience and background separated them, they had this in common. His story was a revelation. He laid bare the foundations on which his sense of self had been built. Losing the setting for his life had made his memories of it indelible. This was something she recognized; she remembered the smallest tidbit of her mother's tenderness. For different reasons, his misery echoed hers.

Once arrived in Germany, Heinrich's family faced the dilemma of where to go. Since the revolution and civil war in Russia, Berlin had become a sort of stepmother of Russian cities; Berliners referred to the Charlottenburg district as "Charlottengrad" and grumbled that in the Wilmersdorf section only Russian was heard on the streets. But the family had relatives in Dresden, and family connections were critical. That was where they would settle.

Dresden was beautiful, a fine place for enriching the mind and educating the eye, and they quickly settled into a pattern that did both. They were penniless, but the city's beauties were free, the doors of its picture galleries and museums open. As soon as they arrived, the children dropped their bags with a relative and set off to see Raphael's

Sistine Madonna. On Saturdays, they heard Vespers sung by the famous Dresdner Kreuzchor boys' choir. Soon Margarethe was rehearsing Bach or Mozart with a choir one or two evenings a week, and the Royal Court Chapel offered glorious music. Evenings, Papa read aloud—biographies or his beloved Russians—and on Sundays there was more glorious music. What they had lost was very lost, they all felt it, but they never regretted settling in Dresden.

A relative found work for Papa at the Interior Ministry, but this good fortune was short-lived. In 1920, a right-wing putsch against the Weimar Republic failed, but succeeded in putting Papa out of work. He tried selling insurance, but salesmanship was alien to him; he would rather be a night watchman, he said, where at least he would not have to force himself on people. Finally, he went to work for Leo-Werke, a company that made Chlorodont, the first toothpaste in a tube, with subsidiaries in Moscow and Paris. He was responsible for Russian and French correspondence, a painfully modest assignment.

The first years were bleak, and the news from home was terrible. Bolsheviks had rounded up relatives who stayed, and shipped them off to Siberia in cattle cars with BARIN—GENTRY—chalked on the sides. Papa's brother Emil, the lively flutist who'd brought shell casings for the boys, was shot, ending up in a mass grave, leaving his Lili with five young children. It was almost too much to bear. Then his mother died, and soon after, his sister Marie.

But for Papa, the hardest of all was seeing his Mima in their present life. She never complained, but silent tears sometimes ran down her cheek, and he blamed himself. When someone from the old days visited, her tears give way to smiles and chatter. Otherwise she withdrew into her memories, where the beloved rooms of home spooled, enfilade. A letter of Heinrich's, written from Providence in 1924, recalled her birthday at Ottenhof in September 1918:

> Out as the sun rose out of the mist, to gather chrysanthemums, bright phlox heavy with dew, the last pale roses, I carried my heavy burden into the silent house. I filled the big bowls in front of the salon mirrors with asters. The phlox went into your

flower room, roses to the ancestors, to the library, chrysanthe-mums to Papa and to the hall, while the gardener decorated the dining table and your desk.

It was already eight, but I hurried out again into the blue Sep-tember morning, to bring you something special before everyone gathered to celebrate. By the cold frames near the orchard, I found mignonette, covered with pearls of dew. Dashing up the house's broad steps, I saw the birthday table, the burning candles, shining faces, but you were not yet there.

Slipping up to your room, I saw you reflected in the dressing table mirror, pinning the brooch with pendant pearls on a silver-blue dress. The sunny fall morning, your grace, the blessed free-dom after Saint Petersburg, and your beloved silver hair made me inexpressibly happy.

Handing you the dewy bouquet, I suddenly sobbed. For joy I said, when you asked, but we both knew it was not just happiness. You took me in your arms and we got a little sentimental. I re-member this birthday so clearly. That morning was so blissfully still and beautiful, our last peaceful celebration in the old nest. Do you remember, Mama?

Papa could not forgive himself for Mima's desolation. At home in Russia, he had been busy at work, in the church, and certainly at Otten-hof. There had been a future. But here he was a little factory worker. He erected a wall of modesty around himself, a bulwark against admiration, maintaining it with the same passion with which he praised his adored wife. That wall became his one pride, and his children sometimes had trouble finding the father they loved and admired hidden behind it.

Adapting to their new circumstances was easier for the siblings. Mlle. Sophie's offer of work for Heinrich in Providence was a financial godsend, and things brightened. The Nicholson File Company was not what the twenty-year-old Heinrich had in mind for himself, and he wrote home saying that he felt captive to less-than-captivating employ-ment, but Providence offered consolations, and beautiful Hope Cary was only one of them.

Heinrich's daybook of that time is full of social engagements and girls' names: *Ball at Agawam Hunt Club, May 23; Charity Ball and Nancy; Sunday—Julia at church.* One nameless young thing is memorialized with multiple variations on her initials, S.V.R., interspersed with notations like *"L'amour est l'unique extase; tout le reste pleure!"*—"Love is the only ecstasy; all else weeps." Everything testifies to a young man quick to respond to a charming smile or an agile mind, but hardly neglecting his intellect. Quotations from Rilke, Li Po, and Rupert Brooke rub elbows with Russian citations, Hugo's *Les Miserables,* and text from Handel's *Messiah*: "Why do the nations so furiously rage together?" In December 1924, he wrote to his parents:

> Ever since the great balls of late November, life is swirling around me: I am perched on a wave of glittering winter nights— parties, concerts, dances and dinners. All this won't last. The long lonely trips in the snowy north will begin, and the bright images of today will seem a garden of wonders. My trip [to Scandinavia] has been postponed, and that's fine with me. I am penetrating deeper and deeper into the wonders of language, and many people here who were merely acquaintances are becoming friends to whom I will always be able to return.

His captivity in less-than-captivating employment had served its purpose. His parents and siblings were eating better, and he now had the funds to pay for study.

6

I Never Knew—Ooh, Ooh—
What Love Could Do—Ooh, Ooh . . .

Pedaling and picnicking through the countryside, Heinrich and Aimée saw some of France's famous and lesser-known treasures in the area: Azay-le-Rideau, a jewel-box castle with peaked roofs and airy turrets that belied the solidity of its corner towers shimmering like a mirage over water; the cathedral at Tours with its brilliant flower of a rose window; Chambord, with a glorious gallimaufry of pinnacles, dormers, towers, and chimneys.

When the French program concluded, the little château began to empty. Soon there was room for her; she said her farewells to Mère and Père Fenique, and Heinrich helped her move into a high-ceilinged room looking out on the park barely touched by fall. But the miraculous summer was coming to an end. In early October, on the morning of her birthday, she was still luxuriating in bed when there was a light knock at her door. He had picked her a bouquet of the wild cyclamen that carpeted a shady bank in the park, their small pink heads nodding in dappled sunlight. The room was very still. As he knelt by her bed, the clear fragrance of the little flowers blossomed out in a rush, exuding a power that ensnared them both. The silence between them grew, engulfing them in an immensity of feeling that could only mean a shared future.

Heinrich had to leave. His dissertation was waiting for him at the university at Marburg. On the way, he would visit an old uncle—Mikhail Basilevitch, affectionately called "Buddha"—at Toffen, a small château in Switzerland. He was also planning a trip to England to talk to G. P. Gooch, a recognized authority on the origins of World War I, about his new book on European diplomacy, a topic of particular interest for his dissertation. But "today," he wrote from Toffen, "I have nothing to say to you but love, love, love! Lucky you are not here; I fear your ribs would not be safe in my embrace."

She would not go back to the States yet; she needed time to consider a future that looked both wonderful and terrifying. But she would at least stay on the same continent as Heinrich. With money from her mother's trust, she was free to do as she pleased.

On their way through Italy, she and Hope had seen Mary Russell, her friend from the Art Students League, in Florence. Now she wrote Mary, suggesting she join her in France and discover the delights of bicycle touring Heinrich had introduced her to. Mary needed no persuading, and Lestion became their base of operations for touring the Loire and its châteaux. Young, attractive, and obviously foreign females, they zipped through the fall countryside, occasionally scandalizing old ladies, which only added to their delight. In late October, she wrote Heinrich from Paris:

> I'm miserable that you have not received my letters. I can't bear for you to think that I would have deserted you for so long. Your own letters are so infinitely dear to me. How wholly beloved you are. I put my face between your hands and the tears are tears of great happiness.
>
> Somehow I have to bridge those heartbreaking miles between us and this wretched pen is the only thing I have to do it with. Tonight I must tell how dearly, dearly I love you. The window is open and I can hear the night wind in the poplars. If I close my eyes I can almost believe you are kneeling beside me, your head on my breast, your arms around me so, your kisses on my mouth. Oh heart, heart, the time is so long.
>
> I've just spent two perfect days among drifts of yellow leaves, wandering along the *quais*, shopping, eating filet of sole twice a day and generally enjoying myself. In a day or two I hope to go to Nantes at last.

Nantes was a special errand. After World War I, France was awash with orphans. The Red Cross and American welfare committees were determined to help their devastated former ally by arranging long-distance adoptions to deal with the problem. Among Americans who could afford it, such adoptions were seen as the "decent" thing to do, and became quite fashionable. For several years, Aimée had been corresponding with and sending money to Anna Malé, her *fille adoptive*. She had written Anna from Paris to say that she would like to meet her at last.

Off the main street of the pretty town, she went up a very steep stairway, down a narrow corridor, and turned a big brass knob at one door. A distant bell rang. Hesitant footsteps, then *"Qui est-ce?"* A small child sniffled audibly. The door opened, and Anna, dark and wiry, holding a teary little girl of about two, led Aimée down a dark hallway. A bedroom and bath lay off the corridor that opened into a larger room. A crib in one corner held a small bundle with a head of dark, shining curls. By the window, where the light was good, stood a sewing machine, a basket of fabric, and sewing miscellany. Nervously, Anna offered tea.

Aimée had a toy for the child, and some small gifts for which Anna was effusively, embarrassingly grateful. For half an hour Aimée sat awkwardly over her tea, then quickly got up to go when the baby began to fuss. Many farewells, thank-yous, and promises to write, and she was gone. The visit left her wondering whether she was actually doing any good. She had written often, sent money regularly, but she had had no idea that there was a second baby, and there was no sign of a husband. Anna's sewing was bringing in something, but with two babies . . . She would send more money. What else could she do? It was a relief to find sunshine in the city park, where a fresh wind blew away gloomy questions.

In Paris, she and Mary settled into an apartment in the house of a slightly eccentric, genteel, if ever-so-slightly-down-at-the-heel count and countess on Rue Louis David. Heinrich dreamed of a career in the diplomatic corps. If she was to be part of his life, working on her French was crucial. She signed up for private French lessons, for art classes, rented a piano, and even took a few tentative German lessons at Berlitz. That would keep her occupied while he worked on his PhD.

Busy with this self-improvement campaign or not, away from Heinrich, she was visited by doubts. Absent her letters, these can only be inferred from the pattern of reassurances in his. Apart from sharing a life completely taken up with his studies, he labors to calm her fears about her inadequacies, their continental divide, and their future:

Often mountains prove to be clouds when one approaches them. Uncle Bill is wrong. I could not find a better wife than you. We would be fools not to marry! One thing you can be sure of: You can trust me to the end of my life. . . . If you think you can marry me, I shall love you truly and continuously. . . . The things I want are so rare, so precious. They are above nations. . . .

Before he goes home to Dresden for Christmas, he begs her to meet him in Kassel. She mustn't worry about not speaking German; the train from Paris is direct and he will meet her at the station. "I am preparing a small gift for you, very modest, but rich in love."

Of course she would come. But in Saarbrücken, the "direct" train to Kassel went elsewhere. She would have to get another train. French occupation of the Saar coal basin, a legacy of Versailles, was causing deep resentment in the local population, and given the mood, no one was willing to speak French. English did not seem to work either. Not being in control of her situation always made her uncomfortable. Now, feeling increasingly uneasy, she realized that she was getting an education in the tensions that were fraying Europe's temper.

Marching into the stationmaster's office, she pointed to the train schedule. She needed to know: what train to Kassel, what platform, what time? After much gesticulation and a noisy, frustrating exchange, she knew it would be a three-hour wait. Pushing on the heavy brass bars across the glass door of the station restaurant, she found a small table, pointed at random at the unintelligible menu, and settled in to wait. She knew where she wanted to go; now at least, she knew how to get there.

As the train pulled into Kassel, she leaned anxiously out the window and, to her vast relief, saw Heinrich on the platform. Not knowing what else to do, he had simply waited and waited. Throwing himself into the compartment, he scooped her into an enthusiastic embrace and rushed her out of the station. Daylight was fading; there was no time to waste. He wanted to show her the great ruined castle high above the city.

In the snowy woods surrounding the ruin, he asked her to walk ahead a bit—he would catch up. Thinking he needed a private moment behind a tree, she walked slowly, then heard him call her back. Candles flickered tentatively on a small fir tree dusted with snow. On its branches hung pictures of his family: Mimama, Papa, Mira, Ebba, Margarethe, and Georg. This was his Christmas present. He was very poor, he had nothing else to give, but he was giving her his greatest treasure: his family. They would become her family too.

She had always felt orphaned, and he was inviting her into his warm and intimate family circle. It was a circle she did not yet know, but it felt like coming home. This was a true gift, an extraordinary gesture suggesting that a huge heart lay behind it. She was overcome with happiness, tears, nerves—it was hard to know exactly what. She had never encountered anyone capable of such emotional freedom. The sentiment, the unconventional largesse of it, spoke directly to her heart.

This was a new emotional sphere, and her every instinct hungered for a life lived differently. She had a choice between two worlds: the old but familiar one of stiffness and strictures, empty apart from loving, unchanging Uncle Bill; this new one, full of unknown challenges, but with an extraordinary man and love at its center. It was frightening, dizzying, but hesitating could only make her more unsure. She would take the leap—joyously.

Back in Paris, a cable from her friend Anita invited her to join her and her mother in Algeciras for Christmas. She accepted happily, glad for the distance, glad for the time it would give her with these two, not back in her "other world" exactly, but a reminder of good things from her past. It would let her weigh, balance, and even bolster her confidence in her sudden and terrifying leap into commitment. A cold Algeciras made them take ship for Casablanca, thinking Morocco might be warmer, then rumble through the North African countryside to Marrakesh and the sumptuous Mamounia Hotel. With them, the gap between the old and the new seemed less daunting. She felt that the whole world was spreading its wonders at her feet, engulfing her in miracles.

Happily among his family meantime, Heinrich imagined Aimée in that charmed circle beside him. His letter, forwarded from Paris to Algeciras, then back to Paris, is full of wedding plans. They will honeymoon at Ottenhof. Why did he not think of it before? It is a ruin now, but he longs to show her the place where his heart lives. Camping in a bare room, their windows will open to the "spring night, the scent of lilacs and the song of the nightingale." They will have the river for a bathtub, the lake to sail on. They will read in the park; old Jaeger, the overseer, will give them lunch.

He has had a long, delightful conversation over tea with the Nostitzes, and another with his cousin Oswald, counsel to the Foreign Office and working closely now with Germany's president, Paul von Hindenburg. Things are looking up: His inquiries at Berlin's Wilhelmstrasse about a future in the diplomatic service are getting serious; he feels cheerful, hopeful, and greatly relieved to have her letters from Marrakesh. He had imagined horrors: "Oh my dear, my dear, where are you? Where is your dear heart beating at this moment?"

Anxious about the problems they faced, about whether his family would accept her, she had been "lining up the dragons [he] has to slay this year" while he finishes his studies. The unloved, motherless little girl from Hartford worried about being up to snuff: intelligent enough, educated enough, attractive enough. And she doesn't speak German! But he is all reassurance. His family knows he's hard to please, he admits; their only concern will be for her nobility of spirit. For them, aristocracy lies in the moral person. Intelligent enough? "I never noticed you were anything but intelligent, but I shall be glad to find that what I considered brilliant were your dullest moments." As for language, she need not worry; "everyone knows French."

He maps out twenty-two pages of options for overcoming their "long painful separations, and rare, short, hectic meetings." The daunting programs involve her coming either to Dresden or Marburg, and take everything into consideration: living arrangements, suitable chaperones, companionship, ways to keep her engaged, educate her, help her get to know his extended family, people and culture, and—best of all—give them more time together. His conclusion: During their engagement she should join him in Marburg and learn German.

By page nineteen, he is exhausted. It is past midnight. He feels the constant pressure of work. She must realize that he has been hers since that morning in the little church at Lestion. But, he writes, "if you can find somebody who can make you significantly happier than I promise to do, follow him. While my heart and life will be broken, I shall bless your happiness." Next to these words, a note in the margin: "Fine plot for a tragedy or an etching!" Even in exhaustion, humor has not deserted him. He is delighted that she has bought beautiful things in Paris. His mother shares their secret, he says, but no one else, and closes with words that speak directly to the motherless child in her: "My mother will open her arms and her heart to you. God keep you until that day."

In late January 1928, he writes that she must continue her French studies. While he is in London in March and April, she should also take the Sorbonne's *Cours de Civilisation Française*. She is eager to learn; he is eager to teach and share everything. "Oh my dear! What a world with you!" He advises on what to study at the Sorbonne and with whom. As a long-distance docent, he offers enthusiastic, painstakingly detailed advice on what to see in Paris's many museums, but finally concludes: "Henry, stop now! You are getting crazy. Do you really want to kill poor, darling Aimée? BASTA!"

While she is improving her French and furnishing her mind, he is studying, reading, doing exercises—little stick figures engage in push-ups on the page. He has also been taking serious riding lessons—she must do the same to strengthen her legs and back. Yes, she fell off a horse badly once with Everest, but she must try again. The bareback exercises are so effective that she will never fall off a horse again. Then they will ride together in the forest at Chantilly.

But not all his letters are lectures on self-improvement. There are repeated snatches of what may be a popular song, or his own creation: "I never knew—ooh, ooh—What love could do—ooh, ooh. . . ." After Chantilly they will go to Marburg, where she will be under Daisy von Pritzelwitz's motherly wing. They will walk together for an hour each evening and he will come for one meal a week at the "Pension Daisy." When he has the time, they will make fabulous excursions into the countryside. Soon her German will be good enough to sit in on lectures.

Mary Russell, sharing Aimée's apartment in Paris, hoped to remedy her perennially precarious finances and dependence on Aimée's habitual generosity by breaking into modeling. She enlisted Heinrich's help

because of his contacts in Paris's fashion world. He wrote on Mary's behalf in February 1928:

> Here are two cards: Mainbocher, editor of Paris *Vogue*; very
> fine, delicate creature, charming, exquisite taste, *Vogue* from
> "top to bottom," and he must be taken that way. He lives at 18
> Rue de l'Université, but see him at his office. I advise Mary to see
> him first, and to see George [his cousin, the photographer George
> Hoyningen-Huene] only on Main's advice. If Main is not in Paris
> and not about to return, Mary should see George, but *telephone
> first*! George is always very busy, in a hurry, hard working. Best
> time: 4–5. I am writing to both.

For Aimée, he has also copied out pages from Maurice Paléologue's
memoirs of his time as France's last ambassador to the imperial Russian
court. According to him, "Baltic barons" swallowed up all the high court
offices, much of the army, administration, and diplomacy. "By furnishing tsarism's most devoted servants . . . the Baltic feudal caste consti-
tuted the regime's principal armature and was responsible for the
triumph of autocratic absolutism." Harsh words; Aimée must remember
that Paléologue was French, that the memoir was written during the
war, and that "I can fairly say he is not objective."

Possibly not, though Heinrich's own family could certainly testify to
the German influence at court. A few days later, responding to a plaint
from her: "If French grammar bores you, some consolation: your love is no
better off." Reading fifteen hundred pages on *"l'évolution du système ban-
caire en France"*—the evolution of the French banking system—for a paper
he must deliver at the Institute of Economics has scrambled his brain. Taking a break, he has been reading Colette, and composed the Ballad of Mme.
Colette: "The Story of Mme. Colette-Willy, Telling Who she is, What she
does, Whom she married, and Whom she loved" in English doggerel:

> They produced seven books, or ten,
> She wrote, he corrected and never neglected
> The public, both women and men.

He was right, for these books had success.
He was wrong, for she in distress,
Said "My life is a bore! I'm your sweetie no more!
I can't bear that my books wear your dress!"

Colette continued to write
Books more delicate surely, than bright
But in France of our day, please believe what I say—
In the desert of art, she's a light!

"*Mon Dieu!*" countered Aimée. "Who is Colette? I shall never be a success with my French teacher if I am ignorant on that subject."

The *New Yorker,* a weekly magazine . . . has this theatrical review of *The Merchant of Venice*: "The only other person who stands out is Hope Cary, a velvet-voiced newcomer who plays Jessica." Read it and weep! Isn't it grand! How I would love to see her.

I didn't realize that I had written "not sure yet about Holland" [the rendezvous, planned earlier]. Such flippancy on such serious matters! For myself, when I am terribly tired or thirsty, I always wait, do a thousand little foolishnesses first, and then take my cool, clear drink. Is that being gourmet or super-gourmand? Yet, it would be kinda nice to see the golden-haired shepherd boy. Only, O Heihohne, isn't it better that we have separate rooms if I come? I'm positive and think you will agree. Three days—I insist on going to a concert or the opera. I have such an ache to put on my best clothes and go on a bat with you. Truly, it must be most romantic to have a young and ravishing female following you all over the map of Europe. How anxious I am to see you, to know you more, to talk with you as an intelligent human being instead of as a lovesick lady, who may be human but is seldom intelligent.

In London he has found documents not available in Germany, and met with British historians. His letter puts us back to the planned rendezvous, and for ten days, the cross-channel mail debates the merits of sharing or not sharing a hotel room. He cannot afford it, but does not want her to pay for a separate room for him. He insists they should share because

I have more and more things to tell you. If you insist on banishing me to another corner of the hotel, don't be amazed if I knock at your door at 2 past midnight because my heart is frozen in loneliness and my brain chock full of things that can only be said between 2–4 in the morning. I promise to be very obedient and a true knight.

As the big day approaches, questions and suggestions:

What time are you arriving (so that I can count on you 5–12 hours later—am I not mean)? Whoever arrives first makes arrangements at the hotel, and, if the concierge winks, goes to meet the other at the station. Here is a flower from my garden.

Sending Hope's engagement announcement, she says: "Claude looks smug, Hope has a curious, unreadable expression. What was going on behind those eyes?" Everything about the time that the three of them spent in Paris told her that Heinrich had been captivated, even in love with Hope. Then, as their relationship deepened at Lestion, he confessed that he had been besotted. At this news he writes:

I had asked that she forget the things I could not give her, forget them for love. But the things I could not give her mattered more to her than the things I could. My pride was hurt. In those moments of weakness, dishonesty, sentimentality, poverty— both inside and out—there you were, my dear, calm, serene, kind, wise, intelligent, mature, cool, understanding, and the whole sentimental affair with Hope vanished like a cloud, to bring forth the calm, more impassioned, yet deep, immeasurable love I wanted: not flirting, playing, chatting like Hope . . . but the way my mother and sisters look at life—never fearing to lose many things in this world—because to us they simply *do not* amount to anything. My mother has lost those things and I have never heard her complain, and she has not grown an inch smaller for it. . . . I do want you sometimes to be simpler, more ascetic in things. . . .

I want you to be Aimée and nothing else, in rags if you please.

He objects to the "heiress" in her, some privileged debutante posture—a taste for fine clothes perhaps—but he always appreciates her generosity.

One letter, clearly written at the end of a long day, is reflective, prayerful:

Evening has come silently into my solitude. I have nothing to tell you but what you know already: I love you. I hear no sound but the running of time. The glow of my fire is extinct. My heart is quiet in this silence, all my thoughts rest in you.

He seems to have made a complete recovery from beautiful Hope, and spring had come to London.

What can I do with pen and ink to tell you how happy you make me? My heart bubbles up into my throat, my breath is short. There is so much growing within me. I can almost understand what it must be like to feel a child growing inside.

London will be in full spring when you come. The sun is just setting in clouds à la Turner.

He is making wonderful contacts: dinner with old friends, the Buzzards; their son in the Foreign Office; a bigwig in the War Department with his Russian wife; the establishment portrait painter, the Honourable John Collier. The Buzzards know Lord Haldane, Gooch, Bernard Shaw, et al.—a whole list of British luminaries of the time, and not least: "Luncheon with a man who put me in touch with the right hand of Stresemann [Weimar's foreign minister], up to my standard: brain, heart, all in good form."

Walking into Barclays Bank, he asked to see Mr. B. himself. It was an impromptu request, sparked by his own family connection to Barclay de Tolly, the Russian field marshal who fought Napoleon. The curiosity and directness of approach were typical and disarming, as was the charm that often guaranteed that such out-of-the-blue requests were met with enthusiasm. And sure enough, not only was he admitted to Mr. B.'s inner sanctum, he was also invited to the family country house for the weekend, the beginning of a relationship that lasted for many years.

Spring was returning to Paris too, as Aimée wrote on April 1, 1928, to Oxford, where Heinrich was pursuing his work:

> I have written at least five letters and one after another has found its way into the wastebasket. This enforced solitude weighs so heavily and yet Paris is beautiful. A pale green mist of buds and a frosty breath of blossoms are in the Blois. A bird sings in the garden with a sob of ecstasy in his throat. But all these things belong to someone else. I think it must be "us." Oh my Darling, someday they will.
>
> . . . It is curious how your happiness becomes my happiness, and what an extraordinary comfort I derive from knowing that you are among charming people. Your letters have been more than ever precious to me. Such letters to such an unworthy object, and yet—*mein Liebes, Liebes,* I love you.

Then, writing from the Grand Hôtel du Nord the following day:

> Rouen under an Italian sky. I am all alone for the first time in months and so happy. The cathedral is perfect, but not as a temple to religion. I held up traffic for half an hour, having fallen into the profoundest of meditations in the middle of the street. Those soaring stones against the same throbbing blue glimpsed through the temples at Agrigento! Was any other world so beautiful or any other life so sweet!

His almost daily letters are full of what—apart from his studies— he's thinking and reading: Colette's *Chéri* and *La fin de Chéri.*

Her manner is the most delicate and sensitive I know in the literature of today—what Marcel Proust did in his more intellectual analysis, she achieved in the impressionist method, beautiful, finely chiseled language!

April 11, 1928
34 Great Ormond Street, London, to 18 Rue Louis David, Paris:

I am in real bachelor's chambers here—books around me and in the misty grey of an old London street below, children yelling and playing. Once in a while beggars pass by, playing a tune on a violin. Sentimental songs, the gaiety of children under a grey sky—it charms my heart. I love it and feel at home.

I am waiting for you.

This was impossible for Aimée to resist. She dashed to London to meet him, later writing to Mary:

My Dear Squeedunk, Calais, snow on the ground, the crossing a polar expedition, ice on the mast, snowflakes on the eyelashes. London. Aimée in three shirts, two pairs of stockings, two sweaters, my nose the color of shoe trees. Gladys [Mary loathed her "ordinary" name, so Aimée often invented alternatives], what have I done to deserve this? Still, a nice life. A rather complete tour of the National Gallery and the Tate: Uccello, Mantegna, Rembrandt's *Philosopher,* Rubens' *Chapeau de Paille* . . . We've traipsed all over London, theatre every night, and tragedy. . . .

As to the Bolshevist prayer meeting, it was a great failure. Henry had hoped to catch a few intellectuals but instead got a small crowd of morons. But the Russian—tall, ravishing, with a mop of long black hair and a great sweetness and intelligence. The three of us went to Hyde Park on Sunday. Orators on all subjects; no charge, but brains at a premium. Then home to tea, then supper. Henry and Arkangelsky talked for four hours while the idiot sat by, chewing her fingernails with excitement and despair.

I finally went to Kenilworth and Warwick. Long vistas of lawn sliding down to a misty river, little English daisies like a terrestrial Milky Way, old walls, immense trees in their first breathless green—that was heaven! For a day or two I decided that I could not marry anyone but the Earl of Warwick, but when I got back to London I forgot all about it.

Henry dashed off to Oxford at the last minute, then two days on the way to Germany. We stopped off in Cologne and saw three churches and a museum in two hours—we have got this down to a science. The cathedral is pretty fierce on the outside, rococo gothic, unsoftened by time, but the inside is tremendous, larger than even Milan, I believe, with a breathtakingly lovely choir. The other two churches were very early, 11th and 12th century, one with the skulls of 2 legions of Roman soldiers massacred in the 4th century, as they were Christians. The skulls were saved from an earlier church destroyed about 900—St. Gereon. They were the first Romanesque churches I have seen—with a breadth and depth to them—a great calm, almost a "stretching of the soul," after the soaring, mystic gothic. The gothic strives, but these strengthen. The day after I got to Marburg, it snowed!

7

Life Is a Beautiful Dream

Marburg was a picture-book town, the embodiment of medieval Germany, all steeples, turrets, and gables—a fitting place for the Brothers Grimm to have studied. Steps helped pedestrians cope with the steep climb from the river to the picturesque castle looming above it all. In fact, Jacob Grimm insisted that the town had more stairs than its half-timbered houses. The Gothic town hall's rooster flapped his wings every hour, and on the market square a fountain splashed agreeably at the feet of Saint George. Aimée wrote Mary, entranced:

> Life is a beautiful dream. Marburg is a mass of lilacs and frail apple blossoms bursting out of sooty twisted branches. Dozens and dozens of pigtailed little girls with the pinkest cheeks imaginable, peasant girls in enormous petticoats and great twisted shining yellow braids, and hundreds of students with many-colored caps, audible in harmony in the wee hours, perpendicular cobbled streets staggering up to the old castle and a grand view across a tossing sea of flowers. The name of this ditty is "Love in Marburg in the Spring."

The town and surrounding countryside, so obviously inhabited and lovingly tended by generations over the centuries, spoke to her. This was an old civilization; signs of a rich past were everywhere. Even the humblest, most utilitarian article merited some carefully crafted beautification: carved heads on newel posts, inventive, whimsical—a fiddle-playing hare—or often outrageously irreverent gargoyles at every church downspout. The wrought-iron support for the gilded cluster of grapes announcing the inn *Zur Goldenen Traube*—the Golden Grape— sprouted sinuous arabesques of tendrils and vine leaves. The chimney sweeps wore black suits and stovepipe hats, just as Heinrich had said, and carried the ladders and brushes of their trade. Some narrow alleyways and steps could be navigated only single file or, in their case, by squeezing wonderfully close, as the great bells of Saint Elisabeth's Cathedral reverberated in happy cacophony over their heads.

She delighted in the peasant costumes, so ornate, so varied according to region or village, so unlike the old blue serge at Dobbs and the flapper outfits of her crowd in the States, so utterly, wonderfully different. She had escaped Hartford and landed in a fairy tale that included a handsome prince, but she never forgot Mary in Paris.

> Dear Petronia, please tell me how things are working out. If you don't, I shall send another hundred dollars. . . . Anna, dear heavens! is having another baby—now what do I do?

The welfare agency through which she had adopted Anna had been sending notes extolling her "kindness and sympathy for the fatherless children of France" at regular intervals for almost ten years. The war had done its damage; now Anna was about to produce a third fatherless child of France. There was no way money could undo the damage, but recalling the dim, jumbled apartment, the two wailing little ones, and Anna's huge, fearful eyes, she sent more money. It could not hurt.

Money went to Anna and to the consistently financially distressed Mary. Heinrich was grateful for a check—already sent on to Riga. Whatever it was—monies for a needy relative or for repairs at Ottenhof—money is part of a pattern of financial help that surfaces repeatedly: money for big things like a new roof for Ottenhof; money for little things, for Anna's new baby, a signet ring for Georg.

That spring, without telling the family the reason for her visit, Heinrich's mother came to Marburg to inspect her prospective daughter-in-law. Though it was hard to imagine, the siblings suspected that Heinrich must be in some sort of trouble. Why else would Mimama undertake the trip? And why not Papa? They were beside themselves with curiosity. With her usual quiet diplomacy, Mimama avoided particulars, and arrived in April to meet Aimée.

Mima within the family, Mimama to her children, Marie Emilie Olga, born Countess Sievers in 1873 in Saint Petersburg, was a majestic figure, clothed in a still serenity. To everyone who knew her, she displayed the same steady calm, gentility, and warmth. Her deep blue eyes were set in fine, long features, her silver hair was swept up in a turn-of-the-century style accentuated by high collars, and always, she wore a fichu or a black ribbon with a cameo at her throat. As a girl at Saint Petersburg's Smolny Institute for daughters of the aristocracy, she had learned a measured, gliding walk, almost like skating. Before her marriage, she never combed her own hair. After war, revolution, and years of poverty, she still exuded dignity, an inner stillness and gentle surety. She was like a visitation from an angel. Heinrich was right: Aimée had found her mother again.

On her return to Dresden, Mimama dropped the bomb: Heinrich was engaged. She had met his fiancée, an American woman, living in Paris. First stunned silence, then questions: Does she paint her face? Does she smoke? What other clichés of Americanism did she represent? At this point, the truthful answer to the first two questions would have been "yes" and "yes," but Mimama did not know the truth, and she dealt with the family's anxieties about their golden one with aplomb.

Heinrich, meantime, wrote to the focus of his family's anxiety.

Do you realize that yesterday was the anniversary of my love? I am glad the "14 Juillet" is over but I shall never forget that day and how sweet it was to bring you that first shy flower of my affection for you, which has grown ever since and is growing still.

I feel a burning thirst to read, read, read and widen my horizon. There is an enormous responsibility in politics; you can rely on your instincts only if you have a precise, reliable understanding of history. I cannot permit myself as much leisure as other people. I get up early and by noon, 5–6 hours of work are already behind me.

Here are a few linden blossoms. I wish they could bring you some of their scent that I love so much. Ottenhof is full of it at this time of year and our honey comes from the linden trees in the old park and around the orchard.

With Aimée in Marburg, Heinrich's family began to come into the picture in various ways. Mimama thought that since Heinrich was so busy, Aimée should have daily sessions with an eccentric, antique aunt—one of the many. It would be an excellent way for her to learn German and become acquainted with the family's history and a good deal else an American girl needed to know to fit into her environment-to-be.

Heinrich had described his aunt, Princess Ada de Tolly-Weymarn, as "highly intelligent and a grand lady of the old days," warning Aimée only that she "talked a bit much about God." In fact, she was an extraordinary mix of Christian piety and utter worldliness. Her title was inherited—everything about her said "Princess"—but the personality was entirely her own: a vivid mind in an infirm body. The minute anyone came into her salon, she would sit forward in her armchair, seize a notepad and pen, and wait expectantly for whoever entered to say something worth noting. Her mind then pounced, masticated, and either noted and digested it or tossed it aside as unworthy.

Nearly everyone, except possibly Heinrich, found this deeply intimidating, but for someone with educational insecurities and desperate to pass muster, whose native language was not German (or French), it was torture. The daily sessions were unlike anything at Dobbs, or any deb-party torments where the lingua franca was gossip, supplemented by fashion chitchat and weather. Those earlier experiences had often been dull and awkward, but the discomfort she'd felt then paled in comparison to the excruciating experience of having this tiny old woman claw at her mind to glean tidbits of substance to sustain her intellect and spirit. Aimée had no doubt that she would be found seriously wanting.

Uncle Bill responded to news of her engagement, saying he had heard that everyone seemed to be marrying Russian princes these days, but who knew what kind of people they were? Colorful, surely, but he was concerned. He wanted to look this one over personally, so he and Aunt Marion were coming to Marburg for an inspection. Aimée felt deeply grateful. He cared. In her desolate childhood years, he had always been there, gentle and warm, trying to fill in for her mother however he could. Now he cared enough to play a protective role that would otherwise be unmet.

Seeing Uncle Bill and Aunt Marion was wonderful, and, as expected, the "Russian prince" passed inspection. When they returned to the States, Aimée went with them. She needed to arrange her affairs and collect her things, and it was also a graceful way of cutting short her sessions with the formidable aunt. Stopping in Paris, she then wrote Mary from the *Mauretania* in late June 1928:

> Well, you saw what left the Gare St. Lazare. Here we are, bootleggers and their wives and the rest of the idle rich—me. So snooty am I that while the rest of the world walks the deck in their new shoes and Paris models, I turn out in my good old faithful browns, my rose-colored spectacles, and my Cyrano [the long nose she hated] in the air. Alone, I consider myself an adult infant, in such company, Socrates.

The flowers she sent Daisy in thanks for her Marburg hospitality arrived when everyone was at dinner. Heinrich reported: "Tableau: 'Ahh! Oooh! How beautiful! So Miss Ellis will be with us for some time yet.'" At this, all Daisy's guests looked at him, and he "blushed like a tulip. Daisy was so glad to meet Uncle Bill, Aunt Marion. 'They were so real, so nice—100% American.'"

> I went out to get some flowers to put in this letter. The enclosed St. John's wort reminded me that this is St. John's day—the summer solstice. At Ottenhof tonight they will build a fire high up in a tree in the park. Everyone wears wreaths and sings the old songs around the fire. Out after supper to listen, we were given wreaths too. My father would give a feast in the big carriage house where the floor was good for dancing. The sun was up almost all night.

A few days later, he realizes that she has made him reevaluate his attitude toward Germany.

> I feel more and more at home in Germany, no longer a critical stranger, but a loving—if critical—friend. You have helped me a good deal to come to love this country. How long is the list of all you have done for me?

The refugee from Hartford had persuaded a refugee from Saint Petersburg to come to love Germany. She had found things there she had never found before, an exhilarating, all-consuming love and an adventure into a new cultural world, while he had seen mostly what was wanting.

Mapping out a tour to take when she returned—through northern Italy, then back through Vienna and Prague to Dresden, where the family expects them—he asks: "Do you remember the night by the fire in my room with my mother? Strange and sweet that friendship, love and understanding grow in silence, not words." Until now, he had found the comfort of silence only within his family, but now he has found it with her. That is true intimacy. He looks forward to Italy. His work is going well; he is gathering strength, collecting his forces. Enclosing some poppy petals, he signs off "Heinrich = Hercules."

Then his letters sound a new note:

> My Heart's Dearest Love, Where are you? What has happened? It's over a week since I had your letter from the boat and I am trying to persuade myself that this agony of waiting will end as happily as when you came back from Africa.
>
> Coming home, I say to myself: "No, there won't be any letter today. The table will be empty, as it was yesterday and the day before . . . Perhaps the day after tomorrow, or next week. Don't be impatient. . . ."
>
> I cannot think you want to test my love; you know it is yours forever. But you said one day you would not marry me if you had a child. I protested then, and I protest now. If you tried to go away alone under such circumstances, you would make me very unhappy. My greatest wish is to marry and have children with

you. . . . I could not bear the feeling of having broken your wings, given you a child and abandoned you. . . . I could not bear that responsibility. . . . I do not want to bind you by saying "my wife," but I am your husband. I am not made for a bachelor's existence. I am terribly worried. . . .

He has had no word. He doesn't want to bother her, but he can't concentrate, he can't work, cable is expensive.

Aimée, Aimée! What is it, in God's name? Why not a single word? This waiting is agony. Heaven help me. You left a month ago. Since that day, nothing. If it is what I think it is, please tell me! I want to see clearly.

After weeks of torment, her silence is explained; she is pregnant. His response:

The Lord bless you and keep you. Darling mother! Dear, dear wife, how happy I am! I am looking forward to our child with gratitude and a quiet heart. My only wish—do not leave me! If you need someone to be with you and take care of you, my dear, quiet sister, Ebba, is silent and strong, with the goodness of an angel.

My father loves calm people like you, and my heart tells me he will love you silently and more deeply than others. And is my mother not your mother already? Has she not enough goodness of heart to soothe all the past suffering of your lonely childhood? On our wedding day we shall look into each other's eyes and celebrate our union for life and for our children.

I cannot take my eyes off the darling portraits of you as a little girl and of the dear face of your mother in which there is so much of you. If she is still near you at times, I hope to heaven she would like me. I am quite boyishly in love with you, smiling under that glorious bonnet with the ostrich feathers, those little hands in their white gloves. You look so kind and serious, there is all your wisdom and goodness of heart.

Above all, she must not worry about the effect of this development
on his plans and their future. She had said earlier that if she were pregnant, she would not marry him at risk of jeopardizing his career ambitions. "I am not bound hand and foot to diplomacy." Another, written to
the SS *De Grasse*, French Line Pier, New York, sailing August 30, 1928:

> I doubt whether this letter will ever reach you but I want to
> give my happiness to the winds that blow in your direction, that
> some of it might reach you. If, suddenly, you feel happiness com-
> ing to you, you will know it comes from me. I am so happy, so
> strong. I feel as if I have sunshine within me to last a life-long
> winter. Here is a modest flower for you from my garden. Do not
> suffer, do not worry, my own one. Don't you think I am strong
> enough to make our way, yours and mine?

"Mary, Mary," Aimée wrote her friend in an infuriatingly undated
letter, "love has not only to do with desire. Is the 'importance of living'
only the desire of the moment? Desire alone is without meaning and
'hateful wedlock' is an idea that does not touch on this. You said contra-
ceptives, I said abstinence. I knew Heinrich's ambition, I knew, or should
have guessed the consequences, but I was weak. . . ."

Bearing the "consequences" en route to her future aboard the SS *De
Grasse*, she remembered lying in that fragrant May meadow, trying to
marshal every ounce of her native toughness to resist his urgency. They
must wait. But the flowers and grasses bending over them, the stars
turning in the night sky, had conspired with her own desire.

Her mind had been made up long since that there would be no family
plot for her, at least not in Hartford. Now there was no doubt whatever.
Buoyed by the exhilarating tumble of Heinrich's letters, only her natural restraint kept the great bubble of anticipation she felt from bursting
through. Asked by a smartly dressed fellow passenger when she planned
to return to the States, her emphatic "Never!" elicited a sharp look, a
turned back, and heels clicking off across the deck.

8

Abie's Irish Rose

Meeting Heinrich's entire family for the first time, Aimée wrote Mary, was like entering a time warp, a life arranged according to 1890 norms. Tradition ruled a household of enormous simplicity, and a deep, slightly formal mutual respect between family members forged a sense of harmony she had never experienced. At the end of meals she often found alarmingly skimpy, each family member in turn kissed Mimama's hand, a gesture of respect and gratitude to the lady of the house, whose thought and effort had provided the meal. As children, Heinrich said, they had always kissed Papa's hand as well, until one day Papa would not have it anymore.

Money played no role here. Heinrich's cherished younger sister, Margarethe, told Aimée that when they were growing up, their father often said that whatever they thought they wanted, they could also do without. The lesson had held; their life was spare, even Spartan, but money did not mean here what it meant in Hartford. They had learned to live without it, and Dresden was the perfect venue for living richly on slender means. Then again, as she wrote Mary before the wedding,

Oh Myrtle! Ravenna, Verona, my dear, dead youth and the crazily beautiful time we might have had. Still, I relinquish my complete freedom with nothing more than an anguished sigh, but I shall never relinquish my right to vagabond. I shall probably turn up on the doorstep of your Turkestan villa one of these days with my galoshes, clutching a bag of books and a cardboard hatbox of shoes.

If you could see me, a dazed mutt in the center of literally hundreds of sisters, aunts, uncles, cousins, their husbands and wives, stared at and vivisected, your heart would ache at the sight. Heinrich marrying an American! Isn't it aw-w-ful! And with all our German girls needing husbands. I am going to feel like the sacrificial lamb at the wedding, surrounded by high priests. It's humorous—Abie's Irish Rose, but thank heavens, it is *not* Hartford. Only ten more days of being AE.

The eve of the wedding—the *Polterabend*—friends and family acted out skits of telling incidents in the past lives of the bride and groom. Margarethe appeared as the young Aimée, in rain boots and carrying an umbrella, bending again and again to pick something gently off the ground and place it tenderly to one side. Mira as Mis' Walker peered through an empty-picture-frame window, looking puzzled. Whatever was her little charge up to? Aimée had told Heinrich about her affinity for earthworms, and here she was, rescuing earthworms stranded on Prospect Avenue's rainy sidewalks to put them on the grass. Already she exhibited the caretaking tendencies that eventually involved more than just the humblest of God's creatures.

An incident from Heinrich's past had his younger brother, Georg, in the leading role. Entering stage right, he taps his head in an *aha!* gesture. He has a brilliant idea. He goes off to find his sister Ebba, stage left, with a bicycle for sale. Just what he is after; a bicycle will save money on tram fares. He pays, climbs aboard, and wobbles off, stage right. Asked how he got it home, he says matter-of-factly, he rode it. It had never occurred to him that he had to learn how to ride the thing—an example of his blissful lack of awareness that anything could stand in his way or might go wrong, a trait his bride encountered often in their married life.

They were married on her twenty-fifth birthday, a brilliant blue October day, arriving at the church, she wrote Mary, in a "small black coach lined with ivory satin, drawn by two white horses, and attended by two buff-liveried gentlemen of most picturesque mien." She had hoped to be alone with Heinrich on the way to the church, but a little nephew was so taken by the vision of the fairy-tale coach and dancing white horses that it was impossible to deny him. She wore her mother's wedding dress, its appliquéd satin daisies a nod to her mother's nickname.

The altar of the Gothic Sophienkirche was decorated with autumn leaves and trailing vines, the dark nave lit only by candles. Traditionally, bride and groom sat on two little chairs in front of the altar during the ceremony, but she insisted on standing. Worriers fretted that she might feel weak during the ceremony, but she was adamant; surely, for one of the great moments of her life, she could muster the strength to stand for twenty minutes. If worst came to worst, she had a good strong man to hold on to. The service was in German and she understood almost nothing, but the good strong man was there to poke her and prompt her proper responses.

"Afterwards, surrounded by every possible relative, near or distant relation," she told Mary, "I smiled and drank, and smiled and ate, and smiled, and smiled again for six hours." Heinrich, a genealogy buff, knew all the relationships of this immense family, and had given her thumbnail sketches of who they all were. The names of the cousins, uncles, and aunts she was dealing with that day, from the various branches or "houses" of the family—Ottenhof, Heimar, Echmes, Lelle, Navvast, Addila, Lechts, and so on—run to forty-five pages in the genealogical table of German nobility. Their convoluted relationships bewildered even initiates; for a novice operating in a foreign language, they were incomprehensible.

"From now on," Heinrich said on the train en route to their honeymoon, "we speak only German." They had always spoken English, sometimes French. German had terrified her since the Saarbrücken incident, but it was too late for terror now. She would learn German, and quickly. There were other things too. Her hair was bobbed; she smoked; she painted her lips. But *"Eine deutsche Frau schminkt sich nicht"*—A German woman does not wear makeup. She would let her bobbed hair grow; the German would require more effort.

Honeymooning, she wrote Mary about Bamberg—"walks along autumn roads to old monasteries"—and Heidelberg, "the most glorious

ruin, walls flaming with woodbine . . ." And from Toffen: "a small castle, turned chateau." Their windows opened onto a walled terrace garden
and an astonishing view of meadows and villages toward the Jungfrau,
"alps along the horizon, and in the dawn, the sound of cowbells coming
down from above." She described its "carved Renaissance room, a long
gallery in *cuir de Cordoue* [embossed leather panels, painted and gilded],
hung with superb ancestors," citizens of a distant age, with starched
white ruffs or a soldier's breastplate, hands on a globe or books, peering
down on the young pair, some benign, some dour. According to Tante
Margot, their hostess, some were there to make sure there was laughter
within Toffen's walls, the others to make sure the laughter did not get
out of bounds. "Now I've written pages without mentioning Heinrich,
but he is responsible for all wealth and happiness. . . ."

From Breslau, the newly married woman wrote Mary:

> I don't dare tell you the horrors of our domestic existence.
> We're so broke it's painful, but you are well-acquainted with my
> present state, it happens every three months [when the income
> from her mother's trust was paid]. But this time it has been gor-
> geous for I had wedding presents to spend. We bought a candela-
> brum, a carved chest and an old chair in Berne [near Toffen] and
> beautiful old Strasbourg faience. In Dresden, a whole service of
> flat silver, an elegant old engraved glass, a superb painted tray
> and, I nearly forgot—a French Renaissance mirror in silver which
> we had no business buying but which was so extraordinary that
> we did. Then Aimée spent 24 hours in Berlin, bought a comfort-
> able chair and a sofa, came home, did her accounts and immedi-
> ately went to bed.

Newlyweds on a buying spree, to create a country of their own, far
from any sense of exile. Flush with wedding-present funds, they were
determined to furnish a new life with glorious things—plant a flag, lay
claim to their future. She had no reason to doubt that these purchases
were an affirmation, enduring feathers in a permanent nest.

9

In a Thousand Ways an Exile

Heinrich's dissertation adviser, Professor Siegfried Kaehler, was leaving Marburg for a prestigious post at the university in Breslau, and according to custom, Heinrich would follow him. An ancient city with a long history of changing rule and shifting cultural influences, Breslau had become a bit of a backwater after World War I, but with an excellent university.

After their honeymoon, they settled at Beethovenstrasse 21, Breslau, living modestly, but as she wrote Mary, "Yes, we have a study, and *Gilles* [Mary's gift of a print of a Watteau painting] looks out over Heinrich's beloved head." Her things came from America, and busy in expectation of their baby, involved in her new life, she was unaware of much going on around her. Even if her German had let her manage the newspapers, they might not have clarified the political chaos of a country splintered between so many parties, prey to any enemy, particularly internal weaknesses. The Hartford debutante was about to be enlightened.

Communists marched in the streets with red banners. Their rallying cry, "Hunger!" was understood throughout the country. Germany was starving; people died of malnutrition. The war, the humiliation of Versailles, and a disastrous inflation had wrecked the dreams of the young and confirmed the grievances of the old. There seemed to be nothing to hope for and no politicians had any convincing answers. Only Aimée's money stood between them and the fate of many.

Even with Aimée's help, Mary's finances could not sustain her in Paris, and Aimée wrote:

> Knowing that you are leaving Paris closes—even more than my departure closed it—a long and uneven chapter, not devoid of human interest: a friend betrayed; a lover rejected; an acquaintance

hurt; a friend found; two deep loves created. You wrote the rest of the chapter quite by yourself (or perhaps it was a new chapter). Anyway, it's over, and the books of our lives well begun. I would like to write chapters and chapters of deep happiness into yours, but perhaps someone else will do it for me.

In Breslau, Aimée was on her own. Heinrich was always busy. He was a husband now, about to be a father, and he must finish his degree. Russian archives relevant to his dissertation were newly available; he was excited, working steadily. For her, this meant that he was hardly ever at home and had little time for her when he was. Her German, improving but still meager, made her self-conscious. She felt isolated and lonely. Still, they were young, they were in love, newly married, and expecting a child. It was all something of an adventure, and there were bright spots.

For their first Christmas alone together, "We bought the tree with as much care as one might give to buying an estate, and decked it with candles." A fresh snowfall on Christmas Day inspired them to "grab our toothbrushes, bundle up and go for a glorious weekend in the country, sledding like schoolchildren," trundling her expanding belly down the hills. Back home, from the roof of their house they watched the majestic, transatlantic *Graf Zeppelin* drift by, "beautiful as a Grecian urn." Addicted to travel as they were, the zeppelin's planned round-the-world trip in 1929 seemed miraculous. "The thought that it can make the trip to America in three days is amazing—one might be in China in ten days to two weeks—Fabulous."

They were both refugees, she from America, he from a lost world that now existed only in memory. He had told her once that he knew how important it was to move on, to look toward the future. Memory must not harden into myth. Still, no matter how engaged in the present or ambitious for the future, he inhabited a landscape of exile. Part of him was locked into a longing, backward glance. His exile was emotional, with an edge of sorrow, restlessness, and frustration. Dante, he said, had described it perfectly in *Paradiso*: First, you leave everything you cherish most; then you discover that the bread of exile is salty, that it is hard to climb another's stairs.

They shared an outsider status, though she had volunteered for this part of it. Her life now was more that of an expatriate than that of an exile; she was only as cut off as she wanted to be. He had opened a door she had never been able to find. This marriage was her passport to a life of family, of belonging to something, of kinship. The tight circle of his family, bound by shared experiences, was sometimes hard for her to penetrate, but she had enlisted in the life he dreamed of creating, and she would put her energies into making it reality. "Never!" she had told the woman on shipboard asking when she planned to return to America. She would not go back. But oh, the language!

Most shopkeepers were friendly and patient with her very halting German. The grocer, Herr Wenig—Mr. Just a Little—an aptly named wisp of a man as thin and fragile as a Meissen teacup, was always very welcoming in his diffident, modest way. *"Frau Baronin spricht gebrochen Deutsch"*—"The baroness speaks broken German"—he would say kindly, always taking the trouble to be encouraging without abandoning the truth entirely.

In late February 1929, they went to hear Wanda Landowska and next day, she gave birth to a baby boy, convinced that Landowska's music would be an important influence on this new life. Papa announced that this grandchild was a wonderful, if slightly early, birthday present for him. The boy was named Friedrich Alexander, after Heinrich's grandfather. Now she had a real family.

The winter was bitterly cold, a once-in-a-century kind of winter. People claimed that trains froze to their tracks. Versailles's peace terms meant that coal from the Ruhr was going to France, and even in Breslau, an area rich in coal, there was little to be had for love or money. Only through their stalwart cleaning woman did they manage to get any warmth at all. With her large purse clutched tightly in both hands, her sturdy, worn shoes slapping the pavement with the intensity of her purpose, Frau Dombrowski marched off to announce to her coal-business relatives that there was a newborn in the family; they simply had to have coal and her mission was to see that they had it—now. She returned with a small bag of coal, and some came every week thereafter, not enough to make the apartment cozy, but enough to keep the geraniums alive.

The economic fragility and hardships of that winter created a volatile mix of desperation and anger. As Aimée was walking from the beautiful Gothic central square to Herr Golandowski's butcher shop one day, with the baby in his carriage, a strange young woman she had seen occasionally suddenly rushed at her: "*Steinreiche Amerikanerin!*"—"Filthy rich American!"—she hissed, spitting and sticking out her tongue for emphasis. The venom from this unhinged creature was a reminder of how much of Germany was faring.

That spring of 1929, one of Heinrich's professors invited several of his students to his country house near the Czech border. They spent time outdoors in spring sunshine during the day; evenings after dinner were filled with talk in the comfortable living room, much of it political, naturally. The big windows onto the garden were open and soft air was moving through the room when one of the students jumped up and paced nervously, declaring suddenly that the first priority was to get rid of the Jews.

He might as well have thrown a firecracker into their midst. The room held its collective breath.

"Oh," their Jewish professor said mildly in the pained silence, "so you've got to throw me out?"

The Jews were smart, the student said apologetically, even sheepishly. They had cornered the good jobs. They were doctors, lawyers, professors, and that was the problem. It left no work for anyone else, or for him. His tone turned truculent again. People were out of work and in trouble, all because of the Jews.

Aimée leaned forward in her large chair by the open window. "Do you mean you are not smart enough to get a job," she asked, "or just not as smart as the Jews?"

There was an uneasy quiet in the room. She had done it again, she realized. She had opened her mouth when she should have kept it shut. This was a forum for doctoral students, not for her. She was there by special invitation, and had no business inserting herself into what was obviously a fraught discussion. Terrible times had produced fear and resentment. Her husband's position was infinitely better than that of most of his friends and fellow students. After all, he had married a rich American.

The sense that Jews were more intelligent, more focused, often dominant in their fields, was alive, she knew, even in intellectual and academic circles. In a sense, it made Jews victims of their own success. But the idea that somehow they were just smarter and better than anyone else seemed impossibly simplistic. She balked at the notion that they were the beneficiaries of some mysterious wisdom come down from generations of forebears hunched over massive tomes, far from worldly pursuits. Still, at that moment, whatever resentment this fellow was not directing at the Jews, he was directing at her.

"I'm sorry. Please forgive me," she said, excusing herself from the room and leaving embarrassed murmurs behind. She would walk in the garden, where there was little danger of alienating anyone, and calm down. Then she would go to their room and write some letters.

Escaping Hartford left something to be desired after all. The émigré experience was liberating, but isolating. Heinrich was always lighter, quicker on his feet, far ahead of where his circumstances warranted. She wanted to be there with him but he was temperamentally better suited to finding his way into almost any situation than she seemed to be. And he spoke German! Her kindergarten German frustrated her efforts at conversation and real relationships among the few people she did know. Breslau offered little to make up for the lack of companionship, like fashionable clothes or shoes to set off her elegant feet. And Heinrich was always so busy—with work, with fellow students, professors, and friends. Letters were her lifeline. If her friends did not write, she was wretched, as she told Mary.

Ah, Myrtle—If only I could wring your neck—but no. Have you sailed to China or Japan and forgotten your old hanger-on in Breslau? My son is in long pants, and whiskers, Heinrich has just been proclaimed Kaiser, and I have had my face lifted—Why the hell don't you write? Only in my adored *New Yorker* that you send where you scrawled something in the margins now and then. Otherwise, nothing. I feel in a thousand ways an exile. If you cherish a last gram of affection or shred of memory for many glorious days spent together, write me.

Breslau is a cross. We might as well be living in Kalamazoo. Heinrich never fails me, but I fail myself sometimes. The son is also a help, but one does so want to speak English with a blessed female like yourself.

Betty Judd [an old acquaintance] and her newly acquired husband met us in Berlin and I didn't let the poor girl open her mouth. Nobody had any chance at conversation save me. Berlin was very nice, everyone was very kind and gave us parties, but next November we move there and Heinrich must *commute* to Breslau [five hours] every week for three months, coming to Berlin for the weekends or every other weekend, leaving me alone with the cook. I contemplate it only with horror.

I have met a few older women and an American girl who married a German and is just dying to get back home. She thinks that people who let themselves be Europeanized are dreadful!

Write, write, if you have an ounce of pity!

They did escape for a whirlwind trip to Paris, which was having a Russian moment; revolution had brought an influx of fugitives—the cream of Moscow and Saint Petersburg salons. Some aristocratic émigrés had managed to stash a few remaining jewels and still had a bit to live on, but most were falling back on whatever talent, style, or exoticism they could muster to help make ends meet. Chanel had aristocratic fingers embroidering collars or cuffs on the Russian-style peasant tunics—*rubashkas*—she was showing with such success. "*Pauvreté de luxe*," fashion designer Paul Poiret called it.

Some émigrés scratched together their few remaining rubles and cachet to start fashion houses, naming them by concocting exotic amalgams of initials or syllables of their own. Irina and Felix Yusupov created Irfe, and Roman de Tirtoff became Erté. Those in the know could play the guessing game of who was behind this or that boutique or house. Heinrich's cousin George was working as a photographer for *Vogue* and *Harper's Bazaar*, and did a typically elegant portrait of the young pair in his characteristic chiaroscuro. Aimée was pleased with Heinrich's likeness, but no happier with her nose in the photograph than she was in real life. George knew the entire cohort of artists, designers, and theater people in fashionable Paris, and took them around to his friends. His "garret" apartment was simplicity itself, pared down to refined tranquility. His sister, Betty, designed and sold accessories for her fashion house, Yteb, on the Rue Royale, among them the silk scarves Nina Sievers was producing in the south of France. Some old networks were at work, even in exile.

Paris was definitely not Breslau. At Vionnet, Aimée succumbed to a sleek, bias-cut black satin dress, though she worried that she might never have an opportunity to wear it in Breslau. At one dark little *boîte* full of artists, designers, and photographers, she discovered the delights of blini and caviar. Though French could substitute, Russian was clearly the lingua franca, but she barely minded understanding only bits and pieces of the swirling conversations. After the drear of Breslau, she was giddy with the glamour and excitement.

Hurrying along on the Île Saint-Louis the next day, Heinrich suddenly stopped dead. He turned to the great portal of an *hôtel particulier* and rang the bell. When Aimée asked what he was doing, he said he had seen the house years before. It was particularly lovely, and he wanted to show it to her. Did he know the owners? No, but . . . At that moment, a servant opened the door. Heinrich explained that he had visited this wonderful house once, earlier. Would it be possible to show it to his new wife? The servant disappeared.

She turned to him in disbelief. Did he realize how embarrassing this was for her? But when the servant returned and ushered them in, she followed meekly through the beautiful rooms, pondering the amazing creature she had married. It was a matter of temperament; convinced that every path would be cleared, he met life with a high heart and perpetual optimism, unclouded by the possibility that he might be refused, or that things might not turn out for the best.

In Breslau, she recapped the heady days for Mary, who was planning to be married.

I've just been to Paris and seen underwear! I want to start on
your trousseau. Still, I want to be practical as well as beautiful;
send me your measurements! [The sumptuous underwear intended for Mary's trousseau would be stitched together by Russian princesses and countesses down on their luck.]

Yes, Paris—mad and glorious days with Heinrich. He knew I
was fed up with Breslau, but not how much, and Paris saved my
life. He was pursuing a job that has not yet materialized [an
opening at the Foreign Office]. It was so nice to be gay in Paris.
Approaching it from the continental side, I looked at the place as
if for the first time. Rue Nicolo [around the corner from their old
apartment] gave me a twinge, only it seemed to have acquired an
added bit of well-to-do, and seemed more beautiful than before.
When one grows too familiar with objects or places, one loses
oneself in picking out details and flaws; the whole vanishes. Only
Heinrich remains unchangeably beautiful in my eyes, with the
character and disposition of an archangel. How much happiness
has been thrown at me!

Mary had worried about repaying "loans," but Aimée insisted:

Don't worry about any of it. As for the hundred, it is yours to
buy yourself a temple, the Peacock Throne, or anything else you
might like for a wedding present.

It is June 1929, Friedrich is lying beside me under an acacia
tree, his feet waving wildly . . . he coos in the most angelic ac-
cents, low and sweet—only a cherub could utter them. I have
been polite about other people's children; I find mine beautiful
beyond expression. How strange that according to the world Friedrich's being is wrong. So beautiful a thing should only be right.

Have I told you Heinrich is marvelous? With tremendous
spiritual and moral power based neither on ignorance nor popular
philosophy—extraordinary in this world where strength lies in
blindness and weakness is seeing. I am so undeservedly happy. . . .

Mary, Mary, when are you going to China [to get married]?
You can't treat me as I treat you. It is so great an event in your

life. In more inspired moments I see you on the boat, sailing sailing into a strange future, probably a stranger one than I sailed into. I only wish you a happiness as complete as mine. It will be different, but cannot be vaster.

Walking in Breslau in early October, she saw a stark notice in a shop window: STRESEMANN DEAD. Foreign Minister Gustav Stresemann had worked hard to reconcile with Germany's former enemies, lighten some conditions of Versailles, and restore Germany to international respect. With help from his French counterpart, Aristide Briand, he had been remarkably successful, and the two innkeeper's sons shared a Nobel Peace Prize for their efforts to rebuild a Europe shattered by World War I.

Heinrich was devastated. Stresemann had nurtured a new liberal idealism among the young hoping to push beyond the doubts and gloom of the recent past. The French newspapers Aimée read and all but the most hysterical extremists recognized that his death was a huge loss. Among the fifty or so political parties, there was no one of stature to tame the monsters that fed on misery and political chaos. Heinrich worried that squabbles between parties hoping to inherit even a shred of his legacy would bring a shift to the right; the country could lurch toward dictatorship. Three weeks after Stresemann's death, whatever progress he had made toward stabilizing Germany's economy disappeared in the 1929 depression.

Still stinging from the terrifying inflation of the twenties, Germany plunged into catastrophe. Wages for industrial workers were lower than in 1914. Five million of the country's sixty-four million people were out of work. Businesses collapsed. People were hungry, with little faith in the system such as it was, and almost no expectations for the future. Heinrich's generation thought they might never find work, never afford marriage, home, or family.

"Our plans are as foggy as ever," Aimée wrote Mary. "Next month, Berlin, this winter, Heinrich's PhD. Spring, you, summer Ottenhof, hope for the FO [Foreign Office] fainter than ever—everything subject to change. How I wish I knew what was happening to you! Please, please write."

10

No Ground Under Anyone's Feet

Adolf Hitler seemed an unlikely candidate to save the country. He did not look the part of national savior, nor did his shrill, bellicose rhetoric sound particularly promising. That spring of 1930, many considered him a very small man. Since winning less than 3 percent of the popular vote in May 1928, he had been scrambling up the political ladder, blaming all Germany's ills on either Bolsheviks or Jews.

Anti-Semitism, if in a more genteel form, was familiar to Aimée from childhood. When Mr. Wise of the Wise, Smith Department Store on Hartford's Main Street began building a house next door on Prospect Avenue, people said he was Jewish, adding quickly that of course they didn't know him, but he was said to be "rather nice." She knew only that his store carried her favorite drawing pencils, those Uncle Bill had given her for Christmas one year, that meant so much to her. At Dobbs the very Christian Miss Masters explained that the school could not accept Jewish girls, because if it did, "the parents of so many of our girls would take them out." Even at fourteen, Aimée thought that odd; Jesus was Jewish, and the disciples, even the saints. It did not fit with the love-thy-neighbor ethic. Even at Dana Hall, Jewish girls were referred to as French or Austrian.

But the anti-Semitic rants of a marginal politico were not uppermost in her mind. As she wrote Mary that spring, she had her own worries:

Ah, but I shall be glad to leave Breslau! This summer we all hope to go to Ottenhof and then probably to Berlin where H. will do his law exam. I hope it won't be the F.O.—Foreign Office. I saw a bit of that life in Paris—two or three teas a day, and receptions— Oh, Myrtle—I couldn't! We will try to make him Minister of Foreign Affairs. Travel is heaven, but moving is the devil itself! I want too much: five children, an estate, interesting and brilliant people, and then, above all, this for Heinrich. Daring to consider even one of these desires is a form of presumption.

She lamented having to pack so many books and shoes, her two passions. "All I can see are books, books, books, the odd shoe, packing cases, and books!" while Heinrich went to Berlin to "hold a lantern over my head," as he put it, to find work.

Diogenes's odds of finding an honest man with his lantern were better than Heinrich's odds of finding work in Berlin. He met with his cousin Oswald, experienced as counsel to embassies in Stockholm and Belgrade, and in Berlin's Foreign Office, and now working with Reich president Hindenburg. But things did not look promising; the Foreign Office was closed to newcomers for the foreseeable future. Like thousands of others, Heinrich found only closed doors. His letter to Aimée from Berlin's Hotel Kaiserhof on the mood in the capital encapsulates the era's dissonance: extravagant frivolity afloat over a thousand fathoms of anxiety.

The hotel is completely full. There is a beauty pageant, and the place is as animated as a beehive. In all the corridors are beauties—or such as would like to be beauties—of every imaginable variety. Next to them: old men; young men; youths with monocles, cigars, armbands. These men live on beauty, tending it as one might tend flowers, and then let them be photographed. The judges pass as the lovelies dance, wander, or glide by. Then the announcement of the prizes; the electric suns are lit, and the beauties smile into the cameras.

Outside, the big city is at work. A zeppelin circles in the dark sky, beaming down advertising. The nights now are bright with balls and concerts, but there is no ground under anyone's feet.

Older Germans often said that anyone who had not lived before 1914 had never tasted life's sweetness, and things had been hard since the Great War's opening shots. Heinrich's family had known hunger already in Russia, and arrived empty-handed in January 1919, in a country reeling with unemployment, its own hunger, and political unrest. In 1921 the mark dropped

from four to the dollar to seventy-five. By late 1923, it had plummeted to
trillions to the dollar. A reputable upper-middle-class salary of 65,000
marks brought home on Friday could not buy cigarettes on Monday. Prices
went up so quickly that putting money aside was pointless. At nineteen,
Heinrich had outgrown everything. His father's shoes were too small, but
no amount of scrimping and saving put new shoes within reach. Bicycling
past the shoe store one day, he saw shoes at a price they might manage. He
raced home for the money, then returned to find them marked up and out of
reach again. His story reminded Aimée of the porter in Hamburg with his
suitcase of bills—a few hours' tips.

In June 1930, Aimée, Heinrich, and all his siblings gathered at Ottenhof,
working hard to make the contrast between the place now and in former
days less glaring before their parents arrived. The intervening years had
drawn a leafy curtain across the garden veranda's view to the river, so
Heinrich and Georg spent days clearing brush and sawing off branches
to open the vista again. Thanks to Jaeger, the long drive had been weeded
and raked. Fresh paint hid the beer accounts scribbled on the walls of the
white salon, pictures the biggest holes and mysterious dark patches. The
remains of the great chandelier were turned into sconces.

When Papa and Mimama arrived, peasants and villagers gathered to
greet them, many trying to kiss the hem of Mimama's dress. She
thanked them for their welcome, but insisted that the time for this custom was past. Soon Papa was outdoors: "The oak I had planted should be
just here. . . . Look how beautifully it has grown!" And so it went. He
was immediately full of new plans. An old peasant came to repay a loan
that had been weighing on him since 1918. They bathed in the river,
drinking in the air of home.

For Heinrich, the visit reawakened his visceral attachment to the
land. For Aimée, it brought home an awareness of how different the
ethos informing this family's life was from that which had shaped her
own. Personal wealth and grandeur were not the issue. Everything was
underplayed. Land was in stewardship for the future; traditions were
maintained for the next generation to cherish, maintain, and pass on to
a new generation in turn.

Papa was charming to Aimée, trying to make her comfortable in their close circle and acquaint her with the family's history and ways. He reminded her in some ways of her own father, so shy and constricted. But unlike her father, he was gregarious and warm, and with patient coaxing, he began to emerge. Quietly, in her much-improved German, she encouraged him. As he opened up to her, he was full of stories about his life, about earlier, happy times, invariably assigning starring roles to his bride, a brother, aunt, or sister. He was diffident about his relationship to a bride better placed than he, and after thirty-two years of marriage, he spoke about his Mima as a besotted, reverent bridegroom.

He told Aimée that on their wedding day in 1898, he and his brother Emil had delivered the groom's bouquet to the bride's house. Then, with the May sun glittering on the Neva, their smart-stepping bays whisked them off to Saint Peter's Church. Sitting alone in the first pew, he waited, his heart full.

Papa stopped, looking down at his hands. How distant it all seemed now. And everything had turned out so differently from their expectations. He smiled ruefully; he must be boring Aimée with details from long ago. She insisted she wanted to hear everything. She had never heard such stories from her own parents, and these stories were the backdrop of a life that was dear to her. They gave her the family lore and history she needed, as important to her as to his grandchildren.

He was silent for a time, looking at his attenuated fingers splayed across his knees. Over the years, his thick wedding band had left a deep groove. It occurred to her that until she suggested it, it might have been impossible for him to imagine a future with grandchildren taking their place on the continuum of generations—a family that replicated something like his own happy early life, surrounded by siblings, cousins, uncles, aunts, grandparents, legions of relatives and family friends. But now, with his children gathered at Ottenhof again, with a grandchild, with Aimée promising a new roof for the place, perhaps, in spite of everything, it really was possible.

He had been in the thick of things when revolution ruptured his life. His professional life had been on the upswing, the title of Excellency had awaited him. But it was Ottenhof that had been his passion, and he'd been full of plans. Twelve new buildings had gone up, housing for workers, and new stalls. A series of canals were dug to drain the moor and some fields. The park was taken in hand, a wood planted, the stock improved. They had planned a new house for family and guests—the more the better. The children must be educated, and travel. Already, the first ball had been given for Mira, the eldest. Her dark hair gleamed that night, he remembered, satin against the satin of her shoulders and white dress. She was radiant during the opening waltz. But Mira's first ball was the last; now she was being sent out as a governess—a bitter necessity he found hard to accept.

When revolution made realizing the goals he had set himself as a young man impossible, he saw everything as lost. He was forty-seven, too old to start anew, too young to give up when so many depended on him. A trained, experienced lawyer, he had drafted legislation to establish constitutional norms. Now all that was of no use; his accomplishments had been erased. He had lost his purpose in life, and what purpose remained—supporting his family—was one he felt he was not meeting. The one thing he had made a success of in his life was his choice of a wife.

Describing the hard, hungry early years in Dresden, he told Aimée that over time, they had learned to fend for themselves and make do with very little. But music was a passion: Schubert, Schumann, and the Beethoven sonatas that his sister Marie had played so beautifully— though she was dead now too—and the rich church music Dresden offered so liberally. Frugality, always a habit, now became nearly an obsession. But his fare-saving walks to Leo-Werke were long, letting him replay the pleasures of the old days, the glorious hunts in the great forests of home, so different from those in the west. He revisited endlessly, and at no cost, the glorious hunt party at snowy Neshnovo, its deep evergreen forests reaching to the icy sea, the servant Gerassim bringing the lynx he had shot on a sleigh, and his beloved dog Unkas.

His self-deprecating stories, so rich with feeling, deepened Aimée's understanding of this vanished world that was so much a part of Heinrich. The small details brought a different timbre to Papa's voice and a spark to his mild eyes that she had rarely seen there—as if the past rekindled a nearly extinguished fire.

11

Such Fearful Need

By September 1930, Germany's unemployment was more than 15 percent by some estimates. The accompanying hunger and bitterness gave Hitler a bigger hold on the electorate than he had ever had. The opening of the Reichstag that October ended with massive Nazi demonstrations. Thugs smashed department store windows along Leipziger Strasse and on Potsdamer Platz, police on horseback rushed to disperse adolescent rowdies shouting *"Heil Hitler!"* and *"Germany awake!"*

The day after Berlin's December premiere of the American film version of Erich Maria Remarque's *All Quiet on the Western Front*, Nazi protesters beat moviegoers, claiming that the antiwar film belittled Germany's greatness and threatened public safety. It was the Nazis and their poisonous reaction that threatened public safety; it felt like civil war.

Aimée and Heinrich's new apartment was in Berlin's Wilmersdorf section, home to a sizable cluster of Russian émigrés. Considerable funds and effort went into improving it, and after much debate, they even cut down the tree shading a good-size patch of walled garden behind the house to bring sunshine into their outdoors for their almost-two-year-old.

Gardening was entirely new to Aimée, but friends recommended Herr Liebig, older, competent, and friendly. Slight and a bit bent, perpetually under a battered cap, Herr Liebig was a gentle soul. The money was a great help to him and his family, but it was clear from the start that more than money was involved. Plants were his true love. Quietly, ably, he shared his love, opening her eyes to the green unfurling from a bare rose stalk, small, pale shoots poking up into sunshine. They communicated in a language that demanded none of the hellish agreements between verbs, nouns, and gender that bedeviled her German. Wordlessly, Herr Liebig demonstrated; wordlessly, she watched. They became a team.

Settled, elegantly furnished with wedding gifts, Persian rugs, and a

Chinese lacquer table she had bought in Paris, the ménage at 16 Burg-grafenstrasse was completed by a cook, a cleaning woman, and a nurse. In May 1931, a second son was born. "Michael is completely adorable," she wrote Mary. "I lie watching sleep flow and ebb in him like a barely perceptible tide. How I would love to lay Michael in your arms. I am so proud. . . . I want to have twelve! I've wished you here a thousand times."

But they were living in a different world from most of the population:

> I've never fought for anything. Life picked me out to spoil. I sometimes wonder if she isn't playing with me and will come with the reckoning before long.
>
> Everywhere around me is such fearful need. People are so poor. Anna Malé, my French "orphan," has a son. Last month he gained 300 grams and she is so pleased. Friedrich gains 3,000 grams a week! Friedrich has a nurse—we are most elegant. She is an angel, excellently educated, 23 years old, pretty, very intelligent, and more of a friend than a nursemaid, but she does everything: gets breakfast and suppers, darns my stockings, arranges flowers, waters the garden, dusts, cleans, turns back the beds at night, everything luxurious, makes clothes for the infant. I was so impressed with her capability and her goodness that I gave her $2.50 more a month. She is not emotional or sentimental by nature, but when I told her, she suddenly burst into tears, seized my hand and kissed it. How frightful! The opulence one sees in the street is of a cheap, tawdry variety. Almost without exception, one sees poverty in every face.

She sent money to Jean Heurteloup, a poor Paris neighbor. "I can see his pinched face, his green, faded overcoat, [see him] standing in the rain, telling me how it was to be old and poor." Sending thanks, "his rusty pen sputtered great inkspots of gratitude all over his touching letter. I would send it to you, but I can't bear to part with it. He had savings in Russian bonds—gone forever. As for Heinrich's family, they live on macaroni and coffee, his father walks an hour and a quarter each way to work to save carfare. We try to help, but it is difficult."

. . .

Visiting Hartford briefly, Aimée hoped to see her friend Anita, but Anita called from a Paris honeymoon, hoping to see her in Berlin. What a disappointment! She had so wanted her old pal to see her new home ground and show off her little ones. Back in Berlin she wrote: "Heinrich comes home only to go like a whirlwind through the house and out again. There is little enough peace and quiet here, though compared to New York, Berlin is a country village."

Of course Berlin was not a country village, but a city of big stolid gray buildings and much gray sky, yet restless and throbbing with excitement. In many ways it reminded her of New York. Artists and aspirants of every inclination—the brilliant, the promising, the merely hopeful—flocked to Berlin, producing an electric mix of talent, power, and sleaze completely at odds with the solemnity of its architecture. The city's arteries pulsated with life—high or low: politicians, pretty boys, frowzy landladies, and prostitutes—a full complement of Isherwood characters. Berlin was seen as an apostle of Americanism—the ultimate in modernity, everything that was fashionable and fun. Jazz represented a liberated, open, antiauthoritarian world. To some, this implied admirable, if frightening, mechanization; to others, mongrel vulgarity and an assault on European cultural values. Josephine Baker, fabulous, titillating, exotic, racially charged, was a huge success. But beneath the glitter and extravagance lay a terrifying poverty, largely out of the casual visitor's sight. Poverty, propaganda, and agitation made for a tense mix, and Berlin was now under threat from the Nazis.

Attending a rally on Wittenbergplatz, young louts emerged from the darkness, shouting the now familiar "Germany awake!" She and Heinrich heard a narrow, unpleasant-looking man ranting that everything was the fault of the Jews; society must be unified in proud nationhood by blood. The skeptic in Aimée heard only rare, insubstantial positives clearly aimed at the desperate, who might clutch at any proffered straws.

She was in Hartford in October 1931, when Heinrich wrote of possible "good and promising work" for him. Political factions, "Stahlhelm and S.A.—Storm Troops—Catholic and Protestant services, also some elements from the right," were meeting at Bad Harzburg, hoping to settle on a joint candidate for president in the upcoming elections and rectify recent failures in German politics. "A new government might be built on this basis." Herbert von Bose, a conservative, anti-Communist pressman with little hope that the Nazis would save Germany, had suggested Heinrich as second secretary of the new government, "responsible for a Press Service in English, Spanish and Italian. I will be very close to the heart of things, can learn and see a lot and make my way in the world of politics without being tied to any party and without compromising my future."

Building a seaworthy ship of state is usually challenging; in Germany's 1931 political waters, the projected "joint cabinet," spare parts held together by expedient alliances, sank instantly. A cartoon showed Hitler and Alfred Hugenberg, political allies for the moment, hats in hand at the Chancellery door, both hoping for employment. There was no job for Heinrich in this rickety political phantasm.

The depression triggered by the Wall Street crash was in its third year. All Germany was reading Hans Fallada's *Kleiner Mann, was nun?—Little Man, What Now?*—the story of Johannes Pinneberg, the little man of the title, and his beloved *Lämmchen*—Lambie—trying to survive Germany's pitiless depression. Fallada's previous book had sold well, but *Kleiner Mann* had Germany in thrall. Heinrich brought home a copy, convinced that Aimée could manage the German. Her heart sank, but the language was simple, the characters, teetering on the edge of catastrophe, were real, tender, plainspoken. She delighted in reading the story that had captured the public's heart herself.

The world was eyeing Berlin partly in anticipation, partly in dread, occasionally even with hope. But poverty bred political unrest, making what some called the "center of the world" increasingly unruly. Unemployment stood at nearly 30 percent. The weekly *Berliner Illustrierte Zeitung* was running grim, telling pictures of the dark side of Berlin's notorious glitz: squalid dwellings of the city's poor; its loitering, unemployed youth. Of the two principal options in the endless stream of elections—Communists or Nazis—the Nazis were gaining ground. Daily street brawls between factions escalated and political murder was commonplace. The aged Reich president, Paul von Hindenburg, was a totem, incapable of effecting change or even holding his ground in the turmoil.

One economic crisis followed another. Almost every day brought bloody confrontations between Nazi riffraff with swastikas on one side of the street and grim-faced Communists waving red flags and singing "The Internationale" on the other. Berlin had become a battleground of warring propaganda. Political parties other than the Nazis scrambled to compete with Joseph Goebbels's artful constructs of endlessly repeated phrases about Red bosses and wire-pulling Jews.

Yet, Aimée wrote Mary: "After living in deepest seclusion, I am suddenly overcome by a great American migration." She had missed Anita, but her stepmother, Molly, was bringing her stepbrother, Gordon. "Heavens, how will I keep him amused?" Uncle Bill, Aunt Marion, and Corson's "darned nice" mother-in-law had come and gone; she was expecting her sister-in-law, Roberta any minute. Corson had married into a Chicago family, the Thornes. In 1873, Grandfather George Thorne had put down five hundred dollars to join his brother-in-law Aaron Montgomery Ward in a nascent mail-order company. Penny postcards requested catalogs of corn shelters, saws, threshers, sewing machines. Business grew, Montgomery Ward and the Thornes prospered, and Corson's wife, Roberta, was accustomed to living very well. Aimée was used to living well too, if not quite that well. To Mary, she wailed:

One must give them parties, the eternal museum viewing is wearing, and these people live in taxis and orchestra seats, while I am at the bottom of the money bag.

Try to combine this with an undisturbed day so that Heinrich can work in peace and you have a vague idea of my existence. If only I didn't feel 90 percent of these people were only interested in us for the most superficial reasons. But Heinrich believes everyone is intelligent until proven otherwise, and proving otherwise takes a lot of time.

Then her old New York beau, Everest Haight, was keen to see Germany and Berlin's excitement, and meet the man who had won the girl he once thought might be his. As they toured, Everest, present only as the camera's eye, filmed everything: sheep moving across country roads from one meadow to another, horse-drawn carts, Heinrich holding beer bottles and bananas in an attitude suggesting an imminent, antic juggling performance as he and Aimée arrange a picnic. Schoolchildren gape and wave at car and movie camera—both exotic novelties. Everest's film documents a vanished world of little girls with immense white hair bows, schoolbooks riding high on their backs in neat leather packs; veterans marching with the paramilitary Stahlhelm; sheep trotting through the half-timbered medieval town of Dinkelsbühl.

That spring the death of Aristide Briand dimmed Heinrich's hopes for a peaceful Europe. Briand maintained that war should no longer be an instrument of national policy, and had worked to forge a peaceful European union. With both Stresemann and Briand gone, Heinrich felt that international suspicions and belligerence were sure to flare again.

His personal schedule, meanwhile, was a close approximation of the chaos at large. He was always rushing, and together he and Aimée seemed to be always running: late for trains, late for dinner, late to the movies. Finally at the movies, he found waiting for the likely satisfactory outcome of the conflict between white hats (heroes) and black hats (villains) nearly impossible. Aimée's attempts to reassure him by saying "It's going to be all right" were often met with a furious "How do you know?"

Easy enough to predict a happy outcome at the movies, but elsewhere, the nerves and anxiety seemed warranted. It was less and less clear that things would be all right, and there was little she could say or do to reassure him. He was in perpetual motion, pursuing any and every job opportunity, but without result. Whether Berlin was the center of German hopes, there was no work. His vast, extended family, well educated and once well connected, was of little use now. Revolution had affected them as a diaspora, and the context in which their connections could have been useful, introductions made or strings pulled, had vanished. Inflation, penury, and political instability made matters worse. Besides, the present environment called for very different connections that simply were not there. All his energies went nowhere.

A cloud had passed over the sun. Berlin's élan and vibrancy had given way to gloom and anger. Nazis loomed large; brawls and bloodshed were everyday business. The Germany people had thought of since the early nineteenth century as a nation of *Dichter und Denker*—poets and thinkers—was now the Germany of *Richter und Henker*—judges and hangmen. Berlin had become joyless and they were alarmed. With two children and more planned, they wanted a calm and healthy environment, and Berlin was not it.

Looking for an estate somewhere within easy reach of the city, Heinrich wrote to Aimée in Hartford, reflecting on this and their future:

> Things look grim for German agriculture, but if everything else fails, we will still have security. . . . How grateful I am to your parents for this feeling. If we want, we will have *our* soil beneath our feet, and that thought brings security and peace.
>
> You have taken the fear out of my life. I stand so firmly with you; you are the present, our children our future. Half our life is already fulfilled in our family, and work will come too. I feel new powers constantly awakening in my soul.

Terra firma had been missing. Just the idea suggested security. With their "own soil" beneath their feet, they could make the life of *Bildung und Besitz*—culture and property—he hoped to build for his family. Every instinct hungered for a return to the old, conservative values of land, family, and community. With land, he could aspire to Frederick the Great's definition of a great man: one who makes two ears of corn grow where only one grew before; with luck, maybe more. In this one place, the clock might be turned back, or at least stand still. The sense of homelessness would stop. They would re-create his lost life on a smaller scale. Founded on the same principles, funded with American dollars, they would provide for their children the happy childhood that he had lost and that she had never had. In this place, they would create a refuge, a monument to continuity, a patch of stability in a wholly unstable world.

Conditions Are Terrifying

In the spring of 1932, in all innocence—some of their friends called it naïveté—they bought Blumenhagen, an utter ruin of a big farm in the Mecklenburg region, about one hundred kilometers north of Berlin. After a guided tour, a cousin of Heinrich's sniffed, "*Ça ne vaut pas la peine*"—"It's not worth the trouble." But they were young, full of romantic and noble ideas, and convinced that their energy could make something of it. And the place was beautiful—sweeping farmland, forests and lakes under rolling clouds, a languid undulation of hills with an occasional copse tucked into a fold of the broad landscape. Below the house lay a lake fringed with silver willows. Aimée's money would bring the *Besitz*—property. Together they would see to *Bildung*—education and culture. It would be paradise.

At least to some extent their vision was in tune with the Nazis' agrarian romanticism, a glorification of the land and farming that Goebbels linked tirelessly to his myth of blood and soil. Yet as it turned out, the romance of agriculture was anything but. The summer of 1932 was glorious, long golden days of perpetual sunshine. It hardly ever rained. Only later did they realize that in fact it rarely rained at Blumenhagen. Rain in the nearest town was almost certain to stop at the lakes that lay between town and the estate. Local people said that rain had to be rowed across the lakes by boat. Maybe it had to do with electrical polarization, but whatever the reason, rain was scarce. Without it, growing the oats, wheat, rye, barley, flax, and sugar beets they envisioned flourishing in the broad fields was a struggle. It would take longer to turn Frederick the Great's ear of corn into two than they thought.

Heinrich said that their French Mademoiselle used to quote an old expression: "You must learn to flower wherever God planted you." But God had planted him in Saint Petersburg and Ottenhof, and the saying offered no advice on what to do if you were torn out by the roots. He had worked hard to flower in Berlin, but the work he had been so sure would come did not. He was doing translations. It seemed a repeat of his father's miserable position translating toothpaste brochures. He had trained for a life in the big world, and itched to play a part—even a bit part—in shaping its future. The lack of opportunity was frustrating, emasculating. His family's life was being shaped by his wife's money. Restless in the role of gentleman farmer, he was frequently off to Berlin, and looked for comfort in an affair.

Aimée had signed on to Heinrich's agenda. Her money had bought a big place to stand in for his lost Ottenhof. She would produce enough children to replicate his family and meet the demands of any dynastic notions. She would help provide an intense cultural focus. It was certainly an improvement over the two children, two cars, bridge, tennis, and family plot that had awaited her in Hartford. It suited her and she did not regret it, but it had its drawbacks, and now this. Having given her all to this man and this marriage, she felt wounded and unspeakably alone.

But she refused to take up the role of injured wife, go home to Hartford, and prove the naysayers right. In a moment of misery, she had confided in Heinrich's sister Margarethe, but she did not want to involve his family. She was not prepared to deal with the startling dissonance between his family's deep piety and a class tradition that accepted such behavior. What had gone wrong? Where would she find the balance between love, hope, and hurt? And what of the children? She could not just leave; besides, she loved him.

Scrawled in the margin of her recollections, this in quotation marks: "Surely you are not naïve enough to think that one woman is enough for a man?" Was this Heinrich's question? Or was it Margarethe, ever loyal to her adored brother and shocked by Aimée's refusal to share his bed for a time after this infidelity? Her view that a woman had no right to refuse her husband under any circumstances seemed to Aimée to date from another era, but hardly surprised her. She had written Mary once that to some men, "the marriage bed is a bed." To a few (Heinrich presumably among them), "it is a shrine, giving divinity and meaning to the mysteries of life." In this case, the marriage bed and ordinary sex were apparently worlds apart. She loved him, but the hurt was profound.

It may not have been Heinrich's first, nor apparently his last, infidelity. In later years the older children joked occasionally about the sudden departure of one au pair or another, and about the cook's expressive eyebrows when elegant females from Berlin came to Blumenhagen for weekends. One daughter concluded that the Baron Maximilian von Heune in the film version of *Cabaret* was a not entirely veiled reference to their man-about-Berlin father in those years. "A baron!" rhapsodizes Sally Bowles. "Class!"

After this wrenching crisis, Heinrich decided to take up the role of gentleman farmer full-time. It was a family tradition, the life his father and grandfathers had pursued—at least during the summer. Unable to find work in Berlin as they had in Saint Petersburg, he would devote himself completely to Blumenhagen and make amends to his wife. In time, work in Berlin might come too.

In June 1932, Aimée was visiting Hartford again when Heinrich sent a hectic cable. He had been asked to come to Berlin for "the perfect job." President Hindenburg had appointed Franz von Papen chancellor, Papen was gathering "a cabinet of barons," and Heinrich, in a minor capacity, was to be one of them. So were Herbert von Bose and Edgar Jung, both anti-Communist and anti-Nazi, part of a coterie of conservative revolutionaries. This was the long-awaited government post at last, an outlet for Heinrich's energies and interests, yet he hesitated.

He had promised to make amends to Aimée and settle into life as a *Gutsbesitzer*—gentleman farmer. Still, there are many ways to make amends, and he knew that she wanted for him what he wanted for himself. Knowledgeable circles greeted Papen's appointment with disbelief. He might well bring conservative, centrist support to parliament, but he was also ambitious, malleable, and at odds with political realities and parliamentary democracy. It was an agonizing decision, but wary of compromising his future, Heinrich stayed off the political stage.

They were gutting and renovating Blumenhagen's run-down house, a typical old North German brick, with a deep, tiled gable roof and dormers.

Two immense linden trees flanked the front door, great green spheres balanced on thick trunks. In blossom, they were alive with delirious bees, humming and droning like an organ in full voice. The air was heavy with their perfume; the scent seeped into open windows, saturating the whole house with an almost tangible presence that delighted Heinrich with memories of Ottenhof. At the back of the house, land sloped down to a willow-fringed lake for fishing, swimming, sailing, and, in time, skating. Roebuck and wild boar roamed forests of beech and oak that lay beyond.

Making their capacious ruin habitable was a first priority, but there was much else to be done too, as Aimée wrote Mary in early August:

> Forgive me for not writing, but the baby is coming so soon, and we are living in a disorder that is hard to believe. My brother-in-law drove a nail through his foot, and the doctor said, "Are people actually living in this house?" There is so much to be done and not enough to do it, no extra money, and flies and squalling children (no wonder), the toilet paper sitting beside the butter, and wasps in everything. Dirt, flies, disorder, a heat wave, and no chance of getting rid of any of them. Eight grown-ups to be fed, and fruit and vegetables to be put up for the winter, for we must live from Blumenhagen—there is no other wherewithal. Preserves and the inspector's dinner must all be cooked on one tiny ramshackle stove—it is a nightmare. No john apart from the *vase de nuit*—chamber pot.

> We have rented a room from one of the villagers for the great event. That is the only refuge of quiet, cleanliness and order. It is all so grotesque and crazy it's laughable. The whole day is work, and at 8:30 bed and up at 5:30. Today, I've called a short halt, for I've been too energetic and I'm scared to death that the baby will arrive before the midwife, on the 25th. I must hold out until then.

> More days have gone by, the 25th among them, and still no baby. This is almost the hardest part. I am fidgety and tired. But Blumenhagen is marvelous in spite of all discomforts, and we are all in love with the place. *Hagen* is the old word for woodland, and the farm lies between lakes and state forests. Deer and wild boar are here in abundance—oh, you shall hear all about it some day soon. Friedrich and Michael are lords of creation, and all is as it should be.

Her friend Lore Adam, a midwife who had attended Michael's birth, came from Berlin, and a third son, Christian, was born.

During the building of a stone dam linking the estate to the main road, a local archaeologist unearthed heavy silver chains, neck rings, bracelets, earrings, beads, and several hundred coins, some Byzantine, in the remnants of a wattle-and-daub hut near the edge of the forest. Dating from the tenth and eleventh centuries, they had been hastily tossed into the ashes to keep them from whatever ancient enemy or marauding tribe was already pouring over the brow of the hill. The treasure was attributed to the Wends, a Slavic people who once inhabited the region; whoever buried the treasure never returned.

As Blumenhagen's soil yielded up more of its past, other items joined that chieftain's hoard at the local museum. Spring plowing revealed the outlines of ancient hearths, dark against the lighter soil. Near the font of a church that had once stood on a nearby hill, they found urn burials with iron fibulae. Plowing also unearthed a newer graveyard, bringing up skulls, teeth worn but intact. An ancient village had stood between the two lakes. Six hundred years later, the Thirty Years' War ravaged what had once been sturdy farm buildings. It was exciting to be the inheritors of such a storied patch of earth.

Gradually, the house took shape: Terraces and gardens were laid out; a greenhouse and pigsty built; orchards planted. Outside their peaceable kingdom, the country reeled from crisis to crisis. Berlin roiled. People longed for order, normalcy, and stability, but all familiar social reference points seemed at the point of obliteration. A sea of swastikas battled a tide of Communist banners. Franz von Papen foundered amid political machinations, some of his own making, and within six months, he was forced to resign as chancellor. Heinrich and Aimée were well out of it. Berlin, a scant one hundred kilometers distant, seemed light-years away.

Back from her recent U.S. visit, and glad to be out of Berlin, Aimée wrote Mary:

I can't get awfully excited about the depression in America . . . only furious that you are caught up in it. Here it's dreadful and this morning a letter came from Anna Malé saying that she was killing herself and her children. Oh, why am I telling you such things? There's no work, no work of any kind whatsoever. Conditions have become terrifying.

In January 1933, a senile Hindenburg appointed Hitler chancellor. Papen, now in the vice-chancellor slot, imagined himself pulling the strings in a coalition that would have Hitler cornered and squeaking in no time. Many of their friends had believed that even if Hitler came to power, he could never keep his promises, his political fireworks would fizzle, he could not last. But the surprises began almost immediately.

Days before an election set for March 5, the Reichstag burned. Hitler's hysterical preelection speech, accompanied by the customary processions of torchbearers and swastikas, laid blame on a favored bogeyman: the Communists. The result was a big National Socialist gain at the polls. In glorious, intoxicating March weather, Hitler moved quickly, muzzling the press and stripping the Reichstag of its powers. Now only a Nazi cabinet could legislate. His political opponents became the first inmates of newly established concentration camps. Almost immediately, whether out of enthusiasm, a desire to be on the winning side, the realization that there could be no work or advancement without Nazi Party membership, or thinking that they might shift the party's stance, there was an epidemic of political capitulation—the "March Casualties."

In April, uniformed SA—Sturmabteilung—troops in Sam Browne belts exhorted Germans to boycott Jewish-owned shops. All rival political factions and unions were banned. In May, books were burned to cleanse the nation of insufficiently Germanic works. Heinrich claimed that the nineteenth-century poet Heinrich Heine's observation that there was only a small step between burning books and burning people had been prophetic. Bruno Walter, one of Germany's preeminent conductors, was locked out of his concert hall because he was Jewish. Hermann Keyserling, a Baltic exile who had lost everything to the Bolsheviks, claimed that compared to the Nazis, the Russian Revolution was "as a flea to an elephant"; philistines were elbowing out the intellectuals. Only cheese-mongers and pickle vendors counted for anything anymore.

Heinrich's family was of mixed minds about Hitler. Papa regarded the man as an imposter, a vulgar braggart not to be trusted. To Mi-mama, who had already seen a good deal of madness and upheaval, this did not seem very different. Serenely apolitical, she glided through the turmoil on a plane that would have denied such an upstart so much as a glance. Her deep piety allowed her to accept whatever came with relative equanimity. Margarethe shared this piety, saying, "What is, is right."

Too tidy and succinct, said Aimée. She shared neither the faith nor the acceptance. By this credo, if whatever was, was God's will, there was no point in taking a stand against anything or ever trying to improve things. Mimama and Margarethe had seen their lives upended by forces beyond their control, but in Aimée's view, life demanded participation, taking steps, not acquiescence. Her effort to forge a new life had de-manded a nerve-racking leap, but it was the only way she could live.

Despite a shared sense that this regime could not last, 1933 alone brought more than two hundred laws and decrees strengthening the Nazi hold. Between blared fanfares and the "Horst Wessel Lied," radio oratory ruled the airwaves. That summer, another summer of endless sunshine, was a clear turning point. They had settled at Blumenhagen at last, but the precious distance was not enough to keep awareness of the madness out. Bawling, congratulating himself and the party on their accomplishments, Hitler made reckless promises, with clenched fist on his heart, and alternated them with threats, thrusting the same clenched fist belligerently at the crowd. The intensity alone was unnerving.

Still, Hitler did put people to work. He put shovels in people's hands and set them to digging ditches, draining fields, building roads. That simple fact offered many a glimmer of hope. He also embarked on a massive program of rearmament. Corson wrote from Chicago that while he had never heard Hitler speak, he had read the speeches, and he seemed to be a remarkable man. Reading the speeches might make them easier to take, Aimée thought, but it left out the element that made people lis-ten. Without the hysteria, the arm-waving and vocal pyrotechnics, the speeches were mind-numbing, repetitive, jingoistic jargon, heated ramblings about *Volk* and honor and blood.

By late summer a new Protestant *Reichsbischof* had been "elected" and a new brand of "German Christians"—Nazis all—put into positions of power. In September she spotted a notice in the newspaper. Small, and way down on the page, it was nothing like a headline, but the message was clear: From now on, for the sake of "cultural coordination" and the promotion of German culture, all plays, books, paintings, films, and newspapers produced in Germany would be vetted by a *Reichskulturkammer*—Reich Chamber of Culture—under Goebbels, Minister of Public Enlightenment and Propaganda. The little note set off alarm bells. Culture had become the handmaiden of ideology.

Just after Aimée's October birthday, Hitler withdrew Germany from the League of Nations. Both she and Heinrich were surprised by the Allies' silence; it seemed almost like collusion. Then he dissolved the Reichstag and regional parliaments. In a matter of months, Germany descended into dictatorship, tyranny, and violence.

A fourth child was born in January 1934, a daughter, named Brigitte Anita after Aimée's Hartford friend. That spring, while the United States was in a tizzy over Bonnie and Clyde, Hitler had made his methods and aims totally clear. In the space of one year, relentless propaganda, intimidation, and bald brutality had much of the population firmly under control.

Yet disappointment with failed Nazi programs made for unrest. Among workers in particular, the stiff-armed salute mandated the year before lost fervor and favor. People sized each other up; if they recognized a like-minded soul, the masks would slip. Jokes about party bigwigs—always a sign of popular discontent—began to circulate. There were demands for an end to the arbitrary arrests, the harassment of Jews and the churches. Hindenburg urged Papen, still vice-chancellor, if in name only, to try to smooth over the tensions that were creating so much fear and distrust.

In June, Papen gave a speech at the university in Marburg written for him by Edgar Jung. Belatedly denouncing the new government's "mendacity, beastliness, and arrogance," he called for an end to violence, a return to civility, the rule of law, and "fraternal friendship and respect for all our fellow countrymen." It caused a sensation. American ambassador William Dodd observed that after the address, an irreverent "Heil Marburg" reverberated throughout Germany. But Hitler banned publication of the speech, only a few clandestine copies circulated, and the popular upheaval against the regime it was meant to bring about never materialized. Papen did not insist otherwise, and the revolt never came.

Hitler responded with his preferred measures. On June 30, 1934, in what became known as "Reich murder week," the SS—Schutzstaffel— shot Bose at his desk and arrested and murdered Jung. Another "colleague" was imprisoned for weeks while no one knew whether he was dead or alive. Released at last, he and his wife took off for China—as far as possible from Hitler's reach. For Heinrich, the job with Papen would not have been the "perfect job" after all.

Successive Januaries brought more changes. The January 1935 Saar plebiscite returned the coal-rich region to Germany after fifteen years under the French—a major coup for Hitler, yet dissatisfaction with the Nazis still ran strong. Jokes satirizing important Nazis proliferated—in private. Goebbels, scrawny and dark, with one leg shorter than the other and a clubfoot, was known as the nachgedunkelte Schrumpfgermane, roughly if not tidily translatable as a "dark, shrunken Germanic gnome."

Visiting Blumenhagen, Heinrich's sister Margarethe wrote her parents that there were four children plus a small cousin there now—five children—wonderful, but difficult, and Aimée was looking forward to a long visit in Dresden, to savor city life away from the tumult. Heinrich's cousin Oswald had been named ambassador to Portugal, and came to Blumenhagen for a good-bye visit—yet another reminder of Heinrich's own thwarted ambitions. He had grown up in a world ensnared by nineteenth-century conventions and expectations. The Bolsheviks had stolen his assured place in that world, and by the time he arrived in Germany as a fourteen-year-old exile and hungry outsider, that world no longer existed.

He had worked hard to take part in shaping Europe's future and a life to meet the expectations of his youth, but Germany had become a political wasteland, and his efforts had availed him nothing. If they were living out of context, in a world that no longer believed in the things Heinrich had grown up believing and still believed in, at least they had Blumenhagen. Bismarck had once said that when the end of the world came, he would go to Mecklenburg, where everything happened a hundred years later. Still, Heinrich chafed at his enforced inactivity. He was not cut out to be a country gentleman, and it was unlikely that their rural Eden could elude Hitler entirely, and certainly not for one hundred years.

He needed work and a future, and was finding neither. The absurd propaganda could not be taken seriously; the party's extremes would surely self-destruct. Yet he joined the party in spite of Aimée's skepticism. The optimist in him hoped that Hitler could get Germany back on her feet and forge a new, more effective political order, some improvement on the Weimar Republic. Besides, the party's animus toward the Communists played directly into his deepest fears. Over Aimée's serious objections, he even joined the SA, arguing that if more people like him joined, they might be a civilizing force and the thuggishness would wane. To her, this was harebrained; the SA was not an outfit quick to recognize his qualities and rush to reform. One plus could never cancel out ten thousand minuses. Whatever hopes had led him into the party, both they and his party membership were short-lived.

In their early days of power, the Nazis were too busy establishing control across the spectrum to pay much attention to the church, but as the church showed signs of resistance, that changed. Initially, they settled for Teutonic ersatz: Runes replaced Christian symbols; the months lost their Latin-derived names to take on archaic Germanic coloration. November became *Nebelung*, a poetic confabulation of *Nebel*—fog— and *Nibelung*, with its connotations of Norse mythology and Wagner. Under party leadership, the church was infused with an eclectic, neo-pagan Aryanism featuring a blond Christ, more avenging militant than proponent of love and forgiveness. Then *Deutsche Christen*—German Christians—were installed in critical church offices. A poster depicted Hitler, hair slightly mussed by some apparently divine exhalation, holding a fluttering swastika; above him glowed an eagle in a nimbus of light. The iconographic parallel to the newly baptized Christ, with the dove of the Holy Spirit hovering overhead in heavenly radiance, is unmistakable. Now Hitler was not only absolute dictator, he was also becoming the new Messiah.

By early 1935, the Nazis were taking substantive steps against the churches. Protestant clerics who refused to fall into line broke away to form what became known as the Confessing Church. Hundreds were denied the right to work, and arrested. Concentration camps began to fill with clergy. By flouting Christian ethics, Hitler had begun to knit together disparate forces of an opposition.

In this tense atmosphere, the new vicar at the local parish preached an Easter sermon reminding his flock that Christ, not the party representative, was the arbiter of spiritual matters. He was summoned by the party higher-ups and chastised. Then the tone escalated. When parishes were informed that *Mein Kampf* would replace the Old Testament, a local clergyman insisted that *Mein Kampf* might serve for politics, but he would continue to preach the Bible. He was arrested. The new vicar was denounced and forced out.

Papa had watched the Nazis' moves against the church with burning interest. When the *Kirchen Kampf*—church struggle—turned into open warfare, he said that he would gladly put his life on the line in this matter. When Heinrich intervened on behalf of the ousted vicar, he was immediately embroiled in a controversy pitting traditional Protestant "believers" against the new Nazified brand—a political minefield. On July 15, 1935, he was thrown out of the party and into jail, where he wrote a letter that spoke of his family's long, pious tradition. Yes, he had signed the red card denoting his adherence to the Confessing Church. The swastika and the cross of Christ were two different things, and he took exception to mingling the two. As a reserve officer, he had sworn an oath to fight and perhaps die under the sign of the swastika as a symbol of the people, but he hoped to be buried under the Christian cross—the only symbol of redemption. "Hearing the Deutsche Christen confuse the Führer with Christ makes me ashamed, for both Führer and the church."

The farm, meanwhile, was barely surviving. The plentiful roebuck and wild boar they had thought so romantic when they bought the place ravaged the scanty crops, and reducing their number became less sport than necessity. Heinrich did shoot them, but economically, Blumenha-gen still struggled. A lot of Aimée's money had gone into its apparently never-ending demands, and very little was coming out. They grew most of their own food, made their own sausages and preserves. It was work, it was draining, and she felt up to it, but there were worries. She was in up to her neck, the water already pushing her chin up, and she had no idea when, where, or even if it would stop. When a school friend asked Friedrich what his father did, the boy answered, "I don't know exactly what my father does, but my mother delivers milk."

The government also made demands, meticulously enforced by Meck-lenburg's agricultural inspector. Every year, wheat and potatoes of a cer-tain weight and quality had to be delivered to the *Winter Hilfe*—Winter Help program—whose posters proclaimed in bold Gothic script: "No one will go hungry! No one will be cold!" A contemporary cartoon shows an old Berliner in earmuffs and his friend looking at the poster. "Oh," says one, stamping his feet for warmth, "so now they've forbidden that too!"

In late 1935, Aimée wrote Mary, who had predicted years ago that Aimée would have four sons and two daughters:

> Happy to know the fourth son arriving the beginning of Feb-ruary. I assure you that between the children, chickens, the drop of the dollar, the price of wheat, the horse with the colic, the apple orchard we are planting, the new pigsty and the burning ques-tion: "Will the tractor pay for itself?" life is full to the brim and overflowing. I've never been so useful or so necessary in my life.

With the Berlin garden, Herr Liebig had planted the seed of a passion for the soil and growing things. Aimée remembered the long-ago Swiss governess who had taught her the Latin names of flowers, a discipline she had maintained. But the Latin names of flowers were only rarely required now. Instead, with a husband off on other ventures more often than not, the little Hartford "heiress" was working on a much larger canvas, learning to run a big, struggling farm. She needed to know the seasons for planting, details of herd maintenance, and how to make wise investments in machinery. But as usual, she was solicitous of her friend:

I'm sending through the Hartford Bank $30.00 for concerts and theaters. My very much alive ghost will be listening with you. This is for Christmas, my dear, but if you send me so much as a toothpick I shall send a real check when I get my next income and make you swallow it. If the *lieber Gott* would only do a bit more looking after you!

Our world is deep in snow and the children are like wild Indians and Christmas and Santa Claus so near—If only you could come when we are singing around our candlelit tree. Your ghost would be so warmly welcomed with Pfeffernüsse, and apples and an armful of children.

The predicted fourth son turned out to be a second daughter, named Dorothée, after her American cousin. Home movies from that time at Blumenhagen roll out a bucolic idyll: Aimée on sunlit grass surrounded by a tumble of children and dogs; golden children toddling down to the lake, or riding, fishing, sledding. Less than one hundred kilometers away, Hitler jabbed at the air, shouting relentlessly about Germany's enemies.

Even in paradise, all was not well, as Heinrich wrote to Mary:

Aimée had a grave breakdown in July, due to overstrain, but a two-month stay in London, where she was taken by very good friends of ours, George and Marjorie von Harten, helped her greatly and she came back to Blumenhagen for her birthday.

If you come to stay with us, I have in mind some literary work I want to do with you: translation of some German novels into English for some American or English publisher. As it is, I am planning to do the reverse, and must ask if you could help me.

He would be so grateful if she could find "worthwhile novels of deeper value" or some "good political biography . . . a biography of Lincoln, for instance . . . a book alive to the problems of the day," that he could translate. A good friend, a Berlin publisher, is interested in publishing such things in Germany, and Heinrich has time for such work at the moment. Perhaps something is planned for the Christmas market? "I know you would enjoy our growing little family: Friedrich who is much like Aimée,

Michael, very much a little Yankee, Christian, a sturdy little peasant, Brigitte my flirt, a sweet little girl, and that darling Dorothée."

There is real urgency here. He had done translations for his publisher friend in 1931, among them *These Russians*, by William C. White, vignettes of Russians and Russian life. At the time, he thought translations would fill the gap until real work came along. In late 1937, he was hoping for translations again.

Long before Hitler annexed Austria or invaded Czechoslovakia, he had taken over Germany. The regime intruded into every crevice of life, and rather than creating the celebrated Nazi *Volksgemeinschaft*—folk community—it caused thoughtful people to withdraw into a private sphere. Language was retooled and perverted for political advantage. On the radio, the chief instrument of Goebbels's expert propaganda machine, imperatives vied with superlatives for supremacy over the airwaves; imperatives bludgeoning listeners into submission, superlatives lifting them up again. The smallest, least expensive model, the *Volksempfänger*—People's Receiver—popularly known as Goebbels's *Schnauze*—snout—spouted continually about the regime's successes, the Führer's unparalleled wisdom and beneficence. People responded to the glut by designating the smallest unit of energy needed to turn off one hundred thousand radios simultaneously as one "Goeb."

Every town and village was to plant a thousand-year oak, a symbol of the Reich to come, the typical blend of agrarian and folkloric notions, with Hitler a demiurge at the center of a hodgepodge universe. The party machine rediscovered Hermann Löns, a forgotten poet who had died in France in World War I, and resurrected his romantic poem, *"Blut und Boden"*—"Blood and Soil"—as a rallying cry. Endless speeches about *"Deutsches Blut, Deutscher Boden"*—"German blood, German soil"— cluttered the airwaves. Almost instantly, the typically irreverent Berliners abbreviated this into waggish shorthand as "Blubo."

On the surface, Heinrich and Aimée's move to Blumenhagen was in tune with Blubo's ideological glorification of land and agriculture. But Nazi rearmament had drawn workers into munitions, seriously depleting farm labor, and domestic politics were turbulent. Tensions between the Nazis and the Wehrmacht—armed forces—erupted in a scandal manufactured to discredit the Wehrmacht, and Hitler took over as supreme military commander. Pastor Martin Niemöller of the Confessing Church was interned at Sachsenhausen for "subversion." Then came the Austrian Anschluss. Thousands were taken into "protective custody": Communists, dissidents, petty criminals, Gypsies, "antisocial types," homosexuals—and more and more Jews ended up in Dachau.

In May 1938, Heinrich wrote his uncle at Toffen:

> Aimée was quite ill a year ago, from overexertion, particularly after the birth of our little Dorothée, but now she has good help at home, can rest and will go on a longer trip to recuperate.
>
> By bending every effort these last years at Blumenhagen, we have accomplished a great deal. Unfortunately it will still require additional work, so I have engaged an experienced overseer. For me, in the long run, the estate was neither satisfying nor profitable. But the family will stay here until I am firmly in the saddle in Berlin, and I will come home weekends.
>
> My ambition leaves me no rest, and I hope—before I'm too old—to make the right connection and accomplish something in the field that coincides with my education and interests. The younger generation has not had the same education I enjoyed, and people [like me] are occasionally sought out. I very much hope it works. Otherwise, I still have other possibilities *in petto*—up my sleeve—but I very much hope for a state, political function. So, one way or another, I will be in Berlin in the fall.

He adds word-portraits of the children: Friedrich, slender, lively, and showing artistic tendencies; Michael, imaginative, adventurous, gifted in school; and Christian, sturdy, loyal, and cheerful—the farmer among them. Brigitte a coquette, who strokes his cheek, saying, "I love you, Papa."

When the jousting between Hitler and British prime minister Neville Chamberlain—the sword versus the umbrella—over Czechoslovakia ended with Chamberlain's capitulation at Munich in September, Aimée's friend

Marjorie wrote from London, saying that it was being celebrated as the *Pax Umbrellicus*. Much of Germany felt celebratory too, grateful that there would be no war. Privately, Heinrich said it seemed a mercy in the short term, but a political slap from Chamberlain to set Hitler back might have served a larger purpose.

The *Pax Umbrellicus* coincided with an incident that became part of family lore. On her way to town one day, Aimée saw her nine-year-old Friedrich giving an enormous box kite he had built a trial run in the field between house and road. The kite rose slightly, returned to earth, bumped along, and went up again, the boy tugging on the line or letting it out. Suddenly the kite took off, the slim boy racing behind it until his feet began to leave the ground.

If she knew her son, he would never let go of that kite. She stopped the car, running to grab his feet and bring her wayward aviator back to earth. Once he was safely grounded, she went on her way, reflecting that the boy's relationship with the kite paralleled the international community's relationship with Hitler. Friedrich thought he controlled the kite, but it wasn't so. Like the big kite, Hitler pulled and pulled. Jerked back, he would let up, then pull some more until, to everyone's great surprise, he could take off, taking with him so much that was hugely important.

Heinrich was away so much that Aimée suffered from a dearth of real news that was isolating but also provided insulation against troubling realities. Farm and family, the normal mix of work, children, pleasures and anxieties, large and small, kept her fully occupied. To the locals she was an oddity. She spoke idiosyncratic German, but she was "Frau Baronin" after all, and that commanded respect. Yet she never hesitated to lend a hand or do the most menial task herself. That commanded respect too, but also added to the confusion. The farm's workers could never figure her out. Most people understood her situation—a woman with five children—but given the Nazis' growing paranoia, her foreignness, no matter in what guise, might provoke some xenophobic encounter and become a real threat.

Increasingly, she found herself relying on two women who had entered her life by happenstance in 1937. At the clinic in nearby Fürstenberg after her breakdown—whether from postpartum depression, accumulated

exhaustion, worry, or Heinrich's frequent absences and her lonely awareness of his Berlin escapades—Aimée met Dr. Helma Kahnert, one of the
doctors charged with her care. Over time, Dr. Kahnert became a friend,
even getting to know the children who were occasionally brought to visit
their mother. On one such visit, Aimée showed Brigitte a picture postcard
of the RMS *Queen Mary*, with three gloriously red smokestacks, suggesting that someday they would get on that ship together and go to
America, an escape fantasy that left a captivating and indelible impression
on her little daughter.

Dr. Kahnert stayed in touch and visited Blumenhagen often. In
1939, she took a position at the hospital in nearby Neustrelitz, and eventually came to live at Blumenhagen, bringing with her the nervous
twenty-five-year-old the Reich Labor Service had assigned to her as an
assistant at Fürstenberg. Dr. Kahnert had taken young Lo Meyer, grap-
pling desperately with the effects of her mother's suicide, under her
wing, and would not abandon her. So both women came to Blumenhagen, each in her own way bringing companionship and in-house moral
support. Their presence became a fact of life, an extension of life in
Heinrich's family, where estates with plenty of room and help meant
that long-term relatives and guests were common, part of the great web
of relationships.

War Anxiety

All Europe suffered from war anxiety that unusually hot summer of 1939. Poland was acutely aware of its precarious position between two monsters. In Prague, children rode a merry-go-round featuring not the usual prancing ponies or gilded chariots, but tanks and motorcycles. The French voiced Gallic political I-Don't-Care-ism, grumbling, as they dug air-raid shelters beneath the Eiffel Tower, that dying for Danzig seemed hardly worthwhile. England stocked up on flashlights and black-out material, while schoolchildren being outfitted with gas masks delighted in the discovery that they made wonderfully rude noises. Berliners awaiting August holidays sought relief from the heat in slow foxtrots at tea dances on the Wannsee, one of Berlin's many lakes.

Heinrich had been looking for work in Berlin almost continually since 1931. Now, suddenly, there was a job with the *Kolonialbund*—Colonial Office. Pressing for lost African colonies while Europe was fraying at the edges seemed a long way from the realities of the day, but restitution of the colonies that the Versailles Treaty had stripped away fit with the regime's push for expansion and *Lebensraum*. Besides, it was work, and it relieved some of the pressing anxiety over their situation and Heinrich's hopes.

Returning from errands at the end of another dry August, Aimée stood with her bundles on the sunny village street as a military column rumbled past. Housewives came out to watch, wiping their hands on aprons. Children shouted and whirred in excitement at the clanking, grinding progress of dust-covered trucks, artillery, and soldiers. She stared at the dusty boot of a young officer on a motorcycle stopped just feet away, idling due to the column's halting progress. For some reason, she did not want to see the face that went with the boot, but looking up in spite of herself, she met the gray eyes of a very young soldier. They both looked away quickly, but in that moment she thought that she saw in his eyes the same turmoil and fear that she felt must be in hers.

Moving troops east hardly fit with the recent, noisily publicized Nazi-Soviet pact. But Hitler claimed that thousands of *Volksdeutsche* living in Poland were being harassed, and the British were not pushing Poland hard enough to force acceptance of his demands: return of the Baltic port of Danzig, and improved access through the "Polish Corridor," a swath of land—now Polish since the Versailles Treaty—separating Germany from Danzig and her eastern province of East Prussia. Party presses bellowed that Poland was mobilizing feverishly, threatening the peace. Heinrich was in the reserves. If there was a war, he could be called up. He was at the point of packing for Africa when Germany woke on September 1 to the news that the country was at war. Schools were closed; listening to foreign news was forbidden.

Hope was widespread that maybe, in spite of long-standing commitments to defend Poland, England and France would do nothing and it would all be over quickly. There was no enthusiasm for war, no war fever. Another war meant rationing, blackouts, air-raid alarms. According to Aimée's friend Lore, when loudspeakers announced that Britain had declared war, the crowd on Berlin's Alexanderplatz stood numb. The citizenry had learned to be cautious about talking politics in public.

France also declared war and Britain announced a blockade. Goebbels brought the sound of air strikes, heavy artillery, and machine gun fire—a touch of the Polish front—to German listeners in their living rooms, yet Poland's allies fired hardly a shot. Within weeks, Warsaw capitulated; the easy victory was astonishing. Then, just as it seemed the war was over and there was talk of peace, Stalin marched into eastern Poland. Between them, the two dictators had wiped Poland off the map. The Nazi press claimed that since Poland no longer existed, there was no need for England and France to intervene on her behalf. The reasoning was backward; it made no sense. But Aimée was inured to assaults on rational thinking. She hoped Heinrich could shed some light on this when he came home.

For the time being, all bets were off. Heinrich was not going to Africa after all, though at least he was not being mobilized. But for him, the German border, now so close to Latvia, roused old boyhood dreams. Blumenhagen had never carried the same emotional weight as Ottenhof; its soil held no ancestral footprint, no trace of venerated earlier generations. Aimée wondered whether Ottenhof's gravitational pull was powerful enough to seduce him into forgetting that the life of the gentleman farmer had not met his expectations, that he wanted and needed intellectual and worldly stimuli. Maybe the huge obstacles that kept Ottenhof out of reach no longer seemed so enormous. Maybe the drastic methods already set in motion to overcome them were not as frightening as they looked.

October 1 was a day of thanksgiving for the harvest, the radio assuring Germany that the harvest was indeed a good one and that the British blockade could not starve Germany as in World War I. It was also the day for bestowing the *Mutterkreuz*—Mother's Cross—an honor that carried the Führer's gratitude, the privilege of being greeted with the Hitler salute, and a seat on public transportation. Aimée was eligible for the *Mutterkreuz* Third Class, in bronze, for mothers of four or five children. Very small, very round, very nearsighted, the earnest official bestowing the honor stretched to bring the ribbon and its pendant medal up over her head and delivered his carefully rehearsed speech about her contribution to the Reich. It was a hateful intrusion into a personal sphere; she had produced five fine children, but certainly not for the Reich.

Her birthday a few days later was a day of warm sun and crystalline sky, the great lindens by the door just beginning to turn to gold. Resistance in Poland had all but collapsed, and at noon, Hitler addressed the nation about his peace offer to England and France, ending on a note that made acceptance sound inevitable. Buoyed by that hope, the family gathered for the traditional birthday *Kringel*, and to hear Heinrich read a letter from his brother, Georg, who was farming the last remaining fifty hectares at Ottenhof.

Georg wrote that the radio announcement of Hitler's proposed "resettlement" of Baltic Germans had run through his family like a lightning bolt. They were to leave Ottenhof in eight days, taking only what they wore and a small suitcase, to be resettled in areas of Poland newly under German control. Hitler had traded Latvia and Estonia to Stalin in return for Polish provinces under Russian control. Of Ottenhof, 3,600 hectares had already been expropriated without compensation. Now the remaining hectares were gone too, lost even more irredeemably than before.

Heinrich's voice had gone hoarse and the hand holding Georg's letter dropped to his lap. The letter was dated late September. Georg, Karola, and the children were probably gone by now, the house already empty. Ottenhof was abandoned again. He could not go on. The children looked at their father in nervous silence. Aimée took up the letter. " 'I dread this last week in Ottenhof,' " she read, " 'but once the treetops of our beloved park have sunk into the distance, it may be a bit easier.' "

Hitler immediately launched a campaign of massive, ruthless dislocation, expelling Poles and Jews from Polish provinces to repopulate these areas with Germans and "ethnic" Germans uprooted from the Baltics and central and eastern Europe. His push for a Germanized utopia in the east shuffled millions across the wartime chessboard like meaningless atoms. Children were separated from parents, making a mockery of the publicly extolled sanctity of the family. Georg's family, lucky enough to be considered "highly valuable," was still intact, but there were no words for Heinrich's sense of betrayal. The Baltics had been abandoned; Stalin had won.

At dinner with their friends the Gersdorffs one evening, Heinrich mentioned a rumor making the rounds in Berlin that the neutral countries, perhaps even the pope, would ask Roosevelt to broker a peace with Britain and France.

Renate turned to Aimée, asking urgently, "Is this true?"

Of course she had no idea. How could she? She had no more news than anyone else. Real news had been obscured long since by the impenetrable murk of propaganda. Newspapers were written in code and studied like chicken entrails. The western front was consistently described as quiet, but there was no peace.

Days grew shorter, rationing tightened. Hitler's October "peace offer" to England and France was without response, and the hope that had brightened the darkening days faded. Everything was unsettled. There was a sense of suspended animation, of loose ends and hoping for a real

peace before Christmas felt absurdly unrealistic. Real war seemed almost inevitable, just a matter of time. Some evenings Aimée and Lo sat
by lamplight, sewing a deerskin vest from a deer Heinrich had shot. If
he was drafted for a real war, the vest might warm him. If not, he could
wear it happily at home.

Christmas that year was shrouded in snow and sleet, but they were determined to savor the season's private pleasures. They had evolved their
own tradition—a mix of Old World and New that satisfied them both
and was establishing a new one for their children. On the first Sunday of
Advent, an enormous wreath of fir boughs with four fat red candles—
one for each Sunday till Christmas—was suspended by four broad red
ribbons in the big square stairwell, and the family gathered there to
sing. War and weather were banished.

Marta, Blumenhagen's cheerful cook, housekeeper, and factotum, rolled
up her sleeves and set up a big table in the kitchen for the Christmas baking. Each child was given a large lump of dough to roll out, shape, and decorate according to whim. Heinrich took the older children into the woods
for the perfect tree, Brigitte perched on his shoulders, feet tucked into his
pockets for warmth, the boys trudging alongside. The tree went into a corner of the music room, which was then closed and not open to the children
until Christmas Eve.

Aimée had imported miraculous popcorn, and American-style Christmas stockings were hung. On their first Christmas together, she had told
Heinrich about mistletoe, and he now sent Friedrich out into the wintry
woods to find some. Eventually the boy found the elusive parasite in a
gnarled birch and delivered his find, and his father's poem about his quest,
to his delighted mother.

Christmas Eve morning everyone gathered on the big parental bed.
The stockings' pleasures kept the children occupied until, toward evening,
Heinrich corralled them in the darkened library next door to the music
room. Under Aimée's coaching, they had memorized "'Twas the Night
Before Christmas," and recited it together in an excited, if bumpy, chorus.

By the light of a single candle, Friedrich solemnly began to read,
"And it came to pass in those days that there went out a decree . . . " The

reedy ten-year-old voice did not diminish the majesty of the words. Michael and Christian were shepherds, determined to go to Bethlehem to see what the angels had prophesied. Brigitte was Mary, and little Dorothée was all that could be asked of an angel. When a small silver bell sounded next door, it was Christmas.

Heinrich flung open the door, and the children rushed into the music room. After the darkness, the majestic tree cast its spell, the radiance from its countless candles miraculous. Gilded walnuts and stars hung from the tree boughs, turning slowly in the candles' warmth. Glass globes, with a soap bubble's iridescent rainbow hues, were hung as a reminder of God's promise to Noah never again to send a flood. Aimée at the piano accompanied the carols and hymns, German, American, and English.

Then the children were bundled up against the cold to scan the dark for Saint Nicholas's lantern. As they hopped on the terrace in anticipation and to keep warm, Heinrich always seemed to have disappeared. But at last—a faint gleam on the frozen lake. Yet the gleam came no closer. Perhaps Saint Nicholas needed help? Aimée sent Friedrich off to reconnoiter. The boy was past believing, yet his heart pounded as he hurried across the ice toward the light.

Saint Nicholas *did* need help: Gifts had tumbled out of an unseen hole in his sack, and Friedrich helped him back to the house. Warming himself by the fire, Saint Nicholas listened to verses the children had memorized in his honor. Then he dispensed gifts, each accompanied by a short, impromptu rhyme. At last, when the sack was emptied of its last treasure and he was cheered with food and drink, Saint Nicholas disappeared into the night to continue his rounds, the children waving him off. Turning back into the light and warmth, Michael told his mother that Saint Nicholas's shoes were just like his father's.

The winter of 1939–40 was bitter. Roads were sheet ice. The lake was frozen, of course, but so were the Danube and other vital waterways, and frozen transport systems created a coal crisis. To try to keep the population moderately warm, schools, theaters, even factories were closed. The Führer's "peace offensive" was obviously stalled, yet oddly enough, for the first time since the war began, there was renewed talk of Germany's right to colonies and her share of the world's riches. Perhaps Heinrich would go to Africa after all.

Snow was still on the ground in March. If cold stood in the way of military operations, fine. England and France had both declared war, though for lack of armed hostilities, Germany had dubbed it the *Sitzkrieg*—sitting war. But spring might turn *Sitzkrieg* into the real thing. The big propaganda guns Goebbels had long aimed at the British now thundered at France. Hitler's press charged that Roosevelt and his "camarilla" of Jewish plutocrats was forcing Germany into war. Until the Reich's essential *Lebensraum* was secure, there would be no negotiated peace. Bulletins hinted darkly that a "decisive strike" was imminent. Aimée knew that antiwar feeling was strong in the United States, but worried what would become of American neutrality. It was nerve-racking.

She loved Blumenhagen and her life, but the mood was anxious and the future refused to come into focus. She felt out of her depth. She was tired of the tensions, the rationing, the cold. What would become of them all, of everything she and Heinrich had worked toward? The war effort had swallowed her car, and the easy friendships it afforded her went with it. Mary had written to say that she had used some of Aimée's Christmas money to hear Bruno Walter, who had recently immigrated and was causing a sensation in the States; Aimée wished she could have heard Walter with Mary. She missed her car. Most of all, she missed the feeling of having some control over their future, of solid ground under her feet.

Events rocketed unnervingly between war and no war. As the farm edged into a new growing season, the radio announced Germany's attack on British warships and bases at Scapa Flow, action both sides had avoided so far. But now the British retaliated. At Easter the customary family visits were seriously crimped; Reich trains were needed for critical transport. Bright satin chocolate boxes displayed in shop windows provided passersby only illusory respite from the national angst. The boxes were empty; chocolate was in short supply. War had killed the Easter Bunny.

By the time Germany marched into Denmark and Norway in early April, the fields were showing green. Radio bulletins on resistance and

British troop landings in Norway concluded with "We're Marching Against England." Naming the foal born that spring Narvik, the strong-sounding name of the Norwegian town that resisted Hitler's invasion, felt futile, silly except for the wonderful name. Buildup to war had taken on a horrible momentum. Germany was being told that this war would be won, her colonies returned. Between the Colonial Office and increased duties at his regiment, Heinrich was hardly ever at home anymore. Then he was mobilized. Aimée thought of the deerskin vest she and Lo had made for him, every stitch sewn in the hope this would not happen.

The curve of the fields, recently just serrated furrows of dark earth picked out by a dusting of late snow, now lay under new green. She welcomed another season in a cycle that felt utterly dependable, yet always surprising, miraculous. Everything looked normal, predictable, but the already less-than-solid ground under her feet now felt like quicksand.

More's the Pity

The train taking Heinrich to war in France sped through the Rhine Valley's vineyards, castles, and Lorelei's crag. Visiting relatives at Koblenz, he sat up "until 2:00 a.m. reading diaries and letters of family members who had been in France in 1814, 1870, and 1914. The 1813–1814 diary of a young lieutenant in the Napoleonic Wars, later a general, is on its way to you." It made him feel a part of history.

He wrote again from Luxembourg, where he looked up "Cousin Franz in his pretty little château."

Luxembourg,
May 23, 1940:

> Cousin Franz has a big terrace, with enormous trees. From there one looks down into a deep valley and up a steep rise on the other side, to a road on which German columns were marching in. Just as I saw the first of them, two British fighter planes flew in to strafe the column, but were gone almost immediately. One was shot down and crashed—just like in the movies—the other one turned back.

It sounded like a report from a holiday: nice views and some action—at a remove—just like the movies.

He arrived at Division HQ by bus, one of two shiny new buses he chartered from the city of Luxembourg to transport his ninety men to the mustering point, passing column after column marching west, faces already browned by the sun. It was hardly a warrior's entry into battle. In fact, Heinrich's role as an infantry lieutenant in the rear guard may have been left over from a Wilhelmine dictate that fathers of children—five for him at that point—ought not to be in the front lines. But after the long and frustrating search for work, years of feeling sidelined and underutilized, he was glad to be doing something, even if it was only marching. Marching from 7:00 a.m. to 7:00 p.m., forty-five kilometers and more a day, writing home during rests, sometimes in staccato for lack of time. His letters are full of sunshine and enthusiasm; he sounds like a teenager finally released from the boredom and restlessness of home. And the countryside was glorious.

> We are resting in beautiful green country. Above us, bombers flying west in a blue sky. The men are gathering clover for the horses. Black and white cattle graze. The villagers are friendly, some shake hands. Children wave, girls smile and bat their eyes. It is clogged up ahead. Larks above, wind from the west. Thirty-seven kilometers yesterday.

At the end of one long day, he found wonderful quarters in the village of Marbay, with "lonely, 74-year-old M. Léonard, 7 children away, 2 in the war, wife dead," who had no news at all, no mail, no newspapers, no radio. "*Oui, oui,*" he said, when he heard how things stood. "It's all the fault of the British. They always want everything. In my day, they fought the Boer War to get the gold mines." Then he mustered his old neighbor lady to make Heinrich a *pouisse*—eggs—with some milk and bread, and sold him his entire store of dried winter apples.

Here was Heinrich the attentive listener, the undercover historian, sitting companionably as M. Léonard's bent old neighbor concocted an omelet for this personable fellow who never saw himself as the enemy—a report that meshed seamlessly with the German propaganda exploiting the ancient French animus toward the British. Heinrich himself could easily have served as poster boy for Goebbels's posters proclaiming, "*Fidez vous des soldats Allemands*"—"Put your trust in German soldiers." He was absolutely correct in all ways. His French was excellent; his manners impeccable; he paid for everything.

For him, difficulties were of the camping-out variety. "Our tent was too hot and close for me, so I slept wonderfully out in the open. When a thunderstorm brought rain, I had to crawl in my sleeping bag, inching along like a caterpillar, to take shelter. The chewing and snorting of the horses accompanied my dreams."

His first real taste of war came as French and British soldiers were already wading toward rescue across the wide beaches of Dunkirk. High in the Ardennes under a steady drizzle, the route was littered with dead horses, burned-out trucks, broken trees, and trampled, singed trails where panzers had crashed through deep woods before they too burned out.

Caesar himself had recognized the dank and gloomy Ardennes as a place of terrors. To Heinrich, "this immense, eerie forest of death" has eclipsed sunshine and high spirits. "The historic battlefield of Sedan unfurls below, in the faint gleam of pale sun. A distant growling thunder of big guns, nearby, a thrush sings over a fresh soldier's grave." In gray drizzle near Neufchâteau, "thousands of prisoners cluster around smoky fires of damp wood—ragged colonials of different colors and dress—slippers, sandals, women's hats, a fox fur piece. Some push along baggage, some have stacked plunder on baby carriages, carts or bicycles, one with a fox fur piece, a sad sight."

A French plane shot down, lying in a field of high grass like a great, dead bird. I will send some of the singed white silk from the parachute. We've only seen two French planes and the one shot down, but we see German planes by the hundreds every day, their shining bodies glinting in the sun. They fly in splendid order, forward, then back again.

In the ragtag muddle of defeat that the French called *la catastrophe*, he now saw signs of hard fighting. The village of Signy-l'Abbaye was completely shot up, the little châteaux in ruins. Sections of railroad track had been jammed into the earth of the park to deter panzers, but the panzers had simply taken the road. "Moving through this empty country, through abandoned villages and farms, is eerie. Cattle wander over pastures, chickens and dogs among the houses. A broody hen with chicks she has hatched somewhere, standing on a manure pile. Tame rabbits hop through gardens, nibbling on lettuces, pigs look for food, grunting as they go." Abandoned cows, udders bursting with milk, were relieved to be milked directly into the passing army's mess pots.

Still, everything is lush with the gleam of early summer, peonies nodding heavy, bright heads in village gardens. He savors every moment, describing the exquisite châteaux dotting the infantry's path in detail, sometimes enclosing picture postcards. At the end of a day's tramp along the hard-packed *chaussées* of the Aisne and Champagne, his men are covered in the chalky dust of French limestone country and looked like millers' apprentices.

La Sauge aux Bois was intact, but its houses wrecked by French and Moroccan troops, leaving shoes, drill jackets, pictures of girls behind. "The beautiful old château, empty now but for the furniture. Beautiful stone terraces, Louis XIII turrets, hedges, rosebeds, espaliered trees . . . ," all designed to please the eye and delight the senses, yet sad and, with no one to take pleasure in its delights, abstract and pointless. "Straw and hay everywhere, feathers and chicken heads in the greenhouse. A brook ran clear and green from the woods through the garden, faced in stone. As soon as my men were taken care of, I bathed there—wonderful after the hot dusty march."

Refreshed and civilized, Heinrich scared up old copies of the *L'Illustration* weekly in the attic, and a leather-bound volume of Corneille "to read in the Rococo paneled dining room until the light failed." The place was a reminder of the riches still to be found in France, a private cultural heritage and wealth. Roaming through this wonderful house, picking up the odd book from the library, might have reminded him of the unwelcome strangers who must have roamed through Ottenhof as he was doing here.

Absorbed by the moment, besotted with the beauties of France, he wrote his family that he was not in any danger, just happy to be involved in something that made demands on him. The demands were mostly mundane—finding quarters and provisions—but the division was moving so quickly, some five hundred kilometers in fourteen days, that this was usually a daily task. French opinion seemed unanimous. As one Frenchman told him: "This war is a great misfortune for France; the capitalists and the English had got them into this pickle; it should be over as quickly as possible." During the phony war, Goebbels had used France's age-old suspicion of England to his wartime advantage. Cartoon flyers depicted British soldiery abandoning the French "ally," and now blamed England for France's present-day troubles. "Asked about the English, many French draw an index finger sharply under their chin."

On June 1, 1940, he wrote that he had never been in any real danger, "but now there is no need to worry at all. The big battles in the north are over. Occasionally, there is the thunder of distant artillery," but France was on the verge of collapse. He hoped for a push to Paris, "where I was in 1926, and where the great-grandfathers who fought to defeat Napoleon joined the victory celebrations in 1815." Paris would represent a nice, historical rounding out. Instead, he was pulled out of some heavenly days of rest to report to the division command post. His life was about to undergo a complete change.

Next morning, while everyone else was still asleep, he sat shaving in dewy grass, then was driven off through a glorious landscape to a nearby town to meet the commandant and staff officers, breakfasting in the bright salon of the *mairie*—the town hall. He spells out both the excitement and embarrassment over his transformation from weary, if game, foot soldier to intelligence officer:

> Everything is new: new surroundings, new work, new people, new quarters. I went back to get my things and say a quick good-bye. It was embarrassing to swoosh around in a fast, shiny Mercedes in front of the fellows with whom I had endured so much dust, thirst and heat. Still, I am very happy. The people are intelligent, the work is interesting and will become even more so. My domain: regional intelligence, politics, land and people. I'll adjust quickly.
>
> It's wonderful here. Such good, intelligent people, the work so suited to me. Contrasts: Saturday I slept in my sleeping bag under a heavy truck, my head on a haversack. Now I'm sitting at MY table, in MY room, with a mirror, washbasin, fireplace, easy chair and a bed with real linens. With a rug—yes, a rug!

The camaraderie of the open road had been exchanged for recognition of his capabilities and a new sense of purpose. He would be able to use his head rather than just his feet and his French. After the inactivity and the long, fruitless search for work, it was a relief to be doing something other than waiting, marking time, hoping. He was part of something; there was forward momentum, and a real bed.

Alexis von Roenne, a senior fellow officer in the Potsdam Infantry Regiment 9 may have been among the "good, intelligent people" Heinrich mentions, and responsible for the small miracle of his transfer. Slight, with sharp features and a lucid intelligence, Roenne became a close friend who played a crucial role in his life. Their shared Baltic background, deepened by religious and moral convictions, was a strong bond.

Heinrich is relieved to have his first letter from Aimée. She reported that it had rained at Blumenhagen—a good thing, since all too often, promising rain clouds failed to deliver. He had written every day; had she received his letters? At a critical time in the farming year, he may have had more time to write than she did, in spite of long marches. He offers reassurance about America joining the war, and beautiful France, their personal Eden, being despoiled. Practically, he says, American entry into the war is problematic, and militarily, France is already kaput. She must not worry; this war is less gruesome than 1914–18; only a few places are hard hit. Laon and Saint-Quentin are untouched, and "about me, you need have no worries at all. For me, my love, the war as trial by fire is over, but there is still a great deal to see and hear." He has found a British light pistol for the boys. The small chess set she sent is always with him.

His work is interesting, his colleagues wonderful. On the night of June 4, they sat up late with wine by the open windows of the great salon. Around eleven-thirty, the radio brought Hitler's proclamation about the end of the great battles in the north. Heinrich wrote

An old world is sinking, but even in ruin she is beautiful. Yet the real, the pure, the eternal will survive. The sun will continue to shine on the gardens of Oxford and Cambridge, on the white chateaux of the Touraine, through the bright windows of the great cathedrals. The spirit, the word, and art will remain. What is passing is a political system that no longer had blood in its veins and cannot survive. The path to the future is wide open.

Ascribing this outburst to too much French wine at the end of a long day makes some sense. Aimée often said that he was a romantic and a naïf. The period was also rife with such high-flown talk, and the thrill of quick victory was not lost on him. Yet Italy's declaration of war meant less to him than the beauties of the landscape:

> The Carolingian fortress and the mighty cathedral of Laon surging like an Acropolis out of misty sunlight that bathed the wide plateau before me. In my deepest thoughts, I am always with you. I delight in every bit of news from you, so write as often as you can.

On one evening of brooding heat, he wrote from a ruined village struggling up the slope toward the Chemin des Dames—a historic ridge running between two river valleys. The little church behind him, already rebuilt after the last war, had been hit again. The schoolhouse next door was littered with French radio equipment, abandoned weapons, clothing, and gas masks. He had been on the ridge above, where an immense stone crucifix towered over dead French soldiers, "its pain-filled features bowed under the evening sky, shedding peace over the world's suffering."

When Dunkirk officially surrendered, the Ninety-Sixth Infantry Division, which had been moving west, turned south, pressing forward in ever longer, ever more hurried marches. One soldier, giddy with the rush and confusion, shouted in passing, "We are marching all the way to Marseille!" Still, Heinrich wrote every day, sometimes in telegraphic haste, sounding young and game. His attention always lingers on the landscape, architectural treasures, or the comical: a mule looking out from a kitchen door, the floor strewn with apples the creature had pulled down for itself. Here a mule, there a horse, sometimes a donkey without a bridle joined the moving columns. "Their soldiering blood allows them no rest. If their own troop has disbanded in defeat, they attach themselves to whatever battalion comes along next."

Though their doors were marked with messages in chalk urging French soldiers to respect civilian habitations, village houses were often in terrible condition, kitchens and wine cellars looted. Beds were torn apart, frame, mattress, pillows, comforters, and bolsters muddled among empty bottles, broken glasses, underwear, blue and khaki coats.

The collapse of France's defensive line on the Somme and the Aisne set off an exodus among the civilian population. Retreating French troops had hurriedly bombed bridges and set roadblocks, complicating movement for German troops and French refugees alike. Camped at the site of the Fort de la Malmaison, the scene of bloody battles in 1914–18, Heinrich watched soldiers, sunburned and full of energy and life, milk cows among the wheat and knee-high clover while others acted as burial details. It was a study in contrasts, he wrote: life and death, victory and defeat, side by side.

The names that crop up in his letters resonate with history, all scenes of past glories or ignominy, depending: blood-soaked Verdun, fought over since Attila, in the Franco-Prussian War, then in World War I; Sedan—long a gateway for invaders. Napoleon's retreat had stalled at Craonne on the Chemin des Dames, where Barclay de Tolly had marched triumphant Russian dragoons, hussars, Cossacks, and cuirassiers toward Paris for a victory parade in 1814. A hundred years later, a bitterly contested Craonne cost innumerable lives, ignited a mutiny, and inspired an anti-military song that did nothing to stop new bloodshed. The historian in him saw past wars everywhere. For nonhistorians, a monument on the road to Igny-Comblizy spelled out the wretched story: At this point the invader was halted in 1915. Farther along, white roses blanketed a vast military cemetery from that war with extravagant blooms.

After another long, sweltering march, soldiers gathered around a basin of flowing spring water under the plane trees in the village square at Coulanges. Seeing their young, half-naked bodies gilded by sun and glistening with water, Heinrich found the "heroic figures of our soldiers, naked to the waist, washing and splashing, a joy to watch." The image smacks of Nazi adoration of Aryan flesh, but the local population seemed to agree. The village consensus: "Quand même, ils sont des beaux gars"—"Anyway, they're good-looking fellows."

At Ronchères, only "five old people, one lone old woman, and one

warden, *'toujours ivre comme un cochon,'*"—always drunk as a pig—
were left, villagers told him, adding that it was all the fault of the capitalists and the English. The age-old grudge lived on. First, England had
been too slow to commit to the defense of France, then she had failed to
put sufficient muscle into that defense. Still, they were resigned, wrote
Heinrich: *"Tant pis pour nous, tant pis pour vous, tant pis pour tout
le monde"*—"More's the pity for us, for you, for everyone!" one old
woman said, and then added, "But at least you are human."

After many marches under relentless sun, dust and heat gave way to
a day of rain, a great relief. On the foggy morning of June 14, he wrote
propped against a gravestone in a crumbling churchyard. Sitting up late
the night before, he had heard French premier Paul Reynaud's desperate midnight appeal to Roosevelt, asking him to declare war and save
France, "the advance guard of democracy." Then they were ordered to
move on, and left in darkness at 3:00 a.m. That day, German tanks lum-
bered down the Paris boulevards in a grim show, four abreast. The
Reich's banner flew over Paris. What France had called the *drôle de
guerre*—funny war—had become deadly serious, and ended so quickly
in humiliation. Reynaud's appeal had been in vain. The only question
now was when he would capitulate.

Pressing farther south, the battalions continued their march in spite
of heat and pain, even by moonlight, the horses' heads nodding in rhythm
with their step. Thirsty, hungry, tired, with little sleep, and resting only
when jammed roads caused delays, they marched 144 kilometers in two
days. Heinrich was moving so fast that he could not write much. In the
Forêt d'Enghien, among the rubble, his men found orders left behind by
the French Twenty-First Battalion: to defend the place, with no thought
of withdrawal. Evidence of recent, terrible fighting was everywhere. In
the marketplace at Romilly-sur-Seine, a shelled monument still lifted a
battered arm over burned-out French and German tanks. Propaganda
trucks blared triumphant marches; Strasbourg had fallen. Amid the noise
and chaos, an exhausted driver slept on a chaise longue.

Refugees were everywhere—on foot, with carts and baby carriages,
often on big two-wheeled wagons with three horses, loaded with beds,
sacks, pots and pans piled high, with old people, women, children, even

dogs atop it all, or in the dust, on a string between the wheels. Sometimes a car—useless without petrol—was tied on behind. Early mornings, refugees stood by the road, their horses harnessed, hoping to get through the German columns. With no way to tell them that the troop column was three days long, he wrote and distributed flyers urging them to wait, let the column pass, then go home. Meanwhile, the tattered, limping remains of France's army—Frenchmen, Africans, Asians—began offering the stiff-armed salute.

Now that the disaster was complete, a wave of finger-pointing engulfed France. Troops blamed their commanders, who blamed the politicians. The right blamed the left and the Communists, and vice versa. One consequence of this domestic rancor was that some of the loathing that might have attached to the invader was now directed at the French body politic. Goebbels urged the French to put their faith in the German soldier, and since, according to Sartre, the German soldier surrendered his seat on the Metro to little old ladies, made way for people in the street, showed kindness to small children, paid for his food and drink, and was, all in all, "correcte," many did. Atrocity stories faded; perhaps the Boches weren't so bad after all. Heinrich's passage was eased considerably.

He reported such news and details of the campaign as he knew, but he knew nothing of the bitter relations between the British and French forces except as they were reflected in the populace. He had heard Reynaud's appeal to Roosevelt. When he began getting reports from Fremde Heere West (Foreign Armies West)—German military intelligence for the west—he knew a good deal more, not shared in censored letters home. It was always on the countryside, the people, the beauties of churches and châteaux, that his letters lavish loving attention, transfixed by the douceur de vie that France offered in abundance, even in wartime. Heady stuff, combined with the flush of victory.

The roses are pale in the cool darkness, vines glint dimly around the tower wall, fresh air breathes into the open windows surrounded by their tendrils. The last messenger has gone, only the spring still gurgles in the silence. I am sitting on a stone bench under the roses to catch my breath, to calm my soul. Good night.

. . .

The footsteps of the watch crunch on the gravel; he breathes in the beauties of France, feeling like a benign conqueror, wholly attuned to the culture. The letters are a love song to France, a romantic travelogue; if they relieved his wife's workaday isolation and tedium, so much the better.

At Champvallon, near Joigny, while the general worked in the billiard room to typewriter clatter, Heinrich and other officers sat late by the fire in the grand salon, talking about the future of Europe. A Europe under German dominion? Or the kind his hero, Briand, had proposed at a 1929 lunch "between a pear and some cheese"—a "United States of Europe," with no more wars? After World War I, there were high hopes for a new, united Europe, with justice and democracy triumphant on a continent blessed with peace. And now—were they at the threshold of that new world?

Next day, June 17, a violent cloudburst ended the long string of sunny days that had lasted through much of the French campaign—*la débâcle*, the French called it. Shortly after noon, in the midst of the downpour, Marshal Pétain's thin, old-lady voice came across the airwaves to announce to his shaken compatriots that "*il faut en finir*"—it was time to put an end to—hostilities. He was taking the reins of government. For many, this sapped whatever morale and resistance remained; arms were tossed aside, soldiers headed home. Despite some relief, the conditions for peace were still unknown. France felt dishonored and enslaved.

The recent marches in blazing heat were over. Very late that evening, Heinrich and Major Schipp stood under a full, milk-white moon, mirrored in the broad moat of the château where they were billeted, wondering what fate was "being decided in the heart of the 84-year-old Marshal Pétain, as the silent moon shines on his homeland, and ours?"

Searching for new quarters in the quiet between two fronts, his car speeding through a park of old trees, Heinrich felt transported into the eighteenth century, the car breaking into the peace of the place "like Martians or modern knights in armor." Pulling up to a white château with wide wings, he saw curious faces behind the panes. An elegant white-haired lady stepped out, white lace around her shoulders, a heavy pearl necklace against her black silk dress. Next to her stood a tall old gentleman, and behind them, two slender young girls, the young *comtesses*. "They were the perfect French count's family, at once rural and seigneurial, with all the hallmarks of a long-gone era. It was like an apparition out of a fairy tale."

This was a family he recognized. A photograph of his mother— white hair drawn up in a now outmoded style, a fichu and cameo at her throat—could stand in for the old lady he described. He was delighted to have found someone of his own ilk. The old gentleman stepped forward "with the consummate good manners of old Europe. Here the dealings between friend and foe were those of a chivalrous culture, now disappeared. It was like talking to like. We understood each other completely."

Did this vision and his nostalgia for an earlier, courtlier time let him invest this encounter with recognition and kinship that the old count's family may not have felt? Despite his impeccable French and his manners, these people may not have seen this tall invader in his Wehrmacht uniform as a kindred spirit. The week before, the German army had entered a crushed, half-empty Paris. By midday, the swastika fluttered from the Eiffel Tower; men wept openly as the Germans marched into the City of Light. The letter goes on: "These isolated folk of an old culture may have seen something they had found lacking in a Republic gone base. For them, the German uniform embodied principles of order and tradition."

Maybe. When his father left Saint Petersburg in 1918, the sight of German uniforms had represented welcome order and civilization after terror. And when the German army withdrew from the Baltics, the Bolsheviks brought an end to his world. Now, twenty-two years later, French villagers were offering wine, insisting on drinking brandy together, and maintaining that their own troops brought disorder and looting, but "you are human, like us. You are good fellows." What could account for such surprising bonhomie toward an invading army? Was it true, at least in the early days, or was it just an ingratiating posture toward the invader?

At Osmoy, near Bourges, a last prisoner, a terribly young lieutenant, fresh out of Saint-Cyr—France's military college—was caught when he came out of hiding to fetch water. He knew nothing of the cease-fire and the change of government. News of the war's disappointing end left him sad and silent. "When I told him that Marshal Pétain had called for a cease-fire 'with a heavy heart,' he sobbed, then sat for a long time, still and sunken into himself, his heart filled with sorrow for his defeated country."

Now, though he would hardly have thought it possible, the pace picked up even more. His days turned into an exhausting welter of local problems: POWs, officers, the mayor, refugees. Every minute was packed; he had nearly given up sleep and there was no time for meals. At Bourges, he was put in charge of a POW camp—2,600 men of every stripe and color: French, Walloons, Flemish, Alsatians, Slovaks fighting under the French flag, Poles, Moroccans, Senegalese, and Indochinese all stepped up to the French bugler's call. Whites wandered around in khaki; others, in turban or fez, squatted under trees in the dust. Horses and mules were without fodder. Storehouses were full of plundered clothing, tools, munitions, arms, rotting meat. Just as he was beginning to make sense of it all came the order to evacuate.

In light of the armistice, he told men over forty to go home to their harvest or business. But he needed one doctor to accompany the others' sixty-five-kilometer march, and requests for a volunteer brought only reasons why it was impossible for each of them. At wits' end, he said that one of them must accompany their comrades. It was their affair; he would leave it to them. In the end, they volunteered one of their number—asleep and unable to protest—for the unwanted duty. Unaccustomed to command, he confessed that it never occurred to him to simply order one of them to go.

As adjutant of the administrative Kommandantur at Bourges, "if one can call this battle with chaos that," he was charged with finding accommodations for an endless stream of wretched civilians, evacuees, and refugees. He was so busy he gave up eating entirely, writing, "But it's good; responsibility and work. Order will come out of this chaos." After another long day, the magnificent cathedral's bell tower clock outside his window struck half past midnight. But this hectic work would not last. Refugees were being channeled through Bourges and home as quickly as possible. He will write to Roenne to see if he might get a liaison staff position for the denouement, so that he could "still be useful and learn things." After no word for a month, he has finally had her letter. "Waiting was a lingering hurt. Please write!"

Getting refugees home made sorting out snarled railroad traffic urgent, and the many blown-up bridges made matters worse. As he threaded his way through the pitch-dark Bourges station to meet with French railroad officials, only the glow of his flashlight kept him from stepping on the arms and legs of refugees sleeping there. Negotiations took place in a dim, narrow room, while a radio bleated, *"O mama! O mama!"* in a pitiful, monotonous refrain. The French official in charge looked utterly broken and managed only an occasional sighed *"Oui, oui."* On his way back through the station, "gloomy with the sorrow-laden sleep of the refugees," he remembered that "in 1919, we knew that sleep ourselves."

"The misery in which these unhappy refugees live—here, there, wherever they find a place—is terrible." After another long day of finding accommodations for thousands, the commanding general put him in charge of refugees. He had been part of this cruel cycle; he knew their plight well. They were everywhere, in Blois, Chaumont, and Chenonceau, standing, staring, waiting. In the surrounding countryside, the charred remains of burned-out vehicles littered the roads "like camel skeletons on a desert caravan route." The daybook he kept in Providence had quoted from Handel's *Messiah*: "Why do the nations so furiously rage together?" Now he comforted himself for the miseries of war and human fate with the view of "the river Cher in its broad green valley, like a silver ribbon in the evening's gold."

During his new assignment as refugee tsar, one incident struck a particularly personal note. At Bourges he was living in the house of a Major Brochard, a POW, whose family hoped to escape to the country. Of their seven children, they had no news of their twenty-year-old, who was in the army. Heinrich drove one car, accompanied by the sixteen-year-old son, the older children, and untold boxes and suitcases. Mme.

Brochard, the rest of the family, and more baggage went with Mademoiselle in the family car. As their little caravan made its way through the
rich country of the Berry region, he was relieved and happy to get his
charges through the demarcation line with the password. But it felt
strange, "as an enemy officer wanting to help—to drive up to the well-
tended old manor house of people who might just as well have been
named Huene—who could as easily have been us."

Then suddenly the long days at Bourges were over. The battalion was
headed home. Evening light gleamed in the reflecting pool on the château's terrace, and an elegiac mood hung over the farewell ceremonies.
Memories of shared days and the joy of going home brought a lump to
many young throats. Heinrich would be transferred back to the division
staff. On July 13, the eve of France's national holiday, an irony that cannot
have escaped him, he wrote one last letter from the French campaign.

Dearest wife! Your wonderful long letter about your life, the
full house and the boys' swimming came yesterday. I can never
tell you how grateful I am for what you are, for everything you
accomplish, and what you have achieved. You are the children's
mother, the caring wife, and now, the farm manager. You are the
one who has won the war, our war—within and without. My part
was easy, you are the one who bears the burden.

Intermezzo

Germany celebrated the fall of France with an orgy of bell ringing. Flush with victory, Hitler offered Churchill peace, and hopes ran high. Heinrich even wrote from France saying he hoped to visit George and Marjorie in London. But hard-pressed as Churchill was, his no was immediate and firm.

When Hitler took half of Poland, Stalin had taken the other half and then moved into the Baltics, and with Hitler preoccupied in France, Stalin incorporated the Baltics into the Soviet Union. For Hitler, this was a blow to his ego and his economy. For Heinrich, it meant that Ottenhof was truly gone, more gone even than when Georg had had to leave it the autumn before. Stalin would make a tabula rasa of the region where his family had lived for six hundred years. The Bolsheviks had won. His desolation took shape in a poem:

Wo meine Wiege stand, weht jetzt der Wind.
Die Fenster meiner Kinderzeit sind jetzt blind.
Unser Vaterhaus, unsere Heimat hat der Krieg in Asche gelegt.
Wer kann die Wunden zählen, die das Schicksal der Völker
*   schlägt?*

Where once my cradle stood, the wind now blows.
The windows of my childhood have gone blind.
The war has turned our fathers' house, our home, to ash.
Who can count the many wounds Fate deals mankind?

With France safely under his thumb and the British back across the channel, Hitler launched the "Battle of Britain" to soften Churchill's stance, or perhaps serve as prelude to invasion. But his generals balked;

invasion was simply not feasible. When the relentless bombing did not affect British morale as he had hoped, he decided that the time was not quite ripe for invasion after all.

Heinrich was home from France, but not for long. His letter to Roenne had had the desired effect; he was transferred to OKH (Oberkommando des Heeres—Supreme Army Command) in France, where they would work together at FHW (Fremde Heere West—Foreign Armies West) gathering intelligence on western countries. It was a stroke of luck. For an historian with language capabilities, it was ideal: a desk job with interesting people and—at last—a chance to put what he knew to some use. Under Roenne's sponsorship, he had found his métier.

Some new colleagues became friends, particularly Roenne, who brought him into the Tafelrunde—a clear reference to King Arthur's Round Table. It was a gentleman's club of twenty-five officers from Fremde Heere West who gathered to eat and savor talk among men like themselves at Fontainebleau, the site of Francis I's famous château. Francis's device, a salamander with the motto *Nutrisco et extinguo*—I nourish and extinguish—referred to a myth that salamanders not only feed on flames but also extinguish them. By extension, Francis claimed to nurture good and extinguish the bad. The Tafelrunde's adoption of his motto probably meant that they ate well, extinguished thirst with good wine, and shared talk of common interest.

Knowing that Heinrich loved daybooks for recording thoughts, ideas, and bons mots, Aimée had given him a leather-bound one imprinted with a salamander. If he did not already know the salamander's meaning, his curiosity would have made him research it, and his delight in such connections would have caused him to recommend it as the device for the officers' club at Francis I's Fontainebleau.

The Tafelrunde was an interesting crew. At the head of the membership list—arranged by rank, then alphabet, was Lieutenant General Kurt von Tippelskirch, *Oberquartiermeister*—Senior Quartermaster, Intelligence. The offshoot of an old military family and a World War I veteran, his brief now was vetting reports and analyses, and liasing with the upper reaches of the army command, where intelligence and policy intersected. Another World War I veteran was Major General Gerhard Matzky, a

student of philosophy, history, international law, and economics who had
served with the League of Nations. A cheerful, multilingual extrovert
and a lover of French food, Matzky welcomed the Tafelrunde's fare after
the wretched field rations he and his staff had been served at Zossen
during the "phony" war. Colonel Ulrich Liss, chief of Fremde Heere
West, a fellow anglophile and Mecklenburger, had worked with Roenne
at the FHW bunker at Zossen, outside Berlin, maintaining the so-called
Kuhhaut—cowhide—actually a large-scale, constantly updated terrain
map of all German and enemy forces, in preparation for the French campaign.

Brilliant and meticulous, Roenne considered Hitler's policies irrec-
oncilable with his own moral and religious convictions, and did little to
disguise his feelings. From aerial photographs, Roenne's sharp eye had
led him to conclude that enemy forces were thin along the Ardennes.
This detail, critical to the early success in France, had earned Roenne
special recognition; his word carried weight. Though some found him
hard to befriend, he and Heinrich shared values and a Baltic background,
with all that this entailed—a strong bond. After more colonels and ma-
jors, next to last on the Tafelrunde list was First Lieutenant Hoyningen-
Huene, who felt privileged to listen and learn.

Especially in Paris. For months, Maurice Chevalier's hugely popular
"Paris reste Paris"—"Paris Is Still Paris"—floated on the airwaves, and it
still held true, if now with a touch of defiant pride. The light over Paris's
daytime roofs still had the same nacreous sheen; scudding clouds still
pulled along in constantly shifting arrangements. Aimée had told Heinrich when they first met that in Paris the sky was like a Ruysdael painting in motion. There were still the odd treasures to be found among the
old book dealers along the Seine, still the lingering smell of fresh bread
outside the *boulangeries*. The river Cher, now marking the border between German-occupied France and Vichy France, still reflected Chenonceau's arches in the same double image Heinrich had seen with Aimée.
The thirteen intervening years had changed the world in ways he never
imagined.

Writer Ernst Jünger's itinerary through France touched several spots
Heinrich went through, Bourges among them. In Paris, Jünger likened

certain groups of like-minded colleagues to "shining cell[s] of spiritual chivalry" at the heart of the military machine, in the very belly of the beast. Threads of resistance were stretching through the military networks, particularly the OKH.

FHW had had a quiet if palpable anti-Hitler bent for some time. In the late thirties, as Hitler turned one nation after another into a potential enemy, stepping up intelligence operations became a priority. In laying the groundwork, old-school soldier Carl-Heinrich von Stülpnagel made no secret of his anti-Hitler views. His successor, Tippelskirch, privy to General Staff concern that the French campaign could easily end in disaster, routinely cautioned colleagues and younger officers to be circumspect when talking of bringing about "basic changes" in German leadership. Current FHW chief Colonel Ulrich Liss's criteria for FHW staff—a range of experience, travel, languages, exposure to a world beyond Germany—effectively precluded a fanatical Nazi mind-set. Heinrich was fluent in Russian, French, and German from childhood and had traveled widely. He spoke excellent English, had a more than reasonable command of several other languages, and held a PhD in history. It all fit.

Russia had shimmered in Hitler's ambitions for years, a phantasm of endless promise. With France under control and England on hold, now was the time for him to act. For Heinrich too, Russia was a phantasm that had never lost its luster. Stalin's takeover of the Baltics had thrown a dark shroud over it, but now Hitler proposed to lift that shroud. The war was escalating in a way few had imagined, taking on the momentum of a fearsome machine. Official rationale left much unanswered, yet Heinrich felt himself being drawn in. As the eldest son, it was his duty to return to his parents the vitality and joie de vivre the Bolsheviks had taken from them.

Circumstance had set him down in an awkward place. Uncomfortably perched between two eras, one foot in an era completely eradicated, the other in an age not yet fully formed, he could not move freely in either. For someone of his intensity and ambition, this was difficult terrain to inhabit. As a boy of fourteen, he had begged his father to let him enlist in the fight against the Bolsheviks in the Baltics, as his cousin

George had done. Papa had refused, but this was his chance to recapture that moment, and the vestigial teenager in him longed to settle a personal score with the Bolsheviks; where the boy had been denied, the man would act.

Yet for a romantic, this war was a conundrum, harnessing him to forces with no patience for romantics or idealists, where only arrogance and force counted. Liberating Russia from Stalin would be a good thing, but could such a war be sustained, or even won, and at what price? Optimism, energy, and idealism suggested it might be possible. Considering the unanswerable questions through a deceptive, deeply personal lens did the rest; he volunteered for the Russian front.

Was launching himself into this war a desperate salvo against fate, his last hope for the future and a place in it? If he saw Hitler's Operation Barbarossa as an attempt to liberate Russia and recapture his lost patrimony, serious misgivings about the plans for a merciless war pulled in a direction opposite to the stubborn tug of those dreams. Yet those misgivings and others—where, when, and how it would all end—were superseded by the simple fact that Germany was at war. Breaking the sworn oath of allegiance to Hitler was a matter for soul-searching; breaking it in time of war was unimaginable. War smudged the line between patriotism and conscience, duty and honor, making it hard to discern, and more difficult to draw. The chasm that had opened between public duty and private morality now seemed big enough to swallow Germany whole.

Wilfred Owen had called Horace's famous line *"Dulce et decorum est pro patria mori"*—"It is sweet and fitting to die for one's country"—the "old lie." The legacy of a classical education, it had seduced generations into marching and dying for king and country, surviving the horrors of World War I to be inscribed on countless war memorials. It also fit Hitler's plan for forging a huge army that was willing to go to any lengths to accomplish his aims.

When Heinrich knew he was going to the Russian front, he wrote a poem. *"In der Bereitstellung"*—"In Readiness"—gives a nod to the Roman notion of *virtus,* the quality of both martial courage and moral virtue. Horace's *decorum*—a certain style, the art of dying well, the military equivalent of savoir-faire—is implicit. But there is no *pro patria* here. Hitler had delivered Heinrich's homeland to Stalin. Still, there is the suggestion that his heart's blood will secure a future—one he had been unable to secure in life. Like ripened grain, his heart is ready for the harvest; in death it will be seed for the future. Death as the price of the future: a wildly romantic idea, in tune with the Zeitgeist, and shared by others. Ernst Jünger's *The Peace*, begun in Paris in 1940, also claimed that soldiers' blood bore fruit in a redeeming peace. Though it circulated only underground for years, Jünger regarded it as his most widely read book.

Heinrich had intimated that with Roenne's help, he might be engaged in an important new mission. When it was definite, Aimée stood studying the big atlas open on the table before her. One index finger on Paris and the other where—Moscow?—she imagined the journey. He would be only one of many thousands rattling by train through a verdant France, past vineyards green-gold under the sun, eastward. If he started from Paris, what cities would the train pass through—Strasbourg, Prague, Breslau, Cracow—couplings banging and clattering whenever cars were added or subtracted? And then? Who knew where he would be or what the ultimate goal was? Farther east, a thousand kilometers and more gliding away under the wheels of the train, the landscape flattening, the population thinning, the stations smaller, grayer, dustier.

She thought back to Mère and Père Fenique. Père must have died meantime, but the redoubtable Mère? It seemed impossible that it was only fourteen years ago. That delirious summer had changed her life. Heinrich had opened a door for her that summer and spilled the world at her feet. His knowledge and excitement over everything he wanted to share had taught her so much. She tried to remember the name of the little restaurant near the cathedral at Tours, where he drew her a chart of the French royal succession. *Monsieur le patron*, in his apron and inevitable moustache, helped fill in the occasional gap, and the local wine spilled on the lineage had done its part. Were German soldiers billeted at the little château of Lestion now, the commandant in the room where Heinrich had brought her his bouquet of cyclamen?

The future was impenetrable. She understood that he was chasing the dream of delivering his home from the Bolsheviks, but understanding did not make it seem any less unrealistic. Her realistic streak nagged at what looked like Heinrich's pie-in-the-sky optimism. The thought of Hitler's juggernaut reshaping the world and history was frightening, but if it did succeed, would liberating Russia and the Baltics from Stalin be enough? Would it reshape Heinrich's expectations? If she ever considered the possibility that he might not come back, she never uttered a syllable about his decision to leave his wife and five children—and soon another— behind, as hostages to fortune.

Officially the attack on Russia was a deep secret, but if there was to be peace, the obvious push for armaments made no sense. Kept in the dark, people provided their own explanations. One rumor—more wishful thinking than political likelihood—claimed that Stalin would lease the Ukraine to Hitler for ninety-nine years. That might head off more war—*if* it were true. Maybe, she thought, life really was just a pause between war and more war, time enough to be born and beget children before the dreadful continuum ground up the next generation. Never mind. Speculation would never get the fields plowed or planted.

Barbarossa

In the still evening hours of June 21, 1941, a vast army massed on the west bank of the stream that was now the German-Russian frontier. Operation Barbarossa began as sound: the somber opening chords of a grim symphony that stilled the lugubrious croaking of the river's frogs; a percussive drumming of boots on bridges; the harsh roar of heavy-caliber artillery shattering a village like a house of cards; the dark, muttering commotion of men and motors stirring up dust and unrest along the roads; a sky humming with Stukas, then a shrill whine as they dove to deliver their load on dreaming babushkas.

The three-part push had a three-part goal: endless grain, the oil fields beyond the Caucasus, and, of course, *Lebensraum*. An eighteen-hundred-mile front was to draw a line demarcating German dominance across western Russia, from Arkhangelsk on the White Sea to Astrakhan on the Caspian. For anyone with an awareness of history, it was impossible not to think of what had become of Napoleon's invincible army that set out against Russia in June 1812. But Hitler was confident, claiming that he had only to "kick in the door" and the behemoth would crumble.

Heinrich was with Army Group Center, the largest of the three prongs of the operation, meant to deliver a lightning strike and bring the quick victory Hitler predicted would be his before fall. According to Heinrich's diary:

A few days before the attack our border guards brought in deserters, Poles from 2 villages beyond the barbed wire, in ragged Polish uniforms. One, barefoot, wet to the knees from the tall, dewy grass, was happy to have escaped the Reds. He had enjoyed his first hours of freedom asleep. Two young fellows had escaped the draft. The third, a settled farmer, had escaped a fate in Siberia only because he was at a neighbor's when his family was dragged off. They seem like hounded creatures.

Along the border, most prisoners are older men, bearded fathers of families, usually collective farmers, drafted for construction battalions to build roads and border defenses. Dressed in rubber boots and soldier's gear with no insignia or arms-training, they worked from 6:00 a.m. till 11:00 at night, digging and carting dirt for a pitiful 9 rubles a month, on scant rations: fish soup, potato gruel, sauerkraut and bread. At home, meanwhile, their families are hungry, their households disintegrating.

General Heinz Guderian's panzers were critical to the quick victory Army Group Center was expected to deliver. Marked by a big white G, they raced ahead to Minsk, then Smolensk, toward Moscow. Jostling along behind came millions of men and hundreds of thousands of horses and vehicles, moving east along the same narrow, dusty road Napoleon had called Moscow Boulevard, not for any resemblance to a Parisian boulevard, but because it was the only real road across those nearly six hundred kilometers to the capital. This rutted track set the pace. In summer heat, suffocating yellow dust enveloped men and horses. A day of rain brought everything to a halt, with troops strung out over sixty kilometers, waiting for the broiling sun to dry out knee-deep mud.

The days were long, the sun an almost constant presence. A glimmering twilight lingered, just as it had during the white nights of Heinrich's boyhood summers at Ottenhof. Now there was room for hope of return, and everything paled before that possibility.

Roenne was seriously wounded just outside Białystok, near the turnoff for Grodno. At the Suraż field hospital, Heinrich helped get him into an ambulance for evacuation. Roenne had made it possible for him to be here, and he was deeply grateful. Both had known that this might be a hard campaign, not at all like France, but both had seen it as their best hope for recapturing what was lost, a hope that trumped the dangers and had brought them here together.

. . .

Stalin had not been seen or heard from since the initial attack. On July 3, in a broadcast monitored by the Wehrmacht, he finally addressed his comrades, citizens, brothers, and sisters to say that the Fascists were not unbeatable. Hitler's troops had captured Lithuania, much of Latvia, western Belorussia, and the Ukraine. They were bombing—here Stalin's flat, powerful voice turned rhythmic, incantatory—Murmansk, Orsha, Mogilev, Smolensk, Kiev, Odessa, and Sevastopol. But their finest divisions and finest air force units had already been smashed on the battlefield.

Stalin's speech was not the familiar call to bolster Bolshevism, but a call to defend Mother Russia. He went on, in a blend of propaganda and fiction, tossing significant facts into the mix: No army was invincible, Soviet political gain might well be lasting, deserters were being ruthlessly shot, the scorched-earth policy was already clear, and his call for partisan action would take dramatic effect. While the Wehrmacht had not yet seen Russia's numberless forces, Stalin promised that it would learn of the huge reserves east of the Dnieper at heavy cost.

Marching, marching, marching, into the sun, under the sun, with the sun at their backs. The road to Minsk passed through a wooden gate, the pre-1939 Polish-Russian frontier, now already far behind them, its Cyrillic sign urging the proletariat of the world to unite. Minsk was smoking rubble, a ruined ghost town, the only hint of humanity there a headless statue of Lenin, toppled from its pedestal.

This was not France. No elegant billets in châteaux, no leather-bound Corneille in rococo libraries. Accommodations were usually tents, preferably on a rise to catch a breeze and offer a view of surrounding territory, with trees for shade and water for men and horses. The army tramped through an immensity of open country, moors, and forests. Oceans of wheat dotted with poppies and cornflowers stretched to the horizon under white July heat, the changes in landscape so slight, so slow in coming, that they made no real impression. If the limitless sea of grain gave way to sunflowers, the troops marched hour after hour between tall stalks, the flowers' golden faces turning slowly as the sun moved from the horizon ahead to the horizon behind.

The occasional tiny villages in the vastness could scarcely have changed since Napoleon passed through them. Peasants watching the long columns roll by had little idea of what to expect, and the invader was equally unsure. Peasants lined the road. Shy blond girls and broad women with kerchiefs covering their hair offered bread and salt, a traditional welcome. Some knelt, making the Orthodox sign of the cross; some presented flowers. A photograph shows officers at a table set outdoors: a tablecloth with a decorative border (requisitioned from the nearest household?), cups, saucers, and a jug with field flowers. Heinrich sits at the far left, turned toward the camera. To all appearances, it is a civilized war.

> The Red Army types—ragged, dirty, often shoeless—are caught in the wheat or brush. Some have thrown their weapons away. Red stars are torn off, even buttons with the Soviet star, or civilian clothes were begged from peasants. They have been wandering, leaderless, singly or in groups, for 3 or 4 days with no food, hoping to find their fleeing units.

As they moved farther east, villagers gawked at the army's typewriters and radios, gathering to hear the box from which came not only music, but also news—in Russian—news of a war they knew almost nothing about. Often they seemed to draw no real distinction between themselves and the "enemy."

Sometimes, under Russian artillery fire, a peculiar camaraderie sprang up between villagers and the invader. As they sheltered together under whatever protection was available, the terrible whining roar of approaching shells turned them into unexpected allies—co-conspirators against death. The explosion, the shrapnel whistling past, the sudden shower of debris, and the pungent burning smell hanging over them created an odd but unmistakable bond; both were trying to survive. An aged babushka, rosy-brown and wrinkled as an old apple, crouched nearby in the illusion of cover that a small shed offered them both. Dark eyes twinkling, she gave a small, quick nod and a smile, such as a mother might give to reassure a frightened child. She had known the time of the Little Father, the tsar. She had weathered Stalin's terror. She was worn, but she had never lost her faith in the goodness of heaven. She seemed Mother Russia herself.

Beyond the villages, in the immensity where sky and horizon became indistinguishable, the commanders who had been in Russia in the last war contemplated the vastness yet to be conquered in silence. Blitzkrieg did not apply here; it was hard not to draw comparisons to Napoleon's campaign. Heinrich knew the history well.

Russian armies had gathered under the command of a forebear, Field Marshal Barclay de Tolly, to fight Napoleon along the same route, also in high summer. Napoleon too had predicted a quick victory; the tsar would be begging for peace within two months. Barclay argued that confronting Napoleon directly with a seriously outnumbered and widely dispersed Russian army was senseless, if not suicidal. Russia could win by retreating into her depths, drawing Napoleon away from supply lines until bad weather gave Russia the advantage.

Barclay's withdrawals spared the army but earned him popular scorn. National pride was at stake. The fact that he was Baltic, of Scottish origin, and spoke accented Russian made matters worse. When Tsar Alexander commanded Barclay to fight at Smolensk, the disastrous result vindicated Barclay's strategy, but lost him his command and turned his name into a derisive pun: *Boltai da i Tol'ko*—all talk, nothing more.

Mikhail Kutuzov, aged and infirm, but thoroughly Russian, was pulled out of retirement to engage Napoleon at Borodino, where the horrific carnage made the wisdom of Barclay's delaying tactics clear, but did not keep Napoleon out of Moscow. In a burned-out city, with no capitulation, Napoleon began his retreat, but he had waited too long. Russia's unforgiving "General Winter" came to her aid, and his immense Grande Armée dwindled to pitiful, straggling survivors. It was a military disaster; Barclay had been right.

Early Wehrmacht victories had infected the German High Command with enthusiasm. Minsk and Lvov had fallen. By July 2, Guderian had reached the Dnieper. Army Group Center had broken Russian defenses;

encircled troops in the Białystok pocket surrendered the day of Stalin's address. General Franz Halder's diary conceded that resistance and the country's vastness might keep the Wehrmacht busy for a few weeks yet, but the war in the east had been essentially won in a fortnight. Soon Guderian's tanks were within 350 kilometers of Moscow, the infantry ten days behind. With no road worthy of the name, they pushed hard to catch up, even at night, when the dispatch rider's lonely light was not enough to keep men and vehicles from lurching into deep sloughs.

"The General's order to move forward to the new command post here came during the night," Heinrich wrote, "[so] we went across moor and stream, with no road, no moon or stars." Descriptions of the bottomless mud that became passable only in freezing weather were familiar to him from French ambassador Paléologue's diaries. Now he experienced it for himself, his car completely, utterly stuck, sinking deeper and deeper into the quagmire, wheels spinning uselessly in spite of his excellent driver. When a heavy battery came snorting and puffing out of the dark, he mustered men and horses to get the car out. Only then could the long column of the intelligence unit move on, behind a dispatch rider, "their lights like glowworms in the dark." Creeping along a narrow log road laid across bogs, men with flashlights on both sides, he imagined that from the air, they looked like "an electrified dragon's lashing tail." Between 11:00 p.m. and 2:00 a.m., they managed four kilometers.

At last we reached a solid road with houses, dusty flowers. Through two wooden gates with the Soviet stars, we reached the RR station by the wood as the sun came up. The General was already at work. Anyone with no particular assignment immediately fell to the ground to sleep in the dust.

Speed was critical. Troops were covering fifty kilometers or more a day. Speed had been critical in France too, but this was different. On July 11, General Gotthard Heinrici wrote his wife that for him, the invasion of Russia meant "running, running, running . . . until our tongues hang out, always running, running running . . . ankle deep in dust." Every step, every moving vehicle, raised impenetrable billows of

Heinrich's mother, Marie "Mima" Emilie Olga, Countess Sievers, in her lady-in-waiting costume: the traditional *kokoshnik* (headdress) and tsaritsa's *shifr* (monogram) in diamonds, c. 1894–95.

Heinrich's father, Ernst von Hoyningen-Huene, and mother on their engagement, c. 1897.

Portrait of Mikhail Barclay de Tolly (pictured here on the outskirts of Paris in 1814), a Russian field marshal who fought Napoleon.

(George Dawe, War Gallery, Hermitage, St. Petersburg.)

Ottenhof in 1907.

Mushrooming picnic, left to right: Ebba, Papa, Mima, Heinrich, Grandpapa Nikolai, Dimenty Zacharievitch, Mira, and others, c. 1909.

Haystack at Ottenhof.
Clockwise from bottom left:
Georg, nursemaid, Ebba,
Mira, Heinrich, and
Margarethe, c. 1909–10

Heinrich's family at Ottenhof. From left to right: Papa, Mira, Ebba,
Heinrich, Margarethe, Georg, and Mima, c. 1911.

Aimée Freeland Corson Ellis, c. 1905. "I cannot take my eyes off the dear face of your mother in which there is so much of you," Heinrich wrote. "If she is still near you at times, I hope to heaven she would like me."

George Ellis and his wife, Aimée, who wears the leg o'mutton sleeves fashionable at the turn of the century.

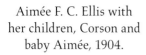
Aimée F. C. Ellis with her children, Corson and baby Aimée, 1904.

Aimée Ellis, c. 1906. Heinrich adored the fashion plate of three-year-old Aimée and her "glorious bonnet with ostrich feathers, those little hands in their white gloves. You look so kind and serious, there is all your wisdom and goodness of heart."

George Ellis with Corson and Aimée on his lap, c. 1909.

Aimée Ellis, 1928.

Mary Russell, Aimée's friend from
the Art Students League, during
their Paris days, 1927–28.

Heinrich von
Hoyningen-Huene,
c. 1925.

Aimée and Heinrich at
their wedding in Dresden,
October 6, 1928.

Schloss Toffen, near
Berne, Switzerland,
where Heinrich and
Aimée honeymooned.

Blumenhagen
under snow and
construction,
c. 1933.

Aimée surrounded
by her children at
Blumenhagen.
Clockwise from
bottom left:
Brigitte, Christian,
Aimée, Friedrich,
and Michael,
summer
1934.

Heinrich and his siblings in birth order, from youngest to oldest: Georg, Margarethe, Heinrich, Ebba, and Mira. Family profiles—taken every New Year's—were a tradition dating back to the eighteenth century, c. 1932.

The family in profile: Brigitte, Christian, Michael, Friedrich, Aimée holding Dorothée, and Heinrich. Blumenhagen, winter 1938.

Heinrich in uniform, c. 1940.

Heinrich (first on left) at a table with other officers during the Russian campaign, June–July, 1941.

(Photograph by Heribert von Koerber.)

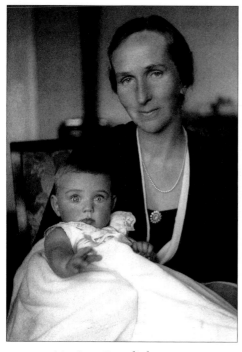

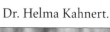

Dr. Helma Kahnert.

Aimée at Sigrid's baptism,
March 1942, wearing her father's
engagement present to her mother:
a diamond daisy brooch.

A costume drama at Blumenhagen with a
cast of cousins, c. 1944.

Sigrid with Pucki, Blumenhagen, c. 1944.

Ran Beardsley's visit to Grosseelheim, 1945. Left to right: Christian, Dorothée, Ran behind her, Aimée, Friedrich, with Sigrid and Brigitte below.

Aimée
reading to
Sigrid,
c. 1944–45.

Aimée with Brigitte, Sigrid, and Dorothée,
before leaving Germany, 1947.

Sigrid's passport photo, 1947.

Lo Nöhring, knitting,
Frankenberg, 1947.

Haying in Maine: Brigitte with rake; Michael driving the truck; and Christian and Sigrid aboard, c. 1949–50.

Lo Nöhring with Snowflake and Jasmine.

The house and garden at Middle Bay Road, 1952.

Mima, 1953.

Aimée at the Great Wall
of China, 1984.

dust, marking the routes with "yellow-brown clouds that hang . . . like long veils." Dust rose from the columns to settle on sweat-covered faces. By late afternoon, thousands of weary eyes in every shade of blue or brown or gray peered out of the dull, tawny mask each face had become.

In the early weeks of the war, often confused, frightened, unsure of what they were fighting for, enemy soldiers surrendered in unexpected numbers. Heinrich wrote

> They come in droves, waving our leaflets from the distance. The Russians with flat, round faces, the bonier White Russians with water-blue eyes, the Mongolian types, the Tungus, Kirghiz, Tadzhiks, Turgut, Chuvash, and Uzbeks. Kazakhs from the wide regions beyond the Caspian, and the half-wild descendants of the Kalmuks, who had fought in the Napoleonic wars with bow and arrow, and came through Dresden on little horses, Tartars and Astrakhans, and Georgians with black curls from the mountainous wildernesses of the Caucasus.
>
> The Mongols speak only broken Russian, their comrades translating for them, or they use sign language. Usually, it is difficult to determine even the number of their regiment. One gentle boy from Uzbekistan with the eyes of a child stepped out of the wheat and stood in the evening sunlight in the dust of the columns rolling past. Holding a bunch of cornflowers that grew among the grain in his delicate hands, he answered to nothing, and only smiled.

These disparate peoples had never become one nation. They resented Russian rule and Soviet power. Little unified them or motivated them to die for Stalin. Their loyalties and sense of belonging lay elsewhere, in Kyrgyzstan, Azerbaijan, Georgia. Those who understood this—Heinrich among them—hoped to see Russia freed from Stalin's dictatorship. That spring, intelligence sources had suggested that in a struggle with a powerful enemy, the Russian people would welcome the Germans. Festering hostility toward Stalin might bring about a popular uprising, the Communist Party would lose control, and the USSR would crumble into independent states. Whether this was based on solid intelligence or wishful thinking, the offensive made no effort to turn any longing for an end to Stalin's regime to its advantage.

> Red soldiers are fighting between 2 fires. The Red commanders' brutal discipline presses them into battle, telling them that capture means mistreatment or being shot. This is confirmed by officers and political commissars, [who] are particularly afraid of being shot and have usually torn off rank insignia or are in ordinary uniforms. They would be shot on return in any case; no distinction is drawn between surrender and capture.
>
> If you raise your head, you are shot at from the front. If you surrender, you are shot from behind. Two had been wounded by their own when they put up their hands, and many others had been killed.

Whether taken on the battlefield, because of propaganda leaflets, or because they simply threw down their arms in panic and exhaustion, by mid-July, prisoners numbered in the hundreds of thousands. The defenders of the Motherland were hungry and hollow-eyed from skimpy rations—soup, kasha, a bit of dried fish, tea. Many had cut off uniform sleeves and pant legs. Some still had their pouches for food and tobacco— empty now—but not one had lost his wooden spoon, the most essential weapon in his personal arsenal, always tucked into his boot, handy for any chance of a bite to eat.

Army Group Center's field marshal Fedor von Bock found them a pitiable sight, "weary unto death and half starving," tottering along for miles in a grim parade. In the villages, silent clusters of women watched them pass, an occasional babushka standing for hours, offering cucumbers, bread, and tears, hoping for a glimpse of a son or husband among the passing columns. With neither system nor resources to deal with such numbers, the skeletal, listless shadows were herded into open camps with no shelter and barely any food. But as only the most recent of many generations accustomed to living under the knout, they were conditioned to accept things beyond their control. Whether the knout was the tsar's or Stalin's or Hitler's apparently made little difference. They seemed indifferent to their fate, more worried about their hungry families and who would now look after home and harvest.

Heinrich's diary records his impressions in a long entry made at a place identified only as O.U.

When I speak to them in Russian, they melt. "That's our man," they say, "he speaks Russian." Then there is much "*Tovarich*"—"comrade"—talk. Even discounting the fear of the last days, their strange surroundings, and their uncertainty for the future, one has the impression that their native energy and joie de vivre are broken. "We are a dark people," they say. "We don't know anything. We live badly. Don't shoot us. We mean you no harm."

Few have kept the simplicity and heart's ease of the Russian of earlier times. Even the illiterates have been "enlightened," robbed of their faith, and hardened by hunger and oppression. Only the hardiest, most extraordinary natures still believe in good. One approached with open arms, saying "*Bozhe budet na vas*—God be with you. I'm coming over to you. I know you are good people."

One strong, blond boy, a peasant from the Smolenk region, was conspicuously clean and healthy. "I don't want to go back to the *kolkhoz* [collective]," he said, standing on hot sandy ground under scrawny pines. "I'd rather you shoot me right here. I don't want to live a life that is not free anymore. My mother told me what it was like under Nikolka—the tsar. How can I be happy working, when the land and cattle are not mine?"

One captured officer, sharply reprimanded when he asked a Russian-speaking German officer where the German artillery was entrenched, explained that he was only trying to help; the German artillery's aim had been consistently off.

From the memoirs of a long-dead relative, a young Lieutenant Uexküll, an officer in the Russian Imperial Guard, Heinrich knew that bonfires of green wood and leaves were lit in July 1812, as they were being lit now, to fend off swarms of ravenous mosquitoes. This was the kind of personal, historical connection that delighted him. The acrid smoke from those fires had probably been just as effective as the present-day fires—driving away both mosquitoes and men.

By July 15, they had reached their intermediate goal, the Berezina River, a tributary of the Dnieper. After bivouac and rest near the village of Murova, they would cross the next day. An evening wind breathed the scent of sun-warmed resin through the tall, narrow trees along the water. Light streamed between the trunks, touching the tiny, sweet strawberries that glowed like scattered rubies on the forest floor. Heinrich was surprised to find a few boletus mushrooms; it was still early for them.

As he scratched leaves away from their fat white stems, the smell of damp earth and decay conjured childhood mushroom hunts with Grandpapa Nikolai. The enfolding safety of those years had seemed immutable, and everything had collaborated to buttress his unsuspecting, childish faith in that immutability. Since that time, he had known mostly shifting ground under his feet, sometimes no ground at all. The intense recall of that shattered past and powerful hopes for the future had brought him to this Russian wood.

Just beyond the trees, the broad, lazy Berezina flowed between banks of white sand—an irresistible invitation to a holiday. Uniforms were stripped off and the river was soon alive with bodies up to their necks in cooling water, drifting, splashing, simply happy to be washing away the dust, heat, and strain of the merciless march.

Crossing the river took the division until well into the next afternoon. Then the road to Orsha, marked on the map in red as a highway, turned out to be pitiless. Engines screamed like living creatures in pain, then failed. Man and beast strained every muscle and nerve, the heat and dust stretching horses to the limit and beyond. Some collapsed and died in harness; others were abandoned by the roadside in mute exhaustion. For their handlers, who had marched endless kilometers by their side, watching the horses buckle with fatigue was anguish. Leaving them behind was only slightly less wrenching, and they faced the road ahead with heavy hearts. When that road proved too punishing, the column veered southeast, through a glorious landscape, toward Mogilev.

. . .

Hitler had told senior officers at the outset that Barbarossa was not just any war, but a war of ideologies that could not be conducted in accordance with old values. He dismissed all argument about violating the wartime code of conduct; in the east, officers must put aside their scruples and overcome outmoded notions of chivalry. His "Commissar Order" detailed specially trained *Einsatzgruppen*—task forces—to follow in the army's footsteps, execute Red Army commissars, and purge POWs and the civilian population of "bolshevized" or other undesirable individuals posing a potential threat to the Reich. Jews and intellectuals figured prominently among those undesirables.

On July 17, Reinhard Heydrich, chief of the SD—Security Service— formalized policy in the east by issuing Operational Order No. 8, spelling out the particulars: Einsatzgruppen, operating independently, would segregate "undesirables" for "further handling"; executions were to be carried out as "inconspicuously as possible . . . free from bureaucratic and administrative influences." Hitler's merciless war made no allowances for old-fashioned niceties.

By July 20, Hitler was buoyant; Russian émigrés in Germany were in despair. The war they had thought was against Bolshevism seemed to be a war against the Russian people. As word of the brutality of the Einsatzkommandos seeped through Red Army lines, any hope that Russia's disenchanted would rise against Stalin and align themselves with the invader evaporated. Resistance stiffened. Hitler's policies turned a dispirited gaggle of halfhearted soldiers into a fierce and inexhaustible enemy, fighting with a savage, vengeful courage verging on the suicidal.

The Soviets had hoped to hold the Berezina, but it was lost. Now holding Mogilev, a crux of trading routes for centuries and a frequent military command post, was even more critical. Panzers had skirted the city in their rush to Smolensk, and technically it was already behind the front, but Mogilev controlled the Dnieper River and the railroad junction. Its importance in this war became more obvious with every passing kilometer on the approach. It would be fiercely defended. Eight kilometers out, the enterprising garrison commander had set up a semicircle of carefully camouflaged field defenses to guard the bridgehead of the vital Dnieper crossing. He had also outfitted a hurriedly organized militia with English rifles and all available ammunition and mobilized the citizenry, arming them with makeshift weapons, improvised from whatever was at hand: bottles, gasoline, phosphorus, and rags—the Molotov cocktail.

The Russians had been set up on the bank of the Dnieper in 1812 just as they were now. If an awareness that this time Heinrich was in the role of invader, not defender, cast any shadow or brought a frisson of unease, it was quickly banished. He mentions no burned villages, no ruthless brutality. He was no alien invader; he was returning to land defended over the years by forefathers. This was a liberation, a return home.

Accounts of the battle for Mogilev are confusing and sometimes difficult to reconcile. In that, they paint a convincing picture of real war. Things look different from one hillock than from the nearby railroad track. Fatigue plays tricks with time; the sequence of events differs for each unit, every vantage point. Establishing a hard-and-fast time line is tricky, but the fight was on.

An attack on the bridgehead began July 20. The general's command post was set up among pines high above the river. A lone Russian *pepecha*— machine gun—delivered its dull, onomatopoetic staccato, then another stuttered into action. Scant undergrowth offered the Russians good visibility and the garrison's artillery unit had obviously been practicing in these hills; they came unnervingly close. Red artillery searching out the big German guns and mortars behind the command post was clearly very nearby— the sounds of firing and strike were almost simultaneous. The next strikes were closer still. The command post moved to a small gully, Heinrich and command post officers following.

Heinrich's diary brackets incidents and observations under the dates they were recorded, occasionally specifying "yesterday" or "today." July 21:

> The infantry assault began yesterday at 08:30, the forward battalion breaking through the outer ring of Russian field defenses in fierce fighting. At 09:00 a shell hit the intelligence unit, wounding

seven, two seriously, and killing the staff doctor. Artillery sang
and crashed all night, with even more dramtic fireworks at about
06:00.

Two battalions of the Ninth Infantry Regiment crossed the Dnieper
in rafts, trying to encircle Mogilev from the south. Pinned down on the
bank between Lupolovo and Mogilev, many officers were killed in an orchard under heavy fire. That evening, the right wing of the Twenty-third
Infantry Division held the southeastern and eastern edge of Lupolovo
and the small bridgehead of Mogilev, while the left wing held the area
just north of Bunichi. In a furious night engagement, a unit of the Ninth
routed dug-in Soviets. The annals of the Potsdam Ninth Infantry Regiment document casualties and captured materiel.

Questioning prisoners, Heinrich was told that they had been hastily
recruited from the Tula region on June 22. Barely educated, barely trained,
they were given old carbines and thrown into the field defenses by officers
to the rear. They had been at Mogilev for ten days, living on five hundred
grams of bread and sorrel soup. Among the prisoners were women—some
in uniform. As soon as they came in, they began tending to their wounded
comrades, kneeling, speaking softly, stroking a hand, or kissing the bloodless lips of a dying boy.

In Heinrich's entry on the twenty-first, from "RR Station Z," death
and the varieties of burial customs he has seen are meticulously recorded.

Yesterday in the evening wind, we buried our staff doctor, to the
howling and crashing of shells. A white, straight cross of birch
and wildflowers on the little mound. Not far off, at the edge of
the woods, I saw another grave. A tablet attached to a little stick
bears an inscription in red and blue pencil: "Here lies buried a
fighter for Red workers and peasants: Babushkin, Vassily Zacharievitch, fallen in the battle against the fascists, 10 July, 1941."

On the march here, I saw all sorts of graves. Our soldiers'
graves always recognizable from a distance, with a white cross
topped by a helmet, covered with the dust of passing columns.
Sometimes they are surrounded by a little fence of birch—the

forest bride embracing the soldier dead in the land of forests. On Guderian's panzer route I saw Waffen-SS graves with a wooden Nazi death rune attached. Most Russian dead or wounded were just left behind, but some were buried by country people, who had jammed a twig into a split stick to make the holy sign visible, as simply as a child might. By the fall, most of them will probably have disappeared into the landscape.

I also saw Russian graves lovingly prepared with the double crucifix of the old Orthodox faith. Even in the Bolshevik oppression, the old villagers held on to their faith. Now they bring their icons out of hiding, returning them to their holy corner, surrounding them with beautifully embroidered cloths. Even in untended cemeteries with crumbling chapels, villagers buried their dead as best they could, without priests, setting new wooden crosses next to old, upended iron crosses "from the time of peace," they say.

Russian artillery had no trouble finding the German general's new command post, and managed another perfect hit on the intelligence unit where Heinrich had questioned the POWs from Tula. More prisoners came in. The field hospital was filled up with wounded; crosses at the edge of the woods began to form rows. Craters and deep black holes bracketed the railway line. Shelling had maimed and broken countless trees. Their singed branches hung at odd angles, shriveled and dying. The intelligence unit moved across the railroad bridge to the woods.

Here we sit, 19:00 hours. It is darkening, a gray sky drizzles. Our artillery's radio is silent, while the Russian infantry's command post signals in code. Up ahead, uninterrupted rumbling and crashing, now and then, a strike nearby, and in between, the sharp, bright nattering of German machine guns. Those of the Reds have a slower, deeper bark. Forward movement is slow; two days already, fighting for Mogilev.

For the reader trying to reconcile accounts, the jumbled detail of war is stultifying; for the soldier, it is an adrenaline-charged nightmare.

France had felt like maneuvers but this shredded nerves. Heinrich sits in a niggling drizzle, his head splitting apart. The mess boy brings a sandwich and coffee, even a swallow of cognac, but it is not much help. After two days of heavy fighting, progress is slow, casualties terrible, the Russian defense system unbroken. Mogilev will not be taken with the forces at hand. More infantry is needed.

On the morning of July 23, both sides pursued the bitter fight. Heavy infantry fire and flak from the "88" antitank gun prepared the Ninth Infantry Regiment's assault to secure a highly visible, one-hundred-meter-long bridge. Under heavy fire, twelve officers and men managed to reach the far side, but their wounded could not be shielded or replaced; those on the far bank could not hold their position, but crossing the bridge would be suicide. They would wait for darkness, and try to swim back with their wounded.

POWs questioned earlier had suggested that a regiment on Hill 96 that had been causing the Germans so much trouble wanted to defect. Perhaps sending out a convincing, sympathetic Russian speaker might encourage them to follow through. At 1500 hours, the Ninth's regimental commander notified the division that he planned to attack to the north and northwest at 1650, to finally break Mogilev's defense system. That evening, Hill 96 was taken.

On July 23, radio commentary supplementing the *Wehrmachtbericht*—the official army news bulletin—remarked on unanticipated difficulties. The campaign was delayed; German High Command had to abandon previously successful tactics. Even Goebbels's *Deutsche Wochenschau* newsreels, with their Wagnerian lead-in, spoke of farmhouses and villages being taken one by one in fierce fighting, with hard battles in huge sectors. By August 1, the German invasion force had been decimated—10 percent wounded, missing, or dead.

17

The Home Front

CBS's Berlin correspondent, Howard K. Smith, suggested that by mid-1941, willy-nilly, Germany had become the most temperate place on earth. Everything was ersatz. Aimée had essentially given up smoking anyway; Heinrich's family silently disapproved and her hands were rarely idle long enough now to deal with a cigarette. When rationed tobacco was replaced with something rumored to be camel dung, courtesy of Rommel's Afrika Korps, she knew it was time to give it up entirely.

That May a poster for a regional party rally showed a sturdy peasant woman guiding a plow. Behind her loomed the huge, ghostly profile of a German soldier on the attack, backed by a cloud and an eagle with the laurels of victory in its talons. Aimée was not actually guiding the plow herself, and she was far too slender to compare with her stalwart German counterpart, though as Heinrich had written the year before from France, she was running the farm and winning "their war." But times were harder now. Herr Liebig, the Berlin gardener, had not taught her anything on this scale, and she did not feel that she was winning at anything. She was pregnant too, and the daily concerns of high summer were more than a counterweight to the triumphant news from the front.

The days passed in a hot, exhausting haze of details and demands. For all the talk of the glories of agriculture and life on the land, war was claiming all hands. With most able-bodied men and boys on one front or another, the labor shortage was acute. Blumenhagen still had Wilhelm Below, the overseer, and Kowalcyk, a so-called *Schweizer*, not Swiss at all really, only called that for his special skills with cattle, and exempt from the draft for the sake of the herd. Otherwise, like all farms, they were stretched to the limit. They still had the horses, and had been assigned some Polish POWs to help the farm keep producing. Glad to be out of the war, they were always polite, always willing, and touchingly grateful for Helma's expert medical attention when it was needed. They more than pulled their weight. Without them, Aimée could not have managed at all. But broken machines essential for planting or harvest went unrepaired for lack of parts, and there was no petrol to be had at any price. "*Kaput, kaput,*" usually accompanied by a little noncommittal shrug, cropped up with discouraging frequency.

Brigitte needed a new apron. With little fabric available but swastika banners aplenty, Aimée bought one at a price clearly subsidized by the Reich. Cutting away the crossed black, spiderlike pieces, she made a cheerful little red and white apron. It reminded her of a snatch of Gilbert and Sullivan, from *H.M.S. Pinafore*. She and Anita had seen it years ago in Hartford, and had taken to humming Buttercup's duet with the captain of the *Pinafore* whenever they encountered some outrageous sham.

> Things are seldom what they seem,
> Skim milk masquerades as cream;
> Highlows pass as patent leathers;
> Jackdaws strut in peacock's feathers . . .
>
> Black sheep dwell in every fold;
> All that glitters is not gold . . .

There were gaps in her recall, but she did remember

> Gild the farthing if you will,
> Yet it is a farthing still.

It was apt: just as false and infuriating as everyday life had become. But it was oddly reassuring to think that Gilbert and Sullivan had seen nonsense too. This was not the only time in history when everything was topsy-turvy, that falseness prevailed, that terrifying people were in positions of terrifying power. Turning the sinister totalitarian symbol into a pretty, utilitarian article for her darling daughter, she hummed the ditty, pleased to be quietly subverting the dark forces.

. . . .

Then came the news: Heinrich had been killed on July 23 at Mogilev. Death from a head wound was instantaneous. The annals of his regiment offer a laconic report:

> Among those killed at the bridge of Mogilev was First Lieutenant of the Reserves, Freiherr H. von Hoiningen-Huene [sic], of the Division's Command Staff (1c), who was encouraging the Russians to stop the fighting via loudspeaker. The Baron was Baltic German. He was buried with the dead of I.R. 9, on the south bank of the Dnieper at the bridge of Mogilev.

Another report states that the day after hearing about the possible defectors on Hill 96, on July 23,

> 1st Lieutenant von Hoyningen-Huene of 1c was killed while encouraging the Bolsheviks to surrender from a truck with a loudspeaker, by the bridge at Mogilev. A Bolshevik sharpshooter's shot to the head ended the life of a father of 4 [sic] children. We are all very sad. He was a magnificent person and a charming comrade.

Instantaneous death from a head wound was the official bromide. Quick, tidy, it cut off speculation on the home front, where appalling alternatives could undermine morale. The party routinely vetted reports of deaths in the field to ensure that proper Nazi phraseology was used to impart bad news, and in spite of improbable odds, few German soldiers died any other death.

First Aimée felt only stunned disbelief; it was not possible. Then a desolate, numbing finality preempted all other thought. Yet gradually, unwelcome images began to flit across her consciousness. A brilliant July afternoon, no breath of air to lessen the heat. Riding in a truck through an open landscape, slight hills baking to dun under a sun at the zenith. Or no—maybe the sun is lower, coming a bit from behind. But its heat still stabs, sending runnels of sweat coursing down inside his field-gray uniform. Dust drifts in the wake of the truck jolting through the countryside. Is it a random shot, or one in a volley, or a sniper, rising suddenly out of ripening, waist-high grain? Or hidden among black pines, taking aim as the truck lurches along a rutted road through alternating sun and shadow? The figure in the truck crumples, the megaphone goes silent . . .

Keeping the images at bay was impossible. They nagged ceaselessly, foraging for detail to delineate or redefine imagined particulars of that moment. Had he sensed—even if only for an instant—the death speeding toward him? Shouting into a megaphone in a language learned in childhood that surrender was the only alternative to life under the hated regime or death in battle would leave little room for awareness of anything beyond the enormity of his amplified voice and possibly the heat. Was this the heroic death he had imagined? Would she have recognized the body that was buried by the bridge at Mogilev? The questions—all unanswerable—would not leave her alone. Variations on that instant replayed again and again in her mind, as if she could somehow change the outcome. In the end it meant only that he died a thousand deaths.

When the telephone rang, she was sure it was Heinrich. One day she saw him get off the bus at the stone dam by the road. He was there—alive! The man moved; he was a total stranger. Understanding what drove Heinrich to volunteer for this campaign had never made it seem any less unrealistic. The old traditions existed only in memory now. He could not reconstruct them by force of will. She had told him at Ottenhof that she could never live there; it was too far from the world, her world and his too, the real, modern world, in which he burned to participate. Blinded by his dream to the demented forces loosed by this war, had he tempted fate by trying to rewrite history and turn back the clock? Chasing his dream, he had died for another's delusions. But it hardly mattered anymore. Speculation was pointless. Where she and the children fit into this scheme, now so drastically altered, was a mystery.

She was thirty-seven, five months pregnant with a sixth child, a furlough baby. The other children ranged in age from thirteen to four. The farm, so idyllic on the surface, represented unending work and bottomless anxiety. It consumed money and innumerable problems that had to be dealt with, alone. Whatever betrayals had wounded her, nothing had prepared her for this. Mired in staggering, numbing grief, she realized that being caught up in everyday minutiae had been a mercy.

She remembered Papa saying that he envisioned Heinrich's life like the ancient oak near Ottenhof, stretching out its branches to encompass an ever-widening circle of enormous circumference. But Heinrich was dead. Music had always been a comfort to her, but now when she sat at the piano and tried to play, it brought only dry, shuddering sobs that changed nothing. His child moved within her, and he was dead.

Her anguish would have sounded like a raw, animal howl, but no sound or words could say it; she was silent. The first time she had felt flutters of a new life within her, afraid that this would crush Heinrich's dreams, his love and optimism had overcome her decision to go it alone. Giddy and hopeful, they had marched into marriage and parenthood together.

Now, whatever lay ahead, no one offered a rosy future. Heinrich was gone; the children were fatherless; she was alone. She had felt that kind of aloneness at her mother's death—bereft, abandoned. But now there were the children, and though she felt hollow and eviscerated, another was growing in her body. The details, the clamoring daily needs, would have to pull a veil over her fears and fill the void, one day after another.

No church service felt right, so she gathered the children; the immediate household; the schoolmaster, Herr Lücht, so close to the children; their neighbor Herr Bürger; and the Gersdorffs for a small memorial service out on the summer fields. They bowed their heads in the sunshine, said the few words they could muster, and sang. It was utterly inadequate, but there was no way to define and seal away this loss.

Shorthanded for the harvest, the men were working in the late summer dusk to bring in the wheat. The air around the mowing machine was a haze of dust. The clatter of the blades, the plaintive creaking at turns, the horses snorting to clear their nostrils, the endless shrilling of the cicadas, was a familiar seasonal symphony, the accompaniment to the turn of another season, another harvest accomplished. In earlier years its peculiar music had always pleased her. Now it was out of joint and unbearably sad.

Weeks later, she received the case Heinrich was carrying when he was killed. In it were two letters from her, pages of a diary, and letters dictated to him by illiterate Russian POWs to their parents, siblings, wives, children, and sweethearts. One of his comrades had translated them for her.

June 26, 1941:   To Dunya Tcherkas, Mestichko Moyniki, Strelitchev:

I greet you, my dear little children, and I tell you that I am alive and healthy, and I wish you the same. I will probably not come home; you probably know what it is about and you know everything. I am en route near Mogilev. Dunya, I beg you, if you can work, work and look after the house. Please Dunyetchka, don't hurt anyone. And now, good-bye—I kiss you countless times. Please don't worry about me; perhaps I will come home.

July 4, 1941:   To Semipalatensky, Novishulbinsk, Tashiavoy:

I greet you, my honored parents, Papa, Mama, Nadia, Tomatchka, Vovochka, Shuratachka. First, I have had some happy moments today. So far, I am alive, though what will be, I don't know. If I live, then we will see each other again, but do not count on it. Please do not hurt or grieve each other, or the children who love you. For now I kiss you all good-bye—Your Bronya.

July 4, 1941:   To Samarka, near Samara:

I greet you, Grusha, Grisha, Mama and Papa—a greeting from Mitya. As you see, I am alive and healthy. It is already 12 days that we fight. From 22 June to this day, we always withdrew and withdrew, but soon we will worm our way forward. We are shot at every day, but so far we have been spared by an unknown power. In Minsk I came into the encirclement and was within 15 paces of the German tanks. So I have already sung the death song for myself, but I stayed alive. Mama must not worry on my account. So—all the best. I have no address, so don't write to me. . . .

July 23, 1941:   To Ryasancher, Pitchkiryaevo, Village of
                               Gorbunovke, Buryakevoi:

I greet you, precious Mother, Vitya, Pasha, Vera, Nina, Lena,
and everyone I know. With these first lines, I want to tell you that
so far I am alive. It is a shame I was not able to have myself photographed. It is not clear whether I will stay alive. Dear Mother, often, very often, Death passes very close by. As long as I am alive,
I will write you. And now, good-bye; greet everyone for me, and
tell them that on the 23rd, I was still alive. Soon, if I live, I will
write again. Good-bye, Mama, Your son, Shura.

As she read these letters, the Bronyas, the Shuras, their mothers, siblings, the Dunyetchkas, the wives and children, emerged from the words
to stand before Aimée as unassuming, heartbreakingly individual ghosts.
Plainspoken and accepting, the writers' resignation to their unknown fate
was wrenching. Heinrich had written these letters on behalf of unlettered
souls caught in the vise of history—for what? They exposed the war's
murderous futility in the simplest human terms. Heinrich had vanished
into nothingness and it was easy to imagine that the letter writers were all
dead too, or soon would be.

In October, Hitler launched a new, all-out offensive. He had just come
from the greatest battle in the history of the world. In two steel pockets,
Germany's Wehrmacht would trap and annihilate the pitiful remnants
of the Russian army. The Soviet enemy would never rise again. Newspapers trumpeted: "Campaign in East Decided! The Great Hour Has
Struck." Bookshops began displaying Russian grammars to help the
conquerors and colonizers of the German empire in the east cope with
newly acquired Lebensraum. It all meant nothing to Aimée. Writing to
Mary, she apologized for her long silence:

Heinrich was killed at Mogilev on the 23 of July. With him died
half my life and such great hopes for the future. Our sixth child is to
be born the middle of November. It's useless to write more; the words
seem empty. Every day makes the loss greater and the thought of the

children is sometimes unbearable. Heinrich's heart was in this campaign, which you can't possibly understand. If you had known him these last years and those who are his friends, you would know another Germany—and the world would seem a very different place.

October turned into November. The baby was due soon. When Heinrich's sister Margarethe came to console and be consoled, the fields were already bare and monochrome. It was dark as she stepped off the bus at the turnoff to Blumenhagen, where seven-year-old Brigitte was waiting for her and slipped her a little welcoming gift—an apple. It felt so firm and solid in her hand, it seemed one of the great wonders of creation: cool, smooth, and capable of satisfying both hunger and thirst. Its solidity was unlike anything else in the world they now inhabited, where everything was slippery, frenzied, and changing, where nothing had real substance or represented itself alone, without apology.

Over supper and pallid tea, Margarethe said that when she received Mimama's letter about Heinrich's death, she could not believe it. They had been so close; how could she not have felt it immediately when he was dead? Needing to be alone, she had run out to the pasture, and the horses had come, licking her hands and face. It had been so comforting. Only later did she realize that they were savoring the salt from her tears. He had invited her to Paris, a wonderful, unforgettable time. They had been so close, she said again; it was unfathomable that she had not felt something at the moment of his death.

She had last seen Heinrich when he came to visit to reassure himself that his younger sister's situation—managing the household of a widowed minister and his children—was not too trying for her. When he offered his arm to escort the young daughter of the house in to dinner, the gallant, grown-up formality had elicited a deep blush and shining eyes. That evening, they went to hear Mozart's *Abduction from the Seraglio*. When Belmonte sang tremblingly of his longing to be reunited with his beloved Constanze in act I, Heinrich had leaned over to whisper, "Listen to how the strings echo each anxious heartbeat." He had taught her so much . . . She trailed off, her teaspoon mimicking those anxious heartbeats lightly against her cup.

Each clear ting of Margarethe's teaspoon against the cup was a reminder that Heinrich had been the brightest light in the family's firmament, their golden hope. They had all known and accepted it. Aimée had not married one of the boys from Yale or Trinity, but full of hope and expectation, had hitched her wagon to that star, a star now abruptly extinguished. The brilliant career she had envisioned was Heinrich's. She would serve willingly as an intelligent hostess, a support, a charming and elegant adjunct, a stance in keeping with the culture and the time. Her money would help get them started, then he would light the world. She had learned to live with Heinrich's absences, learned to run the farm and manage the children, but in her head, he was always the centerpiece. This brutal thrust into the foreground of her life's narrative meant that everything depended on her. How could she alone provide continuity for them all? Now, only she could salvage what was salvageable; there was no alternative.

After the children were sent upstairs, Margarethe went up to say good night. Standing on her little bed, Brigitte flung both arms around her neck, her whole body shuddering with sobs. Across the room, four-year-old Dorothée jumped up and down on her own bed, shouting, "You're crying because of Papa! But he's coming back! He's coming back!" Margarethe gathered the children to her, and they held each other tight. The closeness brought a bit of comfort, little enough given the heartbreak, but comfort nonetheless.

Aimée's labor pains began on a day of unusual cold for early November, frost riming the willows edging the lake and a transparent sheet of ice across its expanse. While all the children had been born at home, Helma insisted that this child be delivered at the hospital; they would take no chances. A third daughter, Sigrid, was born, but for Aimée, death had written the central character in the family drama out of the script. Just after the child's birth, Aimée needed minor surgery. Slipping into unconsciousness, she hoped God would forgive her for asking never to wake up.

Vigorously denying "lies about Russian victories," the newspaper gave no accounts of losses. Yet the long trains coming into Berlin from the east on the maze of tracks and semaphores at the Potsdamer Platz Station were all marked with a red cross. Surveying the sight, an old Berliner deep in his cups remarked recklessly to Howard K. Smith: "From France we got silk stockings. From Russia, this. Damn Russians must not have any silk stockings."

Public sentiment, always a more accurate barometer of the popular mood than the press, could be gauged by tallying the number of *"Heil Hitlers"* that greeted Aimée in shops against the "Good mornings" or "Good afternoons." A chorus of *"Heil Hitlers"* meant either that the owners were ardent Nazis, that they were reluctant to attract the attention of ardent Nazis within earshot, or that the war was going remarkably well. When "Good mornings" outnumbered *"Heil Hitlers,"* the finger on the popular pulse registered widespread "treasonous defeatism."

In cities with frequent air-raid alarms, exhaustion and ill humor took their toll. People wanted a real night's sleep. Friends took to wishing each other a *"Bolona,"* shorthand for a bombless night. Some, of course, still believed in the *Endsieg*—final victory—but even those who distrusted the Nazis completely worried. "Enjoy the war," they said. "The peace will be terrible." Rumors about rancor among party bigwigs reflected popular unrest: Air Marshal Hermann Göring had quarreled with the Führer and was in custody; Hitler had been shot by a disgruntled general. Collectively, they were not far off the mark. Dissension was growing on the inside, particularly between the military and the regime that essentially despised them.

Alexis von Roenne had learned of Heinrich's death only during his own long recovery from his injuries. His condolence letter, a period piece of formality and restraint, is difficult to render in modern English. He told Aimée that the news from Mogilev was the hardest he could possibly have received.

> This last year I had the good fortune to come to know your husband better, living and working with him directly for many months. Looking back on that marvelous, unclouded time, I must tell you that your husband was one of the most impressive

personalities I have ever encountered. Wherever I looked, I saw his even temperament, his modesty in spite of his wide-ranging knowledge and clear judgment, his consistent warmth and feeling, win hearts. Twice I watched him come into a new environment, and saw how quickly his restraint and tact overcame the group's reservations to win him a position much higher than that generally accorded to his rank. For me, he was a telling example of the power of a strong character.

I believe that in him, our country has lost one of its truest and most significant sons. For some time, I, and a number of others, pinned special hopes on him for the foreseeable future. He combined discernment, farsightedness and toughness with a triumphant idealism that is seen only rarely. Yet if I am right, there is comfort in the thought that he will be spared the worst.

When I was wounded, we met by chance at the field hospital at Suraz, and he immediately began to look after me. As I was being evacuated, he took my hand and said quietly how grateful he was to be able to experience all this. I had told him a few days earlier that I was worried because I had made his participation in this dangerous eastern campaign possible. I believe that in that moment, as we said good-bye, he saw his fate clearly, and wanted me to take these comforting words with me.

Whoever believes as we do, that even individual fates are determined by a higher power, ought not to lose themselves in speculating whether Heinrich should have been prevented from participating in an assault as dangerous as the one on Mogilev (though naturally I would have tried). I only know that I will always be grateful to this higher power for leading me to him, and for allowing me such a long, wonderful, marvelously unencumbered friendship with him. The belief in a higher power also holds the happy promise of an eventual reunion; even in these months of heavy losses, that hope has never abandoned me.

In Russia, meanwhile, the first snowfall melted, returning the landscape to a trackless state, the *rasputitsa*—the time without roads—that held everything, the Wehrmacht too, hostage until frozen ground let travel resume at a reasonable pace. Hitler had assured Germany that Moscow would be taken well before winter; there would be no winter campaign. By November, it was winter deep in Russia, and the army was not prepared. During diminishing daylight hours, marching helped generate warmth, but the long dark hours were bitter. Soldiers routinely pulled *valenki*—heavy felt boots—off the feet of dead Russians. They helped, but not enough. Stumbling along the rutted roads dressed in every available piece of clothing, wrapped in blankets, cursing the cold, the men cursed the lack of foresight that had brought them to this even more.

Goebbels demanded that the German people donate every conceivable item of warm clothing to *Winterhilfe*: woolens of any and every variety, warm underwear, sweaters, and fur in any form. Persistent rumors of Hitler's differences with his generals were borne out when he assumed personal control of the war. Challenging herself every day to find things to be grateful for, Aimée found that the sometimes appallingly short list was topped by deep gratitude that Heinrich did not have to endure this brutal winter.

On December 11, 1941, Hitler declared war on America. Berlin went into a tailspin; America had turned the tide in World War I, and that alone was cause for alarm. Combined with the season's reminder of the fate of Napoleon in Russia, it was terrifying. The American consulate called to say that if Aimée plannned to leave, it must be soon. With communication cut, she would not hear from Uncle Bill, Mary, or Anita.

She did not know what to do. For the first time in her life, she felt she had real roots, roots that went right into the soil. This was the home she and Heinrich had been determined to create, home to the children. This was where they belonged; she could not simply leave. And there was Heinrich's family. The thread of common experience with everyone in the States was broken. They could never understand. If the Americans arrived soon, the war should be over quickly.

She wavered. The consul was convincingly urgent. Under American law, he continued, children of a dual-nationality marriage born before May 1934 took the nationality of the father; those born after that date, that of the mother. Her four older children, classified as "enemy aliens," would be denied entry to the United States. The two youngest, as U.S. citizens, would have entry permits. Whatever doubts she had had vanished; she must keep her brood together. She said no. Thank you, but no.

Roenne came to see her and to meet his new godchild that winter. All the children were introduced and Friedrich's thirteen-year-old heart thrilled at the red stripe down Roenne's uniform trousers, designating him as an officer of the General Staff. Alone later in the gathering afternoon darkness, they were silent for a time as the fire crackled and hissed, its light glinting on the tea tray before them.

Tersely, with great reserve, he began to talk. He had understood Heinrich's sense of urgency about joining the Russian campaign, but he was torn. Both had known the dangers, both had recognized that this campaign might be very hard fought, but Heinrich's death had overwhelmed him with a sense of personal responsibility. He hoped that she could understand and forgive. She began to protest, but was stopped short. Then he was silent again, his eyes on the fire. He had seen terrible things, he said suddenly. Terrible things, he said again, terrible, unspeakable things.

As she stood outside to see him off, a cold wind moved through the bare branches of the great trees by the door. Watching the big car pull slowly to the road, its headlights reduced to slits because of blackout regulations, she felt both shattered and relieved. Shattered that Roenne, who had shared so much with Heinrich, was going back. What would become of this deeply moral man enmeshed in this war? But relieved that Heinrich would not have to face the terrible quandary Roenne would face again.

In March, Mimama and Papa came to Blumenhagen for the baby's christening. Papa said very little, spending most of his time with the children, his refuge from the bitter present. Mimama seemed to Aimée to have aged twenty years since the last time she had seen her. She sat with the small white bundle on her lap, peering into the face of this new being, the last vestige of her dead son.

Several months later, returning from a July vacation on Hiddensee, a glorious, slender finger of an island in the Baltic, Aimée, Helma, and the six sun-browned children filled most of the small island bus with chatter and toys: kites, pails, beach treasures. The only other passengers were a couple they did not know. Watching, smiling, wiggling her fingers at the baby, the woman leaned forward: "Where is the father of these enchanting children?" This was always a loaded question. Aimée's heart stopped. She was not sure she could muster the required explanation, but Helma managed a quiet "He was killed on the Russian front." The woman's face reflected her understanding of how deeply they had all been wounded. Heinrich had been dead a year.

The mammoth Russian campaign was sucking up resources. Rations were reduced steadily, fueling endless debate about whether the food situation was better or worse than in 1918. Even potatoes were hard to come by. The radio's usual string of superlatives announcing stupendous victories unparalleled in human history gave way to talk of the true mark of a people's greatness: *Durchhalten*—hanging on in tough times. This was tantamount to an admission that things were bad.

A pop song designed to encourage Germany to hang on—a *Durchhalteschlager*—made it official. By late 1942, a simple, sentimental waltz tune took up significant radio time not devoted to propaganda. Clouds drifting westward turn a lonely sentry's thoughts to dreams of the girl and the happiness he left at home. The refrain that delivered the song's punch line was being whistled and hummed everywhere:

> *Es geht alles vorüber,*
> *es geht alles vorbei.*
> *Nach jeden Dezember*
> *Kommt wieder der Mai.*

Everything passes, it all passes away. After every December comes a new May. The message: This too shall pass. Before long, an underground version changed the refrain's last two lines to

> *Erst geht der Führer,*
> *Und dann die Partei.*

First goes the Führer, and then the party.

· · ·

With no sign that either *Führer* or *Partei* were about to go, at least hanging on at Blumenhagen was easier than in cities. Eggs were not the unheard-of luxury they had become for so many, but times were hard, there was little food. They too were being tested for true greatness. In early November Aimée was convinced that Allied troop landings in Africa would bring a quick end. The baby was a year old; the war would surely be over long before her next birthday. The radio still spewed news of dramatic advances, but the encirclement of Moscow was broken and soon the idea of an invincible German war machine was kaput too. The machine had stopped before Moscow and stalled at Stalingrad. Again, the populace was asked to surrender warm clothing and furs.

By Christmas, the fall's triumphalist propaganda was silent. Soldiers on leave were told to be circumspect about what they said at home because, as the *Völkischer Beobachter* noted sourly, soldiers were inclined to believe the bad rather than the good. But there was no denying the heavy black crosses blotting page after page in the newspapers: *"In stillem Schmerz"*—in silent sorrow; *"Unser geliebter Sohn"*—our beloved son; *"In tiefer Trauer"*—in deep mourning. Column after column: Loving Husband, Beloved Father. Some earlier death notices had used not crosses, but an upside-down Y, the runic symbol the Nazis promoted, adding that the deceased had died for Führer and Fatherland. As the lists lengthened, the rune gave way to the cross; fewer notices added "For Führer and Fatherland."

The retreat from the Caucasus was billed as *planmässig*—according to plan—though the plan itself was increasingly mysterious. Mail from the front was routinely censored, and letters from Stalingrad, collected to make an uplifting anthology for the German public, proved disappointing. Most blamed their predicament on the command, and the command was now Hitler. By the second week of January 1943, the letters consisted principally of pitiful good-byes, and Goebbels, complaining that he was powerless against such "disastrous, indescribable, human weakness," scrapped the project. Home on leave, the son of one of Blumenhagen's farmworkers hanged himself rather than go back to the eastern front. Eleven-year-old Michael told Aimée quietly that he was thankful that his father had been spared Stalingrad. The deerskin vest she and Lo had sewn for him would not have helped.

With the collapse of Stalingrad, the tide turned. Hitler had always escaped direct criticism, but having taken over from the generals, he was now in charge, and people held him responsible. He was not invincible after all. That, at least, was good news. There might actually be an end to this war. In a reversal of the propaganda that transformed every defeat into a triumph, people began to see each defeat as real progress, a step closer to the end. A segment of the officer corps was convinced that there was no other way but to get rid of Hitler; even some uncomfortable with assassination rethought their position. The only question was how. But Hitler's uncanny sense of self-preservation—a dictator's fine-tuned paranoia—had already saved him from several assassination attempts. One member of the resistance held out little hope; there were no young men left in Germany to make revolution.

February. Sleet hissed against the windowpanes. The entire household stumbled through the chilly house, bundled in layer upon layer, fingers blue and stiff, waiting for the inevitable end. Even Goebbels admitted that morale was flagging and declared a state of "total war."

It was hard to imagine how total war would be different from what had gone before, but Aimée had to consider what would become of them if the front moved in their direction and—God forbid—engulfed Blumenhagen. It was all they had left. Where were the Allies? Would they arrive before the Russians? She was afraid, and would have preferred to push the questions away, but she had to do something to protect them all. Calling an insurance inspector to take inventory felt pathetic, like sticking a finger in the dike. What good would an inventory do if total war did come? Yet the simple fact of taking some action gave her a tiny sense of control over what had become an uncontrollable situation.

As lists of soldiers dying a "hero's death" lengthened, Goebbels's diary noted the need to sharpen the anti-Bolshevik line, and 1943 became the year of desperation propaganda. Posters screamed that it would either be victory—happy mother and smiling baby, basking in golden light—or Bolshevism—emaciated bodies tumbling through gloom under the sinister gaze of a caricatured, Semitic face. With Russian operations again bogged down in mud, Radio Berlin announced the discovery of a mass grave with the bodies of thousands of Polish officers executed in the forest of Katyn, near Smolensk. Soviet atrocities, said the Nazi propaganda; if the Soviets won, Katyn would be everywhere.

Aimée's sunny-faced, nine-year-old Christian came home from school one day saying that he and another boy had stayed a bit late, waiting, while two uniformed men who wanted to see them talked with Herr Lücht, the schoolmaster. Next day, the two officials arrived at Blumenhagen, one thin and colorless, the other dark and emphatic, to tell her that her youngest boy had been chosen for the Nazi educational system. Recruiting for schools to inculcate the future leaders of Germany's *Herrenvolk* with the proper SS spirit was well under way among eligible ethnic Germans and Aryans. Only the brightest and the best were offered such opportunities. It was a great honor.

Yes, he was bright, and yes he was Aryan. Yes, she knew it was a great honor, but she declined. This was her youngest son; she needed the boy at home. Turning down one of the Reich's great honors was a risky business. Her status as war widow and mother of six did not give her immunity, but it did offer some defense against an all-powerful state, wishing to bestow an honor and quick to take offense.

It was not long before she offended the state again. When Herr Lücht was drafted, she marched straight to the local authorities to say that the schoolmaster belonged in the schoolroom, not at the front. Even before she had finished, the red-faced little man stuffed into his uniform began to shout: This was the Reich's business, not hers. Unless she left his office immediately and never mentioned this matter to anyone, she would be arrested.

The war lay heavy, huge, and apparently unending over everything and everyone. Fear, whispers, dissimulation, scrounging, and deceit eroded whatever reserves of faith and hope were left. It was hard to imagine that it would ever stop, that things would ever get better, that right would prevail. The overriding sense was that one simply had to endure until the nightmare evaporated. Heinrich had never believed that there was true evil in the world; people were good, noble. She did not share that conviction, certainly not now, when it seemed spun of hopeless, if joyful, naïveté. The question, she thought, was how long could fear keep people in line? How long could this go on?

The gap between the daily details of survival that occupied most of the mind and the abstract was huge. The bridge linking the every day to any philosophical or moral reflection was now so narrow that only news of the regime's most egregious outrages elicited response. The watchwords for civilians had been reduced to *sich organisieren*—organize oneself—and *durchhalten*—hang on—and people devised all kinds of systems to accomplish both. In cities, inhabitants of bombed-out buildings scrawled their names and new addresses on the ruined walls. A sort of jungle-drums network of information allowed people to send even subversive messages. Families under constant bombardment sent children to country relatives if they had any.

Marshaling thousands of skinny boys to shore up domestic defenses by manning antiaircraft batteries and digging tank traps was not sufficiently reassuring, so Germany was reminded that the long-promised but as yet undelivered *Wunderwaffe*—miracle weapon—was on its way. *WuWa*, Berliners called it, less deus ex machina than a toy for preverbal children.

Keep Your Mouth Shut

People knew not to speak openly, not with the grocer, not with a neighbor. Daily exchanges were fraught with potential for betrayal; a careless word might be overheard. In the practical world, language had turned everything into something it wasn't: *Reine Wolle*—pure wool—was known to be fibers made from *Deutscher Wald*—German forest. Fear had created a new language, a code that veiled everything to produce a peculiar sense of unreality in relationships, even between the few couples not separated by war. Relationships with families and intimates were subtly altered. People censored themselves. Everyday spats became a rarity, particularly in constantly bombed cities. Angry words might be the last.

Walking the tightrope between private thought and public conformity called for a perpetual circumspection that deprived people of real companionship. Speaking in the singular, particularly in public, verged on the foolhardy. Deprived of a personal voice, the sense of self wavered and blurred; people lost sight of who they were. Yet no matter how grim the situation, how grotesque the latest edicts and propaganda, how low the popular mood, some vestiges of spirit did survive. As the epicenter of nervy, cynical humor, Berlin was where what remained of the vox populi was heard. Even in the darkest hours, wildly irreverent jokes and verses made the rounds. A random sampling provides the flavor:

"Anyone bringing ten new recruits into the party is permitted to resign. Anyone bringing in twenty gets a certificate saying he never belonged."

An interrogation during the Fourth Reich: "Were you ever imprisoned during the Third Reich? If not, why not?"

Whimsical revenge fantasies took shape in verse:

Mein Auge strahlt,
mein Herz es klopft,
Ich singe ein Te Deum.
Ich sehe Adolf ausgestopft
im Britischen Museum.

My eye it shines,
My heart beats high,
I sing a glad Te Deum.
I see Adolf dead and stuffed,
In the British Museum.

Bringing Berlin's acerbic take on the current situation to Blumenhagen, Lore Adam helped Aimée keep treading water over what felt like a frightening thousand fathoms. The jokes were a welcome relief, a way of defusing the sense of powerlessness and frustration and keeping a grip on sanity. But they also made her uneasy. Maybe they relieved tension just enough to ensure inaction. Maybe the day-to-day grumbling made bowing to the whole of a crushing regime more tolerable, maybe just tolerable enough to sidestep *Zivilcourage*—taking a strong, now wildly dangerous personal stand against the outrages. Maybe without jokes, the deep underlying desperation would have achieved a purposeful focus.

That summer brought a lot of family to Blumenhagen. Margarethe had married her widowed minister, and sent a teenage stepson, Winfried. When Mira, four children, and their nurse came to escape the daily, fact-of-life bombing in Münster, the household swelled to ten children and eight adults. With luggage and boxes set down under the great linden trees, the children were hopping excitedly at seeing their cousins, when they heard the rumble of aircraft. All heads tilted to watch a huge formation of Flying Fortresses lumber past, glittering in the sun. Four-year-old Otto was transfixed. Airplanes were the terror of his young life; each one represented potential disaster. But they passed over, headed toward Berlin. Planes would not hurt him here, he announced solemnly.

Here he was safe. Then he turned to ask: Did the English have legs too, or did they only fly?

The boy's relief brought more comfort than Aimée had felt for a long time. At least one anxiety was eased. Blumenhagen was still a haven; she still had something to offer. After an often skimpy meal, she could set the horde loose on the cherry trees, where dessert was free for the picking. Friedrich, absorbed by his passion for maritime life, was busy building painstakingly accurate ship models to scale. For the other children, there were picnics, swimming, sailing, and fishing. For them at least, life was good.

She and Lo read aloud to the children and any interested adults who happened by the big library. They organized house concerts for which each child presented a musical offering, vocal or instrumental. With so many people in the house, there were plenty of actors for roles in amateur theater pieces. All the cousins, village children, and any willing grown-ups were marshaled for lively performances of classics—*Cinderella, Snow White*, or new inventions. As director, Aimée cast one little cousin with a particularly high voice in the specially devised role of a piglet, rushing across the stage, squeaking pitifully.

Hearing her cousins talk about their Mami and Papi, her two-year-old flung her arms around her neck one night at bedtime, saying, "You are my Mami *and* my Papi." It touched her heart, but it would never be true. Heinrich's death had been a division, not a multiplication. She was only one—there would be no alternative parental ear to pour confidences into, no other parent to offer support, encouragement, praise, or discipline. Her own mother's death was so clear, so devastating a memory. Now her children faced the same thing.

Her father had never mentioned her mother again. To the child clinging to every vestige of her mother, it seemed as if her mother had been erased, had never existed, only deepening the loss. Maybe her father had been as overwhelmed and desperate as she felt, and was only trying to rein in his misery, but she knew she must keep Heinrich alive for his children. The thought of making decisions on behalf of those children's very different selves alone made her quake, but she was all there was.

So she kept going, always doing: planning, planting, mending, organizing, gardening, knitting, reading aloud. The demands left no time for ego, for self, for second-guessing, or much of anything else, even news or what pretended to be news. Life consisted of unremitting dailiness. The farm needed managing every day. The children needed attention every day. Standards and traditions needed to be maintained. Conversation at dinner was supposed to be in English, her long-standing attempt to raise the children as bilingual, but it meant that, apart from her own efforts, she presided over a "conversation" of minimal requests for "more please." At Sunday services she accompanied the hymns and chorales at the piano. Friedrich now delivered a closing prayer as his father had done, but Heinrich's other task, formulating a personal moral lesson for each week, fell to her. Everyday demands prevented much thought about the future or where all this was leading. The gaping hole between daily doing and abstract moral imperatives was bridged only by ferocious focus, and following through on that moral focus endangered everyone she knew and loved.

Newspapers and radio delivered only propaganda. What passed for news came by word of mouth, spawning rumors. Endless rumors, outrageous or within range of possibility, maybe even with a basis in what might once have been fact, were whispered to a trusted few, then whispered to a trusted few in turn. Listening to foreign radio broadcasts, forbidden since 1939, was treasonous, and "moral self-mutilation," whatever that meant. It carried a minimum five-year prison term, but could bring a death sentence. Aimée did not dare turn the radio on; even heard indistinctly through Blumenhagen's thick walls, the BBC's measured cadences were unmistakably different from the hectic tone of official broadcasts, and there were too many people in the house. She did not know who might report her, or if the children might unwittingly let something slip at school. Posters warned: *"Feind Hört Mit"*—"The enemy is listening too." Ten times a day, Helma muttered under her breath, "Keep your mouth shut! Think what would happen to the children if they took you away."

Keep your mouth shut. All well and good, but in the process, she felt she was losing her voice, losing herself. She was outspoken by nature;

lively conversation was her lifeblood. What had become of her notions of taking a stand, trying to change things? How could she do right by the children without saying anything about what was everywhere, without teaching them that life sometimes meant taking nerve-racking steps? Keeping her mouth shut meant betraying her convictions, yet she knew, and Helma consistently reminded her, that anything but acquiescence threatened those children. At the railroad crossing one day, a train came through bringing *Ostarbeiter*—eastern workers—to work in German factories and farms. In the open door of one car, a raggedy young fellow sat swinging his feet, smiling and waving. She realized she was afraid to wave back. She had become a stranger to herself.

When she first heard talk about German atrocities, she remembered seeing an exhibit of the work of Louis Raemaekers, a Dutch cartoonist whose World War I drawings of women bleeding from severed breasts, children with hands cut off, and boxcars dripping blood had become a British wartime propaganda staple. This seemed like more of the same. Mention of "KZ"—concentration camp—conjured up images of camps like Dachau, where dissidents, clergy, Communists, and a number of higher-ups had been putting in time since 1933. When they began to round up Jews, she asked why, where were they being taken? A thumb jerked eastward. "Somewhere back there."

The questions remained, but questions were dangerous. With the added complication of being an American, however camouflaged, it was best not to attract any attention at all. Better to be blind, deaf, and dumb. The nearest KZ, Ravensbrück, was largely for women, most of them political prisoners. Every day Helma reminded her that she could not afford to be one of them, even if it meant dying an inch at a time. This war had killed Heinrich. It had killed her expectations, and it was now killing her. God willing, it would be over before she was completely dead.

Under SS guard, men shoveled coal by the tracks on which the *Ostarbeiter* transport had run. No one looked at them or said anything. Everyone shared the paranoia that enveloped the regime. Only eyes communicated: "Look, someone is being beaten up," or "the Gestapo is rounding up another hapless creature." All this circumvention added up to leading a double life: one life demanding at least the semblance of conformity and loyalty; true hopes and fears were expressed only in the other life, and behind closed doors. Still the insidiousness seeped into the minutest crevices. Helma told her that party bigwig Robert Ley had boasted that now only those asleep still enjoyed a private life. Yet even in dreams, the helpless sleeper was led down a *via dolorosa* into a fearful, stifling netherworld.

19

Give Me Ten Years

Hitler had once proclaimed, "Give me ten years and you will not recognize Germany." That was a promise he had kept; eleven years later, cities were buried in rubble, and oddly enough, given the drastic food shortages, the distinctly anti-Nazi mood focused less on empty stomachs than on political and military failures. Wartime realities had long since drained away any excitement and élan. Sustaining the Führer myth required successes, and contrary to propaganda, there were none. Hitler had outlived his myth.

Against a brilliant blue June sky, huge formations of Flying Fortresses flew over the farm toward Berlin, straight, calm, unperturbed, unopposed, awe-inspiring. Air Marshal Göring had once claimed that if enemy air-craft ever flew over Germany, his name would be Meyer—the Smith or Jones of Germany. His name was definitely Meyer now, and people were taking childish delight in thinking, and occasionally even saying so. His penchant for elaborate uniforms, gaudy epaulettes, and innumerable med-als had underground humor claiming that one "Goer" was the maximum amount of tin—i.e., medals—that could be pinned to one's chest without causing one to fall flat on one's face.

Heinrich's family was strewn across a map dotted with pins marking disaster; his friends were on various fronts or dead. Germany had be-come a nation of women, and for Aimée, three women, Helma, Lo, and Marta, supplied crucial sustenance. After Heinrich's death, Helma put her strength and intelligence to work on behalf of her surrogate family, providing medical attention, no-nonsense advice, and unfailing support. Her slight frame belied an iron will, and with the children she took a loving hand—firm enough with the boys that they grumbled, secretly calling her "the General."

At fifteen, thirteen, and twelve, they were temperamentally very individual, but put together, without a father's presence, they were a handful, and Aimée was grateful for the reinforcements. Lo, more pliant and still emotionally fragile, was wonderful with the girls, imaginative, enterprising, and loving. Ever cheerful and resourceful Marta was a mainstay, keeping household and kitchen running far more smoothly than circumstances warranted.

When Lo first came to Blumenhagen, she was so thin and anxious, so agonizingly eager to please, that she had been almost like an additional needy child. Her unabashed admiration sometimes made Aimée uncomfortable, but it was also touching and, she had to admit, a bit of a lift to her battered sense of self. Over time, with Lo spelling out her love for the children in a hundred ways every day, she had become indispensible. In the years since Helma and Lo had come to Blumenhagen, Aimée repeatedly thanked God for them both. Marta, a household fixture, a linchpin, was steady, straight, and always cheerful. Still, for Aimée it was a time of too many decisions, and the big ones were hers alone. No amount of advice and support changed that, and she claimed it left her with a lasting distaste for decisions, even the smallest. There had been too many, and in retrospect, too many of them felt wrong.

Storks had always come to the farm, the same pair returning every year to nest on the big wagon wheel set on the roof of the great brick barn for them. They were a part of farm life, a traditional sign of good luck. Village storks had returned some time ago, but there was no sign of their pair, no fresh twigs or nesting material on their uninhabited wagon wheel. No one wanted to mention it; it seemed another bad omen. Then on April 19, with a great clacking of his long bill and flapping of enormous wings, the big male arrived at last. Madame was sure to follow soon.

The entire household rushed outside, the two youngest whirring in circles, flapping their arms in imitation of the welcome arrival. Laying this superstition to rest was a great, if secret, relief—everyone was elated, nearly giddy, the Polish workers joining the celebration. It was spring; the stork had come, the fruit trees were in bloom. Maybe things would look up.

Heinrich had been dead for three years. The pain was intermittent now, not constant. When they vacationed on idyllic Hiddensee again, the sun and the sea made everything seem easier, simpler. With day-to-day cares at a remove, even the big ones seemed less daunting. One evening the children were up later than usual, variously occupied at the big table, when the radio announced that a bomb had exploded in Hitler's eastern headquarters.

The room felt suddenly fiercely hot, as if all the air had been sucked out. The children abandoned whatever they were doing to look nervously at the adults. Complete, breathless silence. Silence was the only weapon the adults could muster against their inner turmoil, and silence in front of the children was always critical. Later, Hitler himself told the German people that Providence had spared his life to allow him to carry out his sacred mission.

Officially, the infamy was perpetrated by a handful of plotters, a tiny "elitist clique of officers without a conscience," yet thousands were arrested. Hitler railed against "all those 'vons' who call themselves aristocrats." *Der Angriff,* the Berlin party paper, announced that in accordance with an ancient Teutonic form of retribution, *Sippenhaft,* literally "kinship detention," families of those who had risen against Hitler would be held responsible, hunted down, dispossessed, and destroyed—"root and branch."

The ferocity of the Nazi response to the plot was in part the eruption of long-standing resentment toward the nobility and its traditional ties to the officer corps. Longtime Nazi Party functionary Robert Ley inveighed against the "blue-blooded swine whose entire families must be wiped out." Goebbels, more restrained but typically also more methodical, simply gave orders for liquidating the aristocracy after the war. Heinrich's regiment, a nexus of anti-Hitler sentiment and resistance, soon had the distinction of having more of its members hanged, shot, or otherwise killed by the Nazi regime than any other outfit in the military.

Down in Blumenhagen's great vaulted cellar that fall, Aimée saw Brigitte come down the stairs. Cool and dim, smelling of earth, the cellar was not a place the children liked much, but the child followed her around in the scant light, trying to look aimless. Something was on her mind. Finally it came out. Why were people trying to kill Hitler? She had been mulling this over since that day in July, when she recognized the adults' silence as important, even portentous. She needed to know what it meant.

Aimée's heart ached for her. She had been in anguish over the loss of her beloved father, and now these questions. It was time for candor, for the child's sake, but also for her own. Hitler was doing terrible things inside and outside Germany, she said. The war was killing many, many people, and destroying so much. Years ago, her father and some friends in Berlin had considered getting rid of Heinrich Himmler, thinking that if Himmler were out of the way, Hitler might be brought under control. His friends tried to persuade him to stay out of it; he had five children. But neither Himmler nor Hitler was brought under control. Friends at the Potsdamer Ninth Infantry Regiment did not like what Hitler was doing, and now things were even worse. People had tried to kill Hitler to stop Hitler from killing others. Brigitte listened in silence. Climbing the stairs together, Aimée was sure her daughter would honor this confidence.

Everyone knew the war was lost. The Americans were in Aachen, the Russians in East Prussia, yet Hitler mobilized all men and boys between sixteen and sixty—women were welcome too—into the *Volkssturm*, a people's militia. Mustering skinny boys and their grandfathers for the Reich's defense was just another indication of how things stood. Soon the idea of creating an "Iron Reserve" of 100,000 sixteen-year-olds to defend the familiar *Deutsches Blut, Deutscher Boden*, was everywhere.

Friedrich was fifteen. The dreaded notice could come any day. In October, he and about twenty boys from his class were ordered to report to Neubrandenburg, bringing sandwiches. The "recruits" were ordered to run back and forth between barracks and nearby woods to soften them up, then given a pep talk on antitank bazookas and wartime exploits to fan their boyish enthusiasm for weaponry and military bravado.

A *Bannführer*—a ranking Hitler Youth type—lined them up by height. The Führer had ordered all boys to join the Waffen-SS, he brayed, and asked for volunteers. Volunteers for a Führer order? It was confusing. With no volunteers, Friedrich, as the tallest, was taken for a private talk. Why was he not volunteering?

He liked ships and the sea, Friedrich said, and would be better suited to the navy. He did not mention that the navy also had a longer training period; the longer the training, the less likely the war would still be going on. His interview over, he was publicly berated as a *Scheisskopf*, reduced to tears, and ignominiously sent home to his relieved family. A school friend summoned a week later reported that the officials had mentioned a pathetic "degenerate blue blood." When Friedrich asked what a degenerate was, his friend replied, "Never mind. It doesn't apply to you." To everyone's dismay, Fritz, the son of Blumenhagen's black-smith, a few months older than Friedrich, was tapped for the Waffen-SS.

As the names of several of the July plotters emerged, some were un-known, some unbearably familiar. The name of Heinrich's friend Alexis von Roenne was never mentioned, but his wife, informed of his arrest, went to Berlin. She was not permitted to see him, but managed access to the courtroom. Hearing his voice, she leaned forward for a glimpse, and was immediately escorted out by the Gestapo. As she stood at the streetcar stop in desperation, a *Schupo*, a policeman, wearing the absurd, cockaded hat seen in films of the conspirators' trials, approached, asking: "Are you Frau von Roenne?"

Sippenhaft! Surely he had come to arrest her. Weak-kneed, she thought of her poor children, but he grasped both her hands, saying only, "I just wanted to tell you that there is still hope!"

Roenne was released for lack of evidence, but then rearrested, tried, and executed. She never saw her husband again. When she wrote to Aimée, his family was under surveillance, their mail monitored.

If there was a god in heaven, Aimée thought, why had he not stopped Hitler? On December 11, 1944, in her still idiosyncratic German, she wrote Roenne's widow what was, in the circumstances, a remarkably brave letter:

> Your letter's terrible news struck deep into my heart. That a man of such spirit, such true and unshakeable idealism, had to walk this bitter road nearly strips away all hope for the future. I have thought of him often in these hard times, wishing I could hear his clear insights, but the thought that such a man was alive, leading and working for Germany, comforted me.

Suffering has become daily bread for us all, but what has been dealt you and your husband constricts my heart. Sometimes, when I considered the threatening future, my first thought was always of your husband, and what might befall him in body and spirit in these times. My little one, seeing my face as I read your letter, immediately began to talk about her father, and that he was dead, as if she knew that something more of him had been taken from us.

After Roenne had recovered from wounds sustained in Russia, Hitler had ordered him back to his earlier posting at FHW, now as its head, distilling masses of intelligence on the Allied war effort. Opposed to Hitler and his racial policies from the beginning, he had become increasingly militant. Though many conspirators were colleagues and friends, on religious grounds he had never participated actively in plots to kill Hitler.

Though the *Wehrmachtbericht* zealously reported the "terror missons" of Allied bombers and disguised what was really happening in the east, all Germany envisioned a ragged line of sons and fathers straggling westward ahead of the Red Army. The hope that the Allies would push east faster than the Russians moved west seemed desperate. Between the bombings and the innumerable deaths, an immense hole had opened in the middle of Europe. If the Russians arrived first, they would flood in to fill it.

Under a lowering sky, with a scumble of rain-laden clouds rolling across the curve of the horizon, Aimée buried some family silver in a far corner of the garden. Blumenhagen's soil had harbored the treasures of other generations long ago, why not these? Whoever had buried the coins and fibulae in the ashes of the ancient hearth had never returned. Would their silver stay buried as long?

In October 1944, the regime had asked fifteen-year-old Friedrich to "volunteer." By January, the "third wave" of seventeen-year-olds was inducted to reinforce the eastern front. If the draft or youthful enthusiasm for uniforms and arms lured them in, a few ounces of pressed metal pinned to their chest compensated them for the loss of an eye, a leg, or life. In February, Hitler approved the drafting of fifteen-year-olds to shore up the rear defenses. Children as fodder for the monster machine seemed to Aimée a violation of basic instincts, counter to natural law. It was madness—like eating one's young.

Dresden was not considered a strategic target in any conventional military sense, but life there was more difficult for Heinrich's parents now. They were slower, the air-raid alarms more frequent. The painstaking precautions, the blackouts, gathering their few remaining valuables for the descent into the cellar, were hard on them. Much of the day and the night could be spent climbing slowly down the stairs, or slowly up again. Margarethe had gone to live nearby to help her increasingly infirm parents, bringing her two youngest stepchildren with her. Recently, assuming that it was a "safe" city, refugees from the east and many old people, women and children like Margarethe and hers, had swelled Dresden's population well beyond its usual 650,000. The letters LSR, for Luftschutzraum—air-raid shelter—were chalked up everywhere, of course, but Dresdeners contended that LSR really stood for "Lernt schnell Russisch"—"Learn Russian fast." In that regard, at least, the family was at an advantage.

The bombs began to fall just after 10:00 p.m. on February 13, 1945. First, one-thousand-pound red flares, target markers, like Christmas trees. Then nearly seven thousand tons of explosives and phosphorus incendiary bombs. People on the streets were trapped in molten asphalt. Their forward motion halted, they either burned like torches where they stood, or were sucked into a firestorm so greedy for air that every living thing within its grasp—and beyond—suffocated. Then P-51s strafed anyone alive enough to flee.

After the first wave of bombing, Margarethe thought things had quieted down, so she and the children rushed out toward her parents' house. At the street corner, she saw Papa leading Mimama by the hand, and a bit behind them, old Tante Nina. No one could manage words; they stood in the street, locked together in a silent embrace. Then came the second wave, then wave after wave.

But they survived. The next day, the house was full of survivors of the infernal ruins, numb and indifferent. Papa's unbending sense of responsibility dictated that he report for work at the toothpaste factory.

Walking, as always, he traversed a mountainous landscape of rubble. The bridge that would get him across the wide Elbe to the office had been destroyed, so he turned and walked home. It was the end of his seventeen-year career at the Leo-Werke, A.G.

He never said anything about his walk to work on that eerily dark morning. He had always been a man of few words, but now, whether he felt unequal to describing it or because his faith in a loving God made articulating the horror taboo, he seemed bereft of any words at all. He was not alone in his silence; survivors in Hamburg, Berlin, Cologne, and other cities were also robbed of language. The sight of the unimaginable left them numb, affectless, apathetic. They walked, finding paths through the rubble of unrecognizable cities, as if they had always looked that way. Kurt Vonnegut had found Dresden "enchanted . . . like a Sunday school picture of Heaven." Now its delights, its gargoyles, spires, volutes, domes, were "crushed . . . disemboweled . . . cremated." Yet Margarethe's memoir makes no mention of mass funeral pyres, of shriveled remains, of a child reduced to the size of a shoebox, recognizable only by an incongruously intact shoe. She speaks only of her relief at finding her parents miraculously alive.

They had survived, but the need was terrible. Ten days after the bombing, Margarethe prepared a special treat for her father's seventy-third birthday: a piece of bread spread with a mixture concocted from their tiny store of what was available, potato and dried sugar beet chips. Typically, Papa would not accept it, saying she should give it to the children. He withdrew even more, deep into his books and his garden. After fleeing Ottenhof, he had often said that one day God might give him a little patch of earth. Now he had that patch and it was there that his spirit healed. After carefully planting a small juniper, he would decide that it was not in the right spot after all, move it, then move it again. Repeated calls to dinner, cheerfully answered, were rarely heeded; some new task in the garden demanded more immediate attention. Planting a birch by the garden gate was done in the spirit of a religious rite; after all, they were planting a birch, the tree of home.

The first refugees had come to Blumenhagen to escape bombing in the west, like Mira's family. Aimée's first indication of the collapsing front in the east was a telegram from a family friend, a photographer who had done wonderful portraits of the children. "I am sending my family to you," Ebba cabled. "Forgive me. There's nothing else I can do." When her mother arrived in Neustrelitz, Blumenhagen's nearest town, with four children in tow, she was greeted by a committee assigned to deal with people displaced by what were termed "events." The three ladies, with no inkling of what to do or what lay ahead, limited themselves to a tone of humbling disapproval: According to the authorities, they said, everything was under control, so why were they here?

They had friends at Blumenhagen, Ebba's mother answered, and for the committee, this crisis, the first of thousands, was solved. For Aimée, it was just the beginning. She found room for them in the farmworkers' village, and they would eat at Blumenhagen. What they would eat was another matter. Then came the flood, an unending stream of women and children, all fleeing the Russians, more family among them: Heinrich's cousins the Weymarns, from East Prussia, then Marie Louise von Krusenstjerna, and more. Somehow, they managed to stow everyone somewhere, mostly at the house. Still the tide did not stop.

Landowners and peasants—anyone with means of transport as well as those without—crowded the highways to head west. Bridges across the Oder were backed up for miles. A large contingent from an estate in East Prussia arrived at Blumenhagen with their prize thoroughbreds, one mare foaling in the barn. A young woman came, cradling a four-year-old dying of dysentery, which had claimed her two other children. An aunt of Lo's had fled Halle in the caboose of a train with two dachshunds. Word of the bombing in her hometown made Lo anxious, but aside from the aunt with the dachshunds, she had no news of her family.

After Ebba's family moved on, the "black sheep" of their family appeared, crawling with lice. The local health department recommended isolation and burning all bedding and clothes to avoid infestation, a remedy circumstances made absurd. One elegant, exotic creature clutched constantly at her two children, murmuring, "You would be astounded if you knew who I am!" But Aimée had no interest in being astounded. Their neighbor Herr Bürger remarked wryly that Blumenhagen must have rubber walls to contain such a bulging household.

One day nearly a hundred French POWs came through, hoping for food. There was little she could do for them. When Aimée's former baby nurse, Ursula, newly married to a widower, appeared with his five children, the house's "rubber walls" were stretched too far. They put away the dining room table that could seat twenty at dinner, spread straw on the floor, and let the ill-assorted gaggle of family, friends, and strangers sleep there in rows. Above the sleepers' heads hung the decorative commedia dell'arte panels from the little rococo game room at Toffen that Uncle Buddha had given Heinrich. Colombina and Arlecchino still played their amorous games, their eighteenth-century gaiety reassuringly impervious to the changed circumstances. Besides, everyone still had a roof over their heads.

Refugees began arriving from the "Wartheland," where Georg's family had been sent in 1939. Aimée stood for hours in Neustrelitz's crowded market square, asking for news of them. Georg had disappeared on the eastern front and Karola would be alone with the children, fleeing the Polish territories they had been sent to "resettle" and Germanize. But there was no word of them. Mira's family had been at Blumenhagen since the summer of 1943, but if flight became the only option, there would not be room for the combined families in the wagon Aimée planned to use. Reluctantly, they moved on.

Potatoes, potatoes, and more potatoes. Still, they were lucky to have them. Food was scarce and already-skimpy rations were being shared with the new arrivals. March was too early for anything from the garden, and though they were better off than many, there were too many mouths to feed. They still had some potatoes, and bread if they were lucky, but the daily battle was exhausting. After one meal consisting solely of cucumbers baked with flour, Marta came in from the kitchen, looking pained. Might she remove the large casserole from which Aimée had been serving for a moment? Sensing that something was wrong, Aimée followed Marta back to the kitchen. The Polish POWs had sent a delegation to complain that they were being fed rotten cucumbers. Cooking had given the cucumbers the odd glassiness typical of rotten or frozen ones. Aimée lifted the cover of the serving dish; they were all eating the same thing.

Everything was rationed. There was no salt, no fat, little flour, no toilet paper. Soap was a dim memory of an almost unspeakable luxury. Privacy, not officially rationed, was not to be had anywhere, at any price. That winter, the kerosene ran out. One small lamp served the kitchen, and the children crowded around another at a big round table to do their homework and were then sent into the otherwise dark house to play cops and robbers. To them, playing cops and robbers in the dark seemed just as it should be, but next day, when Aimée found pictures askew on the walls and chairs toppled, it felt more ominous than just the aftermath of rowdy games. They were living in a real darkness that shrouded a question she was afraid to acknowledge for fear it might paralyze her.

Blumenhagen had always had dogs, all kinds of dogs: retrievers, a shepherd, Sambo the dachshund, two Scotties, an Airedale. It had become very hard to feed them, and now there was only Pucki, a little fox terrier. For a long time there was no dog food at all, but inexplicably, in early 1945, it was suddenly available again. Turning to the woman behind her in line, wearing what had once been quite a chic, dove-gray hat, Aimée said, laughing, "Who knows? In a few weeks we may be happy to eat this ourselves."

The woman drew back, stone-faced, stiff with fury. How dare she say such a thing? Aimée was stunned. Was it possible that there were still people who did not see the obvious? After years of silence, of weighing every word, people were slowly taking heart, allowing themselves a tiny bit of latitude. But for true believers, there could be no latitude—the nearer the end, the more rigid the belief. For years, Aimée too had obeyed the great unseen censor, had never cried in outrage. After years of thoughts never given voice, she had spoken her mind. It was a stupid mistake. She turned to hurry away. How could she explain herself if this woman called the police? What would become of the children?

A Latvian SS contingent had been billeted at the farm for some time already, standing at attention in front of the house every evening, singing "A Mighty Fortress Is Our God" in Latvian, followed by what sounded like a national anthem, with "Latviju" cropping up among otherwise unfamiliar syllables. Though the men and the several women with them seemed unaffected by the threat of a Russian advance, they had dug big trenches in the fields and laid tree trunks across the road.

The hard-bitten young lieutenant in command had taken over Heinrich's old office now. Studying him at closer range, Aimée found his regular, rather finely cut features almost handsome, but he was strangely monochromatic, bloodless. The ash blond hair matched his ashen skin, and only a veiled, malevolent glitter suggested that life lay behind the nearly colorless eyes. Everything about him was sharp, angular: jaw, brows, mouth, the absence of curves underlining an implicit menace. He frightened her.

From Lore, she knew that Berlin was in the grip of what Berliners called *Untergangsatmosphäre*—an avalanche of syllables denoting the atmosphere of going under. The city was bombed beyond recognition, the air thick with sour dust. Collapsed walls surrounded bomb craters, stinking puddles of sewage, and clouds of flies. People lived in cellars, in any corner that provided a semblance of shelter. Brigades of women sifted through the rubble clogging streets, squares, and parks to extract anything reusable: a bit of scrap metal; a dust-choked harmonica; a shirt or a pair of shoes, sometimes with their owner still in them. This was the city for which Hitler had had grandiose plans—a monument to his rule—to be renamed Germania.

At home, everyone knew the end was near. Listening to the children's prayers every night as she put them to bed, Aimée wondered how much time they had left. Heinrich had written and chosen prayers for each child, tailored to their ages and personal challenges. The prayers were serious business, evolving as the children grew. One was a poem by Christian Morgenstern:

> Look not what others do;
> They are too many.
> You will end in a game
> That never leaves you rest.

> Go simply on God's path,
> Let none other lead.
> Then you'll go right and strong,
> Though you may go alone.

Exhorting children not to take their bearings from the narrow range of another's compass but to be true only to themselves and God's path, even if it means going it alone, is not moral pabulum. Nor are the pounding cadences of Goethe's famous "*Feiger Gedanken*": Cowardly thoughts, anxious wavering, feeble hesitation, and frightened lament will never avert disaster or make you free, Goethe says. Stand up against all forces, show yourself strong, never bend—call upon the arms of the gods. Those verses had sent seven-year-old Brigitte stumping bravely through knee-deep snow in early morning darkness on her solo path to school, reciting its recipe for survival in desperate times. Hearing their prayers brought Heinrich's principles back every evening.

She had not found new prayers for each of them yet, but thinking on an immediate, practical note, she had insisted on an addendum, "Corson-Ellis-Lake-Forest-Illinois-USA. Amen," and heard this little mantra again and again. If all hell broke loose and they were separated, maybe, by some miracle she had trouble believing in, they might find their way to her brother. Secretly Brigitte also asked Uncle Corson to please land his plane on the great lawn to save them, and asked God why the Americans were not here yet, when there was such terrible danger from the east.

As always, the agriculture department distributed seed for the farm that spring. The world was disintegrating, and they were being given seed for a harvest she had little hope of seeing. It was entirely in keeping with the party line: everything was *planmässig*—according to plan. April produced an almost endless string of what was called "Hitler weather"— perfect for devastating bombing runs. Every day was so beautiful that in spite of everything, worrying felt oddly irrelevant. The children were a constant source of delight, and the greening of the gentle landscape felt miraculous—almost miraculous enough to overcome the gnawing question of how many more such days might be left.

Flight seemed the only option, but Aimée had little idea of where to go. West, of course, but how? They knew almost nothing about what was really happening. Getting to British or American lines was critical, but she had only a vague sense of where those lines were. The consensus was that the Western Allies had stopped advancing while the Russians were pushing west, a thought that fueled nightmares. She had only one reliable scrap of information: Küstrin on the Oder, less than 160 kilometers away and in a direct line to Berlin, had been defended against a massive Russian offensive by only a pitiful ragtag assembly of over- and underage Volkssturm recruits.

In the midst of her deliberations, Friedrich received a notice to report for the draft. The boy had just turned sixteen. Tall and thin, he had not begun to shave, but he was ordered to report for three weeks of basic training at a camp near Flensburg, on the Danish border. How could she send him off alone to fight a last-ditch effort in this futile war? Where were the Allies? Might there be an armistice before he got there? But fifteen-year-olds were being hanged as "deserters." Yet another decision; now was the time for a calming male presence and sound advice, and there was none. Uncle Bill was beyond reach, so she examined the problem with Helma and Lo.

The Russians were sweeping west, driving everything ahead of them like animals ahead of a forest fire. There was something utterly perverted about a system that sent children off to almost certain death to fight its battles. But contemplating what could happen if he did not report was unbearable too.

Afraid to send him off, and afraid not to, an anxious cluster gathered under the great linden trees, Michael and Christian a bit apart, silent and awkward. Friedrich had warm clothes, a toothbrush, ten marks, and Marta's sandwiches. Seeing him go was anguish. If they fled, it would have to be soon. If he was not back in time, how would they find each other again? It was impossible. At the end of the drive, the boy turned and waved.

20

Flight

The Regional Council called Aimée to say that leaving, or even making plans to leave, was strictly forbidden. Refugees from East Prussia had been shot trying to get away ahead of the Russians, but had fled by the thousands anyway. Now Herr Bürger had standing orders to hang anyone trying to flee.

She and Lo set off on bicycles to reconnoiter possible escape routes, a mission complicated by the fact that they knew so little. All they knew for certain was that the positive official bulletins were false and people were terrified. The circuitous network that passed along a tiny kernel of possibly real information had a way of shifting emphasis, inflating, dismissing, exaggerating, or rearranging fragments into fable. It reminded her of "Telephone," a game they played at Dana Hall, a circle of giggling girls passing along a bit of whispered gossip to see what came out at the other end. People were torn between the desire to believe something, anything, and a learned, cynical hopelessness that made it impossible to believe anything at all.

Easter fell on another glorious day. They held the service in the music room, Aimée at the piano, Michael on violin, recorders distributed among the other children. As always, they sang. The Easter egg hunt was chilly and short on candies, but in the afternoon, she read aloud from Howard Pyle's *Men of Iron*. She had loved it as a child, and she and Lo had been working on a translation. It was nearly finished, but she wondered whether the children would ever hear the end of the story.

She had heard a good deal about the Russians. Heinrich's Bolsheviks were brutish and merciless, and recent refugees had updated and amplified his stories: Russian tanks pursuing fugitives, rolling over anyone not fast enough on their feet; children shot and left dying at the roadside. Women were routinely, repeatedly raped, their wedding rings removed, then they were killed or nailed to barn doors to die. The motivation for such brutality was not hard to fathom, but there was little doubt about what Germany could expect. Aimée no longer wondered whether the Allies realized what letting the Russians into the heart of Europe would mean. America was blind to the realities faced by countries without oceans between them and hostile neighbors. Soviet artillery was already audible, and she did not plan to wait for them to arrive. But where was Friedrich?

Among the Latvian SS crew, one older man had always seemed reasonable, even friendly to her and the children. She wondered where his family was. Steeling herself to overcome her fear of disclosing her plan, using all the delicacy and circumlocution she could muster, she asked him what he would do if he were in her position. Under his breath, he shot back a terse "Leave!"

Motorized vehicles and fuel had been requisitioned long ago, but she had a wooden frame built as a roof for their best wagon. Two Persian rugs went over the frame as protection against the weather. Food, warm clothes, family papers, musical instruments, and paintings were stowed. Geese and some chickens were slaughtered and slung under the wagon, along with the biggest pots, a pickaxe, and tools to dig a shelter. Michael, always the keeper of the family flame, insisted that they make room for the family photo album. He was nearly fourteen—the same age as Heinrich when his family had fled Ottenhof. Was it only twenty-six years since Heinrich had run back into the house there to take treasured family portraits off the walls? Even her hurried arithmetic told her that history had not given them enough time.

Helma decided to join them rather than stay behind at the hospital, but her tiny, eighty-two-year-old mother feared the trek and stayed, sure she would not be harmed. Aimée, Helma, and the boys had bicycles for mobility. Each of the girls could bring a small box of personal treasures and one doll. Dorothée refused to take any; taking one would make the others feel unloved. When Brigitte was overheard telling her beloved teddy, Brummel, that he had to be left behind, room was found for him far back in the wagon.

The villagers—farmworkers and peasants—were in an uproar,

demanding to come along in spite of all official injunctions. Eager to keep them from calling attention to their planned departure, Aimée said of course they could come. Below's decision to stay behind to look after the estate as best he could stirred debate as to which one of the Polish POWs would drive the wagon. They too were afraid of the Russians, and eager to leave.

Renate von Gersdorff phoned, saying, "Surely you are not leaving?"

"Yes," Aimée replied. "We are leaving very soon."

"Ah," came a sigh at the other end. "I was so sure that you would keep your head."

She was keeping her head, she insisted. They were leaving.

Suddenly Friedrich was home, narrow as a sapling, hungry and worn, but home! She had quaked at the thought of leaving without him, and the relief was huge. Words spilled out of him in a jumble. When he and a few other boys had presented themselves, they were told that the training camp had been disbanded. Not knowing what to do, the official asked them to leave their names and addresses. But hearing artillery from the direction of Hamburg, he and another boy decided that it made more sense to disappear. They had spent the night in a shed and come home by train next morning. The Reich's trains were still running.

Having him back made her feel almost teary with relief but created yet another logistical problem. He had skipped out on the draft. They would have to find a way to hide the gangly boy in case they were stopped and searched. If the wrong people found him, he would be hanged. Next day, a notice demanded that Friedrich report to the Volkssturm. He would not report, she decided. If they left, it would be soon, and leaving without him was unthinkable.

She felt like a cup filled to the brim; any added drop would break the surface tension that held her together. Out of her enthusiasm for Heinrich's family and their enthusiasm for children, she had had six. Children represented a return to normalcy, a renewal, hope for the future. When Heinrich was killed, comforting talk almost always included the notion that he would always be with her in the children. Through them, he would comfort her, and share the burdens. It sounded good, but it wasn't true. After his death, she thought briefly that she sometimes felt his presence, but with time, he had sunk into an enviable unreachability. Except for the many lives that depended on her, she was alone.

April 27 was glorious, the lake still and calm below the house. The apple trees were in full bloom, and tulips stood tall and vivid against new grass. From secret, late-night BBC listening, she knew that the Russians had already crossed the Oder. There would be no hiding in the woods, waiting for the Allies. The frightening SS lieutenant had gone to Neustrelitz for the day, and with luck, the rest of the crew would think that today was no different from any other. The SS had taken over the music room too, so the boys had moved her big Bechstein into the library, where they gathered to sing their staple, "A Mighty Fortress Is Our God," its sturdy cadences implying a stability and calm that no one felt. Reciting the Twenty-third Psalm, she could barely find breath enough or voice to utter the words. Heinrich's family had recited it that dark December night of 1918, when they had fled Ottenhof. Family history was repeating itself.

Most of the villagers had not traveled farther than three kilometers in all their lives, but they were determined to join the trek, even threatening to puncture their wagon's tires if they were left behind. They had piled a hay wagon high with featherbeds and anything else that seemed essential to the two families who were coming. The wagon's high wooden ribs were good for holding hay, but the jumble of family miscellany—pots, pans, a cherished lavender cushion—kept falling out between them.

She gave each child a small chamois bag with Corson's Chicago address to hang around their necks. Putting any hope at all into such a fragile vessel seemed absurd, but she felt compelled to do it. They were headed into the unknown, and the thought of being separated in the maelstrom ahead was terrifying. As they left, she turned for a last look—a mental snapshot of the life she and Heinrich had hoped to build. A tiny vase of bright grape hyacinths on the little table by the window gleamed in the sunshine.

Crossing the cobbled section of the drive to the paved road was grindingly slow. It was nearly impossible not to look back, so she stared in furious concentration at the shoulder of the road instead. The little wild strawberries that grew there were in blossom. For a moment, she felt a savage, irrepressible hope that the children might harvest the tiny, fragrant fruit. Then she pushed the thought away.

Flight was forbidden. Since they could not go through any towns where they might be recognized, they decided to cut across Blumenholz, the neighboring estate. Surely Herr Bürger would not hang them. He had even called to say that he would not be there; he had appointments in Berlin. This made no sense; Berlin was under siege. Was he telling her when and how to leave? Going through his property meant going north-east, toward the Russians, but it would also have them in deep forest almost as far as Güstrow. Moving along under immense beeches, standing tall in pale, new leaf, the horses labored to pull the heavy wagon along the silent, sandy woodland track. By afternoon, it was almost a relief to reach the road.

But what a road—a boiling, seething torrent of people and vehicles. With no time to debate whether to join the tumult, it was the first of several wild days. Roads were gray-brown with the dust of Wehrmacht trucks, motorcycles, and an endless stream of refugee wagons pulled along by exhausted horses, soldiers on foot, and hundreds of people pulling handcarts, pushing wheelbarrows and baby buggies. Anything with wheels was loaded with pots, pans, bedding, even a clock—whatever was thought essential to survival, the future, or that the heart could not leave behind. It was incongruous, unreal. Family essentials and treasures were tied together helter-skelter with rope and often topped off with a baby, supported on the unsteady pile by a grandmother hobbling alongside. Heinrich's letters from France had described just such a pitiful exodus. Aimée was grateful that he would not see this iteration of the cycle, his family in flight—again.

The Dutch word *trek* had described the long nineteenth-century march of the Boers from Cape Town to Transvaal. Nazi propaganda appropriated it to exalt the relocation of uprooted ethnic Germans, like Georg's family, to the newly acquired territories, all crucial to the long-range Nazi plan for "Germanizing" the rich agricultural plains of

Poland and Russia. Now a trek was no longer an eager journey toward a golden dream, but flight from an advancing army into an uncertain future—an accurate reflection of the history of Hitler's war.

They stopped the first night in a barn belonging to strangers, and people seeing the sign they had borrowed from the Weymarns' wagon, giving their point of origin as East Prussia, said, "Oh, but you've come a long way!" She nodded silently. They had probably come less than fifteen kilometers, but it felt like a very long way from home. Marta made them a meal of boiled potatoes with hot bacon fat, served up in the stainless steel, kidney-shaped medical bowls Helma had packed with an eye to eventually reopening her practice. It was hot, delicious, and enormously comforting. They ate greedily, inhaling the aroma, drawing heart from the food and the warmth and from simply being together. When Marta produced another miracle, a custard she had prepared in advance, with rhubarb compote, they were nearly dizzy with delight.

After the tumultuous day, that night was strangely uneventful, though at one point a lone Italian soldier appeared, trying desperately to persuade them to turn back. Why? What did he know? What had he seen? Otherwise all was quiet, until they heard women wailing somewhere in the dark. The next morning, she discovered that the wailing had come from the villagers' wagon. One of the women came to say that they felt they were in alien territory. Feeling lost and afraid, they wanted to turn back, and were willing to battle the tide of refugees. They wanted to go home to what they knew—or thought they knew.

The next day brought a desperate sense of homelessness, of being an insignificant few among thousands of refugees. They were lucky to have horses, but there was no way of knowing how to avoid the throngs and stay far enough ahead to reach Allied lines before the Russians did. Military traffic had nearly stopped, and the enormous stream moved in astonishing silence, broken only by an occasional clink of metal, the complaint of an unoiled axle, or a baby's cry. That night in the park of a large estate, they were dimly aware of another refugee wagon somewhere, but the darkness under the trees was so dense they only sensed its presence. All night they heard heavily laden trains, pulling slowly westward, then a sudden, enormous explosion from the direction of

Neubrandenburg. With Russians outside the old city walls, the army had blown up the depot.

Everyone was bedded down in or under the wagon, but Aimée could not sleep. Her mind was everywhere. The horses had not been watered. What route should they take tomorrow? Michael was restless too, prowling anxiously, worried about the horses. He crept over, whispering that he had heard running water somewhere. Together they felt their way in the dark. More by ear than anything else, they found their way to a small stream and filled their pails with shockingly cold water. The horses drank deeply, gratefully, exhaling warm gusts through tender nostrils. The horses were their lifeline, their only hope. The gratitude went both ways.

It must have been after midnight before she lay down again. She was just dozing off when Michael roused her again, his young, disembodied voice urgent.

"Mother, the other wagon is gone; I think we should leave too." His anxiety reawakened hers. They woke everyone and set off down the almost indiscernible path. Back on the dark, deserted road, they moved westward again, alone.

On April 30, the third day of their trek, they stopped to rest at a small farm to listen to their battery-operated radio. Rigging it up was a nuisance, but the broadcasts helped them decide which routes to take, so Lo and Michael patiently set it up at every stop to hear the BBC report. This time they heard that Neustrelitz had fallen to the Russians.

They had left just in time, and so far, they had chosen their route well. She thought gratefully of Herr Bürger, who had steered them right, and offered a little prayer for his and his family's safety. If they had taken the road to Stemberg, the horses would now be dead by the side of the road. They also seemed to be protected from strafing and the apparently mindless military traffic. Then, somewhere behind them, they heard a mad ringing of church bells, a code the villages had developed; wild bell ringing at a time outside the normal morning, noon, and evening pattern was an alarm, signaling "The Russians are here!" Time to move on.

Looking back from the vantage point of the boys, or Helma or Lo—whoever bicycled ahead to reconnoiter—the picture was almost always the same: Jaczek, the Polish POW, at the reins, with Aimée next to him, one steadying hand on the top wagon rail, her eyes focused far ahead, as if scanning the horizon for a clue to the future. When one horse was not in harness, one of the older children rode alongside.

Christian rode as if he had been poured into the saddle, upright and sure, his bright hair blowing against his face. The boys guarded what they considered their prerogative jealously, insisting that Brigitte could never manage. But once past her initial nerves, the girl looked down from the big horse, proud and happy, liberated from all anxiety. Hair ribbons tucked away because she did not want to lose them, shaking her long, loose hair out of her eyes, she looked like a little Amazon. Aimée had heard enough about Russians raping anything female to make her consider cutting the child's glorious hair and putting her into boys' clothes.

When dirt tracks from the villages reached the road, the stream of people became a slow-moving river. Jostling silently, urgently westward, the muddle inched along with an energy fueled by desperation. One old grandfather, shuffling along in slippers, carried an empty picture frame. It seemed to her emblematic of the entire war. An aged couple, alone, with no possessions, stood at the side of the teeming road and asked her what they should do. What indeed?

Sometimes the stream halted. Only the boys—serious, feverishly curious—were not too tired to speculate. Maybe a ruined tank was blocking the road ahead, or a horse had collapsed. It didn't matter, she thought. Why did they have to know? But they were boys. To varying degrees, they saw this as an adventure, delighting in identifying specific army vehicles or aircraft. If they went ahead to reconnoiter, she was forced out of the lethargy that had seized her, to worry about them until they came back.

In the unsettled afternoon sky, rays of light pierced layers of gray, blue, and black clouds, as if the very finger of God were striking the earth. It looked like a Doré illustration of some ancient cataclysm, a biblical exodus of hunched wretches, driven forward by a merciless unseen force. The strange silence was broken only by an occasional shout or the clang of a utensil tumbling from some precarious arrangement. From

the depths of their own wagon, she heard a barely audible, almost subliminal, repetitive clink that matched the rhythm of the horses' gait.

What was it—the samovar? Had she even packed the samovar? She
could not remember. There had been so many decisions, made hastily
and surreptitiously in constant fear of discovery. If it was the samovar,
what was it chinking against? Friedrich's flute? The questions nagged,
and she strained to hear, listening for that tiny, metallic *tck, tck*. She
heard almost nothing else. It was a reminder of all the things she must
have forgotten, all the ways in which she had failed, was failing, might
fail. She must not let that small sound embody all her inadequacies and
drive her mad.

Fields of sugar beets and spring wheat lay under sun and rain. Occasionally a lone, surviving cow gawked at the passersby, mute or bawling. At
the outskirts of one village, a peasant walked behind his horse, plowing,
oblivious to the throngs passing his fields. It was a year like any other. He
had received his allotment of seed, as always. As always, he would plow and
plant in the furrows. With rain, the seed would germinate, sun would
bring the crop to maturity; someone would reap, someone would eat. Not
everyone would be dead. Not everyone would have fled.

Time was short. They could not allow themselves or the horses much
rest. Low-flying aircraft with Allied stars were strafing the routes
they and the rivers of refugees were traveling. In glorious, clear spring
weather, the sky a relentless azure, the air's transparency offered no
shield from sun or aircraft, no cover at all. When they saw the planes
come in, heard the screeching whine as they dropped down, they abandoned the wagon and dove into the ditches, but with no guarantee of
safety. As they lay facedown, waiting for the *tak-tak-tak* of machine
gun fire, the close grass a minute jungle, the breath of the earth was
sweet and soft. The wait for the rustling of the bullets moving through
the grass, the small thuds as they bit into dirt, or the occasional twang
when something was hit always seemed an eternity, an interminable,
breathless moment, yet oddly abstract and not frightening. It was much
too late to be afraid.

The wagon ahead had been hit; bodies lay in the ditches. Horses pulling another wagon lay dead in bloody harnesses, their owners distraught. Without horses, they would have to leave everything behind. The next time the planes came, Jaczek yanked the horses off the road in the direction of the approaching planes. One stray wagon in a field, he reasoned, was a paltry, low priority compared with total disruption of a heavily trafficked road. By then, the repeated attacks, the planes turning, circling, then swooping down for a reprise, had left everyone exhausted and stupefied.

In some places, soldiers, several of them boys, were hanging from trees, signs around their necks denouncing them as cowards or traitors. Often they were barefoot, their boots taken by their executioners. She trembled at the thought that this was what awaited Friedrich if he was caught. The strafing, the stalled vehicles clogging the roads, made progress excruciatingly slow during the day. Refugee wagons, military vehicles, some still burning, and charred corpses of horses littered the roadsides. So this was the famous *Endsieg*, the final victory of the Thousand-Year Reich they had heard so much about. It looked more like Armageddon. When they had first looked at Blumenhagen, she remembered Heinrich joking about Bismarck's saying that in Mecklenburg everything happened one hundred years later. The Thousand-Year Reich had collapsed in twelve; Bismarck had miscalculated a little.

21

Everything Passes

A haggard group of evacuees in striped prison garb from a concentration camp approached the wagon, wanting to trade chocolate for potatoes, easier than chocolate on stomachs that have been empty too long. Aimée gave them what she could, realizing that the chocolate must have come from fairly high up. By fueling these wraiths with chocolate, the regime hoped to drive them as far as possible from the scene of its crimes. Some refugees were already moving into the evacuated camps; the homeless citizens of a system intent on obliterating all traces of otherness—racial, religious, or political—were taking refuge in the places organized for that obliteration.

Near Schwerin's Lake, a fellow trekker told her that when word of Hitler's death raced through the refugees, an SS officer had overheard one young woman's fervent "Thank God!" She was seized and strung up from the nearest tree in front of her three children. In the hectic violence of the moment, one of her shoes had come off, and her oldest had stood, clutching it to his chest, as his mother's feet dangled at his eye level, above the heads of the younger ones. The thousand-year oak Hitler had ordered planted in every German town and village to mark his Reich was not yet strong enough for such a burden. The irreverent refrain from the 1942 song played in Aimée's head:

> *Es geht alles vorüber, es geht alles vorbei,*
> *erst geht der Führer, und dann die Partei.*

Everything passes, it all passes away, first goes the Führer, and then the party. The Führer, at least, was gone, but the party was very much in evidence.

. . .

One day early in May they pulled the wagon to a stop on a hill near an old farmhouse. They were well hidden under big trees, but low-flying aircraft wheeled wildly overhead, strafing anything that moved. Bullets rattled through the new leaves, bringing down showers of twigs and the occasional branch, fresh, green, broken. Even after the engine roar had passed, the horses stirred and shifted nervously. Suddenly a cry went up somewhere below: *"Die Engländer sind hier!"*—"The English are here!"

If the British had arrived, surely the strafing would stop. Yet the Russians were there too. They were caught between the lines; the shooting went on, from the air and on the ground, and with the British maybe less than a kilometer away, Aimée's one thought was to get to them, through hellfire if need be. The main highway was utterly stalled, so she, Lo, and the boys left the wagon to hurry toward British lines on foot.

At the bottom of the hill: chaos. Caught between the Allies, German troops were tossing radios, weapons, food, and even money out of army trucks. Foolishly, they ignored the money, but oh, the food! Sausages were being tossed to an eager, grasping crowd. Christian slipped nimbly under the truck to emerge directly by the tailgate. He grabbed one sausage, which he threw to Michael, then another. He also managed two sacks of hardtack, iron rations that proved to be a godsend. In the coming months, sooner or later, everyone suffered from wretched, draining bouts of dysentery.

Soldiers threw down their arms, some bitterly, but most in relief. An open truck full of soldiers roared by, an officer furiously trying to pull away the white handkerchiefs they were waving. They were not to surrender; they would be disciplined! For what, she wondered—defeatism? Insubordination? Cowardice? A black Mercedes staff car flying a commandant's pennant crept past, then a lone motorcycle messenger. Neither seemed to know where to go.

Standing by a bridge, Lo and Aimée watched an apparently endless stream of British military vehicles roll past, full of smiling, fresh-faced soldiers. Those on foot looked immaculate, disciplined, like civilization itself,

and jubilant in victory. Lo watched, uncertain and disheartened. Aimée tried
to cheer her: The Nazis' complete collapse was a blessing that would clear the
way for a real future.

Back at the wagon, holding up their sausage and hardtack trophies,
they all talked at once, describing the wild scene below. In the excitement, someone called to Pucki to come and sniff the sausage, but there
was no sign of her. Elation turned to anxious calls and cries. Soon everyone fanned out, calling, "Pucki! Pucki!" With each unanswered call, the
syllables held greater anxiety. If the dog had followed them into that
confusion of people and vehicles . . . It did not bear thinking about. The
children trooped across the hillside, calling. Michael went back into the
melee on the road, calling and calling. As the light faded, desolation
crept over them. The little ones were near tears. Their companion and
tireless source of good cheer was gone.

Lo, tenderly mindful of the children's feelings, sat with the three
girls near the grazing horses. An animal presence, any animal presence,
might soften the loss, but it was a sad little company. The girls, often so
talkative, were very quiet. Then a cold black nose butted Lo's elbow.
Looking for friends and food, the scruffy white, black, and tan dog had
emerged from the nearby woods. Shrieks of joy, shouting, running. Michael, halfheartedly cranking up the radio for the BBC report, dropped
everything. Relief flooded through their little encampment as a leaping
and barking Pucki was welcomed back; home was not entirely gone.

They had won the race against the Russians by a narrow margin.
They had reached British lines, and surely the British would not shoot
women and children. The desperate flight through the countryside, the
fear of the past months, was over; they had some sausage and hardtack.
Maybe they should celebrate. The relief was immense yet hollow. Behind it lay sorrow and uncertainty. This was only a first step and there
was no sense of what the next step would be.

Long ago, Aimée had written Mary that she would never give up her
right to vagabond. She was certainly exercising it now. This primitive,
deracinated life was an accurate reflection of their homelessness. But
they were alive, and life was being lived irremediably, with an intense
commitment to every moment. There was no time for ego, equivocation,

or second-guessing. That was a gift—one aligned with her native
enthusiasm—and something to be grateful for.

Often Lo and Helma bicycled ahead to find a place for the night. Would
they have to knock on door after door, asking to put up in a barn; would
they find friendly, welcoming people? Whether offered grudgingly or
with an open heart, many barns they stayed in were wonderful, dark
and still, solemn as churches. One was special, high and airy, with beautifully constructed cribs for straw and hay and roof beams resting on
massive old stone walls that gave it a faintly romantic touch. At night,
the sound of the horses chewing and shifting their weight nearby was
deeply reassuring, like a parental hand soothing a sleeping child. Bedded
down in a loft still half full of last year's sweet hay, they could catch
their collective breath. Their dining room was the great high space fes-
tooned with swags of spiderwebs. Little chinks in the roof let in the occasional ray of sunlight, alive with dust motes, tingeing everything
with gold. From her nook in the loft, Aimée could see slender birches
swaying against the night sky, soothing her into sleep.

For the youngest, three-year-old Sigrid, those dim barns were both
haven and adventure. Sleeping on hay was itchy, but exciting. Terror
came only once, when harsh voices, disembodied in the blackness behind
bright flashlights, rousted them out of their haven. The fear of the adults
sparked fear in her. The steep ladder she had managed so proudly on the
way up now seemed impossible to go down in darkness. Wordlessly,
horses were hitched and the family set off into the night.

Life was primitive and often cold. Cooking had to be done outdoors
against a low stone wall. When it rained, Aimée held an umbrella over
Marta while she concocted a soup from whatever was available—potatoes
and turnips if they were lucky. But Marta in her ample skirts, her body
thickening with Below's child, was endlessly resourceful, and brought a
miraculous touch to the most common ingredients, usually nettles and
dandelion greens, gathered as young and tender as possible, smelling of
earth and damp.

When the clouds lifted, the owners of the barn where they were staying put them to work among the sugar beets. Both Aimée and Lo had

memorized an immense store of poems that they recited to each other as they hoed and weeded. "Hail to thee, blithe spirit," Aimée would sing out, or Lo launched into her cherished Goethe, the poetic deity of German literature. The cadences—some lyrical, some powerful, with insistent exhortations to courage—gave them a sense of permanence and connection to something beyond the present. The patient, abiding earth under their feet was reassuring. They felt safe and immensely grateful.

One night in the dark, Aimée's head itched and she was convinced that something was moving along her ear. It had to be a louse, she thought. Husband, home, friends, possessions were lost; the future was a gaping void. Every day was a struggle with fear, hunger, and whatever new obstacle presented itself. And now, a louse: the lowliest common denominator of war and misery, the humble emissary of dark forces. She had hit bottom; the critter had stripped away the last precious shred of control.

Then she had an absurd thought. She remembered the Colt factory in Hartford, with its starry blue dome. Colt used to claim that God did not make men equal, Samuel Colt's weapon did. Now the louse was the great equalizer. Much to Miss Masters's mortification, there had been an outbreak of lice at Dobbs Ferry. Well, she had got herself out of Dobbs, and she would get them all out of this too.

That Sunday the radio began to play English church music. The familiar chords sounded much smaller drifting through the lofty rafters of the silent barn than they had resonating over the heads of the congregation at Saint John's on Farmington Avenue, but she was surprised at how easily she could summon the words:

> All hail the power of Jesus' name,
> Let angels prostrate fall.
> Bring forth the royal diadem,
> And crown him Lord of all.

The hymn conjured up another time, standing between her father and Uncle Bill in the family pew, wearing that flowered hat she disliked so much. It was a time when everything had seemed utterly, deadeningly dependable. Suddenly she was struck by the enormity of her situation. Until that moment, there had never been time or sufficient calm to think about it. A rumor that the Russians might withdraw to the Oder had let them hold on to the dream of returning to Blumenhagen. Though she hardly dared to believe it, surrendering that hope completely had been beyond her. But now it hit her like a fist: The Russians would never withdraw; British occupation would become Russian occupation. Blumenhagen was gone, locked away in the Russian sector, possibly forever.

Michael turned fourteen on May 4, a glorious day that suggested summer. Horses grazed in lush meadows, lilacs were in exuberant bloom, and lupines glowed brilliant blue—images of peace and normalcy that seemed incongruous in the prevailing confusion. In fact, a few days later, a policeman came to tell them the Russians insisted that all refugees who had escaped after a certain date must be turned over to them. "I have no choice," he said, as shocked as they were. "They insist that you must be sent back."

Bicycling to the British command in Gadebusch, she barely had time to catch her breath and smooth her hair before she was ushered into the commandant's office. He was small and natty, with a whiff about him of soap and hot water, things she had always considered the basis of a safe and civilized world. He conjured up the unmistakable image of a sunny nursery under the firm hand of a starched nanny. She could almost see the Kate Greenaway alphabet, taste Lyle's Golden Syrup. It had been so long since she had seen anyone looking so neat, so pressed, so immaculate, that she had to force herself not to gape.

Showing him her American passport, she explained where they had come from. She and her six children were staying nearby at the farm of a very kind woman. They must not be sent back to the Russian sector under any circumstances, she said, hoping she sounded more firm than frightened. She needed to know if it was safe to stay here. He must be aware of what was in store for them if they were sent back or this area came under Russian occupation.

"Why are you so afraid of the Russians?" he asked mildly, slowly stroking his meticulously trimmed moustache.

"You simply cannot send us back. I'm afraid of the Bolsheviks," she said, privately congratulating herself for uttering perhaps the only word that might make an impression on him.

"I see." Pause for a ruminative stroke of the moustache. "So you can't go back because you would find no employment there."

"No, no!" she stammered. "That—that isn't it at all!"

"You cannot return because you would have no means of employment there!" he repeated slowly, enunciating with exaggerated precision.

"You don't understand . . . ," she almost shouted, then faltered. His message had penetrated. He was speaking in code, a language prescribed for dealing with jurisdictional disputes over civilians. Feeling humbled and unequal to the demands this new world was making on her, she said quietly, "Yes, that's it. I would have no means of employment."

He turned to his desk, scrawled a quick note, and handed it to his adjutant, saying, "I am not at liberty to tell you whether this area will be turned over to the Russians. But meantime," he said, walking over to a large regional map pinned to the wall, "have you ever visited this little place? It is a charming spot, quite undamaged."

It was a very broad hint. She thanked him and left. Now she knew just where to go. She was grateful for his help, and even more grateful for this reminder that order, cleanliness, and decency still existed. Their encounter had been a return to an earlier, more civilized life she once thought would always be there. He had provided a brief vacation from the present, demonstrating that such a life was still out there, somewhere. Civilized life had been in very short supply recently, and she wanted to find that somewhere as soon as possible.

But first, she went back to tell their hostess what she had learned. That same evening, kind Frau Blomeyer cut a hole in the fence of her beautiful farm and drove her cattle through it to where they would be safe in the future British occupation zone. Relocated to the "charming spot, quite undamaged," Frau Blomeyer spent that night, her first as a refugee in a hayloft, among friends.

They were at a huge refugee camp when official word of Allied occupation sectors leaked out in early June. The borders were vague, confusing, and shifted depending on the source, but there was little doubt that Blumenhagen would be in the Russian sector. Contemplating this hard news amid the hundreds of wagons, tents, people, dogs, and dirt—the war's leftovers—they suddenly saw Below in the crowd. She had never doubted Below's resourcefulness, but finding each other like this was an amazing piece of luck.

Staying on at Blumenhagen had become impossible, but he had managed to break through Russian lines, and here he was. Marta scraped together the makings of a celebratory reunion, almost jolly enough to keep Aimée's mind from the thought of their Blumenhagen marooned in alien hands.

Jaczek had been doing most of the driving and tending to the horses. But now Below was there, and Jaczek wanted to get home to Poland to find his family. They had shared a great deal. Aimée gave him what provisions and money she could. Embracing him, she wished him Godspeed.

They were heading west, hoping to find the Americans. Michael, Helma, and Lo went ahead to reconnoiter about permits and passage across the Elbe. At Hamburg, they were told they would simply have to present the proper papers when they arrived at the ferry. They had no papers, of course, but there was no time to hesitate. Heading straight at a problem was better than nervously weighing the pros and cons in anticipation. Obstacles were easier to overcome on the spot. Map in hand, they moved on.

That night, poised to take a giant step into the unknown, Aimée took comfort from the horses. Standing close to the warmth of their massive bodies, she stroked them and spoke to them. They leaned into her touch, ears swiveling lightly to catch the words. Marushka turned a bit, her soft muzzle searching Aimée's palm for morsels. Everything about them—their noisy exhalations, the dull clunk of hooves as they shifted their weight—was reassuring, all the more for being wordless.

Next morning began bright, but as they moved across the vast, flat landscape, it began to rain. By the time they reached the ferry, they had been in a long line for several hours, only to be told that without papers, they could not cross. The rain was heavy now; it was dark. Seizing that advantage, Below nudged their wagon forward to mingle with other wagons, among them those of an eccentric countess Aimée had spoken with earlier. As they drove onto the ferry, apparently as part of her group, the police asked no questions.

The crossing took only minutes, but they were minutes heavy with feeling. Water and sky were gray, the wind carried a whiff of the open sea. The ship's screws pounded, waves slapped against its side. Being loosed from solid ground brought a moment of strangeness and instability, but there was no time for second thoughts. The land across the river lay flat, gray, inscrutable. She had no idea what part this passage would play in their flight or in their lives. The questions were big and unanswerable. She pressed her lips together, as if that small physical constriction could push them away and quash the fears they raised.

Caught up in the adventure of the moment, Friedrich and Michael stood forward, their profiles sharp against the grayness. Wind blew their hair back from their young faces. The horses were restless, stamping and uneasy at the unaccustomed motion under their feet. Celeste tossed her head, worrying at the bit. With a muted thump, the ferry touched the landing. The vague, misty, silhouetted strip of horizon had become firm ground. Slowly they edged into their new world.

They spent that night in a vast camp with thousands of other displaced people. Next morning, a day of bright sun and wind, they set off on the autobahn, white bands of concrete stretching ahead, broad and straight. One after another, English military trucks roared past. The horses were skittish, nervous in the wind and unaccustomed noise. She too longed for the quiet pace of dirt tracks and country roads.

In a Hamburg obliterated by carpet bombing, foreign reporters clambering over the bizarre, cubist rubble found their vocabulary reduced to the one word applied to nearly all other bombed cities: "indescribable." The city's outskirts crawled with people trying to get across the Elbe in one direction or the other. Margarethe's stepson, Winfried, was there too, hoping for a pass, when he heard someone call his name. Christian's spotting him among the displaced thousands was only one of many improbable encounters among the uprooted millions washing

across Europe. And Winfried had a letter from Uncle Bill! The message
Aimée had sent through an American officer in May had reached him.
His response had reached Ebba, then Christian had spotted Winfried in
the chaos; it was miraculous, obviously a sign from the gods! Winfried
must stay with them, at least until he could find his family.

The boy was seventeen when he was drafted to fight the advancing Russians. Separated from his unit at war's end and moving around on his own,
he connected with an amputee, recently released from a hospital in the
Russian army's path, and having trouble managing on crutches. So Winfried shouldered both packs, and the two made their way slowly, hungrily—
somewhere, anywhere, they did not know exactly where—wherever the
Russians weren't. When they heard that the Americans were turning German soldiers who had fought in the east over to the Russians, they avoided
Americans too. This meant a hard road, through fields and woods. By the
time they reached Altenburg in Saxony, Winfried's amputee friend was
exhausted. It was June; the war had been over for a month and more, but
with no discharge papers, stray SS zealots might string them up as deserters anyway. Too worn out to make it to his family in Leipzig on foot, his
friend decided to risk the train. It was less than an hour's trip.

At the Altenburg railroad station, they were nabbed by the Americans and trucked to a POW camp. The intake officer took one look at the
skeletal amputee and motioned him to approach. If the Americans were
going to spare him, he thought, they should spare his faithful pack carrier too. The amputee grabbed Winfried by the sleeve and pulled him
along, hopping on one leg. What military hospital had he come from?
the officer asked. They had both come from—he named an already evacuated military hospital to the east. Since Winfried was terribly pale and
had inexplicably lost all his hair, the reply was convincing. After less
than two hours' captivity, the two were back at the Altenburg railroad
station with discharge papers.

While his friend waited for a train to Leipzig, Winfried made his
way up the hill to the castle. Friedrich von Saxe-Altenburg, affectionately known as "Prinzlein" for his title and small stature, was an old
friend who might have news of his parents, who had been living in

Posen, but now? If Prinzlein did not know, he would put Winfried up for a few days while he decided what to do next. But Prinzlein had headed west several days before. Guessing that Margarethe's sister Ebba might still be living about 140 kilometers due west, according to the railroad map, he decided to go there.

Finding family in the chaos, no matter how dirty or hungry, was a miracle. Overjoyed to see him, Ebba fed him, listened to his story. She did not know where Margarethe might be, but added quickly that the Americans were withdrawing, and the area would soon be under Russian occupation. He must go now, before the Americans left. She would stay; if her husband came back from the Russian front, he would come here, but Winfried must go, and quickly. She packed him some food, and tucked a letter that had come for Aimée into his pocket, saying, "In case you should see her somewhere along the way."

Winfried's way west was not easy. The Russians had sealed the border with the British and American sectors, and again he went through woods and fields to avoid them. Seeing a man approach on one deserted woodland path, he nearly dove into the undergrowth, but the fellow grinned, and shouted, "I see you made it!" Reaching Hamburg among the tide of postwar flotsam—soldiers, refugees, children looking for parents, parents looking for children, husbands and wives lost to each other—he heard Christian call his name.

Aimée was determined to find the Americans, where her passport might do them some good. But where were they? Celle, Hannover, a ruined Hildesheim, and on toward Kassel. Below and the boys went ahead on bicycles to reconnoiter, hoping for reliable information. As the women and children moved south, the hills got steeper, and harder on the horses. Marushka was always steady, firm, and true. Celeste in harness was a picture of responsibility, always pulling just a fraction ahead of the others, as if she knew exactly how important it was to make the ultimate effort. In spite of the frequent skids, especially on the slippery, cobbled roads that made them uncertain and nervous, they put their all into the effort.

The steep uphill pulls were hard, but the downhill could be even more demanding. As they came down one steep hill near Kassel, the brakes gave out. The horses strained to keep the wagon from pushing them forward, but its weight was too great. Tall firs rose from a deep ravine at the roadside. Any farther, and horses and wagon would go over and be crushed among the trees. Frantically, the women and girls rushed to gather sticks, rocks, anything to stop the relentless roll of the wagon wheels, but the grade was too steep, the weight too great, the horses exhausted.

Grinding up the road toward them, an American jeep came to a screeching stop. Three large black GIs leapt out and, without a word, put their shoulders to the wagon. As it slowed, Lo, Helma, and Marta muscled a heavy rock in front of a rear wheel. Wet with sweat, the horses stood trembling. When strong shoulders were put to the wagon again, the front wheels were turned away from the ravine. Disaster had been averted. Reins in hand, Aimée climbed down from the driver's seat, took their saviors' big hands in hers, and thanked them in effusive English. Eyes wide in shock, they broke into astonished grins, mumbled surprised OKs, jumped back into their jeep, and went toiling up the hill, waving.

At the bottom of the hill, she called a halt. Everyone was in a state of nerves. All of them, especially the horses, needed to collect themselves and rest. In retrospect, she was furious with herself. Why hadn't she asked where the nearest American command post was? But after nearly four hundred kilometers, it was clear that they had almost found the Americans. Or rather, the Americans had found them.

The bright days on the road in the first flush of summer had been beautiful. Except for the awareness that every kilometer was taking them farther from home, they could almost forget the homelessness and the great unknown ahead. Up in the haylofts, it was still warm, but now yellow shocks of wheat already marched across the fields in neat rows. Nights were getting cooler, and in the mornings as they broke up for their journey, a slight, autumnal mist hung over the meadows. Usually two of them bicycled ahead to scout for quarters while everyone else collected the fallen fruit from roadside orchards that Marta, their constant miracle—always doing, always cheerful and steady—turned into quantities of applesauce.

With winter coming, the pretty Hessian village of Grosseelheim seemed a good place to settle. The rich landscape of hills and orderly fields dotted with tidy villages, each with a church tower visible from miles away, looked like illustrations from a book of fairy tales. It was in the American sector. That might make contacting the American family easier, and it was near Marburg, where she had been so happy—really not very long ago. Grosseelheim's mayor would find them refugee accommodations.

August 8, 1945, was their last day in the bright, picturesque wagon with its lovely rose and green carpet roof, pots and pans banging at the rear, and surrounded by children. Roadside apple and pear trees were shaken one more time, pockets stuffed with fruit. During the months when nothing else belonged to them, the road had been theirs—a close companion, a way into the future. After the first hectic days, when they had no control over anything else, they began to feel like rulers of the road. The wagon was home, the horses their unwavering helpmeets. The constant moving had offered at least the possibility that they were moving toward something, of better things to come. Now an enormous sadness hung over their little caravan. They were settling somewhere that was not home, and the prospect of settling, even temporarily, had a terrible finality. It felt like a betrayal, a final good-bye to Blumenhagen and everything it represented.

She and Her Kind

The weeks of nearly unrelieved anxiety had deadened everyone's nerves, though now that the rush and the fear were over, there was no exuberance or relief, only letdown. Still, the American in command at Marburg would help put Aimée in touch with Uncle Bill. She said a private prayer of thanks to the friendly officer who had made sure her letter got to him. Several miracles later, Winfried had brought Uncle Bill's anxious reply. She must get word to reassure him. American headquarters were up in the castle.

Up the familiar steep hill she went to explain her mission. The commandant's secretary was sympathetic, but emerged from his office a few minutes later looking pained. "He won't talk to you," he said. The commandant had instructed him, "Tell this woman that she and her kind are worse than the Nazis."

As she retreated she tried to make sense of this. Who were "she and her kind"? Traitors, nobility, Prussian militarists, what? She was furious with him; he had not even had the courage to tell her himself, but she was even more furious with herself. She should have marched into his office to demand what he meant. Face-to-face, he might well have backed off. Why had she not mustered her forces? Well, that was another day's battle. But her old friend Daisy, with whom she had stayed so happily during her engagement, was still living nearby. Daisy was balm to her heavy heart, and put her in touch with a young American who was headed home and promised to contact Uncle Bill.

Their new life of "permanence" began in Grosseelheim—Great Soul's Home. Saint Boniface had brought Christianity here in the eighth century, saying that here his soul had found its home, and named the place accordingly. The village itself was a giant step back in time, not as far as the eighth century, but at least a century or two, with charming half-timbered houses straight out of stories by the Brothers Grimm. The local peasants even claimed that the nearby forest was where Little Red Riding Hood had met her wolf.

The burgomaster assigned them to different places, wherever there was room to spare. Aimée, Helma, Marta, and Sigrid were housed with the Loebers, one of several well-to-do farmers in the village by the same name. They were allotted a tiny bedroom and one larger room that served as kitchen and living/dining room, where everyone congregated for meals and activities; it sometimes served as sleeping quarters for Marta too. Lo, Brigitte, and Dorothée were across the street, the boys all at a third house, farther along.

The Loebers' farm was typical: House, barns, and outbuildings, built of stone and timbers, formed a contiguous rectangle around a cobbled, raked courtyard centered on a large, meticulously constructed manure pile. Access was only through a large archway, closed at night with an iron gate, like a medieval fortress. Water came from a pump by the horse trough in the yard. Their quarters were tight, crowded with things and people, and surrounded by animals. Emptying a pail meant walking some sixty paces across the slippery court and its manure pile. Reaching the unspeakable outhouse entailed either skidding through a stall with twenty-five hissing and honking geese or feeling one's way past five calves in total darkness at night. The trek had provided practice in primitive living, but this was a shock.

The village women's traditional costume demanded that their long hair be combed and braided into a knot on top of their heads and encased in a small pillbox—black for married women, red for unmarried girls—with wide satin ribbons tied under the chin to hold it in place. With multiple petticoats swaying majestically, the women made their way to a big communal Hansel-and-Gretel oven with a long board of unbaked loaves stabilized on their heads by a doughnut-shaped pillow fitted over their topknots. Spinning and weaving were still practiced. On Saturday evenings, unmarried girls carried spinning wheels in the street to announce that they and their traditional talents were available.

A few kilometers down the road lay smaller, Catholic Kleinseelheim, where the colored bands on women's skirts were of different widths and colors than those in Protestant Grosseelheim, and the women's long, braided hair was wrapped around the back of the head. In Grosseelheim, a Kleinseelheim woman was gawked at as an alien creature. Naturally, Aimée and all the family were aliens too. The kidney-shaped metal bowls Helma had brought along for a future medical practice were now an essential part of each child's survival kit. When they went to the Loebers' house for meals, bowls in hand, the villagers watching them were convinced that the bowls were solid silver. It stood to reason with such grand, titled people.

Using the horses and wagon to haul loads for local people, the enterprising Below soon had a small-scale business going. The boys all helped, and it brought in much-needed money. But the horses covered many miles every day, and their fodder was hard to come by. When the Regional Council allowed fodder for only three of them, there was no choice but to sell one. The parting with Kitty was one more loss: another faithful companion, another bit of the old life, gone.

When Aimée's message reached Uncle Bill, he had immediately contacted her paternal uncle, John Ellis, whose son in-law Ran was stationed in Germany and might help. John replied:

> The situation should be handled with kid gloves. I would not suggest that Ran Beardsley step in, in any way. I have asked Liddy [his daughter] to write him, mentioning receipt of [Aimée's] message and her address. The Red Cross is taking messages to and from, and I am told that similar situations are legion.
>
> Word from the State Department through two different sources in substance advises "There is nothing that can be done." To follow any plans such as Corson suggests might be construed as interfering with military and civil commissions and should not be thought of.

He CC'd Aimée's brother, Corson, and his daughter Elizabeth (Liddy), adding:

Dear Liddy: When you write Ran, tell him we have a message from Aimée which is supposed to read as follows, more or less: "Try to get in touch with us care of Frau Ebba von Kursell (Heinrich's sister), Bendeleben, Sondershausen, Thuringia. Pray for us. We are in trouble. Love, Aimée."

You better recommend to him he handle the matter very, very carefully.

Affectionately your
Father

Ran was stationed near Wiesbaden and well aware of what German civilians were up against. He decided to find Aimée in spite of his father-in-law's warnings, and one Sunday afternoon in late August, a U.S Army car with driver pulled up in the Loebers' courtyard. Soon Ran wrote Uncle Bill:

Dear Grandfather,

I saw Aimee [sic] today. Here is the story. Aimee's former home is in the zone now occupied by the Russians. In spite of that, I thought I might be able to get some information, so I set the wheels in motion. Then your letter came mentioning Frau von Pritzelurz [sic] in a village near Marburg, who might know of Aimee's whereabouts. I lined up Capt. Hahn, a friend who speaks very good German, a car, a driver, Hahn's secretary, a young lady called Carey, and off we went.

In a small village, everyone we asked knew her. She was having lunch outdoors with friends, spoke very good English and was overjoyed when I told her of my mission. She told me Aimee and her children were nearby, in Grosseelheim.

Off we went. Grosseelheim is one of the most delightful little places I have seen. There were chickens, geese, much farm life. We went to the house where we were told she lived and knocked. A young woman answered and went to tell Aimee. When she came out, Capt. Hahn led off in German, but before he finished, I went to her, put my hand out and said, "Aimee." I will never forget that moment. She looked at me, as if to say "Who in the world are you?" When I told her I was Liddy's husband, she grabbed my hand in both hers. "Now," she said, "just as all hope seemed gone." It is something I will never forget.

She told me the story of her trip from Blumenhagen, one step ahead of the oncoming Russians. I took notes so that I could tell you in detail in my next letter. We are going again next weekend with a jeep and a trailer full of stuff: peanut butter, flour, sugar, coffee, cigarettes, canned goods, candy, etc. We'll take sleeping bags and spend the night. We will have more time, and I will go to the military in Marburg to alert them about her, so she can get in touch with me.

You can rest easy about them. It is pretty rugged, but they have a roof over their head and as long as I am here I will supplement what they have. I have plans for helping them further but that will have to be worked out.

Then we went to see the children. Little Brigitta [sic] is a perfect dear. Friedrich is taller than I am, and when Michael was introduced, he drew himself up, clicked his heels and bowed over my hand. Michael is the spitting image of Liddy.

Aimee and Brigitta got in the car and we drove to where Sigrid, Christian and Dorothy were playing near an abandoned American tank. What excitement! Brigitta called to the others, and when Aimee told them who I was, they let out a shout and jumped up and down all around us. What lovely children they are! I look forward to this weekend when I can play with them. I filled my bag last Sunday with two weeks' ration of candy and gave it to them. They thought it was wonderful. They had had no sweets for a long time. Wait till they see what's coming this weekend.

Capt. Hahn and Miss Carey also plan to take stuff up. They are as interested as I am, and had a great time. I had pictures of my children and Aimee enjoyed them no end. She asked all about you and the family. It did her heart good to hear about you all. You will want to write Aimee. I suggest you send letters to me and I will see that she gets them. There is no way for you to write directly.

I feel that whatever I can do to help them is for the good of my country. Those children will not feel so badly towards America, and that should do some good when they grow up and take a place in the Germany of the future, as they undoubtedly will someday.

Ran had an open, friendly, very American way about him, and he brought miracles: Zagnut bars, condensed milk, other food, and soap—heaven! The children were transported, the women deeply grateful. He brought alternatives to the one familiar staple of their diet: *Schiebewurst*—pushing sausage—a tiny sliver of sausage, pushed along with the upper teeth to impart as much flavor as possible to the bread beneath before being consumed. In early September, he wrote again.

Saturday afternoon, Capt. Hahn, Miss Carey and I headed for Aimee's again. We took sleeping bags, and a box containing 40 candy bars, 10 lbs sugar, 10 lbs coffee, cigarettes, toothbrushes, toothpaste, candles, 25 lbs of peanut butter, and lard.

We were welcomed with open arms. Aimee and the girls were at home, the boys were out working, Michael and Friedrich getting the wagon ready for a long trip to Kassel to bring a load of furniture back to Marburg. This wagon is their main source of income and they are kept pretty busy. Christian was working in the fields for a farmer.

Opening the box was like Christmas. While Aimee and I talked, Capt. Hahn and Miss Carey went to see what they could add to the larder. Aimee is very limited in the amount of meat she can buy and eggs and milk are rationed. Capt. Hahn came back with 5 lbs of pork, 5 lbs of veal and some roast beef. He also has his musket bag filled with eggs. Then Christian came running, all out of breath, to greet me. He had seen the car outside on his way home.

There was great to-do between Aimee and her maid, Martha [sic], about what to have for supper. Then we went for a walk into the country to see the sun set. When we got back we moved the table into the center of the room. Two long benches on either side, and a chair at each end, was room for the 12 of us.

After dinner we talked and played with the children. My German got better by leaps and bounds. Soon it was "Uncle Ran" all the time, and I sat with a child on each knee, sometimes changing children, but my knees were always full. I tell you, I had the time of my life. Little Sigrid was very shy at first and would not even smile at me. But before long, she was coming up to me saying "Uncle Ran" this, and "Uncle Ran" that. I don't know which one of them I like best, they are all so nice. Perhaps Brigitta, who first won my heart, and her sidekick, that great working man, Christian. The energy that boy has, and the spirit with which he talks, are really something.

Soon we decided to hit the hay, and that is no fooling, because we had decided to sleep in the hayloft of the barn across from their house. We could have had just about any bed in the village, and Aimee's landlady tried to persuade us to take the best room. But we had counted on sleeping in the hayloft, and were looking forward to it.

With Christian and Friedrich helping carry our stuff, we climbed up the ladder to the loft, and we were soon fast asleep. I woke up at four-thirty. The moon was streaming in on me, and the first rooster sounded off somewhere in the village. He was answered by another, and they kept at it for a while. At about five the church bell rang. A few more animals woke up and I dozed off again. At seven I got up and climbed down the ladder and to the pump out in the courtyard. A drenching under the pump put me in a good frame of mind. The farmer's wife came out with a mirror, which was a help shaving.

I am going back up there to see them again soon. What more I can do to help them I don't know. Of course, Aimee would like to know what has happened to her home and whether there is any chance of their getting back. I do not know what I can do, but I am working on it. Maybe I can get permission from the Russians to take her back for a look. She does not want to come back to America, and frankly, I think they would have a tough time if they were transplanted to the States. Whatever I can do to make life a little easier for them I will do while I am here. When I leave I will try to fix it so that we will be able to communicate with her.

Ran did everyone's heart good, entertaining the children with silly tricks and a gift for making spectacular faces. His recitation of Heine's familiar "Lorelei" in hopeless German had everyone helpless with laughter. And the food! With his sugar and Captain Hahn's eggs, everyone had *goggl moggl*—a Russian treat from Heinrich's childhood: egg yolks beaten with sugar and vanilla, then blended with the whipped egg whites for a frothy delight. The huge, army-drab tin of peanut butter was a peculiar novelty for everyone except Aimée, but it emptied quickly to find a new role as a latrine, a welcome respite from the dreadful outhouse. As welcome as the food was, it revived Aimée's anxieties about the family in the east, for whom there would be no rich Americans bearing gifts.

Marta was noticeably pregnant by this time and Aimée insisted that Below marry her. Friedrich, always handy and inventive, was given the task of creating rings out of what was available: thick copper wire. They were married in the local minister's living room, with the whole family in attendance. When the baby came, it would have its father's name.

Marta gave birth to a boy in November, one of only two women out of the forty in the maternity ward with a husband. Little Erich was baptized at a ceremony in the village church, with the entire congregation in attendance and Aimée standing as godmother. At the Loebers' for a little celebration, the new life soon added a lusty cry to the already crowded quarters.

The Loebers, so solicitous of American soldiers, seemed bent on devising new ways to make the family's life difficult and to extract more money from them. If Aimée turned to the burgomaster for help, he might bring the police, which only raised the level of argument, making the rough spots rougher. The primitive conditions, the lack of privacy, the endless demands, the unknown future, made her long for a place where they could all be together, not beholden to others. Life felt like an exhausting round of mundane detail, floating over an ocean of dread. At least the children were in school—the oldest boys with a private tutor, living in the village with his wife and children while he pursued his studies at Marburg. The five older children had music lessons, but Christian,

Brigitte, and Dorothée were tasting Heinrich's bitterness of exile at the local school; they were singled out as strangers, called names, and even had stones thrown at them. Aimée could not let that go on.

It took time for Grosseelheim's peasants to realize that they had a wonderfully capable and sympathetic doctor in their midst, but then word spread quickly. Helma's practice blossomed. She was completely changed—grateful and happy to be doing real, useful work again. Her patients paid with potatoes or milk, improving everyone's diet and spirits, but without a permit from American authorities, she could not continue to treat anyone. They had to find a place with better schools, where Helma could practice, where they could all be together.

There was little hope of a return to Blumenhagen in the foreseeable future, and the more distant future looked no more certain than it had months ago. But Aimée needed to know if they could ever go home. She and Helma would go to reconnoiter, and perhaps learn something more specific than the usual vague rumors. She had given Friedrich Heinrich's watch, but in early October she asked for it back. She was going to Blumenhagen to see what could be salvaged; Russians were partial to watches, and it might be useful.

They actually managed to get across the border, arriving at Blumenhagen's farmworkers' village in a driving rain. The small red Chinese lacquer table she had bought in Paris stood in front of one of the houses, covered with potato peels. She knocked; the door opened. The woman who had insisted on joining their trek and later abandoned it to return home stood shamefaced, twisting her apron in wet hands. *"Ach, Frau Baronin . . ."*

At the house, French doors to the terrace and garden had been ripped out of their frames; everything was open to the elements. Door handles were gone, books strewn across the ransacked library's floor. Broken glass and china, willfully, randomly destroyed, were everywhere. A photo album open to a picture of a radiant three-year-old Michael lay on the floor, his smile marred by the print of a muddy boot. She later heard that her grand piano, its legs cut off, had been taken to the neighboring estate. How and why? The garden was a wilderness. Everything buried or hidden had been dug up, even the silver. She was glad she had taken some when they left.

Gersdorff, the hospital director, told her that many local people had committed suicide. The food situation was desperate. From May through October, they had had only fifty grams of butter, and the quarter-liter ration of milk for infants under six months had been cut in half. Bread was available occasionally, but there was no meat at all. He estimated that 70 percent of Neustrelitz's population would die of typhus that winter. Friedrich's English teacher told her that he went out every night to steal carrots or potatoes. She had done the right thing, she decided. They had lost a great deal, but there was no comparison.

At party headquarters, she found Herr Koloff, whose years spent in a Nazi concentration camp as a Communist had brought him his new position as regional party boss. After minimal pleasantries, she suggested that if they were allowed to come back, they could run Blumenhagen to feed the community and the Neustrelitz hospital where Helma had worked for so long. Koloff would have none of it. She should disappear, he said, and quickly. If she came back, he would throw her in jail.

He had not changed, she decided; he was exactly the same impractical dreamer and ideologue he had always been. She left, wondering what had become of his little daughter, Lene, a sometime participant in family theater performances, whose photo smiled shyly from their family album.

In Grosseelheim, the family clamored for news. Only Pucki was unaffected by the sad reports of home, lifting her spirits with an excited welcome. Pucki had been with them through it all, embracing everything in the spirit of adventure. They should all take a lesson from her boundless cheer.

The twelve-year-old Loeber boy was very taken with Pucki and began taking her on long walks. Aimée asked him not to. The children were very attached to Pucki; they all were, and if she was lost or anything happened to her, they would be devastated. But the boy took her out anyway. One day that fall, running joyously through the woods, Pucki was shot by American soldiers.

Aimée protested to Herr Loeber: His son should at least apologize. She had lost so much already, he said: her husband, her farm, her land.

Why was she making such a fuss over a dog? His attitude was typical of the village's well-to-do farmers, who found their situation incomprehensible. Land was everything. They had left their land, the only thing that mattered; what sense was there in mourning a little dog? Utterly unmoved, Loeber kept his boy out of sight.

They had encountered much kindness and generosity on the trek, often from poor, hard-pressed people. Yet in this prosperous village, compassion was stubbornly refused and the death of their beloved companion met neither regret nor apology. She could tell herself that in the scheme of things, the loss was small. But in the current scheme of things, holding on to anything dear was so hard that the loss felt enormous.

The children searched out a burial site in a nearby meadow and held a solemn service under an autumnal sky. Loeber complained immediately. The dog was buried on his land. It would contaminate his field, make his cows sick, and bring endless bad luck. They would have to bury it somewhere else. The next day, Michael, Christian, and Lo dug up the small body matted with blood and found a spot in an isolated little hollow. When the family gathered again, Michael took particular pains to arrange a dignified burial, hiding his devastation behind ceremony and big words.

Helma and Aimée were soon on the road again, looking for a practice for Helma, often gone for a week or ten days at a time. They traveled on foot or on trains packed with desperate, emaciated people, part of a miserable human tide. Germany was awash with the displaced: refugees from Poland, the Ukraine, the Baltic, and from all over the country, particularly the east. The wretched of the earth, filthy and traumatized, clung like limpets to the tops and sides of hopelessly overcrowded trains and huddled in bombed-out railroad stations. Locating one old friend in Berlin, Aimée discovered that Margarethe was there too. By some miracle, they had found each other and collapsed, speechless, into each other's arms.

Nights they spent in railroad stations or bunkers, all crammed with itinerants and refugees like themselves—a slack, grimy crowd. Pale children slept on the laps and shoulders of worn, drab parents who looked beyond exhaustion. Occasionally an extraordinary sight interrupted this sad, colorless mass: a Ukrainian peasant woman sitting on her outspread skirts, surrounded by a gaggle of geese tucked into baskets and a flock of flaxen-haired children; a tall, painfully thin Russian Orthodox priest in black, with a tall black hat; or a whole family of Russian peasants, women with white scarves and swarms of children, usually barefoot.

Traveling by freight car, since that was often what was available, Aimée struck up a conversation with a young man on the floor next to her. Up for release from an American POW camp, he was asked his name—von Arnim. The presiding officer refused to release him; a German general had the same name. A few weeks later, a different officer stamped his release papers with a smile, asking, "Wasn't there a poet named von Arnim?" Life, he concluded, was a matter of pure chance.

Rummaging for a pencil one evening, she found a note tucked into a small compartment of her bag. It was from the countess they had met at the Hamburg ferry, asking a friend who lived on their projected route south to give them shelter. She remembered that they had missed the turnoff somehow and never got there. The note ended by saying that although Hitler was dead, "his spirit is still in us and around us." She stared, stunned. It was like a vestige of some remote past, a hieroglyph extolling a forgotten pharaoh.

Ran came for a last visit before going back to the States. He had bad news: Uncle Bill had died. It felt like a body blow. Uncle Bill—her comfort in childhood, a constant, loving presence on the other side of the Atlantic, her hope for love and support in the future. His energy and irrepressible spirit had given her strength in dark times. She longed for his warmth and kindness, his strong embrace, his direct and thoughtful advice, and he was gone. Ran was still talking. To force herself to listen to what he was saying, she turned to face him, desolate. He stopped and leaned over to give her a quick hug—stiff and clearly uncomfortable. She was touched. He knew what this meant to her; he was trying to help.

Frantically, her mind began to riffle through possible alternatives for help, if not comfort. There was Anita. She was there, even if resources were limited. And maybe Corson's wife, Roberta, would help. When

Corson and Roberta announced their engagement, she had given Corson their mother's most extravagant ring—a glowing emerald surrounded by diamonds. Roberta had always seemed kindly disposed, and Montgomery Ward had given them deep pockets. Maybe Roberta would help.

Exhausted, feeling utterly low, she collapsed with a flu. Flattened on the mattress in the tiny bedroom, she felt beaten. Everything seemed hopeless. When Hitler had declared war on the United States, dread of just such a situation had been part of her decision to stay in Germany. But Blumenhagen had still been there then; her pride had still been intact. There had not been the homelessness, the lack of ground under her feet, the pennilessness. If she returned now, she would be poor, tail between her legs, dependent on family charity. From Ran's tone, she knew that her uncle John had been reluctant to make any effort on her behalf. From him, she would be on the receiving end of a good deal of smug, I-told-you-so disapproval.

The season turned. Fields were bare, barns were full, days were short. Suddenly it was winter. The thought of Christmas, a holiday she had come to love, filled Aimée with dread, and the obvious lack of resources was the least of it. More important was her lack of spirit and emotional stamina, a harder gap to fill. She felt their absence almost as a physical pain. Christmas would be quiet that year.

Lo took the children out to find a tree in Red Riding Hood's forest. It would be decorated with the angel and stars Aimée had brought from Blumenhagen. They would take little room in the wagon, she had thought, but provide continuity for the children, for all of them. All her hopes for future Christmases had gone into molding the angel's waxen face, pleating the heavy, silver-blue paper of the skirt, never imagining their present circumstances. Though the angel made the small tree in their "living kitchen" look even smaller, she was as radiant and serene as ever. For presents, Aimée brought out what she had rescued from the detritus at Blumenhagen: a few precious books and one of Dorothée's beloved dolls. A poor family from the village brought them some sausage and tidbits from a pig they had slaughtered, reminding her again that it was always the poor who understood, who shared what they could.

Within a week, she was feeling much better. On the afternoon of New Year's Eve, they all went for a long walk through the countryside, beautiful, if not at all like their expansive, open Blumenhagen landscape. Their celebration started with waffles and real tea—a rare treat. Aimée read aloud from a delightful book she had brought back from Blumenhagen— Waldemar Bonfels's account of his childhood days that made them all laugh as they hadn't laughed in a long time. At eleven o'clock, the two little ones went to bed and everyone else awaited the arrival of the New Year with a little fruit wine and a New Year's wish. Aimée's was for love and rebuilding. Stepping out under the cold, bright winter stars, they heard the church bells from all the nearby villages ringing in the New Year. Gathered inside by the light of one of Uncle Ran's candles, they sang quietly around the little tree, sharing one unspoken hope: a return home. But no matter what happened, she was determined that the coming year would be better than what had gone before.

On a cold day when the slime in the courtyard seemed even thicker than usual, they were startled to see an American jeep pull in, hesitate, and then stop at the Loebers' door with a squeak of brakes. A boyish GI leapt up the steps and rapped smartly at the door. Frau Loeber emerged, listened for a moment, then pointed in their direction. By the time Aimée came out of their living quarters, everyone had gathered to see what this was all about, the little ones behind her skirts, the older children and adults lurking discreetly.

He didn't look threatening—not a day over eighteen. His crew cut made him look unspeakably young, almost naked, like a newborn. It occurred to her that his head must be very cold. Small blue eyes shone under pale circumflex brows. Still, he represented the American military; maybe something was wrong.

"Hi!" The shining pink face exuded health and enthusiasm. "I heard there was a baroness living here." His little speech produced a small, frosty cloud in the cold air.

"Yes," said Aimée, drawing herself together. "What can I do for you?" Calves peered and shuffled in the barn, their smell perfuming the air.

He looked down at his feet for a moment, then reached into the back pocket of his uniform pants for his wallet and pulled out a dollar bill. Would she be willing to autograph it?

"Of course." She was relieved, and suddenly afraid that she might burst out laughing. He was so sweet, the situation so preposterous. A baroness! Was this how he had imagined baronesses, back in the U.S.A.? Life was amazing!

A pen was produced and she signed with as long and impressive a signature as was honestly possible: Baronin Aimée von Hoyningen-Huene. Beneath it, she drew what she hoped would be a smart, satisfying flourish and handed the bill back with a small, ever so slightly imperious smile.

He looked at his dollar, rocked back a bit on his heels, gave a little snort of accomplishment, and grinned. "Gee . . . Thanks!" He turned smartly, jumped back into the jeep where his friend was waiting, and they drove briskly past the manure pile and out of the slippery yard.

The children crowded around. What did the soldier want? Did they have to leave? Why did she have to sign the money? She began to explain, trying to answer their puzzlement in some way that would make sense, but crazy laughter overcame her. Soon they were all laughing with relief, wildly, helplessly, lost in the absurdity of it all.

They had looked everywhere for a position for Helma. It made Aimée nearly dizzy to think of the miles they had traveled on wretched trains and on foot, looking fruitlessly. At Oldenburg, the doctor was ill, there was a desperate need for another, but they had decided on someone else. And so it had gone, all over the map. Then back to Marburg. Then Aimée got sick. Now, suddenly, there was a position in Frankenberg, less than forty kilometers away, where Helma could probably get the necessary American permit. They could leave this place. The next chapter would be better than the last.

A Labyrinth Without an Exit

The move to Frankenberg, a picturesque little hilltop town celebrating its seven hundredth anniversary, was not exactly the "rebuilding" Aimée had hoped for in the New Year, but it was a step forward. An apartment was available on the pretty main street, above Finkelstein's shoe store. Available because of the previous tenant's close Nazi Party ties, the apartment was empty, truly empty. Apart from an enormous wardrobe and a giant hall mirror too big to be moved, there was not a stick of furniture, not a lightbulb, no coal for heat. But there was a stove in the kitchen, a bathroom with a toilet, a washbasin, and—hallelujah—a real tub, cause for rejoicing. The curving street of half-timbered houses ran down the hill to the Eder River valley. When the time came, they could have an allotment garden there—another plus.

Moving was easy—a few shelves, one borrowed armchair, some mattresses and suitcases, most of them never unpacked. Wood, potatoes, and carrots came along too. Below, Marta, Erich, and the horses would stay in Grosseelheim, and Winfried set off to find his own family. They would be a noticeably smaller group, and they would be together. After the low point in Grosseelheim, things were looking up.

While the apartment was turned into living quarters and an office for Helma's hoped-for medical practice, Christian and Brigitte were temporarily put in a nearby children's home with a better school than the one in Grosseelheim, and by late January, they were delighted with the move. Though the cold often kept them huddled by the kitchen stove, the only source of heat, the apartment was pleasant and sunny. The bathtub, that beacon of civilization, sat alluring but coyly unavailable, not connected to any pipes. Considering how they had been living, their disappointment was wildly out of proportion, but the day the pipes were connected was a day of celebration.

Their one big sunny room looked out on the main street, where every day, the town crier's bell signaled a break in the womenfolk's morning housework. With the household's feather beds hung out the windows to air, they sat at their windows, elbows cushioned by down, ready to hear the news, watch the comings and goings in the street below, and gossip. This picturesque spectacle had probably endured for hundreds of years, Aimée realized, a wonderfully reassuring thought. Some things did last.

Christian and Brigitte came back from the children's home, and though the apartment was noisy and crowded, close quarters for nine people and an office, everyone was happy to be under the same roof again. Rumors of a possible Russian withdrawal had kept hope for a return to Blumenhagen alive. They might know more in February. Yet February came and went without resolution, nor did American approval for Helma's practice come from Wiesbaden. They desperately needed whatever food or money Helma's practice could bring in; hunger and tension grew with every passing week. But everything was up in the air and there was nothing anyone could do about it. It was a state of affairs emblematic of the time.

Typically, Helma reacted by stocking her office, determined to be ready when the permit came, while Aimée and Lo struggled to keep the family going. On those dim and hungry winter evenings, *The Three Musketeers* was the most dependable source of relief. When the permit for the medical practice finally came, Helma put an announcement in the newspaper, pasted up notices, and opened her doors. Everyone waited, but patients were few. One day might bring a single patient, another two, then a day with none at all. They would have to wait. Such things take time: patience, patience, patients. At least they had a roof—the same roof—over their heads.

Under that roof, though, everyone suffered from the lack of peace and privacy. As well as his usual flute and recorder, Friedrich had decided to take up the piano. Aimée was delighted that there would be a backup pianist in the family, but it was torment and she prayed that the worst of the beginner-piano assault would soon be over. Still, as cramped as the apartment was, as trapped as everyone felt by close walls and the cold that kept them mostly within those walls, the women kept reminding themselves and each other how lucky they were. Really, she wrote Mary, they ought to be grateful: They were alive, the children were healthy, but

> imagine a small combination living-dining room & nursery, with nine people going in and out, or crawling under tables and chairs, practicing piano or flute, quarreling, playing, etc., etc.

Like many others, they were victims of the housing shortage. Bombing had destroyed millions of living quarters, occupying forces were taking much of what was left, and refugees had nearly doubled the population in the west. The family's sleeping quarters were dormitory-style, most of their things were still in suitcases in the attic, but the few closets were stuffed to bursting, the cluttered rooms in perpetual disorder. Lo took the girls back to Grosseelheim occasionally, not only to alleviate the crowding but to reconnect with Marta, Below, and little Erich. And there were other problems, Aimée wrote Mary.

> You can imagine what conditions are like—no—you can't. No shoes, no stockings, no darning thread, no tubs, no basins, no clothes. No—that's wrong; sometimes there are ten of one article, but you'll never be lucky enough to get one unless you have something to trade or can pull strings. Nor can you move from one place to another. You stay where you are, grateful if you only sleep four to a room. We have walls and a roof, very noisy and squeezed together, but we are thankful. I could write reams, but many things that weigh on my heart would never get by the censor and I haven't the time anyway.
>
> The children are all in school. Friedrich is 6 feet and more, Michael almost as big and growing daily. Brigitte wears my castoffs, though I have nothing to cast off. They grow and grow in spite of slim rations, and are all healthy.

Michael at fifteen was bright and lively, ready to push ahead into life, as Heinrich had been. He was also scatterbrained, starting up at five o'clock, frantically gathering his books, saying, "I almost forgot that I have Greek class at three!" Told it was five, he proclaimed angrily that his watch said two. It was a difficult age; being away might do him and everyone else good. In the tight postwar housing situation, big houses had to be shared; room was found for him with Professor Kommerell's family in Marburg, where he could go to the excellent Gymnasium. The boy thrived, bringing home new friends and a gift for storytelling about the lively Marburg household.

Everyone was thin. Friedrich and Michael each ate for three, and still Michael was at least twenty pounds underweight, and the youngest was looking disturbingly ethereal. Their potatoes, their main food supply, were almost at an end, doubly worrisome as their bread ration had been reduced to two pounds a week—not enough for nine people, growing boys among them. The cheese ration, one eighth of a pound, was, "just enough to sniff at," Aimée wrote Mary. Occasionally she lay down at mealtimes to leave more for others. Twice a month, the two youngest lined up for special ration supplements in front of Frankenberg's turreted town hall. For Dorothée, a lump of gray meat that had surrendered all flavor to someone else's soup long ago was served on a spoon brought from home. The little one brought a tin cup for "cocoa": half a cup of vaguely sweetened watery brown liquid. The supplements were more symbolic than nutritional, but the symbols mattered, suggesting that real meat and real cocoa still existed, somewhere.

Just maintaining stasis was draining and no adrenaline fueled the exhausting daily searches for food, shoes, clothes for the children, a bit of salt or sweet. It almost made Aimée long for the days on the open road, when every day was movement—who knew where, but at least movement. Then, slowly, connections to the United States were reestablished. Even Corson wrote. One wonderful day, the first packages arrived from America, from Aimée's old friend Everest—bless him. Marrying Everest would have meant a different life—a Park Avenue apartment, a horse farm in suburban Bedford Hills, the Metropolitan Opera Club—a *very* different life. But she would not have had the same children, and that was impossible to imagine.

Helma's practice was picking up. Some patients paid with bread, always welcome, no matter how little. Milk was so hard to come by that if a local peasant brought some in payment, they felt fortune's smile. Gradually, more packages—CARE packages, packages from friends and family—got through, each greeted with jubilation. Pudding mix and Cream of Wheat, unimaginable treats, were consumed almost instantly. More food meant that they all had more energy. Aimée was nearly ecstatic when her uncle John sent blankets in response to her plea to use money in her accounts to send help.

Some GIs also began to see that not all Germans were Hitler, that many were decent, hardworking people, worn out, worn down, hungry. Fraternization was forbidden, but thousands of M&M's found their way to the town's eager children. For smokers, though, it was a tough time. Nicotine starved, they chased after army trucks rolling through town to collect *Kippen*—butts—tossed out the back, shredded first, per army regulations. Painstakingly picked from between the cobbles, the bits were hoarded until there was enough to reconstitute them into the semblance of a real smoke. If a softhearted soldier tossed a whole cigarette: heaven. In cities, a mini-industry grew out of collecting carelessly tossed butts. Pooled and re-wrapped, they morphed into currency. Mary's packages sometimes included the real thing, a miracle, since hard currency was denominated in Camels, Chesterfields, and Lucky Strikes.

> The cigarettes are a great life-saver. Yours have meant shoes, butter, eggs and milk. Shoes and food are our greatest worry. The family sends packages now and then, but forget cigarettes' worth. Yours were a godsend; they have financed and fed us, and I still have a heap. You, Everest Haight and Anita are so faithful. Michael is practicing his English, carrying on a lively correspondence with Anita's daughter, Nina, aged 15! The pumps were too high-heeled for me, but I traded them for books on art for the children.

She still needed "new" shoes, but the large-format art books, printed on cheap paper with colored reproductions tipped in, kept the girls content for hours.

Cigarette coupons could buy nearly anything. Aimée commissioned a local woman to produce a beautifully hand-lettered, illustrated "Hansel and Gretel." In their well-lit living room, Frau Richter's tiny scissors flashed through black paper, creating exquisitely detailed silhouette cutouts as if by magic: giant fir trees with tiny birds singing in their branches, clumps of grass, rabbits with puffy white tails, and, of course, a terrifying witch and her oven, all paid for with cigarette coupons.

In their allotted garden patch down by the river, it took time before seeds grew into spinach and peas, but under Lo's careful tending, with help from the girls, carrots and potatoes appeared on the table eventually too. And the garden was theirs, something they could control. That alone was wonderful; the fact that it also helped their diet was almost secondary. Meals were still stretched by every available means, extended with anything available to create the illusion of more.

Letters from America pressed her to return—for the children's sake. Germany was defeated, in ruins, with nothing to offer. Conditions were dreadful and unlikely to improve soon. It was hard to disagree. If there was a future, it was not discernible; the only thing thriving in a hungry, ruined Germany was black humor, like the ditty, sung to the tune of "Deutschland, Deutschland Über Alles," making the rounds.

> *Deutschland, Deutschland ohne Alles,*
> *Ohne Butter, ohne Fett . . .*

> Germany, Germany without everything,
> Without butter, without fat . . .

She worried constantly about Heinrich's family, most of them in the east, and worse off than they were. Several planned trips to Mimama and Papa in Dresden had come to nothing. Then a telegram from Mimama: Papa had died very suddenly. It was high summer but he had been out with his little handcart, gathering wood to ward off the cold he and Mimama dreaded. Preparing for the winter to come, he collapsed and died.

He had died of starvation really, and a broken heart. Margarethe had been with them just days before, and knew how little food they had. There was still a bit of mangel in the garden, but Papa was skeletal, gathering a few remaining cherries to still his hunger. His death, she wrote, made her think of Hugo Wolf's song on Goethe's "Anacreon's Grave": "Spring, Summer, and Fall, the happy poet enjoyed; at last he sheltered from the winter in the hill."

She must get comfort and food to Mimama. The tightly controlled "black border," between the Soviet and western sectors, had been virtually sealed since May 1945. Crossing was against the law, such law as it was, and any trip to the Russian zone was fraught. Lo was hoping to see her sister in the eastern zone too, so they decided to try together, taking Christian. For several weeks, everyone saved as much of their rations as possible to put together a little bundle. Then Aimée, Lo, and Christian set off. At the border, they were picked up immediately by the Americans. Showing them her American passport, Aimée explained that she was trying to get to her starving family in Dresden.

The Americans, "tired of hearing these sob stories," ordered the threesome into a jeep for the drive up a very steep hill to an absurdly romantic old castle, one of many such places being used as garrisons, billets, headquarters, or, in this case, a catchall prison. One large hall housed prostitutes and pickpockets. She and Lo were put into another with women trying to get to husbands, children, or parents on the other side, while Christian was taken off alone to the men's section. He was only thirteen; she worried.

They were held for three days—three days of food, a bed with sheets, hot water, even soap. Had she not been so desperate to move on, it would have been true luxury. But Mimama had lived through revolution, exile, poverty, and hunger. One son was dead; the other had disappeared in Russia. Now Papa was gone too. She had written, describing their diet: Boiled potatoes were peeled, the peels laid out to dry on newspaper in the attic. Cooked up in water, they made what she had called a "nourishing soup." She was obviously starving, and Aimée was afraid she might not see her again. Bringing her food, love, and support was a holy mission. She was frantic, frustrated at being subject to others' priorities.

On the third day, they were pulled out of the prison, a policeman in front, a policeman behind, and marched along the middle of the street to "prevent their escape," though that had never occurred to her. The rigid rules, the painful silence, the sense of helpless captivity, guards front and rear, reminded her of those impossibly long-ago French Walks at Dobbs. As they stood before the judge, he asked what he must have already asked hundreds of others: "Don't you know that crossing the 'black border' is against the law?"

"Yes," she said, "I know."

"Then why did you do it?"

"Because the heart's laws are stronger than other laws." It sounded shamelessly sentimental, but it had a certain ring, and it was true.

The room was very quiet. He seemed to be studying his hand, lying across papers on his desk. He knew that families had been torn apart; people were struggling to be reunited with husbands, children, parents, to get back to the homes they had fled to escape bombs, or Russians, or who knew what.

"Well," he said finally, "if you do try it again, try it somewhere else, or I'll have to put you in prison for three years."

He had shown sympathy. Her throat tightened but there was no time or energy for tears. When they reconnected with Christian, he was putting on a brave face, but it was clear that he had been anxious. They had been on the road for five days, days much like their trek existence, already more than a year ago: one night spent in a rabbit hutch, another in straw next to a chicken coop with an early-bird rooster, and three in jail. Some of the food for Mimama had been eaten along the way, the rest confiscated by the Americans. Their venture was a complete failure. They would have to turn back and try again.

Somehow Aimée managed to acquire a table big enough so that the whole family could eat together. Between meals it provided her the huge luxury of spreading out the letters and papers she seemed always to be working on near the bright geraniums on the windowsill. At meals or when the children had homework, she had to shove it all together and remove it to a corner somewhere, but it was a great improvement. As they were gathered for lunch one Sunday at their grand new table, a giant crash silenced the mealtime chatter. In the hall, the huge mirror lay in glittering shards. Everyone stood for a moment, surveying the wreckage. Seven years' bad luck, she thought; it seemed a skimpy estimate.

The apartment's clutter and close living quarters tested everyone. In the big hall wardrobe hung a dress from America, too small for Dorothée, still too big for Sigrid. But the younger child crept into the wardrobe's stuffy darkness to stroke the dress's miraculous pink velvet in luxurious peace, carving out a bit of privacy for herself there that was utterly unavailable to the adults, and dream.

Dislocation is a dependable suspect in childhood trauma. The lack of predictability and a fixed point affected everyone, but for the youngest, the confusion of itinerant life obscured a great deal. She was little; she lived in the moment, where whatever was happening quickly became the norm. She had no father, but she had not lost one. She was coddled and clucked over, not only by her mother, but also by Lo and Helma, two remarkable women with little hope of children of their own. Buried trauma or no, she seemed to experience little of the durable pain that hung over her older siblings and the adults.

Reaching Mimama involved repeatedly hiding from Russian soldiers; on one train they hid in the engineer's coal box. When she succeeded at last, Aimée found Mimama apparently as serene as always, yet with one worry nagging at her: How could she maintain the graves of her beloved dead? Papa she could manage, but her father and grandfather, buried in the family crypt at Salisburg? She had always brought them roses from Ottenhof. Who would do that now? And Heinrich? Did Georg have a grave at all? This new, recurrent fretfulness upset Aimée, but she could find no honest way to ease it.

She brought out pictures of the children, talked about their very different characters and what they were all doing. Mimama listened, asked questions, but soon came back to her father. Before the railroad, she said, he often traveled the 150 versts from Saint Petersburg to Georgievsk on the Narva road, by calèche in summer, in winter by an enclosed *kibitka*, on runners. In stormy weather, the peasant from whom he sometimes leased horses at Kipenyi used to say, *"Segodnja metelj, werno Graf jed-et!"*—"Snowstorm today, the count is sure to come!" She fell silent, then brightened. She had often traveled this way with her Tante Olga, thirty or forty versts between the Sievers estates, gliding through the snowy whiteness, the *kibitka* a nest of furs and warmth, the Valdai bells jingling with the horses' quick step.

For thirty-eight years, her father was marshal of the nobility, the elected head of a provincial elite that played a significant role in prerevolutionary, rural Russia. As such, he was chairman of the local school board, had power over justices of the peace, and administered the military draft. Being recruited was considered a great misfortune; bribery was common, and the rich routinely tried to buy their sons' freedom. But her father's evenhandedness was well-known. One October, a poor Jewish boy reported to Yamburg, asking anxiously whether the count would be there at the draft. *"Nu, togda ja spokojen!"*—"Then I can rest easy!" he said with a sigh, on hearing that he would.

Memories were taking Mimama away. She was speaking more and more Russian. Her father had been a lieutenant in the Crimean War, she said. She, her brother Georges, and her father's beloved Dimenty Zacharievitch had nursed him in his last weeks. When he died, everyone came, peasants from all the villages for whom he had built a school. As his coffin was brought to Yamburg, hundreds lined the roads, as if a crowned head were being buried, all of Narva, Orthodox priests and pastors walking behind. As it was put on a railroad car decorated with fir boughs for the trip to Ottenhof, it began to rain. People said, *"Grafu jehatje—vot I pagoda!"*—"The count must travel; it is the weather for it."

Mimama could still see Ottenhof's peasant community in their gray, handwoven smocks, singing Lettish funeral hymns in the July heat. After her father was laid to rest, a deafening thunderclap shattered the quiet. Then came the downpour. Mimama looked off into the past. "The count must travel," she said quietly. After a long silence, she said that Papa should have been buried there too, and she could join them. But who would tend her father's grave now?

Aimée realized that she was losing Mimama. If the past offered relief from the desolate present, it was a blessing, but her anxious refrain about untended graves made Aimée sad. It was her one plaint, and she could do nothing about it.

Safely back in the west, she bowed to family pressures and made a stop at the American consulate in Frankfurt on the way home. She should at least find out what was involved if she decided to go back to the States.

As she wrote Mary in October 1946:

> Since I started this letter, I've been to Dresden and back (two weeks on the road). Now for four days, the whole family has been gathering beechnuts in beautiful October sunshine, walking 2 hours to get to the big beeches. For 14 pounds of beechnuts, we get one quart of oil. We've gathered 35 pounds!
>
> I've said nothing of all the things that lie deepest, but I try to think of them as little as possible. It's a good thing one works oneself into unconsciousness.

Helma's practice was doing well now. Miraculously, a patient gave her an orange in time for Sigrid's fifth birthday in November, and everyone at the big table got an orange section. Packages had come from America too, so it was a real celebration. Things were getting better; they would survive.

Lo was resourceful, endlessly helpful, good company, and wonderful with the children. She took up the family's long tradition of amateur theatricals with grace and enthusiasm, writing and directing plays for the children to perform for special occasions, and went to great trouble to search out the perfect backdrop for these productions. With a gift for words and her powers of observation, she wrote sensitive poetry and marvelous letters full of telling detail. Aimée worried that her boundless willingness to pitch in meant that she would disappear into the never-ending needs of this family, now hers by default. Lo should not be swallowed whole by their situation; she must find an outlet for her talents.

The Marburg exchange market was where people went to trade

whatever they had for what they didn't. Some prowled nervously around its peculiar juxtaposition of shoddy junk—old coffee grinders and worn shoes—set out next to a once-glowing Persian rug, well past its prime but still beautiful. Circling to see what was on offer, some kept their own goods under wraps, hoping delay might heighten their appeal or lessen their shabbiness. In the end, volumes of poetry might trade for half a pound of flour, a bicycle pump for barley, a coffeepot for powdered eggs.

Apart from Heinrich's old coat, Aimée had little enough to trade, but she was overjoyed to find a familiar face. Anton Kippenberg, director of the Insel Verlag publishing company and a link to the past, emerged from the ashes. His Leipzig press had been bombed out, and he had relocated to Wiesbaden. After they had caught up with each other's lives, she asked about finding a publisher for some of Lo's poems and children's stories. She should wait, he said. Publishers were either bombed out and shell-shocked or trying to regroup, and they would be wary of taking on a newcomer. Disappointed but not surprised, she traded Heinrich's coat for a suitcase full of his books—a treasure trove.

Her letters to Mary from this time are all stamped with an emphatic OPENED BY MILITARY CENSOR—CIVIL MAILS, but she wrote:

> Parcels from the U.S. come through in good order, so send the clothes! I would be so thankful. The struggle for everything takes so much strength and time. One tries to keep the children from looking shabby and threadbare, though it's not easy. Our things are already old and much worn.

Behind the barbed wire of a military installation, she had seen a small mountain of blue French officers' coats. Weeks went by, and every time she passed, rain or shine, there they were, the pile settling slowly under the effects of weather. They ought to be doing some good, she thought. Remade, they could keep her children warm. Her quick, nimble Christian found a way through the fence and liberated two coats. Refashioned into coats for the girls, they were warm, and not at all shabby—even stylish.

Apologetically, she asked if Mary could send

> one thing for each child that I can't possibly get here for Christmas? For Brigitte and Dorothée, a ball and crayons; for Michael, a pocketknife, for Friedrich, sheet music for his flute—Handel, Bach or Telemann—and for the whole family, a box of marshmallows!
>
> One great wish is for something to keep our youngest busy through the long winter, things to cut out or paste, coloring books, children's cards or dominoes. She's a bright child, damned at the moment to live in a cage, for she has nowhere to play. I seldom have time for her, and I always hope to make a coloring book myself, but I'll never manage it.
>
> Pulled up by the roots, the children are as dazed and homeless as the grown-ups, and every gesture of help and kindness means hope and strength. To them the U.S. is a celestial state, flowing with milk and honey.

Helma's practice had grown enormously; every day, forty or so patients trooped through the apartment to her office, and more came in the evening. She was thorough and caring, the work rewarding, and the money and food it brought was a great help. But she was working too hard and she was exhausted. Then she was diagnosed with a brain tumor.

It seemed the final blow. Or maybe it was just the beginning of the seven years' bad luck the shattered mirror portended. Aimée wanted to be calm and strong, a steady center, but conflict over her ties to Germany, a possible return to America, and now Helma's illness made it hard to maintain even the illusion of calm and strength. At the family's Sunday service on New Year's Day, she spoke about the need to put love before all else and to put every word and deed to work for the best every day.

Leaving the children with Lo, she and Helma went to see a specialist in the Ruhr; for nine weeks she shepherded Helma through tests, surgery, and initial recovery, as she wrote to Mary:

Two days before Christmas my friend Helma Kahnert learned that she had a brain tumor. She was operated on January 23. That's why you haven't heard from me for so long. Everything went well, but it's a hideous operation and it cost us a good deal of our leftover strength and nerve. I'll probably stay 3 more weeks, until my friend can be moved, then bring her to Stuttgart. Then I must go to Frankfurt, and then I'll be getting "home" and will write you a real letter. Here I am day and night nurse and manage the correspondence for both of us. The devil's always loose near us; it seems to be my fate.

In the meantime a package of yours has come. Bless you for your good heart and know how grateful we are for your love. The children are bursting with expectation but we'll celebrate Christmas again when I get back. I'll write you all about it. I always knew you were a decent fellow!

25 February: My dear, you wait daily for a word from me and weeks go by with no sign of life—and that after you've packed half your heart into your packages. But everything conspires against me. My friend went through this fearful operation, and since then I've put all other duties behind me. Brigitte, Dorothée and Friedrich all had birthdays, and I wasn't there for any of them. As soon as I get back we'll have an after-celebration with all your loving gifts. Then you'll get a detailed report.

My friend is still very weak and ill. She can neither read nor write. To leave her alone with her thoughts and her helplessness is more than I can manage. She makes progress so very slowly, but I must go back to the children.

They have no school because of the fuel shortage—a problem for us all. The only blessing is the snow, which keeps them happy outdoors. Then they come back so hungry and our potatoes are almost at an end. Still, we're so lucky with our "care" packages and good shoes and many loving, helping hands. But Helma's illness is a great blow. Her patients brought us bread and milk, and the costs of hospital, sanitarium and convalescence are going to be hard on the bank. But this crazy life has one thing to be said for it: one has so much to worry about that one ceases to worry at all.

On her way home, Aimée stopped at the American consulate in Frankfurt again. They were emphatic. If she was not repatriated within six months, she would lose her American citizenship, and with it, all rights to her American monies. They also reminded her that only the two youngest could go with her.

Sitting in the agonizingly slow train, she had time to consider her problems. She was torn between the dim hope of a return to Blumenhagen, commitment to Heinrich's family, and a future for the children. Yet she had no energy for much feeling. Papa was dead; reaching Mimama was hell. Georg was either dead or in a Russian prison camp. Margarethe and Ebba were in the Soviet sector. Everyone on both sides of the Atlantic was telling her that Germany was in terrible straits, its future obscured by rubble. She should leave, for the children's sake. She had talked to Heinrich's old adviser, Professor Kaehler, praying that he would encourage her to stay, but even he had said, "Go!" The children had no future here, and she could probably be of more help to Heinrich's family from America.

This decision involved so many, and making it alone had become her heaviest private burden. She and Heinrich had decided to build their life in Germany. He was gone, but leaving would mean turning her back on their hopes, on his family, uprooting the children again. She could not imagine staying at 14 Neustädterstrasse, Frankenberg, forever, but where could they go? She had put her money and her whole self into Blumenhagen. If it was really lost, she could not begin to imagine what their finances would be like in Germany. Going back to America, where having money was not only assumed but so important, would be harder still. No one there could ever make sense of what had happened to her life. She would be beholden to others.

If she left, where should she go, how would they live? She had refused to separate her brood before if she could take only her two little ones. Now, without a home, she must go, and bring the older four over later, but how? And Helma? If these past weeks meant there was any hope for her, taking the children to America would be a cruel blow. Aimée felt sick. Even in the midst of the big questions, a small imperative intruded: It was high time to start the garden. Lo had written that the Eder had flooded, and everything was still sodden, if not underwater. But they needed what the garden would yield, especially now, when there were no extras from Helma's practice.

Patients were being told that Dr. Kahnert was having a rest, and many put off appointments till her return, but the story would not hold for long. The family all agreed that the doctor who was filling in, and living with them too, was not only dull but peculiar, which made the usual gathering around the kitchen stove for warmth uncomfortable.

When Aimée finally got "home" in late March, the children were in a state of high excitement. The big room was decorated with fir boughs, and under Friedrich's exacting tutelage, they had rehearsed a musical tribute for her. Food packages had come from America. Lo had baked a cake, Mary's package was opened with great ceremony, and

a general holiday was declared. The children had the feeling of a second Christmas. As my littlest sank into her bed, she said, "It was almost too much!" Her baby doll was the greatest joy of all. She had hoped so desperately and then it came. You should have seen how tenderly she held it. And Friedrich's music; "Mother, look at that!!" And the big coloring book full of never-ending possibilities—a godsend. Crayons, cough drops, pocket-knife, and the girls are never without the little rubber balls. The rest will serve as "Easter eggs," for too much at once spoils them. I bless your name a dozen times a day; everything has made someone happy.

My friend is now in a sanitarium, recovering slowly, but I think I might be sick from the decisions I face. I'm in a labyrinth without an exit.

Helma was dying. Thinking that Sigrid's presence might soften the news that she had decided to go back to America, Aimée brought the child along to visit her. It was a beautiful day in early summer; the enormous rhododendrons in front of the clinic were in impossibly glorious bloom. Helma's short dark curls were gone, fallen to the operation and treatments. "Dying is hard," she said.

Aimée felt she had delivered the bitter coup de grâce. She could answer only that living was hard too. Helma nodded.

June 19, 1947

I'm looking after my friend, distressed over her state and how ill she is. I'm planning to come back to the States (if they'll let me in) in September with my two youngest. The other four, I'll have to leave here for a time. These are difficult steps and have cost heart's blood. I'm sure I'm doing the right thing but the future looks so hideous that I'm ready to change my mind tomorrow. God help us all! To leave Helma in this condition is almost murder.

By September, Helma was dead.

24

America

Passage was booked. First, Aimée and the girls spent several weeks at an American DP (displaced persons) camp in Butzbach, where half the continent's accumulated displacement and sadness seemed to be huddled in the anteroom of the new world. Dingy, makeshift curtains—sheets, really—offered minimal privacy. Canvas Lister bags of warm, musty-tasting water hung from trees in the dusty yard. Meals were served in an echoing cafeteria on pale green melamine trays, with ridges separating mashed potatoes from green beans and some kind of meat. But it was food, ample and steady, a new experience.

Lo brought the older children to say good-bye before they sailed. With no firm date to mark the end of this wrenching separation, no fixed moment to look forward to, they huddled together, close, not wanting to part, yet awkward, wanting this moment to be over. Studying her four oldest, memorizing their faces, she tried to imagine what challenges they would have to meet before she saw them again. Friedrich, so tall and thin, would stay at his boarding school, immersed in his music. He had found a special girl; he would be fine. Michael and Christian would stay with the Kommerells in Marburg, Michael entranced by the lively life there, Christian's energy focused on school, and they would be near enough to visit "home" often. Brigitte, caught in the anguish of full-blown adolescence, worried her a bit, not because of the child or for lack of faith in Lo. Yet part of her felt that this was when Brigitte would need a real mother. Still, she had her great friend Elisabeth, whose mother was a close substitute. Scanning their faces again and again, she tried to suppress an overwhelming fear—a terror that she would not manage to bring them to safety, that another war would engulf them all, that they would never be together again.

An old American C-4 troop transport ship shuttling between Bremerhaven and New York was ferrying the war's flotsam to a new world of hope and—at least in some cases—dreams. "Shuttling" may be the wrong word; the poor old SS *Marine Flasher*, long overdue for decommissioning, was continually plagued by drastic maintenance problems, foul weather, and crew disturbances.

They shared a four-bunk officers' cabin with quiet, middle-aged Frau Weinsheimer. A few days into their passage, she decided that her cabinmates could be trusted, and settled a large, previously unopened suitcase on her bunk. Tenderly removing a large bundle, she peeled away layer after layer of worn and mended sweaters and underwear. Slowly, an exquisite fifteenth-century wooden madonna emerged from her swaddling. The saintly stowaway surveyed her passage to a new world with the same beatific calm with which she had watched centuries pass, the tiny smile on her lips still tinged with rosy pigment. She was a welcome traveling companion. She asked for nothing, and while she did not keep the November storms at bay, they came to think of her as a secret weapon, offering a measure of comfort and protection, a talisman against all future odds.

Their cabin was adjacent to the dining room, but so many passengers were seasick that traffic past the door was light. Dorothée and Sigrid were blissfully unaffected, devouring quantities of acidic green olives from the green melamine bowls that appeared regularly on the long mess tables. The olives' appeal was explained only by their salt and acidity, two flavors lacking for so many years. After meals, they all took up positions on the rain-soaked deck to watch enormous bins of uneaten food dumped over the side and sucked into a greedy sea. Throwing away food, any food at all, was unheard of. Throwing away so much was unfathomable. Aimée explained that the ship had come from America. In America there was more food than they could possibly imagine. Not all the world was hungry.

The girls skittered across decks sloshing with water, up and down stairways, peering into every possible passageway and lifeboat, absorbed by the shipboard adventure. As the ship shuddered and lurched, Aimée lurched between the pain of the recent past and the imponderable future. The cross Friedrich had carved for Helma's grave was still raw, unweathered oak, as fresh as the pain of her death. Lo was valiantly holding things together for the other children, more distant with each angry wave slamming into the ship. Aimée had no idea how she would bring them over, or how she would manage when she did, and Uncle Bill was not there to shine a light into the dark.

There was a time when she had been absolutely certain that, given determination and effort, everything would fall into place. Returning to Europe to marry, pregnant with Heinrich's child, she had been apprehensive, but stirred and excited. Adventure lay ahead. "Never!" she had said cockily to the woman who asked when she planned to return to the States. Whatever deity had overheard that bit of arrogance was humbling her now. That "never" was not quite twenty years later, and she could not even imagine such certainty.

On this passage she was apprehensive too, but only with dread. She was leaving behind everyone with whom she had shared hard times—times that forged unbreakable bonds, but opened a gulf between her and the American family. She remembered her father's sour insistence that the initials of Mrs. C. F. What's-her-name, who lived across Prospect Avenue, stood for "Comfortably Fixed." They were all comfortably fixed, while her life had diverged from their path and fractured. The only things that had ever fractured their cushioned lives were the income tax and "that man" Roosevelt. Mimama's "nourishing" soup of dried potato skins was beyond their wildest imaginings. Aimée knew that she had become someone they could not fathom. They would never be comfortable with her, nor she with them. Looking for understanding was unrealistic, even unfair.

As the ship stumbled through interminable grayness, she revisited the list of people she might be able to count on. Whenever she had contemplated return and tallied the names, Uncle Bill had always topped the list, but he was gone. There was Anita; Anita would be there in Hartford, she knew that. She remembered an old photograph of the two of them, beribboned babies not yet past diaper days, sitting in their respective nurses' laps. Their early lives were lived in tandem; wherever one was, there the other was sure to be. Even distance had made little difference in their relationship. Anita's conspiratorial giggle and unquestioning affection would be there. Then there was Uncle Bill's daughter Dorothy, married to her father's brother, Uncle John. Remembering her kindness to her as an unhappy child, she had named her second daughter after Dorothy. Maybe she was still kind and strong.

As they came into New York Harbor, an early morning mist lifted just enough for them to make out the Statue of Liberty. Edging slowly down the gangway, they were surrounded by others like them, Europe's bedraggled castoffs. Some scanned the crowd below for a familiar face. Others scanned an unfamiliar horizon, hardening themselves against arrival in a new country without a welcome. Sigrid thought it was wonderful. It was her sixth birthday, and here was a new country, just for her.

Among the crowd waving and holding signs and balloons on the pier, Aimée was grateful to see Ran Beardsley's familiar face. Ran knew and understood. The girls knew him as a friend and benefactor. He was a symbol of continuing friendship in their new world. Mary was there too. She had changed her "commonplace" Mary to Marya meanwhile, but Mary or Marya, bless her. She had done all she could to alleviate their misery, and here she was, a huge jar of candies tucked under her arm for the girls. The little welcoming committee warmed Aimée's quaking heart.

They stood on the pier amid the jostle and bustle, a small nervous cluster, eager to move past the awkwardness. Dorothy had offered to put them up in New Jersey, and Ran would take them there. Driving through the Holland Tunnel, he told the girls that they were under the big river they had just seen, a thought both terrifying and delicious. Huddled together on the backseat of the impossibly large, luxurious car, they savored the fright and the candies equally.

As they pulled up to the house in Keyport, Dorothy came out to meet them. She was unrecognizable. The firm contours of her earlier self had blurred, bloated by alcohol meant to ease a miserable marriage. Emotionally she was remote and abstracted, as if she had vacated her life. Uncle John had discouraged Ran from trying to find and help Aimée in Germany, and he was not happy to see the result of Ran's efforts on his doorstep. His reception was icy; there would be no help from him. In fact, he soon presented Aimée with a bill for the army blankets he had sent to Frankenberg.

The immense house was comfortable, but comfortless. They felt unwelcome in the land of plenty. During the hard years, she had sometimes told the children about fabulous food, taste sensations the younger ones had never experienced and that had become a faded memory for the older ones, part of their fantasy lives. The girls had heard about a banana's miraculous, soothing sweetness. Tasting their first one between the giant columns on the brick terrace at the front of the house, they found them green, hard, and infinitely disappointing.

A big living room ran along the entire end wall of the big house, its unused fireplace flanked by windows that looked out on a dun-colored November lawn. Beyond lay a split-rail fence, a pasture, then woods and a stream. Prints of ducks flapping out of rushes implied the sound of wings, but like the rest of the household, the ducks were trapped in sepulchral silence. The room's uninhabited stillness was broken only by the nearly subliminal hum of numerous electric clocks, as if many efficient clocks would speed the empty hours along. Silver cigarette boxes, monogrammed or engraved to commemorate celebratory occasions, gleamed on waxed cocktail tables. The boxes were like artifacts from a past as distant as Troy; it was hard to imagine celebrations in this unhappy house.

Lunch was formal, served by the maid in the dining room, where chipped beef on toast, a salty, WASP staple of the time, kept company with finger bowls. Surprised at the finger bowls, Aimée remarked that it had been a while since she had seen any of those. Dorothy drew herself up and sniffed, "Don't you believe in gracious living?"

The girls suffered through these meals largely in silence. Language was partly to blame, but the real problem went deeper. The youngest sometimes squirmed visibly, and Dorothy presented her with a carved wooden back scratcher to hang from the back of her chair. If Dorothy meant to engage the child, her gesture met with little success. Before long, both girls took to spending time in the kitchen with the cheerful cook until Dorothy told them not to fraternize with the help.

One day in the broad upstairs hall, Dorothy's door opened. Naked, she drifted down the corridor in an alcoholic haze, a strange, mad majesty in her swaying progress. Like a sad, stray balloon, off on its own, the pale, bulky body bumped slowly off one wall, then the other. Aimée had named a daughter after the generosity and lithe grace of the person who had once inhabited that body, but that person, like so many others, was gone.

Still, there were pleasures. For her newly minted six-year-old, her first real balloon—blue was the color of choice—brought hours of delirious happiness, the child running back and forth along the drive, watching it bounce in the wind, or tagging along behind like a faithful friend, as long as she held tight to the string. Aimée had also found a secondhand copy of *A Child's Garden of Verses*, so familiar from her own childhood. On its cover two children in white walked behind stone gateposts and a fancy grillwork gate along a path between deep green hedges. As a child, she had always imagined that path leading to a magical place, hidden, sweet, and deep. This would be the primer to lead her girls into a new language.

"The friendly cow all red and white . . . ," the girls singsonged. The verses were so familiar there was no need for her to look at the pages when they stumbled over the foreign syllables. "In winter I get up at night / And dress by yellow candle-light . . ." "How do you like to go up in a swing, / Up in the air so blue? / Oh, I do think it the pleasantest thing / Ever a child can do." Jessie Willcox Smith's illustrations had provided the children on the cover with a sheltered, golden dusk. How she would ever re-create such days for her own brood was a deep mystery.

One day, overcome by loss and loneliness and in a moment of tears, Aimée was surprised in her room by Dorothy, who demanded to know why she was crying. Why *was* she crying? Her husband was dead, her home was lost, four children were far away; she missed them, and worried. Uncle Bill was gone; her best friend had died just before she left Germany. But for the Dorothy who stood before her, the hammering of carpenters building cabinets in the den represented major hardship. There was no explaining. She felt sad, she said, and left it at that.

At Christmas, the big house was dark and still. There was no tree, no music, no baking, no sense of occasion. She busied herself putting together Christmas packages and a long letter for everyone left behind. On Christmas Eve, they went to the local country club for cocktails and dinner. The next day, she and the girls trudged into the woods and found a small tree to decorate with candles, as Heinrich had done for her twenty years before. Not so many years really, but centuries. They sang Christmas songs, their voices small, unsteady, and insignificant, floating like lonely ghosts among the trees.

Next day the sky went black with birds. When the snow came, it came heavy and deep. The house was even more silent and isolated. She had fled from one nightmare into another. She felt trapped, claustrophobic. She had to get away; she could not stay another day. She would go to Anita.

Dully, repetitively, Dorothy insisted that everything and everyone was snowbound. They would never make it to Hartford. Suddenly Aimée realized that Dorothy was hurt. Her charity, her hospitality, her home as a refuge from the storm, was being rejected. Alcohol had not numbed all capacity for pain. Part of her wanted to embrace Dorothy, to recognize the generous younger self not yet completely buried within this husk, to tell her how sorry she was for her wretched marriage, to thank her and apologize for defecting. But an embrace could never penetrate the years of hurt and the layers of armor put up against it. An embrace would be unwelcome and only make matters worse. Loading their few suitcases onto a child's sled she had found in the garage, she and the girls floundered through deep drifts to the road, and eventually, found a ride to the train station.

The 159-mile trip to Hartford was long and exhausting. The snow stretched a journey of a few hours into many, and by the time they arrived, the bedraggled threesome was completely done in. But the welcome was warm and Aimée was nearly giddy with relief. With the girls fed and put to bed, she and Anita sat together in the kitchen. Their relationship let them take up where they had left off, but there was a lot of catching up to do.

Years ago, she told Anita, she had been convinced that she had some abilities and strengths. Longing to try them out, she had actually hoped for a test of courage and will. She'd had plenty of opportunities since. It reminded her of an old joke about a becalmed sailor who throws a dollar bill into the sky, shouting angrily into the vastness, "God! Send me some wind!" A hurricane blows up, the boat is wrecked, and the sailor, nearly drowned, gasps, "God, if I'd known it was that cheap, I wouldn't have given you so much." She and Anita had a good giggle, with a wry twist, just like old times. God bless Anita. Aimée had found a real haven, at least for a little while.

Anita's architect husband, Merrill, had designed their house and had it built not far from where they had grown up, but farther west, in the newer reaches of West Hartford. The house was pink, Anita's favorite color, though the palest possible buff pink, barely pink at all. It was spacious and comfortable, but with a grown and growly son and a teenage daughter of their own, the Lincolns could not take in this battered widow and her two girls indefinitely. Anita helped put the girls in local schools and arranged a delightful party for Dorothée's eleventh birthday. Anita would watch over her chicks while Aimée set off to find a place to live, a college for the boys, and a way to shape a future for them all.

Uncle Bill had asked his daughters to help Aimée in any way they could before he died. Mildy, the younger of the two, had had rheumatic fever as a child, and Aimée never had the same connection with her that she felt for Dorothy. But now it was Mildy who helped consistently. Her husband John, "Chef," was president of a big electrical company in Hartford; there were ample funds but no children. Mildy drove Aimée to Trinity, her father's alma mater, but they could do nothing in the way of scholarship help for the boys. She drove her to Middlebury, where Aimée was told that they were a poor college, not a poor man's college. She should try Bowdoin, in Maine. They were interested in foreign students.

With Anita, she set off into a snowy landscape of immense pines. The farther north they got, the more she realized that this was where the future lay. It was poor country, and being poor among the poor would be easier for the children. They could still hew to their own path. In the office of Bowdoin's Dean Kendrick, she explained her situation.

His measured and benign response: "If you can find a place to live, and the boys are up to it scholastically, I guess we can help."

When she told Corson, he exploded: "Make sure of one thing: Your children are not foreign. They are American citizens!"

"You're wrong," she said. "America does not regard them as citizens."

When Aimée was about seventeen, a school friend's father had told her that a woman should always be able to support her family. She needed to do that now, but she had no skills, she knew nothing. She felt like a child with adult responsibilities and no experience. But Kendrick had said, "Find a place to live. . . ." She would do that first.

Every penny was precious. She would have to find a cheap old house with land on which to grow food and raise chickens and geese, and woods for firewood. Most of Uncle Bill's modest bequest went into a small, dilapidated farmhouse, three miles from town, with a barn and forty-five acres. The rest went for food and clothes for the family in Germany. On May 1–2, 1947, she wrote Lo and the older children:

I set off by bus, since that is half the price of the train. Hartford was in full-blown spring: cherry trees in bloom, everything was green, narcissus and violets at their height. But I left all that behind, and soon the woods were gray and wintry. A 12-hour trip! Arriving in the evening, I was greeted by the French-Canadian broker, who put me up for the night. He and his wife nearly adopted me. The next day he took me into town, where I bought a spade and a rake, baskets, a crowbar, canned soups (I had brought a small hotplate along), garden clippers and a stepladder. Then we set off, his wife coming along too.

First we stopped at the turnoff to the Middle Bay Road, where I was introduced to Mr. and Mrs. Hummer, who live on a pretty old farm. Across the road was the Grange Hall. The Hummers immediately invited me to stay with them until the house was habitable. I accepted gratefully, and we drove down the little hill, past a pond, and reached our new "home." The family had departed long since, and it was the first time I saw the place without a blanket of pristine snow. What a sight!

The small old Cape Cod, last inhabited by a family with nine children, was the sort of place that anyone who has never seen poverty in rural Maine cannot begin to imagine. Outside, a confusion of rusted chicken wire, a cannibalized car, old shoes, paper, bits of roofing, broken dishes and glass, the remains of a collapsed barn, and two unbelievable sheds. Rubbish everywhere. Stepping into the house itself, the first thing she saw was a chamber pot with dried excrement. Welcome home!

Plaster hung off the walls; the windows, clearly unopened in years, had been painted shut. Inside and out, it nearly made her weep. The central chimney supporting the great principal beam, the house's mainstay, had been ripped out and replaced with a stovepipe. In the attached shed, a two-seater outhouse was so crowded with junk that it was unreachable. *Dear God, give me strength*, she thought, wishing she had Heinrich's faith in God's goodwill and help. Still, there was no harm in asking, and she did need help. As she wrote to everyone in Frankenberg:

> The broker and his wife were horrified. They looked sick at having sold me such a place and wanted to take me back immediately. It had looked so charming under the forgiving snow! But there is no going back—so forward! I waved them good-bye and went in alone.
>
> There I was, and could now begin in my own house. I thought of Blumenhagen, of the beginning and the end, of all of you, whom I miss so bitterly, of my dead, our dead. Then I prayed.
>
> First I had to get to the garden; it was high time to think about peas and carrots. I grabbed a digging fork and began. It was torture. After about half an hour, I heard a "Hallo" beside me and looked up into a pair of bright eyes. Next to their young owner stood another boy. Both were about 11 or 12. "What's your name?"
>
> "James Franklin George Washington Potvin."
>
> "And you are?"
>
> "Arthur Trepanier."
>
> So they were both French Canadian, of whom there are many here.
>
> "Did you buy this house?"
>
> "Yes, and a big mess to go with it."

"We can help you."

"Fine," I said, "pile all that wood up over there, and we'll make a bonfire." I thought they would soon tire of it, but they worked hard. The next day, school, and no boys.

She dubbed the place *Donnerwetter*—Good Grief—Farm. Establishing a minimum of civilization would require a plumber and a carpenter. Mercifully, Merrill had offered to help with the renovation. Heating the house with fireplaces was cheaper than a furnace, and, God knows, they had plenty of wood. But for that she needed the chimney back, so she needed a mason too.

The carpenter and the plumber came to look things over. Much head shaking and chin scratching. Hmmm . . . this was a problem . . . He would come back when Mr. Lincoln was here.

Mr. Ellison, the carpenter, was cheerful and punctual, with steady blue eyes and red hands. He recommended a mason to replace the dismantled chimney-turned-stovepipe with a four-flue chimney. He was eighty, Ellison said, but the only man he knew who used both hands when he worked. The mason's two gnarled hands and those of a young assistant built the requisite chimney—beautifully. But, of course, to heat with open fireplaces, you really needed a hired man to do nothing but chop wood. And so it went.

Two women arrived, wanting to help me in the garden, 80 cents an hour, a lot of money. The boys came back too, and diligently raked up hay and miscellaneous trash. I promised them hot dogs cooked over the open fire as a reward. Heaven! Soon I was known to the whole family. They all wanted to work for me. Yesterday, Saturday, I had 2 men, 3 women and 4 children, either in the house or outside. In the evening, my pockets were empty, but quite a bit had been accomplished.

The broker and his wife came back to see if I was still alive. They felt responsible, and had worried. When they saw what had been done they were amazed. In the evening, stiff with dirt and exhaustion, I went back to the wonderful Hummers. Good food, simple, fresh and clean, like the people themselves. Mrs. Hummer loves to talk—a great deal and often—but she is a sensible soul, and warmhearted. After supper, she pulled a big rectangular tin basin into the kitchen, and I took a heavenly bath in the cozy warmth of the old kitchen stove. Having this refuge is wonderful; the people are so kind and good and unspoiled. At noon, I sit in my ruin, perched on an old clock case, my hotplate on an upside down crate, and heat my soup. I don't dare think too much. Just look ahead and be thankful for everything one is given.

The little ones are still in Hartford until school is out, but we've made a start, and we'll make it work. It will be beautiful someday. God grant that you will all be standing here soon. The enclosed flower is the first wildflower of the spring; it smells wonderful. I picked it for you.

The Hummers were wonderful people. Their son, daughter-in-law, and two grandchildren lived with them. *Life* magazine had discovered the Hummers and sent a photographer to take pictures of a real American farm, a real American farming family, and their American farm kitchen. The Hummers were very proud. The photographer had not noticed the electric iron in his viewfinder; in that respect, 1948 had intruded on down-home America after all. The rarely used living room, like the rest of the downstairs, had linoleum floors. Over the sofa hung a tapestry of Jesus praying at Gethsemane.

The main room downstairs was the big kitchen with a woodstove, usually with a pie baking in it. A large pantry was where they stored pickles and "put up" vegetables from the garden; it also housed the washtub and wringer. In the evenings, Mrs. Hummer's laconic—no, silent—husband, perpetually in overalls, sat by the stove reading his newspaper. Mrs. Hummer, always in a housedress and apron, was round and rumpled, with the demeanor of a loquacious Mrs. Claus. Aimée kept thinking that at some point she would get to the end of her story and take a breather, but there was no end. All her sixty-plus years had to be gone over. She had come to live on nearby Bailey Island as a young bride at the turn of the century. Twenty years later, the islanders still referred to her as being "from away." Then there were her son and daughter-in-law and her grandchildren, Frankie and Mildred, to talk about, and on it went. Aimée sat in the old tin tub, topped up now and then by Mrs. Hummer with more hot water from the stove. Words and water poured over her, endlessly comforting. This lady was getting clean! It was bliss.

Three miles from town, she needed a car. Everyone seemed to be holding on to old cars and there was little to be had, but after a long search she bought an old pickup truck for an astronomical six hundred dollars. What a truck! There was no heater. The front air vent had been sealed, probably to keep the rain out, with at least some success. The windows opened reluctantly, but if by some miracle they opened and the door was slammed shut, the windows broke. But just like the faithful Marushka, still with Marta and Below in Germany, it could haul whatever was necessary. She named it Marushka, hoping for the same stamina and honest effort the horse had always shown.

When school was out in Hartford, Anita and Merrill brought the girls up and went on to visit friends in Tenants Harbor. In a week's time, they would be back for Merrill to consider everything that baffled the workmen. Having the girls was wonderful; they were so game and helpful, and full of stories about school and Hartford. For them, bathing in the icy brook down the hill from the house was a lark. They were a joy to watch, tossing soap back and forth between them, fighting off clouds of gnats. "No-see-ums," Aimée said they were called. Once they understood, they found that hilarious. She had been much alone. She was glad for their company, and they were not so thin anymore.

Mildy helped with funds to drill a well. After a day of taming the wild, weeding, planting, scraping and painting doors and walls, and cooking, Aimée wrote letters, pouring her heart out to Lo, to Margarethe, to Mimama, all so far away, and wrapping packages to send them all. Then she sat down to the mountain of paperwork involved in bringing the four older children over, a slow process being guided along by Maine congressman Robert Hale. Careful, energetic, unwavering, he was always available. In the end, he managed to get a special bill passed on their behalf. She would have her children again.

In July 1948, Aimée and her two youngest went to New York to meet the *Marine Flasher*, bringing another load of the lost and homeless to the new world. They had not seen each other for almost nine months, and the mood was hectic, tearful, and happy. Michael was keen to see New York and visibly disappointed when they went directly to Grand Central Terminal for a train to Connecticut. There was no money for a hotel and sightseeing. Aunt Mildy and Uncle Chef had invited the horde to their summer place on Mason's Island, off the Mystic River. Six excited children represented a huge disruption of their quiet, steady, childless life, but they seemed delighted.

The ease, the plentiful food, the big boat moored below the house, amazed the children. The address—Money Point, so-called because of a rumored connection with Captain Kidd's treasure—was captivating. They ate, swam, explored the shore, and went out on Uncle Chef's tuna-fishing boat. They combed through the grass near the boathouse, singing the hugely popular "I'm Looking Over a Four-Leaf Clover," hoping to find the magical, lucky one. The older four marveled at America and everything American—like the extraordinary cocktail-hour performance of Aunt Mildy's beagle, Becky. A tidbit was put on a small plate for the dog. Told that it cost money, she sat, frozen, until Uncle Chef or Aunt Mildy said, "I'll pay for it, Becky." It was an important lesson; even the dog understood that her evening tidbit was a financial transaction. What an extraordinary world.

On the train from New London, the children all talked at once, all the way to Maine—in German, of course. It was a long trip, and there was a lot to be said. As they clambered off in Brunswick, the conductor held out his hand to help Aimée down the steps, saying, "There was an old woman who lived in a shoe, she had so many children, she didn't know what to do. . . ." On the platform, he doffed his cap with a smile and bowed low. They must have sounded like a real circus, but little did he know, she thought. He'd seen only a tiny piece of the situation. Never mind. They were together, and they were going home.

There was a bit of genius in the choice of rural Maine. The local people were plain and unpretentious, many of them poor. Up the hill were the

Hummers, next door the Bousquets. Every other week or so, the girls went down the hill, over the brook, up through pine woods dotted with lady's slippers, and across a bright pasture to Grandma Prince's farm. Grandma still churned butter on her big front porch, and she was happy to get a bit of money for what was left after churning, perfect for cold buttermilk soup.

In a farmhouse on the way to Brunswick lived Mr. Hollis, a widower of about sixty-five who sold vegetables from a roadside stand under the honor system. You took a pint or a quart or a dozen of whatever it was you wanted, and you left the necessary change. Aimée liked Mr. Hollis; she even copied his spice cake recipe into the back of her *Joy of Cooking*. She turned down his proposal of marriage, but she knew that with neighbors like him, the Hummers, the Bousquets, and the Princes, the children would not feel underprivileged. Access to college and the college community meant music, lectures, theater, and thoughtful educated people to talk to. It was perfect.

She had done it: She had managed to bring all her chickens under one roof again. She had had help, of course, from Uncle Bill, and from Lo, who had managed the older children and the endless details of packing and shipping the household in Germany. She had help from Anita and Merrill and Mildy, and from Congressman Hale. She found herself thanking them all several times a week, especially the ghost of Uncle Bill, who had made the house possible, and generous Mildy. Still, she had done it, and it was no small accomplishment. But she wasn't ready to congratulate herself yet; first she had to keep the roof from leaking and put food on the table.

Knowing what had been everywhere—the broken dishes and glass, the rusty wire, inside the house and out—she still did not dare go barefoot, but the work went quickly now. The girls helped with the chickens, geese, and four newly acquired goats—four charming and very individual characters. That summer, with the boys' strong arms and help from Mildy again, they put a new roof on the house. Aimée decided that it was Mildy's familiarity with trouble that made her so different from Dorothy. Or maybe her generosity grew out of a strong marriage, so unlike Dorothy's unhappy one.

· · ·

The garden was endless work, but she loved it and—thank heaven—it
was beginning to yield. Finding clothes and shoes for the growing horde
was demanding, and the work and the worry never stopped. In the evenings, she tutored the children in English and helped with homework
where possible. If there was any energy left, she readied packages for
Germany. Every minute of the day was totally occupied. It kept her from
being ambushed by memories. But, oh, getting food on the table for so
many hungry mouths, with not much to put in them . . .

For her, cooking had been neither joy nor chore, just someone else's
domain. Now, armed with the 1946 edition of Irma Rombauer's *Joy of
Cooking*, she launched herself into the kitchen with some trepidation.
Irma was certainly not Mimama's одарок молодым хозяйкам—*A
Gift to Young Housewives*, the standard for aristocratic Russian brides
since 1861. Just as well; its recipes and tips on household management—
such as which lesser grades of fish were suitable for servants' meals—
were banned after the revolution as politically unacceptable. Nor was it
the 1876 Mitau cookbook, brimming with Baltic recipes for fish and
game, including duck with oysters to serve eighteen, and menus for
sixteen-course dinners—or simple ones, with only five. No matter. This
was not the Escoffier stakes; she needed whatever help Irma could offer.
But meals were a tiresome treadmill, testing her stamina and ingenuity,
and she longed for Marta.

At least they were settled. Even the samovar, only slightly dented
from its travels, was back in an honored place near the great hearth in
the dining room. Friedrich was taking a year at the local high school to
improve his English before college. Michael was at Bowdoin and the
girls were in local schools. Christian was at a Vermont boarding school
on scholarship, Everest underwriting the rest. Everest's long-standing
generosity was familiar. He had sent packages to Germany consistently,
and now was instrumental in helping Aimée in many ways.

On the way to town one day, very unlike the eponymous horse,
Marushka the truck broke down, her rear end settling abruptly onto
the asphalt. Vital props had given way—rusted out by too many Maine
winters. At alarming expense, she was restored and running again, to

college, on errands, hauling hay and goats, groceries and manure. In bad weather, three could squeeze in front and get to town without getting too sodden or cold. In summer, the entire family and friends went to the beach or the local drive-in, with a bench in the back for grown-ups and everyone else on the truck bed. Marushka brought in hay for the goats, she brought home the old upright piano Aimée bought, and soon, when Friedrich and Michael rattled off to college, she brought their friends home for musical evenings. Life was beginning again.

Inadequate wartime nutrition and poor dentistry had done their worst; Aimée needed new teeth. It was another frightening expense. But suffering through weeks of embarrassing toothlessness did not keep her from pulling the younger children out of bed, no matter how cold the night, to see the northern lights or identify Cassiopeia or the Pleiades. In a clumsy stab at deception, her youngest feigned recognition to be allowed back into her warm bed. Seeing through the transparent fakery, Aimée said that she remembered being dragged out of bed at about the same age, to see Halley's comet in 1910, and had shown the same level of disinterest. Since then she had discovered the glories of the heavens, and wanted to share them. She squeezed the embarrassed faker tight and graciously let her off the hook.

The children did feel different from their schoolmates, but not underprivileged. In the weeks before Christmas, instead of buying presents, they divided the living room into cubicles with blankets, and busy knitters, painters, stitchers, or carvers worked on Christmas gifts in secret. The entire brood took turns needlepointing a sunflower to cover a chubby-legged antique footstool intended for Aunt Mildy while Aimée read aloud from Baroness Orczy's *The Scarlet Pimpernel*: "They seek him here, they seek him there. Those Frenchies seek him everywhere!" Not underprivileged, just different. That was the good kind of different; the other kind was expressed by an open animus that Aimée could not always keep away.

The youngest had been in awe of a Hartford first-grade classmate, Skippy, who brought his dessert to school in what had once been a peanut butter jar with "SKIPPY" in big red letters on the cover. A jar with his own name on it, she told Aimée—imagine! This really was a new country. Then the school reported that the enviable Skippy had yelled at her, calling her a Nazi. A year later, a school assembly program featured a skit on the brotherhood of man. "Ivan comes from Russia," it began; "Gretchen"—Sigrid—"comes from Prussia." A third child came from somewhere else, and "Living on one street we three, are as happy as can be." Aimée thought it was charming; it stood for everything she believed in. To "Gretchen" from Prussia, it meant being the other kind of different, part of being a Nazi. Later, more sophisticated incidents aimed to hurt, and did, sometimes sending her fleeing to whatever cover she imagined her mother's Miss Mayflower persona could provide. But her father's name marked her as a Hun. She even looked the part. There was no escape.

In the kitchen one fall day, Aimée turned from the bag slowly dripping sweet juice for apple jelly into a big pot. Standing straight in her apron, feet together, hands primly folded, she launched into a quavering falsetto—as if an ancient Victrola had sprung into life:

> My mama told me,
> If I be good,
> That she would buy me
> A rubber dolly.
>
> Now don't you tell her
> I've got a feller,
> Or she won't buy me
> That rubber dolly.

Scales fell from her seven-year-old's eyes. The strong, indomitable pillar of her childhood stood like a Kewpie doll, singing a ridiculous song. Once, in the dark ages, this unfailing arbiter of all things had been a little girl, doing childish things, and she had not forgotten how. What prompted this outburst? Life was looking up; she had recovered enough to tap into a reservoir of high spirits long obscured by burdens.

That watershed moment was soon followed by another, as they sat in the chilly truck on the Bowdoin campus, waiting to pick up the boys one dark Halloween. Yellow leaves lay everywhere, their fading glory lighting lawns and pathways. Seeing a student approach in the rearview mirror, Aimée hurriedly pulled on a remarkably convincing rubber witch mask from Woolworth's. The unsuspecting undergrad who glanced into the dark cab was visibly startled by the face that greeted him. From behind the rubber mask came a muffled cackle. As she pulled the mask off, the cackle became a long, unencumbered, full-bore laugh. Her daughter was embarrassed, then surprised, and then burst into unstoppable giggles. A playful person was emerging from an embattled parent. The curtain was going up on someone who had always been there, just buried under sadness, exhaustion, and troubles.

25

The Mail Must Go Through

For Lo, the older children's departure for America left a void. The hectic weeks of checking yet again on stalled visas, of packing the household, sending more than a ton of books in four-pound packages to skirt postal restrictions, of getting assured tickets and shepherding everyone to the ship for a good-bye in the midst of huge anxiety over Germany's currency reform were suddenly over. Sweeping dust balls out of the empty Neustädterstrasse apartment, she felt bereft. As a young woman, her odds of marriage had been made very long by war. Germany was a country with few men and peace did nothing to change that; then came another war. She could go to live with her sister; there was really nowhere else to go, but her sister's husband frightened her a bit. She had survived a war and its aftermath with Aimée and the children. Much of her emotional life lay with the family, and without them, it was empty. In 1950, she took a giant leap across the Atlantic.

For Aimée, Lo's arrival was a godsend. She had worked to exhaustion all day, every day, with little adult companionship, and none at all from anyone who had shared her experiences. At the local agricultural fair, the thought of having her handwriting analyzed had terrified her. Any graphologist would see immediately how close to the edge she felt, and no one must know. Over the past few months, the younger children had asked mournfully again and again when Lo was coming.

Aimée was convinced that Lo saved her from physical and emotional collapse. Lo relieved her of the hated cooking tasks; thanks to Lo, there was time and energy to go beyond the vegetable garden and plant the peonies that fed her soul. Because of Lo, they both joined the local high school's production of *I Remember Mama*, a story about a Norwegian immigrant family at the turn of the century. Papa Hanson is out of work, and Mama is pulling more than her weight, but because, as she puts it, it "is not good for little ones to be afraid . . . to not feel secure," Mama creates a fictitious bank account.

Like Mama Hanson, Aimée created a sense of security, not with a fictitious bank account, but by the steady stream of packages sent off to Europe. The packages made it plain that they were better off than many, certainly the family in Germany: Mimama in Dresden; Georg's family, still hoping for his eventual release from a Russian prison camp; Ebba, Mira, and Margarethe. More than once, the children watched a newly acquired hand-me-down from Chicago cousins disappear into a package destined for Europe, where it was needed more, or so their mother had decided. By sleight of hand, she created the illusion that they were doing rather well—a stretch by any standard.

The illusion was rounded out by every effort to make house and home beautiful, with flowers, paintings, books, and music. They might be poor in rural Maine, they might be slaves to a big vegetable garden behind the barn, to chickens, geese, and goats, but a picket fence edged the house's glorious flower garden. The days when Dorothée hid in embarrassment at the appalling conditions when guests came were over. The *Besitz* might not be much, but there would be plenty of *Bildung*. There were trips to plays, concerts, and lectures, and, of course, there was reading aloud. They were going to be good and civilized.

When *I Remember Mama*'s stage-daughter Katrin wails that she is too upset to play her part as Portia in the school play, Papa insists she go on, no matter how she feels. Among theater people, there is a saying . . . what is it . . . ? He hesitates, trying to remember. In a breathless, heavily accented outburst, Lo, delighted to be involved in something theatrical again, delivered the slightly ditzy Aunt Trina's newly acquired bit of Americana: "The mail must go through!"

"No, no," chides Papa. "The show must go on." But "The mail must go through!" became the watchword for mustering forces in times of trouble, and trouble there was.

Bringing the older four children to the United States meant filing endless papers, and a five-hour interview that asked, among other things, when Aimée had last voted in a German election. She had never been asked anything like this during her repatriation hearings. As the wife of a German citizen, she had dual nationality and German voting rights. Was this a problem? She skirted the issue, but then came clean. She had voted in a local constitutional referendum in Hessia in 1946; it had seemed important to vote against the Communists there.

It took time, but eventually she was notified that with this vote, she had forfeited her American citizenship. She would lose all inherited monies, and she and the four older children would be deported. The younger two could stay.

At her death, her mother had left money in trust for her grandchildren, then still many years from being born. The trust income was to be divided between Corson and Aimée while they lived. Now the Alien Property Custodian seized two thirds of her share of the principal, representing the four older children's share, and her entire share of the income, about $1,500 at the time. This, together with a little from Uncle Bill and what the children earned in the summer, was what they had lived on. Of the money her father had left her stepmother, Molly, to be divided among his children at her death, Aimée's share would now go to the Veterans of Foreign Wars.

She felt like Job on his dung heap. Should she fight the deportation, or just go back to Germany with all the children? There was no money to do either, but they could not stay. If they did go back, they would end up in a DP camp. What would become of the boys' education? Michael had won Bowdoin's freshman English prize his first year in the country. Suddenly, war psychosis closed in on her, and terrors lurked everywhere: War would break out; the boys were of draft age; the Russians would move in. She could not stop imagining new catastrophes, new disasters she could never meet.

Friedrich left college to work for a cabinetmaker in New York and earn desperately needed money. But with the Korean War heating up, she worried that—enemy alien or no—he would be drafted. Tom Means, a Bowdoin professor who had befriended the family, took up their case, putting her in touch with lawyers and writing countless letters attesting to the family's character and qualities. Maine's congressman Hale went back to work, shaping and shepherding another special bill through Congress on their behalf. But it would take time and they were penniless.

If this were a novel, it ought to stop or at least interrupt this catalog of woes here. Plots should be simple enough to be credible, with no unnecessary complications, no *Perils of Pauline*, please. But the luxury of control that fiction offers was not available here, and it was here that the Korean War prompted the U.S. Navy to renew and expand a deactivated airbase in Brunswick. Longer runways were needed, fields for gunnery and practice carrier landings, and their farm was in the way. By dint of eminent domain, the house and land would disappear behind fences and under asphalt. When? "When the first snow flies."

It was another round of upheaval. Everything she had worked for, the home that she had labored to make theirs, was being taken away—first Blumenhagen, now this little house on Middle Bay Road. Should she look for a new house or wait to be deported? For the time it took Mr. Hale to steer his bill through the legislative labyrinth, she and Lo rattled through the Northeast in ancient, heaterless Marushka, looking for a new place to live. She was wrapped in a woolly sack stitched together for chilly trips, but her feet, manipulating the pedals, were out in the cold. "*Eisbein*," they joked—literally, "iceleg," a common German pork dish.

Several months of looking at real estate gave her a good idea of what the house was worth, and she protested the navy's $11,000 offer. They had dug a well, put a new roof on the place. Her boys had done so much; she had pulled the plow herself. "We don't pay for sentiment," the navy replied. Sentiment no, but hard labor, maybe a little. They upped the estimate to $17,500.

She doubted she would find anything for less within easy range of Bowdoin, but they were lucky. Eleven miles from the college, she found an old farmhouse, a big center-hall colonial with a three-seater outhouse in the ell, three barns, several outbuildings, and 175 acres. The place had not been lived in for years. It had no electricity, no heating system, only fireplaces, and a pump in the kitchen. But it had a glorious view and waterfront along the broad Kennebec River, with an old shipbuilding town on the opposite bank. The price: $7,000.

As he showed her the house, friendly Mr. Trott reminisced about his boyhood there. The property had been the site of the last Indian massacre in Maine, he said; the Maine Historical Society had a full account. He hated selling the place, he said, looking out toward the river, but his wife wanted to be in town, and he was giving in. As they talked, one of the house's shutters fell to the ground. A hinge had rusted out. Mr. Trott smiled ruefully: "I'll sell it to you for six thousand," he said. "Call it the one-thousand-dollar shutter."

She paid cash. The rest of the money from the old house went into improving the new one. Every day, Lo and Aimée dropped the boys at college and went to work. On weekends the whole family pitched in, and that summer Anita and Merrill helped too. The grass around the place had not been cut for years; a tangled meadow washed against house, barns, and trees. Anita sat at the base of the great elm by the front door with grass clippers. They had to start somewhere, she said; it might as well be there.

It was another beginning, another storied piece of earth. The shutter was replaced; plumbing and running water were put in. The house was painted; floors were sanded. Layers of paint were scraped from the fronts and backs of thirty-seven doors; shelves were built for a library. Old lilacs were revived, a terrace laid out, a garden planted for vegetables, strawberries, flowers. As civilization took hold, Aimée and Lo established a midafternoon routine, a pause in the constant work. With coffee and a slice of Dundee cake from the local A&P, they settled down to listen to radio soaps, a half hour of *The Romance of Helen Trent* and *Our Gal Sunday*. The heroines' countless travails were deeply relaxing.

Heinrich's old friend "Prinzlein" put Aimée in touch with a relative: Princess Vera Constantinovna Romanov, the ninth child of Grand Duke Constantine of Russia. Prinzlein's family, the house of Saxe-Altenburg, was one in the teeming ant heap of German principalities that had fed a steady stream of marriageable princesses into the Russian imperial family over the years, and Vera's mother had been one of them. In 1945, Vera was living in Altenburg. As the Russians moved west, she fled with Prinzlein, just days before Winfried arrived. Eventually she moved to New York, but summered at a colony of Russian émigrés in nearby Richmond, and Aimée invited her for lunches and outings.

Her twelve-year-old daughter was looking forward to meeting a princess. Sashaying along the path between the lilacs and the mock orange came an old woman with a disorderly muddle of salt-and-pepper hair and teeth in a sorry state. Her bright orange T-shirt, emblazoned with the imperial double-headed Russian eagle, was no help. Vera was hardly what the girl had envisioned, but her stories more than made up for her deficiencies in the Disney princess arena.

She had been born into the last gasp of tsarist grandeur, and it wasn't long before she became yet another orphan of history's storm. In 1914, her family was visiting her mother's family in Altenburg when war broke out and was trapped by the hostilities. Back in Russia, her father died unexpectedly. Most of her brothers were killed, either by the Bolsheviks or in the war. Vera, her mother, and a brother sat out the tense period of the provisional government amid the neoclassical splendors of Pavlovsk, the palace where she was born, surreptitiously selling jewelry to survive. After the October Revolution, they escaped to Sweden, living as itinerant exiles at the invitation of one crowned or no-longer-crowned head or another, until they finally settled in Altenburg. After her mother died, Vera stayed through the war, then fled the Russians with Prinzlein, and eventually came to New York. Apart from an older sister who had taken holy orders, she was the only surviving member of her immediate family.

She was a living chapter of history. Similar stories had swirled through the household for years, of course, but this was different. These were not family stories, but other people's stories, bigger, more important. They carried weight. Direct, utterly without princess-y pretensions, Vera was bemused by the flutter of sentimental nostalgia for imperial glamour that often greeted her. She was an important lesson and, just as Aimée intended, she enlarged the world that her daughter's attempts to fit into rural Maine had narrowed so drastically. And for Aimée, Vera provided the companionship of someone whose experience also went beyond the local horizon.

That horizon had begun to include more of the present than the past, but the past never became bygones. One evening in 1953, before spring had penetrated Maine's winter, the three sisters were washing dishes together when the radio announcer interrupted the Longines-sponsored music programming to deliver the news that Joseph Stalin was dead. From the dining room, where Aimée sat at the sewing machine, came a passionate "Thank God!"

Given their upbringing in social niceties such as not speaking ill of the dead, it was a shocking moment. But the past had visited again and this went beyond the reach of social niceties. Their mother was speaking for Papa and Mimama, for their father, for her former self, for all the lives shredded or extinguished by the pitiless ideology Stalin represented.

Years later, another ghost from the past broke in on Aimée's new life of relative ease—this time in the form of a letter. Dutch POW Leo van Eekelen had been liberated from a German camp by the Russians, in April 1945. As he and his companions made their way west and home, van Eekelen wrote, they stopped to rest near Neustrelitz. In the roadside undergrowth, he had found a German officer's tunic. Tucked into an inner pocket were four letters addressed to Baron Heinrich von Hoyningen-Huene, with French postmarks from the 1920s.

In the unusual circumstances, van Eekelen bypassed his obviously deep, gentlemanly scruples, and reading the letters, he felt he had come upon something unusual. They were unmistakably love letters, in English, and signed only "Aimée." Maybe the addressee had lived in the area, and had fled or been captured by the Russians. He thought they might be from "an English acquaintance or friend of Hoyningen-Huene," he wrote. It was a delicate business; they should not fall into the wrong hands, open old wounds. So he had kept them carefully. More than twenty years later, at a party, he asked a German countess Wester-hold whether she knew a Hoyningen-Huene family. Now that the connection was made, he wrote, he was happy to return the letters at long last. He was sure they would be meaningful for the family.

The years had laid down layers, a carapace of time and distance Aimée had thought impenetrable, but the letters made her tremble. Their return after half a lifetime was utterly improbable, almost fable-like, as if closing a mystical circle. Imagining the trajectory that had brought them back to her was impossible. She knew the last leg of the journey, but the rest was unknowable. Had the letters been in Heinrich's tunic? Or had a friend taken them when he was killed, meaning to return them, and come very close, until he abandoned the tunic at a time when a Wehrmacht uniform could be a death sentence? Or had some lonely soldier found them and occasionally taken surrogate solace from them, leaving the tunic nearby by happenstance?

Surrounded by the summertime hubbub of children and grandchildren, she put them, unread, into the Moroccan box that held Heinrich's letters, wondering if she would recognize the person who had written them, or even the person to whom they were written. It was all so long ago. The letters marked a defining moment, an intense season of love that had shaped her life. She needed courage and solitude to read them.

When at last she did, alone in her bedroom, they read like messages from another world. That world had disappeared, but the time came back with astonishing force and clarity. She could date them only by their postmarks; the historian in Heinrich had always chided her for not dating her letters properly. One was from Lestion, postmarked late October 1927. Somewhere on its travels, in Heinrich's pocket or someone else's, dampness had caused the dark blue tissue lining the envelope to bleed onto the pages, staining the words.

My Darling: I put my face between your hands. The tears are tears of great happiness. How brave I was to wave good-bye to you so gaily. How much I shall have learned about heartache before I see you again.

Oh I have so many reasons to love you and so few words to describe that love to you. But even articulated stumblingly, truth will out, to tell you of the perfect things that are in my heart and sing in my veins. Heart's dearest, I could return your love a thousand fold, for the more love I give you, the more I have. So you see, there is no end to love.

At the window, surveying her own children, riding herd on her grandchildren, toddling, hopping, or loping across the lawns with the river beyond, it was clear that there was no end in sight to that long-ago love.

Epilogue

With the Moroccan box, my mother gave me something I had never had: a piece of my father. It was an enormous gift; his letters revealed some of the magic she and others felt in him. Also tucked into the box was a piece of herself I had never seen—early letters of hers found in the officer's tunic. My father's shockingly alive young voice was no more surprising to me than the breathless creature, overcome with love and longing, I encountered on those pages. The mother I knew was worn, hardened by life, unbowed. But the pale gray paper, pierced with her interlaced initials, *AE*, embossed and enclosed in a silver square, was instantly recognizable. Here was her familiar concern for detail, her implicit level of expectation, later so thoroughly dismantled, though even in the hardest times her standards never wavered. By sharing their love story, she had occasionally made me feel like a voyeur, if a privileged one, and put into my hands the catalyst for this book.

If I set out to understand my parents, I learned that we never completely understand what makes people who they are, and that who they are in fact changes. They are not flies trapped in amber. My father, to all appearances well equipped to cope with life's demands, was trapped by his past, frustrated by unmet expectations and hopes, then cut down, never becoming what he might have been. The mother I knew growing up was not the carefree creature I found in her early letters to Mary. But then, as she often said, life is full of surprises—ready or not. Having thought of herself as a frail vessel, she proved to have courage enough for an army.

This book taught me that there is not one history, but many; that context is everything, and life is far more complex than we ever imagine, especially when history writ large intervenes. I found that despite the stiff-armed Nazi salutes and guttural *"Achtungs"* that came my way, I was not the devil's spawn after all, just the product of two people in a particular time and place, enmeshed in circumstance, their hopes upended.

My father's decision to leave wife and children as hostages to fortune and go to war in Russia, and my mother's prayer never to wake up after my birth, both qualify as fodder for a Freudian picnic. But my father's reasons were determined by forces he could not escape, and my young mother, who once wrote, "I've never fought for anything. Life picked me out to spoil. I sometimes wonder if she isn't playing with me and will come with the reckoning before long," more than made up for any moment of weakness.

When the reckoning came, she had to fight for almost everything—alone. The adjectives she chose to describe her young motherhood were "delighted" and "awestruck." Later, as she met the challenges of an only parent in difficult times, "tireless" and "indomitable" were far more apt. "Outspoken," embarrassingly so for teenage daughters, was also true. "Demanding" would apply too; she never let up in terms of standards for herself or her children. But as life slowly got easier and the dark receded, "enterprising," "adventurous," and "funny" reemerged. In the midst of chaos and hardship, she would declare a family holiday and pack us into the truck for an outing to the beach or an apple farm. And while she had little patience for our minor aches or complaints, she always found room in her heart for the poor or dispossessed.

She never claimed to have shaped her children's very different selves, but her role was a big one. Friedrich fulfilled the musical expectations she had imagined on hearing Landowska play just before his birth, marching through the Korean War as a flutist in the Air Force Band, then winning a Guggenheim Fellowship, an honorary doctorate, and wide recognition as a builder of musical instruments. *Life* magazine captured Michael on the occasion of Bowdoin's three hundredth anniversary, delivering his valedictory address on "The Hope of Europe." He studied under the G.I. Bill, took an MBA, and became an international banker. Christian went on to Harvard to become a doctor. Brigitte still enjoys the affection and reverence of generations of first graders and their parents, whom she also taught. Dorothée took a PhD and is a professor of English. I took a graduate degree in art history at Columbia, lived in Europe for a time, and worked in publishing.

When I was twelve, my mother decided that I was becoming too Americanized and took me to Germany for a year. We visited aunts, uncles, cousins. We visited Mimama, then eighty-three and living with her daughter Ebba, but inhabiting an earlier life untroubled by upheaval and loss. For a girl from Woolwich, Maine's Central School, the Königen Charlotten Gymnasium für Junge Mädchen—and everything else—was eye-opening.

In cathedrals, palaces, baroque churches, tiny chapels, frigid Romanesque monasteries, I got what she thought of as "a firm grounding." She pointed out Marburg's wonderfully irreverent cathedral gargoyles to me as my father must have pointed them out to her. Thanks to her, I met the unmistakably real people with whom the celebrated sculptor Tilman Riemenschneider had populated choir stalls and altarpieces—his wife, his mother, the burgomaster, his self-portrait—all in the roles of saints or sinners. In Bamberg's great cathedral she introduced me to the Bamberg Rider of mysterious identity whom she had first met with my father on their honeymoon. At Toffen, we reached our rooms through the same long halls of ancients she and Heinrich had hushed along by candlelight as newlyweds.

We visited people who meant a great deal to her, places with happy memories. Trudging in the footsteps where her young feet had enthusiastically followed my father's, it all washed over me, but self-involved thirteen-year-old that I was, I was blind to the fact that she was revisiting the landscape of their young love. Only decades later, reading my parents' letters, did I understand what it had really meant to her. My father had nurtured her hungry mind and heart.

Knowing more about my parents intensified my search for that elusive "true" home. On the glittering noon hour when I first saw 820 Prospect Avenue, it had the air of a wealthy suburb slightly past its prime. Deep shade pooled at the bases of old trees. Lawns were wet with the night's drenching rain, the only sound the fluttering of sparrows bathing in the puddles it had left behind. It was peculiar to feel such an intense connection to a great rambling house on a street I had never seen except in my mind's eye. But my mother's descriptions, less physical than emotional, endowed the place with far more than met the eye: pictures of a little girl playing dolls under the snowberry bush; Irish washerwomen chatting and singing in the basement over steaming basins and mountains of linens and her father's stiff collars; of the trolley clanging up the avenue, and romps with Anita in Elizabeth Park. This was where her life began.

Standing in front of that turn-of-the-century Tudor pile with my fourteen-year-old daughter, I felt as if a bond of blood and consciousness— a physical and metaphysical continuum—stretched from everything that had built that house and brought her into being and now touched us. Unable to fill in the blanks in her own family's life, my mother wanted to hear all Heinrich's father's stories, to pass along the history, the story line. The generational continuum should be known and revered in all its complexity and nuance. Just as she had told Papa she would, she had found the courage and strength to push the continuum forward. Much of it had been lonely and hard, not at all the way she had imagined, but she had given us a place there, and we were glad of it.

My grandfather Ernst's memoir described his father's burial in Saint Petersburg's leafy Volkovo Cemetery in 1917: The black plumes of the horses drawing the hearse moved in rhythm with the animals' measured tread. The family followed on foot. The clear May air was filled with birdsong.

Ninety years later, trooping around Saint Petersburg, I was still looking for home. Our driver Sergei had found the elusive entrance to Volkovo in the grimy industrial wasteland that surrounds it now, and armed with a guide to the cemetery bristling with family names, I was convinced we would find Great-Grandpapa Emil's grave. Yet roads clearly marked in the guide bore no relation to the nameless, muddy tracks traversing the tangle of trees and saplings. Late on that gray September day, light was dim under the spindly trees, sectors indistinguishable from one another. Stumbling through weeds and undergrowth, we never found it. I was disappointed, hungry, and tired, but Sergei was a man on a mission, determined to find the massive black marble tomb of another forebear depicted in the booklet. Then our wonderful guide Marina's triumphant shout "Here it is!" brought us together in the gloom.

As Marina deciphered the inscription, ADJUTANT GENERAL WILHELM PETER VON WEYMARN, DEFENDER OF THE MOTHERLAND, Sergei offered his handkerchief to fetch water from a nearby puddle to make this illustrious ancestor's tomb glisten, at least temporarily. When I declined his sacrifice, Sergei was flummoxed; every inch of his sturdy frame registered incomprehension.

Here, under my feet and the weeds, lay the remains of kith and kin: my great-great-grandfather, his wife Christine, baby Alexandrine, dead in 1839, her brother Nikolai—"Kolla"—dead at eight, and Alexander von Weymarn de Tolly. Great-Great-Grandmama Christine had requested a low, square marker for the comfort of future visitors, so I sat, a visitor from across generations, feeling the way I had always felt: in this world, but not of it, a sense that Anna Akhmatova's poem encapsulates.

> This cruel age has deflected me
> like a river from its course.
> Strayed from its familiar shores . . .
> into a sister channel.
> How many spectacles I've missed:
> the curtain rising without me . . .
> How many friends
> I never had the chance to meet. . . .
> The grave I go to will not be my own.

No cruel age had deflected or uprooted these lives. For a moment, I envied them, safely tucked in their own graves, their bones firmly planted in native soil, surrounded by family and friends.

Like much of Saint Petersburg, the house where my grandmother was born was being refurbished by some neo-plutocrat, its arched passageway to the courtyard blocked by a lorry full of building materials. A lanky youth lounged in a gaudy leather jacket, smoking, waiting for fellow workmen. Ringing a doorbell here would not take me up from the porte cochere to the sunny salon with the immense porphyry urn, gift of one tsar or another to Great-Grandpapa Nikolai. Behind the lace curtains and ubiquitous Saint Petersburg snake plant, I would find only signs that life had moved on.

Down a few steps, low, vaulted rooms once housing kitchen, potatoes, and wine are now ПAПAPAЦЦИИ—Paparazzi—a café and bar. Looking for home, I had borscht in the company of life-size photo cutouts of Churchill, Ursula Andress, Tony Curtis, Princess Di, and—of all people—Al Sharpton. Grandpapa's memoir never helped me locate home on any map. The whirligig of recent Russian history has restored the last tsar's ill-fated family to icon status, but could not give me what I was looking for. Home was not there anymore. For me, as for many, "home" has become an imaginary place, "homemade," if you will—internal and eminently portable.

Blumenhagen had been my mother's true home, but she never went back. She preferred to plant a tree wherever she was, or exercise her hankering to "vagabond" elsewhere: in England, Spain, Egypt, or Greece, and, in her eighties, in China. Eventually she moved to Arizona—not to some retirement community, but to a house with a garden and a whole world of new plants that delighted her. As dimming eyesight and diminished hearing narrowed her world, she would totter along on uncertain legs, singsonging Robert Browning's "Grow old along with me! / The best is yet to be, / the last of life, for which the first was made . . . Who saith, 'A whole I planned, / youth shows but half . . . ,' " and trail off with a wry laugh.

This book began as a venture in personal archaeology but gradually became much more than that—an act of reverence and gratitude, even a bit of finding home. Passing through Hartford recently, my daughter stopped at the house at 820 Prospect Avenue, where we had stood together years before, and sent home pictures. It touched my heart. Mirabile dictu: Unwittingly, I had moved the continuum forward to the next generation. And without sounding too grandiose, I felt that a tiny fragment of history itself had been rewritten.

"One lives so many different lives," my mother often said. She spoke from experience. Lives others invented for her represented life's abundant, amusing ironies: A Chicago newspaper's social column chronicling her visit to her brother, Corson, made Heinrich a general, her a countess, and the farm "their castle"; or the DAR scholarship awarded Dorothée for *Mayflower* descendants resident in Maine. "If only they knew about the other half!" my mother said, laughing. So many lives. Yet in the end, against all odds, she lived only one life, fiercely, fully, to the very end.

Acknowledgments

Writing is said to be a solitary profession. It is, but I was lucky I had a host of companions on that lonely road, accompanied by my young parents, and by aunts', uncles', and grandparents' memoirs. Some who helped later were short-timers; others were in for the long haul. To all of them: Thank you.

To my siblings who remember more and different aspects of this story, and have been endlessly generous with their recall; to my cousin Otto Eberhardt, whose memories I tapped into during several wonderful, post–Hurricane Sandy days. Thanks to Simone Amescamp, faithful reader, supporter, giver of feedback; to Professor Volker R. Berghahn, who encouraged my first queries and, with encyclopedic knowledge, supplied valuable bibliographical material and advice; to Adelheid (von Roenne) Döll, who kindly supplied information on our fathers' relationship, particularly during the Paris FHW period, and who read the manuscript and offered much help and detail. Also to Corson Ellis, for his work on the American side of the family tree; to Joan Ellis, for her tapes and transcription of interviews with my mother; to Peter Freed, for his musical savvy; to Tony Morollo, for help with idiosyncratic Russian translations; to Anne Nelson, Tatyana Olyphant, Linda Rae, Virginia Stotz, and the many who contributed suggestions, information of interest, offbeat titles, and photographs. And thanks, of course, to those who listened, read, offered thoughts, encouragement, and made supportive noises: Nicky Cass, Doris Chong, Margaret Connolly, Lea Gordon, Kate Jennings, Noel Rae, Marilyn Schaefer. Jamie Grant helped wrestle too many facts to the ground; my husband, Desmond, ferreted out marvelous, unlikely sources for research and listened to my plaints; and my daughter, Alexandra, already somewhat familiar with a story she saw as

"part Edith Wharton, part Jamaica Kincaid," who will push the continuum forward. David Smith and Jay Barksdale of the New York Public
Library provided an invaluable place to hang my hat (and books) at the
library's Wertheim Study and the Shoichi Noma Reading Room. Thank
you all.

Finally, thanks to Edmund White, perpetually supportive, and in no
small way responsible for the cascade of events that let this book see
print. Thanks also to my agent, Robin Straus, for seeing what I had
hoped to depict, and to my editors, Ben George and Kathryn Court, who
believed, and to Scott Cohen, for patiently making the gears mesh.

Glossary

Breslau, Germany: Wrocław, Poland
Comblizy: Igny-Comblizy
Danzig, Germany: Gdansk, Poland
Fellin, Estonia: Viljandi, Estonia
Mitau, Latvia: Jelgava, Latvia
Rujen, Latvia: Rujiena, Latvia
Salis River: Salaca River
Salisburg, Latvia: Mazsalaca, Latvia
Tavrichesky Palace: Tauride Palace
Walk, Latvia: Valka, Latvia

Notes

Chapter 3: Widening Circles

25 "La Marseillaise" replaced the august cadences: Maurice Paléologue, *An Ambassador's Memoirs* (New York: George H. Doran, 1925), April 7, 1917. Paléologue paints an iridescent picture of revolutionary and pre–World War I Saint Petersburg, all available on http://net.lib.byu.edu/~rdh7/wwi/memoir/FrAmb Rus/palTC.htm. To avoid confusion between editions, only dates are given.

30 Swedish Red Cross . . . German, Austrian, Hungarian and Turkish prisoners of war: Gerald Davis, "National Red Cross Societies and Prisoners of War in Russia, 1914–1918," *Journal of Contemporary History*, vol. 28, no. 1 (Jan. 1993), pp. 31–52.

Chapter 5: The Bread of Exile

43 Charlottenburg district as "Charlottengrad": David Clay Large, *Berlin* (New York, Basic Books, 2000), pp. 186–87.

Chapter 6: I Never Knew—Ooh, Ooh . . .

54 "the Baltic feudal caste": Maurice Paléologue, *An Ambassador's Memoirs*, August 11, 1914.

Chapter 9: In a Thousand Ways an Exile

78 Chanel had aristocratic fingers embroidering: Edmonde Charles-Roux, *Chanel*, trans. Nancy Amphoux (London: Collins Harvill, 1989), p. 208.

78 created Irfe, and Roman de Tirtoff became Erté: Alexandre Vassiliev, *Beauty in Exile* (New York: Harry N. Abrams, 2000), pp. 225ff.

81 bring a shift to the right: the country could lurch toward dictatorship: See Harry Kessler, *Berlin in Lights: The Diaries of Count Harry Kessler (1918–1937)*, trans. and ed. Charles Kessler (New York: Grove Press, 1991), p. 367.

Chapter 10: No Ground Under Anyone's Feet

83–84 In 1921 the mark dropped: On inflation in Germany, see Gerald D. Feldman, *The Great Disorder: Politics, Economics, and Society in the German Inflation, 1914–1924* (New York: Oxford University Press, 1993). Also: Sebastian Haffner, *The Ailing Empire: Germany from Bismarck to Hitler* (New York: Fromm International Publishing, 1989); and, by the same author, *Defying Hitler* (New York: Farrar, Straus and Giroux, 2000), p. 55.

Chapter 11: Such Fearful Need

87 rowdies shouting *"Heil Hitler!"* and "Germany awake!": Kessler, *Berlin in Lights*, pp. 399–401.

87 belittled Germany's greatness and threatened public safety: See Large, *Berlin*, pp. 239–40.

89 an apostle of Americanism: Ilya Ehrenburg on Berlin, quoted in ibid., p. 211.

89 Josephine Baker . . . a huge success: See ibid., pp. 212–13.

90 Hitler and Alfred Hugenberg, political allies: Kessler, *Berlin in Lights*, p. 407.

91 Red bosses and wire-pulling Jews: Richard J. Evans, *The Coming of the Third Reich* (New York: Penguin Books, 2003), p. 293.

93 *Dichter und Denker . . . Richter und Henker*: This view, not uncommon at the time in certain circles, is quoted in Otto Friedrich, *Before the Deluge: A Portrait of Berlin in the 1920s* (New York: Fromm International Publishing, 1986), p. 332.

Chapter 12: Conditions Are Terrifying

96 Knowledgeable circles greeted Papen's appointment: André François-Poncet, in *The Fateful Years: Memoirs of a French Ambassador in Berlin, 1931–1938* (New York: Harcourt Brace, 1949), draws a glittering portrait of Papen as "vain, crafty, an intriguer."

99 epidemic of political capitulation: On the so-called March Casualties, see Pierre Ayçoberry, *The Social History of the Third Reich, 1933–1945*, trans. Janet Lloyd (New York: New Press, 1999), pp. 84ff. Also Gordon A. Craig, *Germany, 1866–1945* (New York: Oxford University Press, 1978), p. 577.

99 Hermann Keyserling, a Baltic exile: See Kessler, *Berlin in Lights*, p. 455.

101 the stiff-armed salute . . . lost fervor: According to Victor Klemperer, *I Will Bear Witness: A Diary of the Nazi Years, 1933–1941* (New York, Random House, 1998), vol. I, Bavarians reverted to their customary *"Grüss Gott."*

101 Papen gave a speech at the university in Marburg: On the fracas over the "Marburg Speech": William L. Shirer, *The Rise and Fall of the Third Reich* (New York: Simon and Schuster, 2011), pp. 217–19. Also Peter Hoffmann, *The History of the German Resistance, 1933–1945* (Cambridge, MA: MIT Press, 1977), pp. 28–29.

104 knit together disparate forces of an opposition: Allen Welsh Dulles, *Germany's Underground* (New York, Da Capo Press, 2000), p. 109.

105 meticulously enforced by Mecklenburg's agricultural inspector: See Klemperer, *I Will Bear Witness*, vol. I, p. 56.

107 Language was retooled: On Nazi language, see Victor Klemperer, *The Language of the Third Reich: LTI, Lingua Tertii Imperii: A Philologist's Notebook* (London, Athlone Press, 2000); and Ayçoberry, *Social History of the Third Reich*, pp. 1–2, 67–73.

107 Goebbels's *Schnauze*: See Alfred Joachim Fischer, *In der Nähe der Ereignisse, als jüdischer Journalist in diesem Jahrhundert* (Berlin: Transit, 1991), p. 370.

107 one "Goeb": Richard Grunberger, *The 12-Year Reich: A Social History of Nazi Germany 1933–1945* (New York: Holt, Rinehart and Winston, 1971), p. 334.

107 On the surface: On rearmament and the depletion of German agricultural labor, see Detlev J. K. Peukert, *Inside Nazi Germany: Conformity, Opposition, and Racism in Everyday Life*, trans. Richard Deveson (New Haven: Yale University Press, 1987), pp. 92–93.

Chapter 13: War Anxiety

112 England and France would do nothing: William L. Shirer, *"This Is Berlin": Radio Broadcasts from Nazi Germany* (Woodstock, NY: Overlook Press, 1999), pp. 75–160.

113 farming the last remaining fifty hectares: Under pressure from the League of Nations, newly independent Latvia allotted former landowners fifty hectares, without further compensation. For analysis of the chaos in the Baltics during and just after WWI, see Artis Pabriks, *From Nationalism to Ethnic Policy: The Latvian Nation in the Present and in the Past* (Berlin: Berliner Interuniversitare Arbeitsgruppe "Baltische Staaten," 1999); also Gert von Pistohlkors, *Deutsche Geschichte im Osten Europas Baltische Länder* (Berlin: Siedler Verlag, 1994), and A. Schwabe, *Grundriss der Agrargeschichte Lettlands* (Riga: Bernhard Lamey, 1928).

114 push for a Germanized utopia in the east: See Ayçoberry, *Social History of the Third Reich*, pp. 228–31.

115 Christmas that year was shrouded in snow and sleet: Joseph Goebbels, *Goebbels Diaries, 1939–1941*, trans. and ed. by Fred Taylor (London: H. Hamilton, 1982), Dec. 26, 1939.

117 Germany's right to colonies: See Shirer, "*This Is Berlin,*" p. 184.

117 War had killed the Easter Bunny: Ibid, p. 234.

118 concluded with "We're Marching Against England": Ibid., p. 242.

118 this war would be won, her colonies returned: Ibid., p. 253.

Chapter 14: More's the Pity

119 More's the Pity: Sources for France between the wars and in the early phase of German occupation are many and varied. Especially recommended are Clare Boothe (Luce), *Europe in the Spring* (New York: Alfred A. Knopf, 1940); Marc Bloch, *Strange Defeat*, trans. Gerard Hopkins (New York: W. W. Norton, 1968); Carmen Callil, *Bad Faith: A Forgotten History of Family, Fatherland, and Vichy France* (New York: Alfred A. Knopf, 2006); Ian Ousby, *Occupation: The Ordeal of France, 1940–1944* (New York: Cooper Square Press, 2000); Antoine de Saint-Exupéry, *Flight to Arras*, trans. Lewis Galantière (New York: Reynal & Hitchcock, 1943), and *Wartime Writings, 1939–1944*, trans. Norah Purcell (New York: Harcourt Brace Jovanovich, 1986); Jean Paul Sartre, *Paris sous l'Occupation*, various editions of this brief account; William Shirer, *The Collapse of the Third Republic: An Inquiry into the Fall of France in 1940* (New York: Simon and Schuster, 1969).

128 was, all in all, "*correcte,*": See Sartre, *Paris sous l'Occupation*.

128 perhaps the Boches weren't so bad after all: See Saint-Exupéry, *Wartime Writings*, p. 51.

130 the swastika fluttered from the Eiffel Tower: Shirer, *Collapse of the Third Republic*, p. 778.

Chapter 15: Intermezzo

134 a blow to his ego and his economy: See Norman Rich, *Hitler's War Aims, Ideology, the Nazi State, and the Course of Expansion* (New York: W. W. Norton, 1973), pp. 206–7.

136 had been served at Zossen during the "phony" war: See David Kahn, *Hitler's Spies: German Military Intelligence in World War II* (New York: Macmillan, 1978), p. 421.

136 maintaining the so-called *Kuhhaut*: See Ernest R. May, *Strange Victory: Hitler's Conquest of France* (New York: Hill and Wang, 2000), p. 245.

137 "shining cell[s] of spiritual chivalry": Thomas Nevin, *Ernst Jünger and Germany: Into the Abyss, 1914–1945* (Durham, NC: Duke University Press, 1997), p. 108, n. 18.

137 bringing about "basic changes" in German leadership: For details on FHW, see May, *Strange Victory*, pp. 254ff.

137 Official rationale: On March 30, 1941, Hitler laid out his plans for the East to his General Staff. General Franz Halder noted "ambiguous strategic aims . . . war of ideology and race that precluded principles. . . ." See Franz Halder, *The Halder War Diary, 1939–1942*, ed. Charles Burdick and Hans-Adolph Jacobsen (Novato, CA: Presidio Press, 1989).

139 Ernst Jünger's *The Peace*: See Jaimey Fisher, *Disciplining Germany: Youth, Reeducation, and Reconstruction After the Second World War* (Detroit: Wayne State University Press, 2007), pp. 110, 155. Also Nevin, *Ernst Jünger and Germany*, pp. 229ff.

Chapter 16: Barbarossa

141 Barbarossa: Among the many sources on Hitler's Russian campaign, one, not widely known, is of particular interest to this story: Fritz Gercke's *Nach Hause geschrieben . . . Aus dem Feldzug 1941 gegen Soviet-Russland* [Written Home, from the 1941 Campaign against Soviet-Russia]. Gercke, a transport and supply officer with Army Group Center, collected information from various comrades, and the booklet was privately printed in 1941, with photographs by Heribert von Koerber. Enthusiastic, propagandistic, his vivid, detailed account of movements and activity during this time is especially apposite, as he and Heinrich von Hoyningen-Huene apparently worked in proximity. I have made much use of his account.

141 In the still evening hours: Gercke, *Nach Hause geschrieben*, p. 11.

142 Roenne was seriously wounded just outside Białystok: Ibid., p. 19, though Gercke mentions Roenne only by his initials and staff designation.

143 the Fascists were not unbeatable: See www.ess.uwe.ac.uk/documents/stalin1 .htm.

143 was not the familiar call to bolster Bolshevism, but a call to defend Mother Russia: See Richard J. Evans, *The Third Reich at War* (New York: Penguin Books, 2009), p. 191.

143 The road to Minsk . . . Cyrillic sign: See Gercke, *Nach Hause geschrieben*, pp. 28, 31.

144 cups, saucers, and a jug with field flowers: Ibid., p. 145, photo by Heribert von Koerber.

144 villagers gawked at the army's typewriters and radios: Ibid., p. 21.

145 earned him popular scorn: Adam Zamoyski, *Moscow, 1812: Napoleon's Fatal March* (London: HarperCollins, 2004), p. 246.

145 Baltic, of Scottish origin, and spoke accented Russian: Ibid., p. 239.

145 Barclay's strategy . . . a derisive pun: Michael Josselson and Diana Josselson, *The Commander: A Life of Barclay de Tolly* (New York: Oxford University Press, 1980), p. 118.

145 his immense Grande Armée dwindled: Zamoyski, *Moscow 1812*, p. 536.

146 "running, running, running . . . ankle deep in dust": Johannes Hürter, ed., *Ein deutscher General an der Ostfront: Die Briefe und Tagebücher des Gotthard Heinrici, 1941–42* (Erfurt, Germany: Sutton, 2001), p. 68.

147 "yellow-brown clouds . . . like long veils": Ibid., p. 63.

147 "They come in droves, waving our leaflets": De Tolly had also distributed leaflets along Napoleon's route in 1812; see Zamoyski, *Moscow 1812*, p. 249.

147 resented Russian rule: Richard Overy, *Russia's War* (New York: Penguin Books, 1998), pp. xviii–xix. Also Catherine Merridale, *Ivan's War: Life and Death in the Red Army, 1939–1945* (New York: Metropolitan Books, 2006), pp. 91–92.

147–48 USSR would crumble into independent states: Kahn, *Hitler's Spies*, pp. 390, 454.

148 pouches for food and tobacco: See Nikolai Amosoff, *A Surgeon's War* (Chicago: Henry Regnery, 1975), p. 140.

148 lost his wooden spoon: Merridale, *Ivan's War*, p. 58.

148 "weary unto death and half starving": Fedor von Bock, *Generalfeldmarshall Fedor von Bock: Zwischen Pflicht und Verweigerung, das Kriegstagebuch*, ed. Klaus Gerbet (Munich: Herbig, 1995), p. 298.

148 babushka standing for hours: See Vasily Grossman, *A Writer at War: Vasily Grossman with the Red Army, 1933–1945*, ed. and trans. Antony Beevor and Luba Vinogradova (New York: Pantheon, 2006), based on Grossman's notebooks, war diaries, personal correspondence, and articles, p. 24.

149 German artillery's aim had been consistently off: See Hans-Heinrich Herwarth von Bittenfeld, *Against Two Evils* (New York: Rawson Wade, 1981), p. 227. Also Overy, *Russia's War*, p. 233.

150 An evening wind: For the scene at the Berezina, the road to Orsha, horses, etc., I have relied heavily on Gercke, *Nach Hause geschrieben*, pp. 36–39.

151 violating the wartime code of conduct: For details and responses to Hitler's edict, see Joachim Fest, *Plotting Hitler's Death: The German Resistance to Hitler, 1933–1945*, trans. Bruce Little (London: Weidenfeld & Nicolson, 1996), pp. 169ff.

151 Operational Order No. 8: Raul Hillberg, *The Destruction of the European Jews* (New Haven: Yale University Press, 2003), vol. I, pp. 346–47.

151 Russian émigrés in Germany were in despair: Ulrich von Hassell, *The Von Hassell Diaries, 1938–1944: The Story of the Forces Against Hitler Inside Germany* (Garden City, NY: Doubleday, 1947), July 13, 1941.

151 technically it was already behind the front: See Paul Carell, *Hitler's War Against Russia: The Story of the German Defeat in the East*, trans. Ewald Osers (London: George G. Harrap, 1964), pp. 85–88.

152 phosphorus, and rags—the Molotov cocktail: Ibid., p. 80.

153 just north of Bunichi: Wolfgang Paul, *Das Potsdamer Infanterie-Regiment 9, 1918–45* (Osnabrück, Germany: Biblio-Verlag, 1983), p. 184.

154 another perfect hit on the intelligence unit: Gercke, *Nach Hause geschrieben*, p. 44.

154 field hospital was filled up with wounded: Ibid., p. 42.

155 France had felt like maneuvers but this shredded nerves: Halder, *Kriegstagebuch*. Also Alan Clark, *Barbarossa: The Russian-German Conflict, 1941–45* (London: Hutchinson, 1965).

155 assault to secure a highly visible . . . bridge: Carell, *Hitler's War*, pp. 80–88.

155 regiment on Hill 96: Paul, *Das Postdamer Infanterie*, p. 184.

155 encourage them to follow through: Gercke, *Nach Hause geschrieben*, p. 44.

155 the Ninth's regimental commander: Paul, *Das Potsdamer Infanterie*, p. 185.

155 10 percent wounded, missing, or dead: Evans, *Third Reich at War*, p. 199.

Chapter 17: The Home Front

156 become the most temperate place on earth: See Howard K. Smith, "Valhalla in Transition *Last Train from Berlin* (New York: Alfred A. Knopf, 1942), pp. 143ff. Also Large, *Berlin*, pp. 328ff.

156 rumored to be camel dung, courtesy of Rommel's Afrika Korps: Ibid., pp. 330–31.

158 "buried . . . on the south bank of the Dnieper at the bridge of Mogilev": Paul, *Das Potsdamer Infanterie*, p. 186.

158 "1st Lieutenant von Hoyningen-Huene of 1c": Gercke, *Nach Hause geschrieben*, p. 44. The translation is mine.

162 Russian grammars to help the conquerors: Overy, *Russia's War*, p. 95.

165 "Damn Russians must not have any silk stockings": Smith, *Last Train from Berlin*, p. 151.

166 the *rasputitsa*—the time without roads: Overy, *Russia's War*, p. 113.

169 the food situation was better or worse than in 1918: Large, *Berlin*, p. 331.

170 warm clothing and furs: Ayçoberry, *Social History of the Third Reich*, pp. 336ff.

170 *Völkischer Beobachter* noted sourly: See Ruth Seydewitz and Max Seydewitz, *Unvergessene Jahre: Begegnungen* (Berlin: Buchverlag der Morgen, 1984), p. 87.

170 retreat from the Caucasus . . . planmässig: Ruth Andreas-Friedrich, *Berlin Underground, 1938–1945* (New York: Holt, 1947), January 1943, p. 85.

170 such "disastrous, indescribable human weakness": For Goebbels's view on the subject, see Ayçoberry, *Social History of the Third Reich*, pp. 315–16.

171 no young men left in Germany to make revolution: U. von Hassell diaries, quoted in Ayçoberry, *Social History of the Third Reich*, p. 339.

171 Posters screamed: For a comprehensive collection of Nazi posters, see http://www.calvin.edu/academic/cas/gpa/.

172 Radio Berlin announced the discovery of a mass grave: See Marie Vassiltchikov, *Berlin Diaries, 1940–1945* (New York: Vintage Books, 1988),
pp. 100ff.

172 inculcate the future leaders of Germany's *Herrenvolk*: On Napola and
cultivating an SS spirit, see Ayçoberry, *Social History of the Third Reich*,
pp. 210ff.

173 The watchwords for civilians: See Christabel Bielenberg, *Ride Out the Dark*
(Boston: G. K. Hall, 1984), p. 145.

Chapter 18: Keep Your Mouth Shut

174 "gets a certificate saying he never belonged": See Klemperer, *I Will Bear
Witness*, vol. 2, 1942–1945, p. 256, Aug. 1943.

175 "*Mein Auge strahlt, / mein Herz es klopft*": Noel Annan, *Changing Enemies* (New York: W. W. Norton, 1996), pp. 238–39.

178 "Look, someone is being beaten up . . .": See Klemperer, *I Will Bear Witness*,
vol. 1, 1933–1941.

179 still enjoyed a private life: Peukert, *Inside Nazi Germany*, pp. 236ff.

Chapter 19: Give Me Ten Years

180 one "Goer" was the maximum amount of tin: Grunberger, *12-Year Reich*,
p. 334.

182 destroyed—"root and branch": See Shirer, *Rise and Fall of the Third Reich*,
pp. 1069ff.

182 Robert Ley inveighed against the "blue-blooded swine" . . . Goebbels . . . orders for liquidating: Grunberger, *12-Year Reich*, p. 143.

183 The Americans were in Aachen . . . "Iron Reserve": Ayçoberry, *Social History of the Third Reich*, p. 331.

185 "terror missions" of Allied bombers: See *Die Wehrmachtberichte, 1939–
1945* (Munich: Deutscher Taschenbuch Verlag, 1985), vol. 3, pp. 370–371.

187 also robbed of language: W. G. Sebald, *On the Natural History of Destruction*, trans. Anthea Bell (New York: Random House, 2003), p. 42.

187 "enchanted . . . like a Sunday school picture": See Kurt Vonnegut, *Slaughterhouse-Five* (New York: Dial Press Trade Paperback, 1999), p. 189.

187 "crushed . . . disemboweled . . . cremated": Kurt Vonnegut, *Armageddon in
Retrospect* (New York: Berkley Trade, 2009), p. 36.

Chapter 22: She and Her Kind

227 huddled in bombed-out railroad stations: See Large, *Berlin*, pp. 388–89; also
see Dagmar Barnouw, *Germany 1945: Views of War and Violence* (Bloomington: Indiana University Press, 1996).

Chapter 23: A Labyrinth Without an Exit

236 Nicotine starved: On cigarettes, *Kippen*, etc., see David Stafford, *Endgame, 1945: The Missing Final Chapter of World War II* (New York: Little, Brown, 2007), p. 479.

Epilogue

281 "This cruel age has deflected me": Anna Akhmatova, *Poems of Akhmatova*, selected, trans., and intro. by Stanley Kunitz with Max Hayward (Boston: Atlantic–Little, Brown, 1973), p. 129.

Bibliography

Akhmatova, Anna. *Poems of Akhmatova*, selected, trans., and intro. by Stanley Kunitz with Max Hayward. Boston: Atlantic–Little, Brown, 1973.

Almedingen, E. M. *My St. Petersburg*. New York: W. W. Norton, 1970.

Amosoff, Nikolai. *A Surgeon's War*. Chicago: Henry Regnery, 1975.

Andreas-Friedrich, Ruth. *Berlin Underground, 1938–1945*. New York: Holt, 1947.

Annan, Noel. *Changing Enemies*. New York: W. W. Norton, 1996.

Anonymous. *A Woman in Berlin: Eight Weeks in a Conquered City: A Diary*, trans. Phillip Boehm. New York: Metropolitan Books, 2005.

Ayçoberry, Pierre. *The Social History of the Third Reich, 1933–1945*, trans. Janet Lloyd. New York: New Press, 1999.

Baranowski, Shelley. *The Sanctity of Rural Life: Nobility, Protestantism and Nazism in Weimar Prussia*. New York: Oxford University Press, 1995.

Baring, Maurice. *A Year in Russia*. London: Methuen, 1907.

Barnouw, Dagmar. *Germany 1945: Views of War and Violence*. Bloomington: Indiana University Press, 1996.

Bartov, Omer. *The Eastern Front 1941–1945: German Troops and the Barbarization of Warfare*. New York: Macmillan, 2001.

Berghahn, Volker R. *Der Stahhelm: Bund der Frontsoldaten, 1918–1935*. Düsseldorf, Droste Verlag, 1966.

Bielenberg, Christabel. *Ride Out the Dark*. Boston: G. K. Hall, 1984.

Bloch, Marc. *Strange Defeat*, trans. Gerard Hopkins. New York: W. W. Norton, 1968.

Bock, Fedor von. *Generalfeldmarshall Fedor von Bock: Zwischen Pflicht und Verweigerung, Das Kriegstagebuch*, ed. Klaus Gerbet. Munich: Herbig, 1995.

Boothe, Clare (Luce). *Europe in the Spring*. New York: Alfred A. Knopf, 1940.

Browning, Christopher. *Ordinary Men: Reserve Police Battalion 101 and the Final Solution in Poland*. New York: Aaron Asher Books, 1992.

———. *The Origins of the Final Solution*. Lincoln: University of Nebraska Press, 2004.

Bruhns, Wibke. *Meines Vaters Land*. Berlin: Ullstein, 2005.

Bunners, Michael, and Erhard Piersig. *Mecklenburgia Sacra, Jahrbuch für Mecklenburgische Kirchengeschichte*, vol. 3. Wismar, Germany: Redaria Verlag, 2000.

Callil, Carmen. *Bad Faith: A Forgotten History of Family, Fatherland and Vichy France*. London: Alfred A. Knopf, 2006.

Calvocoressi, David, and Guy Wint. *Total War: Causes and Course of the Second World War*. London: Harmondsworth, 1974.

Carell, Paul. *Hitler's War on Russia: The Story of the German Defeat in the East*, trans. Ewald Osers. London: George G. Harrap, 1964.

Clark, Alan. *Barbarossa: The Russian-German Conflict, 1941–45*. London: Hutchinson, 1965.

Craig, Gordon A. *Germany, 1866–1945*. New York: Oxford University Press, 1978.

Dagerman, Stig. *German Autumn*, trans. Robin Fulton. London and New York: Quartet Books, 1988.

Davis, Gerald. "National Red Cross Societies and Prisoners of War in Russia, 1914–1918." *Journal of Contemporary History* 28, no. 1 (Jan. 1993): 31–52.

Dulles, Allen Welsh. *Germany's Underground: The Anti-Nazi Resistance*. New York: Da Capo Press, 2000. First published 1947 by Macmillan.

Ehrenburg, Ilya. *The Fall of France, Seen through Soviet Eyes*. London: Modern Books, 1940.

———. *The Fall of Paris*. New York: Alfred A. Knopf, 1943.

Evans, Richard J. *The Coming of the Third Reich*. New York: Penguin Books, 2003.

———. *The Third Reich in Power: 1933–1939*. New York: Penguin, 2005.

———. *The Third Reich at War: How the Nazis Led Germany from Conquest to Disaster*. London: Allen Lane, 2008.

Feldman, Gerald D. *The Great Disorder: Politics, Economics, and Society in the German Inflation, 1914–1924*. New York: Oxford University Press, 1993.

Fest, Joachim. *Plotting Hitler's Death: The German Resistance to Hitler, 1933–1945*, trans. Bruce Little. London: Weidenfeld and Nicolson, 1996.

———. *The Face of the Third Reich: Portraits of the Nazi Leadership*. New York: Da Capo Press, 1999.

Fischer, Alexander, et al. *Russische Sozialdemokratie und bewaffneter Aufstand im Jahre, 1905*. Wiesbaden: Harrassowitz, 1967.

———. *Der Militarische Widerstand gegen Hitler u.d. NS Regime, 1933–1945*. Herford, England: E. S. Mitler, 1984.

Fischer, Alfred Joachim. *In der Nähe der Ereignisse, als jüdischer Journalist in diesem Jahrhundert*. Berlin: Transit, 1991.

Fischer, Conan. *Stormtroopers: A Social, Economic and Ideological Analysis, 1929–35*. London: Allen & Unwin, 1983.

———. *The Rise of National Socialism and the Working Classes in Weimar Germany*. Providence, RI: Berghahn Books, 1996.

Friedrich, Jörg. *Der Brand: Deutschland im Bombenkrieg, 1940–1945*. Berlin, Propyläen, 2002.

Friedrich, Otto. *Before the Deluge: A Portrait of Berlin in the 1920's*. New York: Fromm International, 1986.

Fromm, Bella. *Blood and Banquets: A Berlin Social Diary.* New York and London: Harper & Brothers, 1942.

Gaddis, John Lewis. *The Landscape of History: How Historians Map the Past.* London: Oxford University Press, 2002.

Gercke, Fritz. *Nach Hause geschrieben . . . Aus dem Feldzug 1941 gegen Sowjet-Russland,* with photographs by Heribert von Koerber. Privately published, 1941.

Gildea, Robert. *Marianne in Chains.* New York: Metropolitan Books, 2002.

Gill, Anton. *A Dance through the Flames: Berlin between the Wars.* London: J. Murray, 1993.

———. *An Honorable Defeat: A History of German Resistance to Hitler, 1933–1945.* London: Heinemann, 1994.

Goebbels, Joseph. *The Goebbels Diaries 1939–1941,* trans. and ed. by Fred Taylor. London: H. Hamilton, 1982.

———. *The Goebbels Diaries, 1942–1943,* ed., trans., and intro. by Louis P. Lochner. Garden City, NY: Doubleday, 1948.

Grossman, Vasily. *A Writer at War: Vasily Grossman with the Red Army, 1941–1945,* ed. and trans. by Antony Beevor and Luba Vinogradova. New York: Pantheon, 2005.

Grunberger, Richard. *The 12-Year Reich: A Social History of Nazi Germany, 1933–1945.* New York: Holt, Rinehart and Winston, 1971.

Haffner, Sebastian. *The Ailing Empire: Germany from Bismarck to Hitler.* New York: Fromm, 1989.

———. *Defying Hitler.* New York: Farrar, Straus and Giroux, 2000.

Halder, Franz. *The Halder War Diary, 1939–1942,* ed. Charles Burdick and Hans-Adolph Jacobsen. Novato, CA: Presidio Press, 1989.

Hastings, Max. *Armageddon: The Battle for Germany 1944–1945.* New York: Alfred A. Knopf, 2004.

Herwarth von Bittenfeld, Hans-Heinrich. *Zwischen Hitler und Stalin.* Frankfurt: Propyläen, 1982.

Hiden, John W., and Patrick Salmon. *The Baltic Nations and Europe: Estonia, Latvia and Lithuania in the Twentieth Century.* Rev. ed. London: Longman, 1994.

———, and Thomas Lane, eds. *The Baltic and the Outbreak of the Second World War.* Cambridge: Cambridge University Press, 1992.

Hürter, Johannes, ed. *Ein deutscher General an der Ostfront: Die Briefe und Tagebücher des Gotthard Heinrici, 1941/42.* Erfurt, Germany: Sutton, 2001.

Ignatieff, Michael. *The Russian Album.* London: Chatto & Windus, 1987.

Jackson, Julian. *The Fall of France: The Nazi Invasion of 1940.* New York: Oxford University Press, 2003.

Josselson, Michael, and Diana Josselson. *The Commander: A Life of Barclay de Tolly.* New York: Oxford University Press, 1980.

Keegan, John. *The Battle for History: Refighting World War II.* New York: Vintage Books, 1996.

Kershaw, Ian. *Der Hitler-Mythos: Volksmeinung und Propaganda im Dritten Reich.* Stuttgart: Deutsche Verlags-Anstalt, 1980.

———. *Popular Opinion and Political Dissent in the Third Reich: Bavaria, 1933–45.* Oxford: Clarendon Press, 1983.

———. *Hitler: A Biography.* New York: W. W. Norton, 2008.

Kessler, Harry. *Berlin in Lights: The Diaries of Count Harry Kessler (1918–1937),* trans. and ed. Charles Kessler. New York: Grove Press, 1999.

Klemperer, Klemens von. *Germany's New Conservatism.* Princeton, NJ: Princeton University Press, 1957.

———. *German Resistance against Hitler: The Search for Allies Abroad.* Oxford: Clarendon Press, 1992.

Klemperer, Victor. *I Will Bear Witness: A Diary of the Nazi Years, 1933–41, 1942–45,* 2 vols. New York: Random House, 1998–99.

———. *The Language of the Third Reich: LTI, Lingua Tertii Imperii: A Philologist's Notebook.* London: Athlone Press, 2000.

Knappe, Siegfried, and Ted Brusaw. *Soldat: Reflections of a German Soldier.* New York: Orion Books, 1992.

Krockow, Christian von. *The Hour of the Women: A Young Mother's Fight to Survive at the Close of World War II,* trans. Krishna Winston. New York: Edward Burlingame Books, HarperCollins, 1991.

Large, David Clay. *Between Two Fires: Europe's Path in the 1930's.* New York: W. W. Norton, 1991.

———. *Berlin.* New York: Basic Books, 2000.

Liddell Hart, B. H. *The Soviet Army.* London: Weidenfeld and Nicolson, 1956.

Lieven, Anatol. *The Baltic Revolution; Latvia, Lithuania, Estonia and the Path to Independence.* New Haven: Yale University Press, 1993.

Lieven, D. C. *Russia's Rulers Under the Old Regime.* New Haven: Yale University Press, 1989.

———. *The Aristocracy of Europe.* New York: Columbia University Press, 1993.

———. *Russia Against Napoleon: The True Story of the Campaigns of War and Peace.* New York: Viking, 2010.

MacDonogh, Giles. *After the Reich: The Brutal History of the Allied Occupation.* New York: Basic Books, 2007.

———. *1938: Hitler's Gamble.* New York: Basic Books, 2009.

Meehan, Patricia. *The Unnecessary War.* London: Sinclair-Stevenson, 1992.

Merridale, Catherine. *Ivan's War: Life and Death in the Red Army, 1939–1945.* New York: Metropolitan Books, 2006.

Nabokov, Vladimir. *Speak, Memory.* New York: G. P. Putnam's Sons, 1966.

Némirovsky, Irène. *Suite Française.* New York: Vintage Books, 2007.

Ousby, Ian. *Occupation: The Ordeal of France, 1940–1944.* New York: Cooper Square Press, 2000.

Overy, Richard. *Russia's War.* New York: Penguin Books, 1998.

———. *The Road to War.* New York: Penguin Books, 1999.

Pabriks, Artis. *From Nationalism to Ethnic Policy: The Latvian Nation in the Present and in the Past.* Berlin: Berliner Interuniversitäre Arbeitsgruppe "Baltische Staaten," 1999.

Paléologue, Maurice. *An Ambassador's Memoirs.* New York: George H. Doran, 1925. Online: http://net.lib.byu.edu/~rdh7/wwi/memoir/FrAmbRus/palTC.htm.

Paul, Wolfgang. *Das Postsdamer Infanterie-Regiment 9, 1918–45: Presussische Tradition in Krieg und Frieden.* Osnabrück, Germany: Biblio-Verlag, 1983.

Peukert, Detlev J. K. *Inside Nazi Germany: Conformity, Opposition, and Racism in Everyday Life,* trans. Richard Deveson. New Haven: Yale University Press, 1987.

Pipes, Richard. *The Formation of the Soviet Union: Communism and Nationalism, 1917–1923.* New York: Atheneum, 1968.

———. *Russia under the Bolshevik Regime.* New York: Alfred A. Knopf, 1994.

———. *A Concise History of the Russian Revolution.* New York: Alfred A. Knopf, 1995.

———. *Russia under the Old Regime.* London, New York: Penguin Books, 1995.

Pistohlkors, Get von. *Deutsche Geschichte im Osten Europas.* Berlin: Seidler Verlag, 1994.

Reese, Willi Peter. *A Stranger to Myself.* New York: Farrar, Straus and Giroux, 2005.

Rempel, Gerhard. *Hitler's Children: The Hitler Youth and the SS.* Chapel Hill: University of North Carolina Press, 1989.

Rich, Norman. *Hitler's War Aims, Ideology, the Nazi State, and the Course of Expansion.* New York: W. W. Norton, 1973.

Roth, Joseph. *What I Saw.* New York: W. W. Norton, 2003.

Saint-Exupéry, Antoine de. *Pilote de Guerre.* Paris: Gallimard, 1942.

———. *Wartime Writings, 1939–1944,* trans. Norah Purcell. New York: Harcourt Brace Jovanovich, 1986.

Schiff, Stacy. *Saint-Exupéry: A Biography.* New York: Alfred A. Knopf, 1994.

Schwabe, A. *Grundriss der Agrargeschichte Lettlands.* Riga: Bernhard Lamey, 1928.

Schmemann, Serge. *Echoes of a Native Land.* New York: Alfred A. Knopf, 1997.

Sebald, W. G. *On the Natural History of Destruction,* trans. Anthena Bell. New York: Random House, 2003.

Seydewitz, Ruth, and Max Seydewitz. *Unvergessene Jahre: Begegnungen.* Berlin: Buchverlag der Morgen, 1984.

Shirer, William L. *The Rise and Fall of the Third Reich.* New York: Simon and Schuster, 1960.

———. *The Collapse of the Third Republic.* New York: Da Capo Press, 1994. First published 1969 by Simon and Schuster.

———. *"This Is Berlin": Radio Broadcasts from Nazi Germany.* Woodstock, NY: Overlook Press, 1999.

Smith, Howard K. *Last Train from Berlin.* New York: Alfred A. Knopf, 1942.

Stafford, David. *Endgame, 1945: The Missing Final Chapter of World War II.* New York: Little, Brown, 2007.

Steinhoff, Ilse. *Deutsche in Afrika*. Berlin: Reichskolonialbund, 1941.

Steinhoff, Johannes, Peter Pechel, and Denis Showalter. *Voices from the Third Reich, an Oral History*. Washington, DC: Regnery Gateway, 1998.

Stern, Fritz. *The Varieties of History: From Voltaire to the Present*. New York: Meridian Books, 1956.

———. *Dreams and Delusion: National Socialism in the Drama of the German Past*. New York: Vintage Books, 1989.

———. *Five Germanys I Have Known*. New York: Farrar, Straus and Giroux, 2006.

Studnitz, Hans-Georg. *While Berlin Burns: The Diary of Hans-Georg von Studnitz, 1943–1945*, trans. R. H. Stevens. Englewood Cliffs, NJ: Prentice Hall, 1964.

Tuchman, Barbara. *The Guns of August*. New York: Ballantine Books, 1994.

Vardys, S., and R. Misiunas, eds. *The Baltic States in Peace and War*. University Park: Pennsylvania State University Press, 1978.

Vassiltchikov, Marie. *Berlin Diaries, 1940–1945*. New York: Vintage Books, 1988.

Vonnegut, Kurt. *Armageddon in Retrospect*. New York: G. P. Putnam's Sons, 2008.

———. *Slaughterhouse-Five*. New York: Dial Press Trade Paperback, 1999.

Weber, Eugen. *The Hollow Years: France in the 1930s*. New York: W. W. Norton, 1994.

Die Wehrmachtberichte, 1939–1945. Munich: Deutscher Taschenbuch Verlag GmbH KG, 1985.

Weinberg, Gerhard L. *A World at Arms: A Global History of World War II*. Rev. ed. New York: Cambridge University Press, 2005.

Werth, Léon. *Trente-trois Jours*. Paris: V. Hamy, 1982.

Whelan, Heide W. *Adapting to Modernity: Family, Caste and Capitalism among the Baltic German Nobility*. Köln: Böhler Verlag, 1999.

Zamoyski, Adam. *Moscow 1812: Napoleon's Fatal March*. New York: HarperCollins, 2004. First published as *1812: Napoleon's Fatal March on Moscow*. London: HarperCollins, 2004.

Zuckmayer, Carl. *A Part of Myself: Portrait of an Epoch*, trans. Richard and Clara Winston. New York: Harcourt Brace Jovanovich, 1966.

Index

Aimée and Heinrich are abbreviated in the index as A and H respectively. Because they, along with a number of their friends and family, are treated in the text on a first-name, or familiar, basis, they are entered into the index accordingly. For example, A and H's children, Brigitte, Christian, Dorothée, Friedrich, Michael, and Sigrid, are each listed in the index under their first name. Mimama and Papa, Heinrich's parents, are similarly listed in the index under Mimama and Papa, and so forth.

Africa, 7, 51, 66, 111–12, 117, 170
agrarian romanticism, 94, 107
Agrigento, Sicily, 7, 58
Aimée von Hoyningen-Huene (née Ellis)
    birthdays of, 47, 70, 101, 106, 113
    childhood and youth of, 16–18, 38–39,
        208, 266, 280
    citizenship of, 270
    death of, 3
    as debutante, 40–41
    early travels in Europe of, 7–9, 39–40
    family background of, 16–18
    fears of, 174–79
    first meeting with H's family of, 69–70
    on Hitler, 100
    Hollis proposal to, 263
    H's death and, 158–60, 161, 162–63, 169,
        176, 181, 197
    H's first encounter with, 7–9
    H's shared future with, 47–48
    isolation of, 16–18, 39, 74, 77, 91, 95,
        109–10, 129
    lost love letters to H from, 274–75
    Nazi honor for, 113
    as only parent, 160, 278
    pregnancies of, 67–68, 73, 156, 159, 160,
        162, 164, 251
    subversiveness of, 157
    U.S. visits of, 65, 89, 96

wedding and honeymoon of, 51–53, 70–72
    See also specific person or topic
Akhmatova, Anna, 281
Alexander III (tsar), 8, 27
Alexander Sinclair, Admiral Edwyn, 34
Algeciras, Spain, A's Christmas visit to, 51
All Quiet on the Western Front
    (Remarque film), 87
Allied Commission, Treaty of Brest-
    Litovsk and, 34
Allies, 101, 170, 171, 180, 183, 185, 193
    invasion/occupation of Germany by, 195,
        197, 202, 205, 210–11
    See also specific nation
Anita Dewing (A's friend), 37, 39, 51, 89,
    91, 101, 157, 167, 228, 236, 251–52,
    255–56, 261, 263, 272, 280
Anna Malé (A's adoptee), 49, 62, 88, 99
anti-Semitism. See Jews
Ardennes, 121, 136
Arizona, A's move to, 1, 5, 282
Army Group Center, and H with
    Operation Barbarossa, 141–42,
    145–46, 148–49
Arnim von (German POW), 228
Arkangelsky, 59
Art Students League, 11, 41, 48
Austria, Anschluss in, 107- 08
autograph incident, A's, 230–31

Baker, Josephine, 89
Ballad of Mme. Colette (H composition),
    54–55
Baltic countries
    and buildup to World War II, 112-114
    and German-Russian relations, 134,
        137–40
    German withdrawal from, 35, 130
    Germans in, 7–8, 27, 54, 114, 137–38
    H family departure from, 35–36
    Hitler's proposal about, 113
    H's views about, 138–40
    refugees from, 227
    Treaty of Brest-Litovsk and, 30, 34
    World War I and, 26–28, 30
    World War II and, 137–38
Baltic Land Defense, 34, 137
Barclay's Bank, 58
Barclay de Tolly, Mikhail, 120, 126, 145
Barnard College, 41
Basilevitch, Mikhail (H's Uncle Buddha),
    47, 189
BBC, 177, 197, 200, 206
Below, Wilhelm, 156, 196, 207, 211, 212,
    214, 219, 224, 232, 234, 261
Berezina river, Russia 150-51
Berlin, Germany, 72, 78, 81 111
    A and H in, 82-83, 87–93, 95
    A and Margarethe meeting in, 227
    allied bombing of, 180, 191
    and beginning of World War II, 112
    description of, 89
    desperation in, 92–93, 98
    H in, 83
    H's infidelity in, 95–96, 110
    popular jokes in, 174–75
    Russian refugees in, 43
    siege of, 198
    Untergangsatmosphäre in, 191
Berliner Illustrierte Zeitung, 90
Betty (H's cousin), 79
Betty Judd (A's friend), 78
bicycle touring, 47,48
Bill (A's uncle), 11, 16, 18, 50, 51, 82, 91,
    167, 193, 208, 213, 217, 219–20, 251,
    256–57, 263, 270
    death of, 228
    meets H, 64–65
Bismarck, Otto von, 28, 103, 203
Blomeyer, Frau, 210

blood and soil, 94, 107
Blumenhagen (Mecklenburg farm),
    94–110, 124, 221, 258, 271
    A and H buy, 94
    A's dream of return to, 209, 223, 233, 246
    A's return visit to, 225–26
    and beginning of World War II, 118
    Christmas at, 106, 115–16
    dogs at, 190
    as family refuge, 175–77, 187–88
    final good-bye to, 197, 216
    flight from, 193, 194–203, 204–16
    as home, 282
    Ottenhof compared with, 113
    refugees at, 187–91
    in Russian sector of Germany, 211, 233
    SS at, 190–91, 195, 197
    storks at, 181
    treasures at, 98, 185
    women at, 180–81
    during WWII, 156–73, 175–79, 180–81,
        187–92
Bock, Fedor von, (Field Marshal),148
Bolshevik Revolution (1917), 2, 8, 21–26,
    28, 34, 44, 92, 130, 273
Bonfels, Waldemar, 230
books. See reading
Bose, Herbert von, 90, 96, 102
Bourges, France, and H in military in
    France, 131–33, 136
Bousquet family (Maine neighbors), 263
Bowdoin College, 256–57, 264, 267,
    270–71, 278
Brändstrom, Edvard, 30
Breslau, Germany, A and H in, 72, 73–81,
    82–83
Briand, Aristide, 81, 92, 129
Bridgman, George, 11, 41
Brigitte Anita (A and H's daughter), 107–8,
    110, 115, 116, 157, 192
    and A's move to Maine, 257, 258–60
    and A's return to U.S., 248, 249
    birth of, 101
    citizenship of, 167–68, 246–47, 261,
        269–70
    and flight from Blumenhagen, 195, 201
    in Frankenberg, 232, 244, 245, 257,
        258–60
    in Grosseelheim, 218, 221, 222, 223, 225,
        233, 234

Hitler explained to, 182–83
and H's death, 163, 164
in Maine, 203, 264, 273–74
as teacher, 278
voyage to U.S. of, 262
Brochard family, 132–33
Brooke, Rupert, 46
Brothers Grimm, 61, 218
Browning, Robert, 282
Buddha (Mikhail Basilevitch) (H's uncle),
47, 189
Bürger, Herr (Blumenhagen neighbor),
160, 188, 194, 197, 198, 200
Butzbach, Germany, A in displaced persons
camp, 249
Buzzard family (H's friends), 57–58

Cabaret (film), 96
Carey Miss (Hahn's secretary), 220,
221, 222
CBS, 156
censorship, 99, 101, 170, 174–75, 177–79,
182, 190, 234, 243
Chamber of Culture, Reich
(Reichskulturkammer), 101
Chamberlain, Neville, 108–9
Champvallon (French village), German
troops in, 129
Chanel, 78
"Chef" (Mildy's husband), 256, 262
Chemin des Dames, France, 125
Chenonceau, France, 128, 132
Chevalier, Maurice, "Paris Is Still
Paris," 136
children's prayers, 191–92
A Child's Garden of Verses
(Stevenson), 254
Christian (A and H's son), 107–8,
116, 193
and A's move to Maine, 257, 258–60
and A's return to U.S., 248, 249
birth of, 98
career of, 278
citizenship of, 167–68, 246–47, 261,
269–70
Dresden trip of, 238–39
and flight from Blumenhagen, 201, 205,
212–13, 214
in Frankenberg, 232, 233, 235, 243–44,
257, 258–60

and French officers' coats incident,
243–44
in Grosseelheim, 218, 219, 221, 222, 223,
224–25, 227
at Harvard, 278
in Maine, 263, 264
in Marburg, 249
Nazi honor for, 172
Nazi recruitment of, 172
voyage to U.S. of, 262
Christmas
in Blumenhagen, 106, 115–16
in Breslau, 74
in Frankenberg, 244–45, 247
in Grosseelheim, 229–30
in Hartford, 16
in Maine, 265
in Morocco, 51
in New Jersey, 255
in Saint Petersburg, 12
churches. See religion
Churchill, Winston, 134
cigarettes, 236–37
citizenship
of A, 270–71
of A and H's children, 167–68, 246–47,
269–70
civilization, 130, 205, 209–10, 232, 259,
269, 272
Colette, 54–55, 58–59
Cologne, Germany, churches in, 60
Colonial Office, German, H with, 111, 118
Colt guns, 208
Commissar Order, Hitler's, 151
communists, and Nazis, 90–91, 99, 103, 108
concentration camps, 104, 108, 178, 204,
226
Cone family, 16
Confessing Church, 104, 108
Constituent Assembly, Russian, 28
Corneille, Pierre, dramatist, 122, 143
Cornell, Katherine, 41
Corson (A's brother), 16–18, 37–38, 40, 91,
96, 100, 192, 197, 219, 228–29, 235,
257, 270, 283
Coulanges (French village), German
troops in, 126
culture
at Blumenhagen, 94
in Dresden, 43–44

culture (*cont.*)
  in Maine, 269
  and Nazis, 101
  in NY, 41–42
  See also intellectuals; music; reading
Czechoslovakia, 108, 111

Dachau, Germany, 108
Daisy von Pritzelwitz, 53, 65, 217, 220
Dana Hall, A at, 30, 82, 194
Danzig (Gdansk), 111, 112
Della Robbia, Andrea, 31
De Grasse (ship), A trip on, 68
Denmark, German advance on, 117–18
Der Angriff (Nazi paper), 182
Deutsche Christen, 103, 104
"*Deutschland, Deutschland Über Alles*"
  (song), 237
Dewing, Mrs., 39, 51
Dimenty Zacharievitch, 12, 27–28, 241
Dneiper, river, Russia, 143, 145, 150-51, 158
Dobbs Ferry (Masters) school, 38–39, 64,
  82, 208, 230, 239
Dodd, William, 102
dogs, 190, 206, 226–27, 262
Dombrowski, Frau, 75
Dorothée (A and H's daughter), 107, 108,
  116, 164
  and A's return to U.S., 248, 249–52
  birth of, 106
  birthdays of, 256
  career of, 278–79
  citizenship of, 167–68, 246–47, 270
  DAR scholarship for, 283
  and flight from Blumenhagen, 195
  in Frankenberg, 240, 244, 245
  in Grosseelheim, 218, 221, 222, 225, 229,
    234, 235
  in Hartford, 256, 260
  in Maine, 261, 262, 263, 264, 269, 273–74
  in New Jersey, 253, 255
Dorothy (A's cousin), 18, 252–55, 256, 263
drawing, 11, 17, 42
Dresden, Germany, 43–44, 50, 63, 72,
  86, 143
  A's visits to, 102, 238–39, 240–42
  bombing of, 186–87
  H's parents in, 186–87, 237–39
Dresdner Kreuzchor, boys choir, 44
Duma, Russian, 21, 22, 23

Dunkirk, France, 121, 125
Durchhalteschlager (song), 169

Easter
  at Blumenhagen, 194
  in Saint Petersburg, 13
  and WWII, 104, 117, 194
Ebba (H's sister), 19, 33, 67, 70, 188, 213,
  214, 220, 246, 269, 279
education
  of A in NY, 11, 41–42
  of A in Paris, 49, 53
  A's childhood, 17, 38–39
  A's children in Hartford, 256, 260, 261,
    265–66
  in Frankenberg, 232, 234–35, 236
  in Grosseelheim, 224–25
  of H in Paris, 9
  H's childhood, 33
  and H's PhD, 47, 49, 53–54, 57, 73, 81
  in Maine, 257–58, 263, 264
  recruitment for SS, 172
  See also specific institution
Eekelen, Leo van (Dutch POW), 274
Einsatzgruppen, Einsatzkommandos,
  and Operation Barbarossa, 151
Elisabeth (Brigitte's friend), 249
Ellis, Aimée. *See* Aimée
Ellis, John. *See* John Ellis (A's uncle)
Ellison, Mr. (Maine carpenter), 259
Emil (H's paternal grandfather), 13, 23–24,
  25–26, 280–81
Emil (H's uncle), 12, 22, 44, 85
employment. *See* work
Endsieg, 203
Engelhard-Toróschino, Nina (H family
  neighbor), 21–22
England. *See* Great Britain
Erich (Marta and Below's son), 224,
  232, 234
Erté, 78
Europe
  A and Anita's travel in, 39–40
  A and Hope's travel in, 7–9
  future of, 129
  Germany as hole in, 185
  See also specific nation
Everest Haight (A's friend), 42, 53, 91–92,
  235, 236, 264
exile. *See* outsiders

Fallada, Hans, *Little Man, What Now?*, 90
family
    differences between A and H, 84
    future of A and H, 93
    women as supporter of, 257
    See also names of individuals
farming, 96–97, 105, 109, 113, 156. *See also*
    Blumenhagen; gardening; Good Grief
    farm
father (A's), 16–17, 37–38, 176, 183, 208,
    251, 256, 270, 280
father (H's). *See* Papa (Ernst von
    Hoyningen-Huene)
fear, 76, 101, 111–12, 149, 172–73, 174–79,
    190, 191, 195, 202, 206–8, 209–10, 249
Fenique family, 9–10, 47, 139
Feodorovsk "Belaya Mysa" (H family
    estate), 27, 28
Ferguson, Sammy, 37
FHW (Foreign Armies West), 128, 135,
    136, 137, 185
Finland, H family estate in, 27–28
folk community (*Volksgemeinschaft*),
    Nazi, 107
Fontainebleau, France, Tafelrunde
    meetings at, 135
food, 30–31, 33, 35, 105, 120, 148, 153, 155,
    176, 195, 199, 205–7, 214–16, 221–22,
    224, 229–30, 232–33, 236–39, 242,
    244–45, 247, 249–51, 257, 259–60,
    262–63
    mushroom hunting, 12, 150
    scarcity of, 29, 169–70, 180, 189–90,
    226, 235
    See also hunger
Foreign Office, 80, 83
Fort de la Malmaison (France), 126
France, 47, 114, 117
    and beginning of World War II, 112
    blame for downfall of, 128
    British relations with, 120, 122–23,
    127, 128
    and buildup to World War II, 111
    declaration of war by, 112
    German occupation of, 119–33,
    134, 137
    H at war in, 119–33, 135–37
    and Russia, 142–43
    surrender of, 129, 134
    See also Paris; World War II

Francis I, 135
Frankenberg, Germany
    A in, 232–48
    Christmas in, 244–45, 247
    Helma's medical practice in, 231, 232,
    233, 236, 242, 244, 247
Frankfurt, Germany, A's visit to American
    consulate in, 242, 246
Franz (H's cousin), 119
Frederick the Great, 89, 90
French officers' coats incident, 243–44
Friedrich Alexander (A and H's son), 78,
    80, 88, 97, 105, 106–7, 108–9, 115–16,
    176, 177, 250–51
    and A's move to Maine, 257, 258–60
    and A's return to U.S., 248, 249
    birth of, 75
    career/work of, 270, 278
    citizenship of, 167–68, 246–47, 261,
    269–70
    and flight from Blumenhagen, 203, 212
    in Frankenberg, 233, 234, 235, 244, 245,
    247, 257, 258–60
    in Grosseelheim, 218, 219, 221, 222,
    223, 224
    and H's watch, 225
    in Maine, 263, 264, 265, 267
    and Marta-Below wedding, 224
    musical talents of, 233, 247, 249, 278
    Nazi recruitment of, 183–85, 185, 193,
    195, 196
    in New York, 270
    voyage to U.S. of, 262

Gania (H family servant), 34
gardening, 87, 105, 177, 187, 232, 237, 246,
    257–59, 264, 268–69, 272. *See also*
    farming
Georg (H's brother), 19, 29, 30, 33–34, 62,
    70, 84, 97, 113–14, 134, 189, 198, 240,
    246, 269
George (H's cousin), 2, 34, 54, 78–79,
    137–38
Georges (Mimama's brother), 241
Georgievsk (H family estate), 27, 28
Gerassim (servant), 86
German Christians, 103–4
Germany
    Allied sectors in, 210–11
    A's flight from, 193–216

Germany (*cont.*)
  A's and Sigrid's visit to, 279
  black humor in, 174–75, 237
  book burnings in, 99
  desperation in, 76, 81, 83–84, 87–93, 102
  as dictatorship, 101
  drafting of youth in, 183–84, 185–86
  economic depression in, 81, 90–91
  elections in, 89–90, 99
  Heil Hitlers increase in, 165
  as hole in Europe, 185
  home front during WWII in, 156–73,
    174–79
  housing shortage in, 234–35
  H's family arrives in, 43
  H's views about, 66
  hunger in, 40, 73, 105
  as nation of women, 180–81
  and public sentiment about war, 165
  refugees in, 227
  ruin of, 192–93, 212
  Russian émigrés in, 151
  Russian relations with, 134, 137–38, 144,
    147–49, 151–52
  transformation of, 180
  See also specific person, organization,
    nation, or topic
Gersdorff von, family (A and H friends),
    114, 160, 196, 226
Gift to Young Housewives (Russian
    cookbook), 264
Gilbert and Sullivan, 157
Gillette, Gilbert, 37
Goebbels, Joseph, 91, 94, 101–2, 107,
    112, 117, 120, 122, 128, 155, 167,
    170–71, 182
Goethe, Johann Wolfgang von, 192,
    208, 238
Golandowski, Herr (Breslau butcher), 76
Gooch, G. P., 47, 57
Good Grief Farm, A's (Maine), 257–67,
    268–71
Gordon (A's stepbrother), 91
Göring, Hermann, 165, 180
Graf Zeppelin, (airship) 74
grave(s)
  A's family, 40
  Emil's, 44, 280–81
  in Grosseelheim, 227
  Helma's, 250–51

in H's family, 240–41, 281
in Mogilev, 153–54
in Ottenhof, 14
in Saint Petersburg, 280–81
Sievers family, 14
Great Britain, 114, 117
  and A's flight from Blumenhagen,
    209–10
  "Battle" of, 134–35
  and buildup to World War II, 111, 112
  declaration of war by, 112
  French relations with, 120, 122–23,
    127, 128
  German relations with, 108–9
  occupation of Germany by, 205, 206,
    209–10
  See also London; World War II
great man, definition of, 93
Grimm Brothers, 61, 218
Grosseelheim, Germany
  A in, 216, 217–31
  autograph incident in, 230–31
  difficulty from Loebers in, 224, 226–27
  education in, 224–25
  housing in, 218
  Lo's and girls return to, 234
  Ran-A's connection in, 219–24, 228–29
  religion in, 218–19
  wagon hauling business in, 219, 222
  women in, 218–19
Guderian, General Heinz, 142, 145,
    146, 154
Guitry, Sacha, 41

Hahn, Capt., 220, 221, 222, 224
Haight, Everest, A's friend, 42, 91, 92 235,
    236, 264
Halder, Franz, General, 146
Hale, Congressman Robert, 261, 263,
    270–71
Hamburg, Germany, and A's flight from
    Blumenhagen, 211–12, 214
Handel, George Frideric, *Messiah,* 132
Harper's Bazaar, 78
Harten von, family (A and H friends), 106
Hartford, Connecticut, 89, 93, 95, 96, 157,
    208, 251
  A's childhood and youth in, 16–18, 26, 37
  A's return to, 255–56
  education in, 256, 260, 261

as home, 279–80
memories of, 282
Heidelberg, Germany, A and H in, 71–72
Heine, Heinrich, 99, 224
Heinrich Alexis Nikolai von Hoyningen-Huene
A's initial interest in, 7–9, 11, 26
A's lost love letters to, 274–75
A's shared future with, 47–49
as busy with work, 63–64, 66, 73–74, 77, 89, 92, 109, 118, 128–29, 131
conservative values of, 93, 130, 139
death of, 158–60, 161, 162–64, 165–66, 168, 169, 176, 181, 196, 240
and FHW, 135–37
as gentleman farmer, 96, 113
as hope of others, 164, 166
infidelity of, 95–96, 110
letters as source for understanding of, 3–4, 277
looking for work, 83, 89–90, 92, 95–96, 108, 111
military activities of, 123, 131–32, 135
in military reserves, 112
military service of, 119–33, 135–55, 278
and Nazis, 103–4, 120, 126, 182
personal background of, 11–16, 19
photographs of, 2, 144
poems of, 134, 138–39
in Providence, 8–9, 44–46, 132
and Russian soldiers' letters, 161–62
translation work of, 106–7
watch of, 225
wedding and honeymoon of, 51–53, 70–72
See also specific person or topic
Heinrici, General Gotthard, 146–47
Helma Kahnert, Dr., 110, 157, 168, 177, 178, 179, 180–81, 240
and A's return to U.S., 246, 247–48
brain tumor, 244–45, 247
death of, 247–48
and flight from Blumenhagen, 193, 195, 199, 200, 207, 211, 215
in Frankenberg, 232, 233, 236
grave of, 250–51
in Grosseelheim, 218, 219, 225, 227, 231
Hiddensee vacation of, 168–69
medical practice of, 225, 226, 227, 231, 232, 233, 236, 242, 244, 247
Sigrid and, 164, 247–48

Heune, Baron Maximilian von, 96
Heurteloup, Jean, 88
Heydrich, Reinhard, 151
Hiddensee (Baltic island), A's vacation on, 168–69, 181–82
Himmler, Heinrich, 183
Hindenburg, Paul von, 35, 52, 83, 90, 96, 99, 101
Hitler, Adolf, 82, 87, 90, 106–9, 112, 124, 141, 143, 151, 162, 191
A's views about, 100, 183
bans opposition, 99, 102
criticisms of, 136–37, 165, 167, 171, 183, 185
death of, 204, 228
as dictator, 101, 104
and drafting of German youth, 183–84, 185–86
German military relations with, 167, 183
and Heil Hitlers increase, 165
H's family view of, 100
named chancellor, 99
peace offers of, 113–15, 116–17, 134
plots against, 171, 182–83, 184–85
and Russian front, 137–40
speeches of, 96, 100–101
as supreme military commander, 108, 167, 170
ten-year promise of, 180
See also World War II
H.M.S. Pinafore (Gilbert and Sullivan), 157
Hollis, Mr. (Maine neighbor), 263
home
Blumenhagen as, 282
Hartford as, 279–80
Ottenhof as, 33
search for, 2, 206–7, 215, 229, 279–81, 282
honeymoon. See marriage
Hope Cary (A's friend), 7–9, 45, 48, 55, 56–57
Horace, 138–39
housing shortage, in Germany, 234–35
Hoyningen-Huene, Aimée von. See Aimée
Hoyningen-Huene, Betty, 76
Hoyningen-Huene, Brigitte von. See Brigitte Anita
Hoyningen-Huene, Christian von. See Christian

Hoyningen-Huene, Dorothée von. *See* Dorothée
Hoyningen-Huene, Ernst von. *See* Papa
Hoyningen-Huene, Friedrich von. *See* Friedrich Alexander
Hoyningen-Huene, George, 2, 54,76
Hoyningen-Huene, Heinrich von. *See* Heinrich
Hoyningen-Huene, Michael von. *See* Michael
Hoyningen-Huene, Mima von. *See* Mimama
Hoyningen-Huene, Sigrid von. *See* Sigrid
Hugenberg, Alfred, 90
Hugo, Victor, *Les Miserables*, 46
Hummer family (Maine neighbors), 257, 260–61, 263
hunger, 29, 40, 73, 105, 148, 233, 238. *See also* food; poverty
Hyde Park, London, 59

I Remember Mama (high school production), 268–69
"In Readiness" (H poem), 138–39
Insel Verlag publishing company, 243
intellectuals, and Nazis, 100, 107, 151
Interior Ministry, German, Papa at, 44
Irina (maid), 21, 31
Isherwood, Christopher, 89
Italy, World War II and, 125

Jaczek (Polish POW), 201, 203, 211
Jaeger (Ottenhof overseer), 20, 52, 84
James Brewster Cone "Jim" (A's great-uncle), 16
Jews, 21, 76–77, 82, 89, 91, 99, 101, 103, 108, 114, 117, 151, 178
jobs. *See* work
John Ellis (A's uncle), 219–20, 229, 236, 252–53
jokes, popular, 174–75
Joy of Cooking (Rombauer), 263, 264
Jung, Edgar, 96, 101–2
Jünger, Ernst, 136–37, 139
Junior League, 26

Kaehler, Siegfried, 73, 246
Karola (Georg's wife), 114, 189
Kassel, Germany

A and H in, 50–51
and A's flight from Blumenhagen, 214–15
Katyn forest, massacre at, 172
Kendrick, Dean (Bowdoin College), 256–57
Keyserling, Hermann, 99–100
King Philip's War (A's father's book), 38
Kippenberg, Anton, 243
kite analogy, 109
Koloff, Herr, 226
Kolonialbund (Colonial Office), 111
Kommerell family (Marburg friends), 235, 249
Korean War, 270, 271, 278
Kowalcyk (Blumenhagen worker), 156
Krusenstjerna, Marie Louise von, 188
Kutuzov, Mikhail, 145

La Sauge aux Bois (French village), destruction at, 122
Landowska, Wanda, 75, 278
Latvia, 113–14, 143, 190–91. *See also* Ottenhof
League of Nations, 101
Lebenstraum, Operation Barbarossa and, 141, 162
Lenin, Vladimir, 25, 143
Leo-Werke (toothpaste company), 44, 86, 186–87
Lestion, France, 9–11, 48, 56, 139, 275
letters
  between A and H in courtship years, 4–5, 55–59
  of A to Roenne's widow, 184–85
  as lifeline, 77–78
  and lost love letters from A to H, 274–75
  Moroccan box of, 1–2, 275, 277
  from Roenne to A, 165–66
  for Russian soldiers, 161–62
  See also Mary Russell
Ley, Robert, 179, 182
Liddy (John Ellis's daughter), 219–20, 221
Liebig, Herr (gardener), 87, 105, 156
Life magazine, 260, 278
Lili (H's aunt), 44
L'Illustration, 122
Li-Po, 46
Lisa Sievers (H's maternal grandmother), 26–27
Liss, Colonel Ulrich, 136, 137

Lizzie (A's great-aunt), 16
Lo Meyer, 118, 171, 176, 180, 188, 237, 240, 244, 263
    and anxiety about war, 115
    arrival at Blumenhagen of, 110, 181
    and A's move to Maine, 257, 258–60, 261
    and A's return to U.S., 246–47, 249, 251, 268
    and flight from Blumenhagen, 193, 194, 200, 205, 206, 207–8, 211, 215
    in Frankenberg, 233, 242, 247, 257, 258–60
    in Grosseelheim, 218, 227, 229, 234
    in Maine, 268–69, 271, 272
    publication of poems by, 243
    Russian zone trip of, 238–39
Loeber family (Grosseelheim farmers), 218, 219, 224, 226–27, 230
London, England
    A and Anita's trip to, 39–40
    A in, 59–60, 106
    and courtship letters of A and H, 4–5, 55–59
    H in, 4, 53, 55–58, 59–60
Löns, Hermann, 107
Lore Adam (A's friend), 98, 112, 175, 191
Lücht, Herr (schoolmaster), 160, 172
Luxembourg, H in military in, 119

Mainbocher (Vogue editor), 54
Maine
    A's trip to, 256–57
    A's home in, 2, 257–67, 268–75
    Christmas in, 265
    education in, 257–58, 263, 264
    Good Grief Farm in, 257–67, 268–71
    second farm in, 271–75
    seizure of house in, 271
Maine Historical Society, 272
Mantegna, Andrea, 59
Marburg, Germany, 60, 61–65, 224, 231, 235, 249
    Americans in, 216, 217, 220–22
    A and Sigrid's visit to, 279
    exchange market in, 242–43
Margarethe (H's sister), 19, 33–34, 44, 69–70, 95, 175, 186–87, 212, 214, 227, 238, 261
    and A's return to U.S., 246, 269

Blumenhagen visits of, 102, 163–64
    on Hitler, 100
Margot, Tante (Toffen hostess), 72
Marie (H's aunt), 12, 31, 44, 86
Marina (Saint Petersburg guide), 281
Marine Flasher (ship)
    A's return to U.S. on, 249–52
    older children's trip to U.S. on, 262
Marion (A's aunt), 16, 18, 64–65, 91
marriage, A and H's
    honeymoon and, 71–72
    and infidelity, 95–96, 110
    and wedding day, 70–71
    wedding plans for, 51–53
Marta (A's cook), 115, 180–81, 189, 193, 199, 207, 211, 215, 218, 222, 224, 232, 234, 261, 264
Mary Russell (A's friend), 41, 49, 53–54
    A's letters to, 5, 48, 59–60, 61, 62, 65, 68, 69–72, 73–74, 77–78, 79–81, 82–83, 88, 91, 95–96, 97, 98–99, 105–6, 162–63, 206, 234, 235, 236, 242, 243, 244–45, 277
    and A's return to U.S., 252
    H's letters to, 106–7
    letters/packages to A from, 117, 167, 236, 247
    marriage plans of, 79–81
    as model, 53–54
mask incident, A's, 267
Masters, Lizzie and Sally, 38, 208
Masters School. See Dobbs Ferry school
Matzky, General Gerhard, 135–36
Means, Tom, 270
Mein Kampf (Hitler), 104
Merrill (Anita's husband), 256, 259, 261, 263, 272
Michael (A and H's son), 97, 107–8, 116, 170–71, 193, 194, 225
    and A's move to Maine, 257, 258–60
    and A's return to U.S., 248, 249
    birth of, 88
    birthdays of, 209
    career of, 278
    citizenship of, 167–68, 246–47, 261, 269–70
    and flight from Blumenhagen, 195, 200, 205, 206, 209, 211, 212
    in Frankenberg, 234–35, 236, 244, 257, 258–60

Michael (*cont.*)
  in Grosseelheim, 218, 219, 221, 222, 227
  Life magazine photo of, 278
  in Maine, 263, 264, 265, 267, 270
  in Marburg, 234–35, 249
  trip to U.S. of, 262
Middlebury College, 256
Mildy (Bill's daughter), 256, 261–63, 265
Millay, Edna St. Vincent, 42
Mimama (Marie [Mima] von Hoyningen-
    Huene) (H's mother), 12, 20, 29–30,
    44-45, 62-63, 66, 84, 130, 186–87, 251,
    264, 274
  A's Dresden visits with, 237–38,
    240–42, 279
  A's first meeting with, 62–63
  and A's return to U.S., 246, 261, 269
  birthdays of, 44–45
  on Hitler, 100
  and H's death, 163, 240
  and Papa's death, 237–38, 240, 241
  struggles of, 44–45, 56, 57, 238–39,
    240–41
  visits A after H's death, 168
Minsk, Russia, 138, 139, 141, 143
Mira (H's sister), 19, 33, 86, 175, 187,
    189, 269
mirror incident, shattered, 240, 244
Mogilev, Russia
  battle for, 151–55, 158–59
  death of H in, 158–59, 165, 166
  Operation Barbarossa and, 150, 151–55,
    158–59
Molly Staples (A's stepmother), 37, 39, 41,
    91, 270
Molotov cocktails, 152
money, 7–8, 16, 53, 62, 69, 73, 88, 94–95,
    105, 117, 164, 219, 222, 224, 233,
    244–45, 259, 261–63
  A's autograph on, 231
  exchange market in Marburg, 242–43
  and expropriation of Maine farm, 270
  expropriation of (by Bolsheviks), 28, 30
  and Sievers's family wealth, 27
  trust from A's mother, 41, 48, 72, 270
  See also hunger; poverty; work
Money Point (Mason's Island), A's family
    visit to, 262
Montgomery Ward, Aaron, 91, 229
Morgenstern, Christian, 191–92

Morocco, 51
Moscow, 41, 74, 134, 138, 142, 161, 164,
mother (A's), 16, 17, 67, 160, 176, 229, 270
mother (H's). *See* Mimama (Marie [Mima]
    von Hoyningen-Huene)
Mother's Cross (*Mutterkreuz*), 113
Mozart, Wolfgang Amadeus, 163
Munich Agreement, 108–9
music, 12, 36, 41–42, 44, 86, 116, 160, 163,
    176, 194, 208, 224, 233, 244, 247, 249,
    263, 265, 269

Nantes, France, A in, 48–49
Napoleon Bonaparte, 8, 58, 123, 126, 141,
    142, 144, 145, 167
Napoleon III, 16
National Gallery, London, 59
Navy, U.S., 271
Nazis, 87, 89, 92, 94, 100, 102, 112
  and anti-Hitler views, 182
  and anti-Nazi views, 180
  Christian recruited by, 172
  collapse of, 206
  and communists, 90–91, 99, 103, 108
  and culture, 101
  dissension among, 165
  educational system for, 172
  Friedrich recruited by, 183–84, 185, 193,
    195, 196
  and H, 103–4, 120, 126, 182
  and Hitler's death, 204
  honors awarded by, 113
  and insults to A's children, 2, 266
  and intellectuals, 100, 107, 151
  and military, 108
  and war deaths, 158, 170
  See also SS (Nazis)
Neustrelitz Germany, 110, 188, 189, 197,
    200, 226, 274
New Jersey, A's visit with Dorothy (cousin)
    in, 252–55
New London, Connecticut, 262
New York City, 11, 40–42, 252, 262, 270
New Yorker magazine, 55, 77
Nicholson File Company, 8, 45
Niemöller, Martin, 108
Nijinsky, Vaslav, 37, 41
Nikolai Sievers (H's maternal grandfather),
    12–13, 14, 26–28, 150, 240–41, 282
Nina (Anita's daughter), 236

Nina Engelhard-Toróschino (H family neighbor), 21–22
Nina Howell (A's friend), 39, 41–42
Nina (H's aunt), 186
Nina Sievers (another of H's aunts), 79
Ninety-Sixth Infantry Division, German, 125
Ninth Infantry Regiment, German, 153, 155, 183
Norway, German advance on, 117–18
Nostitz von, family (H's friends), 52

OKH (Oberkommando des Heeres), H with, 135–37
Olga (maid), 31
Olga (Mimama's aunt), 241
Operation Barbarossa
    and German animosity toward Russia, 151–52
    German setbacks in, 155, 170, 171–72
    and German sympathies, 144, 147–49
    goal of, 141
    H and, 141–55
    and Hitler as supreme military commander, 167, 170
    H's views about, 138
    Mogilev battle during, 151–55
    renewal of, 162
    resources for, 169, 170
    Russian army deserters and, 141–42
    secrecy concerning, 140
    Stalingrad battle and, 170, 171
    winter and, 166–67
Operational Order No. 8, Heydrich's, 151
Orczy, Baroness, *The Scarlet Pimpernel*, 265
orphans, 48–49, 62. *See also* Anna Malé
Oswald (H's cousin), 52, 83, 102
Ottenhof (H's Latvian family estate),
    14–15, 20, 26, 28, 29, 30–31, 51–52, 62,
    63–64, 65, 71, 81, 82, 97, 122, 142, 159,
    160, 195, 197, 240–41
    and Blumenhagen, 113
    expropriation of, 34–35, 95, 114, 134
    family gathering at, 84–86
    Georg at, 113–14
    H's poem about, 134
    struggles at, 34
Otto (Mira's son), 175–76
outsiders, 43, 74–75, 109, 219

A as, 18
A and H's children as, 225, 265
A's family as, 2
H's family as, 2, 8
Owen, Wilfred, 138
Oxford, H in, 58, 60

Paléologue, Maurice, 54, 146
Palermo, Sicily, A and Hope in, 7
Papa (Ernst von Hoyningen-Huene) (H's father), 20–26, 30-33, 65, 67, 84, 88, 98, 104, 130, 137–38, 160, 240, 241, 274, 280
    A's chat with, 85–86
    birthdays of, 30, 75, 187
    death of, 237–38, 246
    and gardening, 187
    on Hitler, 100
    interrogation of (WWI), 23–24, 32
    and visit with A after H's death, 168
    work of, 28, 29, 44–45, 186–87
Papen, Franz von, 96, 98, 99, 101–2
Paris, France
    A and H visit to, 78–79
    A and H's first encounter in, 9, 136
    A in, 4, 9, 48, 49–50, 53, 55–59
    and courtship letters of A and H, 4–5, 55–59, 65-68
    in 1814, 126
    German occupation of, 127, 130, 136–37
    and H in military in France, 123
patriotism, 138
Pax Umbrellicus, 108–9
Pétain, Marshal, 129, 131
Petrograd, 20–21, 24–25
    H family departure from, 30–31
    See also Saint Petersburg
Petrovitch, Grigory, 29
Poiret, Paul, 78
Poland, 111, 112, 113, 114, 134, 198–99, 211, 227
Polish Corridor, 112
Potvin, James (Maine neighbor), 258–59
poverty, 88–90, 258. *See also* hunger
Prague, Czechoslovakia, 66, 111
prayers, H's selection of, 191–92
Preobrazhensky Guards, 22
Prince family (Maine neighbors), 263
"Prinzlein" (Friedrich von Saxe-Altenburg), 213–14, 272–73

prisoners of war
    at Blumenhagen, 156-57, 189, 196
    French, 121, 130–33, 189
    H's letters to families of, 161–62
    and Operation Barbarossa, 147, 148, 149,
        151, 153, 154, 155, 161–62
    Polish, 156–57, 189, 196, 203, 211
    Winfried as, 213
    women as, 153,
privacy, 190, 224, 233, 240, 249
propaganda, 89, 114, 158, 164–65, 169–72,
    174–75, 177–79. See also Goebbels,
    Joseph
Proust, Marcel, 59
Providence, Rhode Island, 8–9, 45–46, 132
Pyle, Howard, Men of Iron, 194

Queen Mary (ship), 110

Rachmaninoff, Sergei, 41
Raemaekers, Louis, 178
Räisälä (H family Finland estate), 27–28
Ran Beardsley (A's cousin), 219–24, 228,
    229, 230, 252–53
rape, 194–95, 201
reading, 12, 17, 46, 54, 58, 83, 119, 122,
    176–77, 194, 230, 236, 243, 265, 269
    A and her father, 37–38
    H and his father, 44
Red Cross, 30–31, 33, 48, 219
refugees, 8, 21, 32, 35, 43, 66, 74, 209–10,
    214, 216
    and A's flight from Blumenhagen, 194,
        198–99, 202–4
    at Blumenhagen, 187–91
    in concentration camps, 204
    French, 126, 127–28, 131–32
    H as director of camp for, 131–32
    housing for, 234
    prevalence in Germany of, 227
    See also specific person
Regional Councils, 194, 219
Reich Labor Service, 110
"Reich murder week," 102
Reichstag, German, 87, 99, 101
religion, 27, 89–90, 101, 103–4, 208,
    218–19
Rembrandt, 59
Reynaud, Paul, 127–28
Richter, Frau (Frankenburg neighbor), 237

Riemenschneider, Tilman, 279
Riga, Latvia, 21, 30, 35, 62
Rilke, Rainer Maria, 46
Roberta (A's sister-in-law), 91, 228–29
Roenne, Alexis von, 124, 132, 135, 136,
    139, 142, 165–66, 168, 184–85
Roenne, Frau von, 184–85
Roma (freighter), H family as refugees on,
    35–36
Romanov dynasty, 13
Rombauer, Irma, 264
Rommel, Erwin, General, Afrika
    Korps, 156
Ronchères (French village), German troops
    in, 126–27
Roosevelt, Franklin D., 114, 117, 127,
    128, 251
Rouen, France, 58
Rubens, Peter Paul, 59
Rudolph (H's uncle), 12, 20, 26
Russia
    A's fear of, 209–10
    and A's flight from Blumenhagen, 194,
        197, 200, 201, 205, 206, 209–10
    and A's return visit to Blumenhagen, 225
    and France, 142–43
    German relations with, 134, 137–40,
        144, 147–49, 151–52
    "Germanizing" of, 198–99
    invasion/occupation of Germany by, 183,
        185, 193, 194–96, 197, 200, 201, 205,
        206, 209, 211, 214, 221
    liberation of, 137–40, 147, 152
    Nazi pact with, 112
    and soldiers' letters by H, 161–62
    refugees from, 209
    winter in, 166–67
    See also Bolshevik Revolution;
        Operation Barbarossa; Petrograd;
        Russian Revolution;
Russian Orthodox Church, 27
Russian Revolutions (1905, 1917), 8, 21, 24,
    26, 86, 100, 264

SA, Stirmabteilung, 89, 99
    H joins, 103
Saar coal basin
    A's incident in, 50, 71
    French occupation of, 50
    German control of, 102

Saint-Cyr, French military academy, 131
Saint Petersburg, Russia
    anti-German sentiment in, 21
    Easter in, 13
    H's family in, 11–13, 20–21, 24–25,
        30–31
    name change for, 20–21
    and outbreak of World War I, 20–21
    Romanov jubilee in, 13
    Sigrid's visit to, 280–82
    World War I and, 29–30, 130
    See also Petrograd
salamander myth, 135
Salvolchino (H family estate), 27
Sartre, Jean-Paul, 128
Saxe-Altenburg, Friedrich von "Prinzlein,"
        213–14, 272–73
Scapa Flow, Scotland, 117
Schipp, Major, 129
school. *See* education; *specific school*
Sedan, France, 121, 126
Semstchina (Russian newspaper), 23
Sergei (Saint Petersburg driver), 280–82
servants, 18, 19. *See also specific person*
Sicily, 7
Sievers family, 27. *See also specific person*
Signy-l'Abbaye (French village),
        destruction of, 121–22
Sigrid (A and H's daughter)
    and A's return to U.S., 248, 249–52
    birth of, 164
    birthdays of, 170, 242, 252
    career of, 279
    citizenship of, 167–68, 246–47, 270
    and flight from Blumenhagen, 207
    in Frankenberg, 240, 242, 244
    in Grosseelheim, 218, 221, 222, 223,
        234, 235
    H and, 1–4
    in Hartford, 256, 260, 280
    Helma and, 164, 247–48
    in Maine, 261, 262, 263, 264, 265–66,
        273–74
    in New Jersey, 253, 254, 255
    Saint Petersburg visit of, 280–82
    visit to Germany of, 279
Schupos, (Protective Police), 184
Siberia, H relatives shipped to, 41
Sippenhaft, kinship detention, 182, 184
Sitzkrieg, "Sitting War", 117

Skippy (Sigrid's classmate), 265–66
Smith, Howard K., 156, 165
Smith, Jessie Willcox, 254
soap, 11, 190, 209, 222, 238, 261
Sophie, Mlle., (H family governess), 8, 9, 45
Sophie (H's aunt), 34
Sorbonne, university, Paris, 7, 53
Le Spectre de la Rose (ballet), 37
SS (Nazis), 89–90, 99, 102, 172, 178, 213
    at Blumenhagen, 190–91, 195, 197
    and Hitler's death, 204
    recruitment by, 172, 183–84
St. Paul's School, Corson at, 37
Stahlhelm (German paramilitary), 92
Stalin, Joseph, 112, 113–14, 134, 137–40,
        143, 147–48, 151, 274
Stalingrad, Russia, battle at, 170, 171
Staples, Molly. *See* Molly
State Department, U.S., 219
storks, at Blumenhagen, 181
Strasbourg, France, 130
    surrender of, 127
Stresemann, Gustav, 81, 92
Stülpnagel, Carl-Heinrich von, General, 137
Suraz, Russia, field hospital, 142, 166
swastika, 91, 99,104, 157

Tafelrunde (Round Table, gentlemen's
        club), 135–37
Tate Gallery, London, 59
ten-year promise, Hitler's, 180
Thorne, George, 91
Thousand-Year Reich, 203
Tippelskirch, Kurt von, General, 135, 137
Toffen (Swiss chateau), 108, 189
    A and H at, 72
    A and Sigrid's visit to, 279
    H at, 47–48
Tolly-Weymarn, Princess Ada de
        (H's aunt), 64
Toròschino, Russian/Baltic border
        station, 32
    H family incident at, 31
    Papa's detention at, 32–33
Tours, France, 139
Travelers Insurance Company, 37–38
Treaty of Brest-Litovsk (1918), 30, 33–34
trek
    meaning of term, 198–99
    See also Blumenhagen: flight from

Trepanier, Arthur (Maine neighbor), 258–59
Trinity College, 40, 256
Trott, Mr. (Maine house-owner), 271–72
Twenty-First Battalion, French, 127
Twenty-Third Infantry Division, German, 153

Ucello, Paolo, 59
Uexküll, Lieutenant, 149
Ukraine, 140, 227
"undesirables", 151
United States (U.S.)
  A as never returning to, 68, 75, 223, 251
  A's connections reestablished with, 235–37, 243–44, 246–48
  A's desire to return to, 242, 246–48
  A's return voyage to, 249–52
  and A's search for Americans, 211–16
  A's visits to, 65, 89, 96, 167
  and citizenship issues, 167–68, 246–47, 257, 261, 270
  dream of, 110, 244
  economic depression in, 99
  German declaration of war against, 167, 229
  and WWII, 114, 117, 127, 128, 167, 195, 251
  See also Allies; Maine; New Jersey; *specific person*
University of Marburg
  H's studies at, 47, 73
  Papen speech at, 101–2
Ursula (nurse), 189

Vera, Princess Constantinovna Romanov, 272–73
Verdun, France, 126
Versailles Peace Treaty, 75, 81, 111, 112
Veterans of Foreign Wars, 270
Vichy, France, 136
Vionnet, Madeleine, A dress, 79
Vogue magazine, 54, 78
Volkovo Cemetery (Saint Petersburg), 280–81
Volkssturm (people's militia), 183–84, 193
Volynsky Guard, 21, 25
Vonnegut, Kurt, 187

Waffen-SS, 183–84
wagon hauling business, in Grosseelheim, 219, 222
Walker, Mis' (A's governess), 17, 70
Wall Street crash, 90
Walter, Bruno, 99, 117
Ward, Aaron Montgomery, 91, 229
Watteau, Antoine, 73
wedding. *See* marriage
Wehrmacht, German, 108, 198
  Hitler's relations with, 159, 165, 183
  See also Operation Barbarossa; *specific person*
Weimar Republic, 44, 103
Weinsheimer, Frau, 250
Wenig, Herr (Breslau grocer), 75
Werner, Anton (Papa's alias), 31–32
Weymarn von, family (H's relatives), 188, 199, 281
White, William C., *These Russians* by, 107
Wilhelm II (Kaiser), abdication of, 33
Wiesbaden, Germany, 220, 233, 243
Winfried (Margarethe's stepson), 175–76, 212–14, 217, 232
Winter Help *Wingterhilfe* program, German, 105
Wise, Mr. (Hartford store owner), 82
Wolf, Hugo, 238
women
  Germany as nation of, 180–81
  in Grosseelheim, 218–19
  as political prisoners, 178
  Raemaekers drawings of bleeding, 178
  rape of, 194–95, 201
  as supporter of family, 257
work
  in Germany, 99, 100
  See also specific person
World War I, 20–36, 138
  in Baltic nations, 26–27
  hunger during, 29
  official end of, 33
  outbreak of, 20–21
  Raemaekers drawings of bleeding women in, 178
  and Treaty of Brest-Litovsk, 30, 33–34
  U.S. role in, 167
  wealth expropriated by Bolsheviks, 28, 30

World War II
  "Battle of Britain" and, 134–35
  buildup to, 111–18
  declaration of, 112, 117, 167, 229
  escalation of, 137–40
  French surrender in, 129, 134
  German home front during, 156–73,
    174–79
  German public sentiment about, 112,165
  H in France during, 119–33
  Nazi collapse in, 206
  no danger in, 122–24
  Nordic nations and, 117–18
  peace efforts during, 113–15, 116–17, 134
  signs of destruction during, 121–22,
    127, 132

  total war of, 171–73
  as war of ideologies, 151
  See also Operation Barbarossa; *specific
    nation, commander or battle*
Wunderwaffe (miracle weapon),
    German, 173

Yale, 40
  Banjo Club, 18
youth, German, drafting of, 183–84,
    185–86
Yusupov, Irina and Felix, 78
  palace, 30

Zacharievitch, Dimenty, 12,
    27–28, 241